A Gross of Pirates

A Gross of Pirates

From Alfhild the Shield Maiden to
Afweyne the Big Mouth

Terry Breverton

AMBERLEY

Page 1: Aruj and Khizr Barbarossa, pirates of the Barbary Coast *c.* 1478, etching by Ignatius Lux, 1659–1713. (Courtesy Rijksmuseum)
Page 2: Life on board a ship was hard work and done in all weathers, whether by merchant seamen, navy ratings – or by pirates. (Courtesy razyphoto)

First published 2018

Amberley Publishing
The Hill, Stroud
Gloucestershire, GL5 4EP

www.amberley-books.com

British Library Cataloguing in Publication Data.
A catalogue record for this book is available from the British Library.

ISBN 978 1 4456 8292 1 (hardback)
ISBN 978 1 4456 8293 8 (ebook)

Typesetting and Origination by Amberley Publishing.
Printed in the UK.

Contents

Contents

Contents

Introduction

This book could be many times longer, featuring numerous other pirates and privateers. A problem of definition is that one country's privateers were an enemy nation's pirates, so both are included. Some were not villains, but anti-slavery heroes; others were truly evil. Piracy is an exciting subject, and I began writing about it with my *The Book of Welsh Pirates and Buccaneers* (2003). In the research, I discovered that the most feared and magnificent of all pirates, Black Bart Roberts, was hardly known, and therefore wrote *Black Bart Roberts – The Greatest Pirate of Them All* (2004). My *Pirate Handbook* explains the nautical terms and techniques used, and also lists some of the more popular piracy exploits. This spurred me on to further research, and by far the most successful privateer was Henry Morgan, so I wrote his biography, *Admiral Sir Henry Morgan – The Greatest Buccaneer of Them All*.

I was then commissioned to translate Exquemelin's *History of the Buccaneers*, published as *The Illustrated Pirate Diaries: A Remarkable Eyewitness Account of Captain Morgan and the Buccaneers* (2008). In my researches I was fortunate enough to discover an unknown privateer, who was incredibly important to American history, the polymath William Williams. Obtaining an Everett Helm Visiting Fellowship to work in the Lilly Library at the University of Indiana, Bloomington, I transcribed Williams' original manuscript of his wonderful adventures when he was marooned on the Miskito Coast. This is an extremely important and forgotten work in American literature, worthy of inclusion on literature reading lists across all ages.

The *Pirates of the Caribbean* film series stimulated public interest for a time, which seems unfortunately to have dimmed, but films should be made of Black Bart Roberts, Henry Morgan and Lewellin Penrose, aka William Williams. For those who wish to pursue research into the colourful characters in this book, there are some wonderful and informative websites, which will direct you towards further reading and research. The website *cindyvallar.com* also gives directions for research into adult non-fiction pirate books. Rob Ossian's *thepirateking.com* is very highly recommended, as is *paulinespiratesandprivateers.blogspot. co.uk*, and there are many other fine websites. If you wish to refer to original texts, most are now available free on the web. A seminal work is by Captain Charles Johnson, the most reliable authority on pirates. His *A General History of the Robberies and Murders of the Most Notorious Pyrates* was first published in 1724. Many editions followed, and much information came from the transcripts of pirate trials of the time, and from accounts published in the *Daily Post* and *London Gazette*. *A General History* was written by Daniel Defoe under the Johnson pseudonym to avoid taxation, and he also wrote about Henry Every and John Gow, and seems to have met some of Black Bart's crew.

Alexandre Exquemelin sailed with Henry Morgan and his Dutch *De Americaensche Zee-Roovers* (*History of the Bouccaneers of America*, 1678) is the best contemporary source for the 17th-century buccaneers. Captain Alexander Smith (perhaps another pseudonym of Daniel Defoe?) wrote from 1714 to 1719 the terrific *A Complete History of the Lives and Robberies of the Most Notorious highwaymen, footpads, shoplifts, & cheats of both sexes, wherein their most secret and barbarous murders, unparalleled robberies, notorious thefts, and unheard-of-cheats are set in a true light and exposed to public view, for the common benefit of mankind*. Don't let the title faze you. Thomas Carey published a useful *The History of the Pirates: Containing the Lives of Those Noted Pirate Captains, Misson, Bowen, Kidd, Tew, Halsey, White, Condent, Bellamy* in 1834. Charles Ellms' *The Pirates' Own Book* of 1837 has inaccuracies, like the above accounts, but is a rollicking read with 77 woodcut images. In the 20th century, Philip Gosse was responsible for two excellent works, his 1924 *The Pirates' Who's Who* and in 1934 *The History of Piracy*. *Privateering and Piracy in the Colonial Period* by J. Franklin Jameson (1923) is an excellent work, and there are many fine writers adding to our knowledge today.

I have included Captain William Kidd and Blackbeard in this volume, not because of their great exploits, but because most readers will expect them to feature, but I have also attempted to include the most interesting 144 pirates and privateers from across the ages and across the seas.

One final note is that the pirate crews of the Caribbean, and the earlier Brethren of the Coast in that area, seem to have been the first known 'true' democracies, where usually everyone had an equal vote, including escaped black slaves. In many ways it was a far more attractive life than in the naval ships and merchant vessels of the time. Most pirate books concentrate upon the Caribbean, but it is hoped that this more inclusive book will stimulate interest in pirate exploits across the oceans.

RECOMMENDED READING

Ayres, Philip, *The voyages and adventures of Capt. Barth. Sharp and others... in the West Indies*, 1684; Baring, C.H., *The Buccaneers of the West Indies in the 17th Century*, 1910; Blome, Richard, *A Description of the Island of Jamaica* 1672; Bradlee, F.B.C., *Piracy in the West Indies and its Suppression*, 1923; Breverton, Terry, *Black Bart Roberts, the Greatest Pirate of Them All*, 2004; *The Pirate Handbook* 2004; *Sir Henry Morgan, the Greatest Buccaneer of Them All*, 2005; *The Journal of Penrose, Seaman – The New Robinson Crusoe*, 2014; *The True Confessions of William Owen, Smuggler, Privateer and Murderer*, 2018; Burney, James, *History of the Buccaneers of America*, 1816; Carey, Thomas, *The History of the Pirates*, 1834; Cordingley, David, *Under the Black Flag* 1995; Cruickshank, E.A., *The Life of Sir Henry Morgan*, 1935; Dampier, William, *A New Voyage Round the World*, 1697; Ellms, Charles, *The Pirates' Own Book*, Portland 1844; Exquemelin, J. Alexandre, *History of the Bouccaneers of America*, 1684; Gerhard, Peter, *Pirates of the Pacific*, 1995; Gill, Anton, *The Devil's Mariner: A Life of William Dampier*, 1997; Gosse, Philip, *The History of Piracy*, 1934; *The Pirates' Who's Who*, 1924; Haring, C.H., *Buccaneers in the West Indies in the 17th Century*, 1910; Johnson, Captain Charles (Daniel Defoe), *A General History of the Robberies and Murders of the Most Notorious Pyrates*, 1724; Kemp, Peter, and Lloyd, Christopher, *Brethren of the Coast*, 1960; Leslie, Charles, *New History of Jamaica*, 1740; Marley, David, *Pirates and Privateers of the Americas*, 1994; Marx, Jennifer, *Pirates and Privateers of the Caribbean*, 1992; Nichols, Philip, *Sir Francis Drake Revived*, 1910; Pringle, Patrick, *Jolly Roger*, 1953; Rediker, Marcus, *Between the Devil and the Deep Blue Sea*, 1987; Ringrose, Basil, *Bucaniers of America ...by ... Basil Ringrose, Gent, who was all along present at those transactions,* 1685; Rogozinski, Jan, *A Brief History of the Caribbean*, 1992; Roberts, W. Adolphe, *Sir Henry Morgan: Buccaneer and Governor*, 1933; Sherry, Frank, *Raiders and Rebels*, 1986; Snelgrave, Captain William, *A New Voyage to Guinea, and the Slave-Trade*, 1744; Winston, Alexander, *No Purchase, No Pay*, 1970; Woodbury, George, *The Great Days of Piracy* 1954; Wycherley, George, *Buccaneers of the Pacific*, 1924. Websites – there are many excellent resources, e.g. *cindyvallar.com*; Rob Ossian's *thepirateking.com* and *paulinespiratesandprivateers.blogspot.co.uk*

The Early Pirates

Alfhild (c.9th century) – the 'Shield Maiden' Pirate

This is the only account in this book without a great deal of verifiable factual content, but is included as Alfhild's descendant martyred King Edmund of England. *Gesta Danorum* (*Deeds of the Danes*), written by Saxo Grammaticus, is a 12th-century account of the early history of the Danes, and is the first account of Alfhild (*c.*9th century), the daughter of Siward, King of the Geats, of Götaland in southern Sweden. Olaus Magnus, in his *History of the Northern Peoples* (1555), added to the story. King Siward wished to marry his beautiful daughter to a powerful prince to form an alliance, and the *Gesta* tells us that 'she continually kept her face muffled in her robe, lest she should cause her beauty to provoke the passion of another.' If she lost her virginity, she would not be able to marry any great noble or

Alfhild, leading her Viking 'shield maidens' attacking a ship.

royal, so her father Siward 'banished her into very close-keeping, and gave her a viper and a snake to rear, wishing to defend her chastity by the protection of these reptiles.' Siward also declared that if any man tried to enter her chamber and failed to 'win' the maiden, he would be executed and his head impaled on a stake.

A Viking prince by the romantic name of Alf, the son of Sigar, King of Denmark, was partially of Geatish descent and had heard of Alfhild's great beauty. He had 'devoted himself to the business of a rover,' so was used to sea raiding and fighting, and travelled to Siward's palace. Alf covered his body with a blood-stained hide to unsettle the serpents, and secretly entered Alfhild's chamber. He had a pair of tongs in one hand, and a spear in the other. When the first viper opened its jaws, Alf rammed the tongs down its throat, and then thrust the spear into its gaping mouth, as it wound around and writhed. Killing the other snake by the same method, Alf asked King Siward for Alfhild's hand. However, Siward told him that he would only accept him if Alfhild agreed by her 'free and decided choice'. Alfhild, advised by her mother, fled from Alf, dressed as a man, becoming a 'shield maiden' – a female warrior. According to the *Gesta* she now 'devoted those hands to the lance which they should rather have applied to the loom.' Alfhild gathered a crew of shield maidens and 'happened to come to a spot where a band of rovers were lamenting the death of their captain who had been lost in war.' They chose Alfhild as their new captain and she gathered a pirate longship fleet, with many female crew, attacking shipping and settlements around the Baltic and North Seas.

Olaus Magnus wrote: 'For she so much preferred a life of valour to one of ease that, when she might have enjoyed the pleasure of royalty, drawn by a woman's madness she suddenly plunged into the hazards of war. Her determination to stay chaste was so steadfast that she began to reject all men and firmly resolved with herself never to have intercourse with any, but from then on to equal, or even to surpass, male courage in the practice of piracy.' Because of her attacks, the Danes sent a fleet under Prince Alf and his lieutenant, Borgar, from Scania (the district around Malmo in Southern Sweden). In a narrow gulf in Finland they met the pirate fleet, and although outnumbered, attacked, boarding one ship after another. Borgar, Alf's comrade, struck one pirate's helmet and it tumbled to the deck. It was Princess Alfhild. The *Gesta* records: 'Seeing the smoothness of her chin, [Alf] saw that he must fight with kisses and not with arms; that the cruel spears must be put away, and the enemy handled with gentler dealings... He took hold of her [Alfhild] eagerly, and made her change her man's apparel to a woman's.' She sailed with Alf to Denmark, where they married, and had a daughter, Gurid. Borgar also married, taking Alfhild's second-in-command, Groa, and Alfhild disappeared from the historical record.

Years later, in a Danish civil war, Alf, his brothers and their father King Sigar were killed, with only Gurid, the daughter of Alf and Alfhild, surviving of the royal family. The new queen Gurid married Halfdan, one of Borgar's sons, and they had a son Harald, who became King of Denmark. The tale might even date back to the fifth century, and be a mixture of various legends and facts. One of Alfhild's descendants might be Halfdan Ragnarsson, a Viking commander in the Great Heathen Army that invaded Anglo-Saxon England from 865 onwards. For a time King of Northumbria, he was killed in Ireland in 877. His brothers were the wonderfully named Ubba, Bjorn Ironside, Sigurd 'Snake-in-the-Eye' and Ivar 'the Boneless'. Ubba and Ivar are the Danish leaders who flayed Edmund Ironside, the English king, before using him as target practice with arrows. There was also a Harald 'Klak' Halfdansson (*c.*785–*c.*852), a king in Jutland, and possibly of other parts of Denmark around 812–814 and from 819 to 827.

Eustace the Monk (*c.*1170–24 August 1217) – Eustache Busket le Moine, the Original Robin Hood?

A younger son of Lord Baudoin Busket, of the county of Boulogne, France, he entered the Benedictine Abbey of St Samer, near Calais, as a monk. In 1190, his father was ambushed and killed, and Eustace left religious orders to demand justice from the Count of Boulogne. To settle the dispute, a judicial duel was arranged and Eustace's champion was killed. In 1200 he was appointed seneschal of the Count of Boulogne during his expedition with Philip of France, to reclaim territories held by King John of England. However, on his return in 1203, Eustace was accused of mismanaging the count's finances. The former monk fled into the great woodlands surrounding Boulogne, and the count confiscated his properties. Eustace thus turned to piracy in the English Channel, and in 1205 took an English ship. King John, instead of punishing him, employed him as a privateer, giving Eustace 30 ships to battle those of Philip of France. Eustace and his brothers now raided the coast of Normandy and established bases in the Channel Islands. When Eustace also raided English coastal villages,

John briefly outlawed him, but soon issued a pardon because he needed his services.

In 1209, Eustace acted as John's ambassador to Count Renaud of Boulogne, but the count promptly outlawed him again. When in 1212 Count Renaud signed a charter of allegiance to John, Eustace, now fearing prosecution as an outlaw by the count, joined the forces of King Philip of France. When English troops seized Eustace's Channel Island bases, he raided Folkestone, Kent, in retaliation. On 10 May 1213, supporting the northern English barons in their rebellion against King John, Philip ordered the invasion of England, but the French fleet was destroyed in a surprise attack by John's navy, and Eustace lost his great flagship, the *Nef de Boulogne*. In 1214 Eustace supplied arms to the northern English barons who had rebelled against John, and by 1215 was commanding the French navy, which now controlled the English Channel. In May 1216, 800 ships, under the Dauphin Louis, sailed to assist the barons to depose John. Louis disembarked from Eustace's flagship on the Isle of Thanet, and only then learned of the death of King John, and of the barons' decision to choose his young son, Henry III, as the new king.

In August 1217, whilst ferrying reinforcements to Louis, Eustace met an English fleet under Hubert de Burgh in the Battle of Dover. At the time ships were little more than floating castles full of soldiers, and decks turned to battlefields when boarded. The primary strategy was to manoeuvre to board the enemy's ships, and fight in a general mêlée until death or surrender. Eustace wrought havoc, until the English part-blinded the French with powdered lime. English troops boarded his ships but Eustace, his flagship, and some other ships, managed to escape. However, Eustace's ship was later surrounded by an English fleet of *Cinque Ports* ships under Philip d'Aubigny, on 24 August 1217 in the Battle of Sandwich. Eustace tried to hide in the ship's bilges and when discovered, he offered huge sums for his life. However, he had made himself hated by the English crews and he was summarily beheaded on board ship. The 1217 Treaty of Lambeth compelled Louis to give up his claim to the English throne and also ejected Eustace's brothers from the Channel Islands.

An unknown poet from Picardy wrote a biography of Eustace between 1223 and 1284, and it mainly concerns his year in the forest of Hardelot after escaping from Count Renaud. From his secret hideout, Eustace began 'duping, ambushing and humiliating Renaud again and again, in different disguises and often stealing his horses.' The tale is set in the time of Richard I, King John, and King Philip Augustus of France, and is linked to the medieval myths of Robin Hood.

> In a series of adventures designed to revenge himself on the Count, Eustache uses various disguises in order to harass, embarrass, and rob the Count: a monk, a shepherd, a pilgrim, a coal-man, a potter, a prostitute, a villain [serf], a leper, a fish-merchant, and a baker. In this second set of episodes, Eustache no longer resorts to magic spells but to trickery and deception instead... In assessing the relationships between Eustache the Monk and the Robin Hood legend, we need to consider their similarities and differences, their dates, and their opportunities for contact. Beyond the obvious shared features – both are outlaws living in the forest, venturing out to punish and humiliate the Count of Boulogne and the Sheriff of Nottingham – there are also a number of episodes too similar to be accounted for by coincidence or common tradition. (Carpenter, 2004)

Jeanne de Clisson (1300–1359) – Lioness of Brittany, '*Lionne Sanglante*', Commander of the Black Fleet

Jeanne Louise de Belleville, de Clisson, Dame de Montaigu, was born in Belleville-sur-Vie in the Vendée, France, the daughter of Maurice IV of Belleville-Montaigu and Létice de Parthenay. Aged just 12, Jeanne de Belleville married the 19-year-old Breton noble Geoffrey de Châteaubriant VIII, and had two children. In 1330, she next married Olivier de Clisson IV, holding the great château at Clisson, near Nantes. They had five children, including Olivier V, his father's successor, known as 'the Butcher', and a future Constable of France.

In the Breton War of Succession, Olivier IV de Clisson sided with Charles de Blois, the French choice as the new Duke of Brittany, against the English-backed John de Montfort. After four assaults, the English captured the walled city of Vannes in 1342. Commanders Olivier de Clisson and Hervé VII de Léon were taken prisoner, but de Clisson was exchanged for the Earl of Stafford. Because de Clisson was quickly freed, he was suspected of not having properly defended Vannes, and Charles de Blois alleged he was a traitor. In January 1343, the Truce of Malestroit was signed between England and France, and under safe conditions, de Clisson and fifteen other Breton nobles were invited to a tournament on French soil. Unsuspecting, they went and were arrested, taken to Paris, then summarily beheaded at Les Halles, Paris, in August 1343. 'And then from there his corpse was drawn to the gibbet of Paris and there hanged on the highest level; and his head was sent to Nantes in Brittany to be put on a lance over the Sauvetout gate as a warning to others.'* His guilt was never proven and the nobility was shocked by the French king having de Clisson's body exposed publicly. This was a fate usually reserved for low-class criminals. In the same year, a French court convicted his widow Jeanne, in her absence, as a traitor and confirmed the confiscation of the de Clisson estates. Almost immediately, Edward III of England granted Jeanne an income from lands in Brittany, which the English controlled, knowing the de Clissons had great support across Brittany. Jeanne swore vengeance against the French king, Philippe VI, and with the aid of most of the Breton lords and people, fought for fourteen years to ensure Brittany's continued independence.

Jeanne managed to sell the disputed de Clisson lands to raise an army and began attacking French forces in Brittany. She is said to have attacked a castle occupied by one of the officers of Charles de Blois, Galois de la Heuse, and killed all the garrison except for one individual, freeing him to tell the French king that she would never surrender. However, Château-Thébaud, 12 miles from Nantes, and a former possession of her husband, was attacked by the French, and she was forced back and fled to England. At sea, one son, Guillaume, died of exposure in bad conditions. Her remaining son, Olivier, was brought up in the English court. With Edward III's financial help, she was joined by other Bretons, and fitted out three warships. Painted black, with red sails, the ships of her 'Black Fleet' began hunting down and destroying French ships in the English Channel. Her men would kill entire crews, leaving only one or two survivors to inform the French King, and she became known as the 'Bloody Lioness' and the 'Lioness of Brittany'. She is also said to have attacked coastal villages in Normandy, looting and burning them. In 1346, Jeanne used her ships to supply the English forces at the great victory at Crecy. When Philippe VI died in 1350, Jeanne still continued to attack French ships, especially looking for noblemen, whom she would behead with an axe, and toss their bodies overboard. After more than a decade of piracy, in 1356 Jeanne married Sir Walter Bentley, one of Edward's military captains, and the victor of the 1352 Battle of Mauron. He had been given great estates in Brittany by Edward III, and they settled at Hennebont Castle on the Breton coast, where she died, probably in 1359. Her son Olivier de Clisson, 'the

---

* Cambridge Studies in Medieval Life and Thought: Third Series, *The Law of Treason and Treason Trials in Later Medieval France*, 18 December 2003.

Butcher', later returned from England to Brittany, and fought with great distinction in the War of Breton Succession.

Didrik Pining (*c.*1430–1491) – The Privateer Discoverer of North America?

A nobleman of Hildesheim in Germany, the Hanseatic League records him as a privateer in the service of Hamburg until 1468, hunting down English merchant ships in the North Atlantic. Pining and his partner Hans Pothorst (also from Hildesheim) were called 'pirates who did much damage to the Hanse towns.' From 1468 to 1478, Pining served as an admiral for Christian I of Denmark. Towards the end of Christian's reign, Pining and his ally Hans Pothorst are said to have been 'not less as capable seamen than as matchless freebooters'. In 1478, Pining became the 'Lord' of Iceland, serving until 1481, when he is mentioned as having 'fared out of Iceland.' Pining then served Christian's successor John of Denmark from 1481 until his death, and Pining and Pothorst were captains in the Anglo-Danish Naval War of 1484–1490. About 1484 Pining took three Spanish (possibly Portuguese) ships, which he sent to King John in Copenhagen.

He was admiral of the royal fleet in 1486, and in 1487 took Gotland Island in the Baltic from Sweden for Denmark. In 1489 and 1490, Pining is described as 'hirdstjore (governor) over the whole of Iceland', in Icelandic law. In 1490, Pining was appointed governor of Vardøhus festning (Vardøhus fortress, in Finnmark, Norway), and was probably commander-in-chief in northern waters. Pining may have been killed near there in 1491, with the *Skibby Chronicle* (dating from the 1530s)

Didrik Pining's explorers fighting Inuit on Greenland.

naming Pining and Pothorst among pirates who 'met with a miserable death, being either slain by their friends or hanged on the gallows or drowned in the waves of the sea.' In 1555, in his *History of the Northern Peoples*, Olaus Magnus wrote that because of their piracy, Pining and Pothorst had 'by the Nordic kings been excluded from all human contact and declared outlaws, as a result of their extremely violent robberies and numerous cruel acts against all sailors that they could catch, whether close or distant.'

In Sofus Larsen's 1925 *The Discovery of North America Twenty Years Before Columbus*, he claims that Pining led an expedition to Greenland in the early 1470s with Pothorst and two Portuguese explorers (João Vaz Corte-Real and Álvaro Martins Homem), possibly navigated by John Scolvus. Larsen believes they sailed from Bergen to Iceland and Greenland, and discovered '*Nueva Terra do Bacalhau*' (New Land of the Codfish), which he presumes to be Labrador or Newfoundland. This seems to have been a joint venture in 1473 between the kings of Portugal and Denmark. We know that by 1476 Pining had visited Greenland and encountered hostile Inuit, but had found no trace of its original Norse settlers, so he may well have 'discovered America' on this voyage.

The Victual Brothers and the
Equal Sharers (1392–1449)

The 'Victual Brothers' were a 'pirate collective', beginning as a loosely organised coalition of German, Dutch, Frisian and Danish privateers. It was hired in 1392 by the German duchy of Mecklenburg, on behalf of the imprisoned Albert of Sweden, who controlled Mecklenburg. Mecklenburg hired mercenary captains to relieve the siege of Stockholm by Margaret I of Denmark, who had imprisoned King Albert. The privateers fought their way through the Danish sea blockade to give food to Stockholm's starving citizens, and acquired their name of the 'Victual Brothers'. In 1392, they attacked Lübeck, the only Hanseatic League city supporting Denmark. Other Hanseatic towns and allies provided the Brothers with safe harbours. However, seeing easy pickings, most then turned to outright piracy, seizing ships of any nation in the Baltic and North Seas.

In 1393, they sacked the Norwegian port of Bergen, and in 1394, took the Swedish port of Malmö, holding it for a time. They then based themselves at Visby on Gotland, Sweden's largest island in the Baltic Sea, from 1394, with the motto: 'God's friends and the whole world's enemies.' They were soon also known as the *Likedeelers* (Equal Sharers), as pirates shared their takings. The pirate collective became a feared enemy, taking many Danish ships, mainly in Baltic waters. They also managed to capture ships from England, Holland, Russia and Germany. Pirates such as Störtebeker, Michels and Wigbold owned fast ships that were easily able to capture and plunder slow-moving Hanseatic League ships, full of cargo. Surviving prisoners were usually thrown overboard. Trade ground to a halt in the Baltic Sea and was also badly affected in the North Sea, so Albert of Sweden and Margaret of Denmark agreed a peace to destroy the brotherhood. From 1395, after Margaret united Denmark, Sweden and Norway into the 'Kalmar Union', she used her position to convince the Hanseatic League to co-operate in defeating the pirates. In 1398, 50 Teutonic Knights and the Prussian towns gathered 84 ships, 4,000 men and 400 horses in Danzig to besiege Visby Castle, and took over Gotland until 1408.

Gödeke Michels (*c.*1360–1402) – *Vitalienbrüder*, Leader of the Victual Brothers, 1392–1402

Gödeke Michels, or Gödeke Wessels, was one of the main leaders of the *Vitalienbrüder* (Victual Brothers), and was said to be a learned man from noble stock. His family connections in Pomerania allowed him to hide out there with Störtebeker and other pirate captains after Gotland was taken. His homeport was Heligoland, a North Sea island, but Prussian cities decided in 1401 to send a fleet to kill him. With a crew of 200, Gödeke and his companion Magister Wigbold sailed to Norway, but in April 1402 he was captured with 80 pirates. They were all taken to Grasbrook in Hamburg and beheaded, just a few months after Störtebeker was executed (*see* below).

Klaus Störtebeker (*c.*1360–1401) and the *Likedeelers* (Equal Sharers *c.*1402–1449)

Many of the Gotland Island pirates known as the Victual Brothers sailed to Friesland, in what is now the Netherlands. These remnants of the *Vitalienbrüder* now called themselves *Likedeelers* (equal sharers), a name they also shared with the poor coastal population of Friesland. The pirates allied themselves with some East Frisian nobles, and carried on piracy for decades. The Hanseatic League tried to completely control the Baltic Sea, while the *Likedeelers* expanded their piracy into the North Sea, and along the Atlantic coast, raiding the Low Countries, France and even Spain. The most famous of them, Klaus Störtebeker (born Nikolaus Storzenbecher), from Wismar, allegedly got his name because he could gulp a four-litre beaker of beer in a single swallow.

In Hakluyt's *Voyages*, there is an agreement made by Henry IV of England and the Hanseatic League, regarding the damage done by piracy, recording many English ships that had been plundered:

> Item, in the yeere of our Lord 1395, about the feast of the nativitie of S. John Baptist, the forenamed Godekins [Gödeke] and Stertebeker [Störtebeker], and others of the Hans [Hanseatic League] unjustly tooke a certain ship of Simon Durham, called the Dogger-ship, and the Peter of Wiveton, laden with salt fishes (whereof John Austen was master) upon the coast of Denmarke. And they caried away the

Klaus Störtebeker. Courtesy of
the Wellcome Collection.

saide Dogger, with the furniture thereof, and the foresaid salt fishes,
to the value of 170 pound. Moreover, the master, and 25 mariners in
the same ship they maliciously slewe, and a certaine ladde [load] of
the saide Dogger they caried with them unto Wismer.

In 1401, Störtebeker and 73 of his companions were tricked into
sailing to Hamburg, and off Heligoland a Hamburg warship and a
small fleet under the command of Simon of Utrecht caught up with
Störtebeker. There was a three-day sea battle, and Störtebeker was
captured with some of his crew, and taken to Hamburg. After a short
trial, they were all beheaded. After Störtebeker was beheaded, it is said
that his headless body rose and walked past twelve of the condemned
crew before he was tripped by the executioner. Their decapitated heads
were spiked on poles along the River Elbe. However, in 1429 these
Likedeeler successors of the Victual Brothers once more plundered
Bergen, burning it to the ground. Not until around 1449 did the
nations of northern Europe organise to exterminate the pirates in the
North and Baltic seas.

Erik of Pomerania (1382–1459) – The King of Three Nations who Turned Pirate

The inept Erik, born Bogislaw, fell from being the king of the greatest
realm in Europe to becoming a pirate on the Baltic Sea. Pomerania

Erik of Pomerania.
Courtesy of National
Museum of Sweden.

is on the borders of Poland and Germany, and he was the grand-nephew and heir of the Danish queen Margaret I. After Margaret's son died, she wanted Erik to become the new King of the Nordic countries; he was only six years old when she sent for him. His name was changed from Bogislaw to be more Scandinavian, and in 1392, the 10-year-old Erik was crowned King of Norway at Trondheim. In 1397, he was crowned King of Sweden and Denmark as well. Eric's full title was King of Denmark, Sweden and Norway, the Wends and the Goths, Duke of Pomerania. Noblemen, bishops and priests from all the Nordic countries witnessed the ceremony, and the 'Kalmar Union' of the three nations was established, making 14-year-old Erik the ruler of the greatest kingdom in Europe. His empire stretched from the Arctic Circle (including most of what is now Finland) to the River Eider and Germany, and west to Greenland. However, the nobility were wary of this non-Scandinavian youth, who was described as 'rash, violent and obstinate'.

Queen Margaret remained *de facto* ruler of the three kingdoms until her death in 1412. She was dealing with a war with Holstein, risings among Swedish peasants and the hostility between Erik and the lords, when she collapsed and died. The Danish nobility wanted

Erik's nephew, Christopher of Bavaria, to be their king, and the Swedes wanted a separate constitution and also a different king. In 1434 Swedish farmers and mine workers began a national rebellion, used by the Swedish nobility to weaken Erik's powers. Holstein and the Hanseatic League also were still hostile. In Norway, a peasant rebellion led to the siege of royal castles. The Danish nobles refused both to accept his rule and to ratify Erik's choice of Bogislaw IX of Pomerania as the next king of Denmark, so Erik left Denmark and settled at his castle at Visborg on Gotland Island, Sweden. This led to his deposition by the National Councils of Denmark and Sweden, in 1439. With Erik isolated in Gotland, the Norwegian nobility also felt compelled to depose him in 1440. Within a year, the ruler of the greatest kingdom in Europe had lost three countries. From Visborg Castle, Erik now became the leader of a group of pirates, the revitalised *Vitalienbrüder*, and 'sent forth piratical expeditions against friend and foe alike'. From 1439 to 1449 he lived on Gotland, making his living from piracy against merchant trade in the Baltic. In 1449, he gave up fighting and Gotland was handed over to Denmark, with Erik returning to Pomerania, where he died aged 77 in 1459.

Pier Gerlofs Donia (*c.*1480–1520) – 'Say this Properly, or Die!'

Pier Gerlofs was born near the port of Harlingen in what is now the Netherlands, and was nicknamed *Grutte Pier* (Great Pierre) on account of his height, size and strength. The 'Black Band', a regiment of the Duke of Saxony, plundered Pier's home village of Kimswerd in January 1515, allegedly raping and killing his wife, and burning the church and Pier's estate. He now sided with the Dutch rebels against the rule of the Habsburg emperors, and led a group of pirates, the *Arumer Zwarte Hoop* (the Black Heap [Gang] from Arum), capturing English, Burgundian and Dutch ships. His following grew, and he sailed with 4,000 soldiers from Frisia and Guelders to take Medemblik, slaughtering many of its citizens and taking others prisoner for ransom. Piers razed the town and then took, and burnt, two local castles. In 1517, his *Arumer Zwarte Hoop* took Asperen, killing nearly all its inhabitants. The Hapsburg Emperor Charles V sent the Admiral of the Zuiderzee to free the region of Frisian and Gelder piracy, but his fleet was eventually defeated, with Pier taking eleven of his enemy's ships.

Next, Pier defeated 300 Hollanders in battle and forced his prisoners to repeat a *shibboleth* to distinguish Frisians from Holland and Lower German captives. He also used it when taking ships. It was '*Bûter, brea en griene tsiis: wa't dat net sizze kin, is gjin oprjochte Fries.*'

Pier Gerlofs Donia, a fairly extraordinary 1622 book illustration.

PIERIVS· COGNO· MAGNVS·
LIBERTATIS· ASSERTOR·

(Butter, bread, and green cheese: if you can't say that, you're not a real Frisian.) Those who could not repeat it with a Frisian accent were beheaded personally by Pier. In 1791, two massive swords were found that were said to have belonged to Grutte Pier and his successor Wijerd Jelckama.* Pier was said to be able to wield his great sword so well that he could behead several people with a single blow. His sword weighs almost 15 pounds and is 7 feet long; it is on display in Leeuwarden. A huge helmet said to be Pier's is kept in Sneek town hall. In 1519, the ailing Pier retired, realising that the Habsburg/ Burgundian forces were too great to resist, and died in his bed in Sneek.

---

* Wijerd Jelckama (c.1490–1523) was Pier's lieutenant and fought alongside him against the Hollander and Saxon invaders. He took over command of 4,000 Frisian soldiers, with little success. Losing men, he and his soldiers took part in acts of piracy and looted many Frisian villages, losing support. The remnant of the Frisian army was captured in 1523 and taken to the Leeuwarden in Friesland, all to be publicly beheaded. It was the last revolt in Frisian history.

The Norman Privateers

Jean d'Ango (1480–1551) – Viscount of Dieppe, the 'Medici of Dieppe'

A native of Dieppe, Jean took over his merchant father's business, entering the spice trade with Africa and India and becoming one of the first French corsairs to challenge the monopoly of Spain and Portugal. He also helped *The Compagnie des Indes Orientales* (French East India Company), was a friend of François I, and was nicknamed the 'Medici of Dieppe' for the splendour of his life and his passion for art. In 1521 he was made Viscount of Dieppe, and in 1533, after the king had visited him in his mansion in Normandy, created Captain of Dieppe. With a fleet of about 70 ships, he seemed to engage in blatant piracy in his early career, and in April 1514 his corsairs took a ship from Lübeck. In 1523, three treasure-laden caravels were heading for Spain when intercepted by Verrazzano, Jean Fleury and Jean d'Ango, who were captaining six ships towards Cape St Vincent. Two were taken, and an obsidian mirror was among what was said to be some of Montezuma's treasure, part of the cargo of a vessel belonging to Cortes. Obsidian mirrors were adopted by Mesoamerican rulers, as objects of divination, a medium through which they could look into the future and connect with the realm of the gods. The 'Inca Mirror' is an important piece in the Musée de l'Homme in Paris.

In 1524 d'Ango equipped the *Dauphine*, in which Giovanni da Verrazzano of Florence explored the east coast of North America, and discovered the site of what is now New York City. In 1529 Jean Parmentier reached the coast of Sumatra in two of d'Ango's ships, the *Pensée* and the *Sacre*, attempting to break the Portuguese spice monopoly. John III of Portugal confiscated one of d'Ango's ships in 1530, and in response d'Ango asked for a letter of marque from the French king. D'Ango now attacked the Portuguese fleet in the Atlantic, and threatened to blockade Lisbon, so the Portuguese paid 60,000 ducats in compensation to halt his raids and surrender the letter of marque. In 1537, d'Ango's fleet captured nine ships near the Azores, bringing silver from Peru. From 1535 to 1547, 66 Spanish ships were captured by French corsairs. On the death of François I, d'Ango was imprisoned by the new king Henry in 1549 for failing to pay taxes on proceeds from privateering, and died two years later at his Dieppe mansion. His successes encouraged French captains to invade the Caribbean.

François Le Clerc (*c.*1520–1563), *Jambe de Bois*, Peg Leg

A native of the Cotentin Peninsula, Normandy, he was born at Reville (Greville-Hague) and in 1547 captained the *Fécamp*. He was often the first to board an enemy vessel during an attack. In July 1549, he was in the expedition of 400 men that left Le Havre for the Channel Islands, and was shipwrecked on the island of Sark. Le Clerc was badly wounded in the arm and also lost his leg in the fighting, but the Normans took Sark for a short time. Despite his injury, Le Clerc was active in the 1550s, fighting for France against Charles V of Spain. He seems to have been the first privateer to be knighted, honoured by Henri II in 1551. In July 1552, he stopped privateering in the English Channel and arrived with 150 musketeers at the Portuguese island of Porto Santo, 30 miles from Madeira.

Le Clerc had been commissioned by the French king, who was envious of the incredible wealth that Spain and Portugal were bringing back from the Americas. Le Clerc's loyal lieutenants were Robert Blondel (*see* below) in the *Aventereux* and Jacques de Sores (*see* below) in the *Espérance*, and they sailed with him to the Caribbean in March 1553. Le Clerc assumed command of seven privateer vessels and three royal ships, the latter commanded by himself, Sores and Blondel. The fleet initially attacked Santa Cruz de Las Palmas in the Canary Islands, after its people dared shoot at sailors who were collecting water. Large ransoms were obtained for the most important hostages. Two ships were taken at Las Palmas, to add to the fleet of six large vessels and four smaller boats, with around 800 men. From late April, they attacked San Germán de Puerto Rico, and burned Spanish settlements at Santo Domingo (now in the south of the Dominican Republic), nearby Azua, Monte Cristi (in the north of the Dominican Republic), La Yaguana (now Léogâne, Haiti), Port-au-Prince (Haiti) and Mona and Saona islands. The privateers sailed to Puerto Rico to plan their next expedition, with a fortune in sarsaparilla (*smilax ornata*, then used as a medicine for arthritis and skin problems, and as a flavouring and tonic), and other precious spices and hides. The fleet had four galliots (small, fast rowing galleys), 'whose oars ensure none can escape them', and half of Le Clerc's 800 men were arquebusiers, skilled marksmen.

A year later, in March 1554, Le Clerc, Blondel and Sores attacked again, inland from San Germán de Puerto Rico; then the flotilla stood off Saona Island, taking Spanish ships, before changing their base to Mona Island. Sores then led four ships and 400 men in the night into the harbour of Santiago de Cuba, then the capital of Cuba, and disembarked 300 privateers. He captured the bishop and six other prominent citizens and held the capital for six weeks in 1554, until ransoms of 80,000 pesos were raised. The French spared the church in exchange for all its hidden silver plate, but destroyed the castle and sacked the city of Santiago before sailing off on 16 August. Santiago was so devastated that it was soon succeeded by Havana as the capital. The pirates next sailed to Hispaniola (now Haiti and the Dominican Republic), raiding the coastline, before returning to the Canary Islands and looting again. It is unsure whether Le Clerc and Blondel were with Sores in the later 1555 sacking of Havana. Le Clerc also took the Genoese carrack (a three- or four-masted large ship) *Françon*, using its cannon to strengthen the walls of Brest in Brittany.

In 1555 Le Clerc sided with the great Admiral de Coligny and the Huguenots in France. (Coligny was to be assassinated in the 1572 St Bartholomew's Day Massacre.) Le Clerc and his remaining crew of 330 men were the first Europeans to settle on the island of St Lucia, where he established a French colony. From nearby Pigeon Island he attacked passing Spanish vessels. In 1560, Le Clerc damaged settlements along the coast of Panama, while waiting to intercept the Spanish treasure *flota*. In April 1562, Huguenots across Normandy rebelled against their Catholic king, and Elizabeth I sent English troops to Le Havre to support the Protestants. Le Clerc joined the English Protestants and now attacked French shipping, fighting for the Huguenots in the First War of Religion, in the company of Jacques de Sores. He joined with Protestant English ships in chasing Catholic vessels, and the English bought his cargo and prize ships. In March 1563, he asked for a large pension as a reward, but

Elizabeth turned down his request, and he sailed to the Azores. He was killed there in 1563 while hunting Spanish treasure galleons.

Jacques de Sores *(fl.*1551–1570) – *L'Ange Exterminateur,* the Exterminating Angel

His French name was Jacques Souries, and he was called a 'Norman Huguenot', but was possibly from La Rochelle on the Atlantic Coast. Sores sailed under Le Clerc (*see* above entry), leading the raid on Santiago de Cuba in 1554. He may have stayed in the region, being renowned for his attack on Havana in 1555, possibly assembling 200 men in the Jardines del Rey archipelago, near the northern Cuban coast, as a base of operations. On 10 July, two ships were spotted near the port of Havana being navigated by a Spanish *renegado*. The Spaniard had agreed to guide Sores to an inlet near Havana. Sores secretly landed a few score men at San Lázaro inlet, less than 2 miles from his target. Heading inland, they burnt the wooden doors of Havana's 12-gun Fuerza battery, forcing its 24 defenders to surrender by dawn on 12 July. The French occupied Havana and took four ships into port to careen them. Sores demanded a ransom of 30,000 pesos, and supplies of meat and bread, in order not to burn the town, as well as 500 pesos for each Spanish prisoner and 100 pesos for each slave. The governor had escaped into the interior, and instead led a surprise attack at dawn on 18 July, leading 35 Spanish, 220 black slaves, and 80 Native Indian volunteers. However, they were beaten back, and Sores ordered the execution of all but one of his 31 Spanish prisoners. On the morning of 19 July, Sores hanged dozens of the black slaves by their heels around the outskirts of Havana, and his men used them as target practice, leaving them dead there to discourage any future assaults.

It is fairly likely that he did not find much gold, the treasure he was expecting, as for a month the pirates ransacked houses in the area, killing Spanish settlers and their African slaves. Sores not only destroyed the fort of La Fuerza Vieja in today's Calle Tacón, but burnt most of the town, along with the shipping in the harbour. As well as organising a play 'to insult the Pope', he burnt villages and crops in much of the surrounding countryside, up to 5 miles inland. The pirates tried to collect ransoms for their most important captives, then left on 5 August with the fort's 12 cannon. The Spanish now decided to make Havana the capital of Cuba. They began a massive refortification programme, building the powerful Castillo de la Real Fuerza to replace the burnt fort, and other castles on both sides of the harbour. In the same year, Sores plundered Margarita Island off Venezuela, in revenge for the non-payment of a ransom.

Sores reappears in history in 1570, trying to replicate his successful 1553 attack (then with Le Clerc and Blondel), at Santa Cruz de La Palma, in the Canary Islands. However, this important city, then known as the third most important port in the world, had been rebuilt and refortified with two castles and a city wall, and he was humiliatingly repulsed. In vengeance, on 15 July 1570 he boarded a ship off La Palma, near Tazacorte, and tortured then threw overboard all its passengers. The '40 martyrs of Tazacorte' were 32 Portuguese and eight Spanish Jesuit missionaries. In 1999 a set of crosses was placed on the sea floor to commemorate their martyrdom.

Robert Blondel (*fl.*1553–1568) – the Corsair who Sailed with Hawkins and Drake

His birthplace is unknown but Blondel was the second-in-command with Sores (*see* above) when François le Clerc raided Puerto Rico and Hispaniola in 1553–1554. It is uncertain whether le Clerc and Blondel were with Sores in the 1555 looting of Havana. Unlike the Huguenots Le Clerc and Sores, Blondel fought against the English occupiers of Le Havre in 1563. Blondel was known to have trafficked slaves from Tortuga to Hispaniola, but his movements are unknown until he led French-commissioned corsairs to join John Hawkins' fleet off the West Coast of Africa in 1567. It was Hawkins' third voyage across the Atlantic, picking up slaves from African traders, and his fleet also captured the Portuguese slaver caravel *Madre de Deus* off Ghana. Hawkins thus had about 400 slaves to sell in Santo Domingo and Margarita Island. (The *caravela*, or caravel, had lateen sails for added speed and the capacity to beat to windward. Small and highly manoeuvrable, they were developed by the Portuguese to explore along the West African coast and into the Atlantic Ocean.)

Apart from carrying out illegal trading, Hawkins, his nephew Francis Drake and Blondel were also determined to attack the supply lines and wealth of the Spanish, and pillaged Spanish ships and settlements. Hawkins commanded the royal carrack *Jesus of Lubeck* (leased from Elizabeth I), Drake captained the barque *Judith*, John Hampton captained the *Minion* and the other ships were the *Angel* or *Swallow*. The caravel *Madre de Deus* was now known as the *Grace of God*, captained by Robert Blondel.

After a year of plundering and trading, Hawkins decided to anchor his ships in the port of San Juan de Ulúa (Vera Cruz, Mexico), on 15 September 1568, for repairs and resupply before returning to

England. The Mexican Viceroy, Don Martin Henriquez, agreed not to engage in hostile activity against the privateers while they repaired their storm-ravaged ships. While reprovisioning, a strong Spanish fleet was spotted, which had arrived to suppress a Mexican independence movement. Hawkins and Drake (*q.v.*) did not expect an attack because of the agreed truce, and also had on board several important hostages who had mistaken the English fleet for a Spanish one. However, the Spanish unexpectedly attacked them in the harbour. The privateers lost the galleon *Santa Clara*, which burnt and sank in the port, while the *Minion* was badly damaged while fighting the Spanish flagship *San Pedro*, which was also crippled. The turning point in the battle was the Spanish capture of the island's batteries from the English, and they now poured fire on the English fleet, which was trapped in the port. The *Angel* was hit and sunk, and the *Swallow* was taken by the Spanish troops who had captured the batteries. Blondel set the *Grace of God* on fire before abandoning her and joining Hawkins aboard the *Jesus*. Soon after, Hawkins gave the order to abandon the stricken *Jesus*, and Hawkins, Blondel and some crew were rescued by a pinnace (a small boat) sent from the *Minion*, where Hawkins now assumed command. The *Minion* and Drake's *Judith* managed to escape two fireships. The remaining crew on the *Jesus* were wiped out. The English had lost four ships and 500 men, as well as almost all of their year's loot, and the escaping *Minion* and *Judith* were terribly overcrowded. It is not known whether Blondel died of wounds or was among the 110 crew left by Hawkins in the Southern United States to surrender to the Spanish. Drake returned to England in January 1659 with about 50 or 60 men, and Hawkins a few days later with just 15 survivors. There was no trace of Blondel.

Guillaume Le Testu (*c.*1509–1572) – Huguenot Privateer, Mapmaker

Also known as Têtu, Le Testu was the third generation of captains and pilots sailing from Le Havre in Normandy. He was known to be with other French privateers based at the small island of Tortuga off Haiti, later to become a notorious buccaneer haven:

> *Seuls les épigones d'Ango (Guillaume Le Testu, Leclerc Jambe-de-Bois, Jean Bontemps, Menjouyn de La Cabane, etc.) continuent à opérer dans le golfe du Mexique et la mer des Antilles, en particulier à partir de l'île de la Tortue.*

(Only the captains of the fleet of Jean d'Ango [Guillaume le Testu, Leclerc Peg-Leg, Jean Bontemps, Menjouyn of the Cabin, etc.] continue to operate in the Gulf of Mexico and the Caribbean Sea, in particular departing from the island of Tortuga.)*

This must have been before Jean d'Ango (*q.v.*) died in 1551. Le Testu had studied navigation at Dieppe, becoming a pilot of a ship on an expedition to Brazil in 1551, and charted as far south as the River Plate. In December, his *Salamandre* was badly damaged fighting two Portuguese ships near Trinidad. However, Le Testu had mapped much of the South American coastline by the time of his return to Dieppe in July 1552. Le Testu next piloted the expedition that founded a small French colony called 'French New Haven' (now São Francisco do Sul) near Rio de Janeiro in 1555. Upon returning to France, he presented Henri II with a world atlas of 56 hand-drawn maps, with a southern continent he called 'not imaginary even though no one has found it'. (Presumably this was Antarctica or Australia, 'discovered' around 1820 and 1788 respectively.) In 1556, his *Cosmographie Universelle* was published, using a collection of charts from French, Spanish and Portuguese sources, dedicated to his patron the Huguenot Admiral Gaspard de Coligny. In reward, the king appointed Le Testu his 'royal pilot'.

After the failed attempt of the French settlement near Rio in Brazil, le Testu returned to France in 1559 and redrew a map of the world with significant improvements upon his original 1556 publication, especially as regards the legendary southern continent. In 1566, his *Mappemonde en deux hemispheres* attempted to show accurate latitudes and longitudes across the world. His atlas also clearly outlines the Baja peninsula (on the Pacific coast of Mexico), the Pacific Ocean, Canada and Alaska, for which he must have drawn upon unknown sources.

In 1567 religious civil war broke out once more in France, owing to Huguenot fear of an alliance with Catholic Spain. Le Testu attacked the Spanish throughout 1567 and 1568, but was captured. In June 1571, Charles IX of France wrote to his cousin Philip II of Spain asking for Le Testu's release, which happened on 30 January 1572, after four years in harsh conditions. Le Testu was now appointed captain of a great 80-ton warship, *Le Havre*, with a crew of around 70 men,

---

* Shady Island Pirate Society – *French Corsairs* www.bbprivateer/ca/?=node157

and was sent by the king to chart the Caribbean and southern waters. In February 1573, off Panama, his crew desperately needed fresh water as they were suffering from dysentery, and Le Testu approached another anti-Spanish privateer, Francis Drake (*q.v.*). Drake sent him provisions, with instructions to follow him to a port for drink and fresh meat. In harbour, Le Testu came aboard Drake's ship, informing him that he had been in France at the time of killing of Huguenots (the 'Massacre of St Bartholomew', 1572), the murder of his mentor Admiral de Coligny, 'and divers others murders'. He asked Drake to take him into partnership, along with his great ship, trained crew and navigational knowledge. Drake only had a 20-ton frigate, a pinnace of less than 10 tons, and 31 men. He thus accepted the offer with real relief, although his crew were unsure of French intentions. However, Le Testu was 30 years older, and more experienced than Drake, and told Drake that one could round Cape Horn from the Atlantic to the Pacific by sailing further south, through an easier passage than the Straits of Magellan. From Le Testu's charts, Drake later used this passage between Cape Horn and the South Shetland Islands, which became known as the Drake Passage. This became the main seaway for rounding South America until the opening of the Panama Canal.

Drake had amongst his crew some 'Cimaroons', black slaves who had escaped from the Spanish; the French, English and Cimaroons sailed for Rio Francisco, on the coast of Brazil. They wished to intercept a mule train of gold and silver travelling from Panama to Nombre de Dios to be shipped in the treasure fleet to Spain. On 1 April 1572, the privateers ambushed 45 Spanish soldiers guarding the loot, and there was

> an exchange of bullets and arrows for a time; in which conflict the French Captain was sore wounded with hail-shot in the belly, and one Cimaroon was slain: but in the end, these soldiers thought it the best way to leave their mules with us, and to seek for more help abroad. And because we ourselves were somewhat weary, we were contented with a few bars and quoits of gold, as we could well carry: burying about fifteen tons of silver, partly in the burrows which the great land crabs had made in the earth, and partly under old trees which were fallen thereabout, and partly in the sand and gravel of a river, not very deep of water.*

---

* Nichols, Philip, *Sir Francis Drake Revived*, Collier & Son, NY 1910.

Drake's force swiftly ran for the ships, believing that a Spanish force was close behind, but in the forest 'the French Captain by reason of his wound, not able to travel farther, stayed [hidden, with two Frenchmen], in hope that some rest would recover him better strength.' Le Testu's share of the booty was reported to be around £20,000. Drake had his own problems, but managed to organise another party to recover Le Testu and the rest of the buried silver. They found one of the two French sailors, who had managed to escape from the Spanish. Le Testu had been beheaded and his head taken back to Nombre de Dios, where it was displayed in the marketplace.

Girard Le Testu (*c.*1545–1 August 1582) – the Third of Six Generations of Privateers

Born in Le Havre, this son of Guillaume le Testu (*see* above) was also a captain and pilot, sailing with a fleet of Anglo-French corsairs. Captain of the 100-ton *Mignonne*, in September 1575, he was sailing from Saffi, in Western Morocco. His cargo was 4 pipes of molasses (a pipe is ½ of a tun, 126 US gallons), 21 puncheons of molasses (a puncheon is ⅓ of a tun, 84 US gallons) and 6 barrels (a barrel is ⅛ of a tun, 31.5 US gallons) of molasses, with 4 puncheons and a barrel of capers, 250 boxes of sugar and 3 bales of ostrich feathers. Le Testu was heading for the Channel Islands and encountered the flyboat *Zealander* (between 70 and 200 tons, used as a warship), which carried a letter of marque from the Prince of Orange. Despite being outgunned, Le Testu refused to be taken, and some of his crew were seriously wounded and killed. The *Mignonne* was captured and taken to Flushing. Le Testu must have been released or ransomed, as in June 1582 he was in a fleet of privateers commissioned to protect the Portuguese Azores islands from the Spanish. Le Testu then set sail to take the islands of Santa Maria and São Miguel, and thus capture the incoming Spanish treasure *flota*, which usually put in at the Azores on its way to Spain. The Spanish in turn despatched the Álvaro de Bazán, 1st Marquis of Santa Cruz de Mudela, as admiral of a fleet to intercept the French fleet off the Azores. The marquis was sent as 'Admiral of the Oceans', sailing his personal galley, *La Loba* (the She-Wolf). The marquis arrived too late to prevent the French from landing on São Miguel, but was just in time to save its capital, Ponta Delgada.

On 26 July the fleets met in battle, with General Strozzi, commanding the flagship in the French-Portuguese vanguard, followed by Le Testu in the galleon *Charles*. Severely outnumbered, the marquis won the

Battle of Ponta Delgada, off Terceira Island, against a loose alliance of Portuguese, French, English and Dutch privateers, decisively deciding the struggle for the Azores in favour of the Spanish Habsburgs. After five hours of fighting, around 80 knights, 30 captains, and 300 French sailors were captured by the Spanish, including Le Testu. On 1 August 1582, the French prisoners were escorted to the public gallows on São Miguel and sentenced to death for breaking the peace between France and Castile. Probably 78 French noblemen, including Girard le Testu, were beheaded, and hundreds of French soldiers and sailors were hanged. Girard's son was Guillaume le Testu de Le Havre II, the sixth generation of captain-pilots from Le Havre; he also commanded many ships, sailing in 1608 to 'New France' to aid Samuel de Champlain in the settlement of Quebec.

The Barbary Coast
1480–1816

Terms such as Barbary Corsair, Moorish pirate, Ottoman Corsair and Saracen tend to be used interchangeably, but they generally describe the privateers who operated out of the Barbary Coast, from bases such as Algiers, Tunis, Tripoli and various ports in Morocco. Muslim pirates had operated from bases in North Africa and Turkey during the Crusades (1095–1295), plundering ships carrying Crusaders and pilgrims, and selling many Christians into slavery. For hundreds of years, they collected 'tribute' from the Christian European powers, as protection against attacks on their shipping. There were later Christian corsairs based on Malta, after Rhodes fell. By the 16th century the Muslim corsairs had established a pirate empire, the Barbary States, in the countries of northern Africa.

The revival of European trade with the East during the 15th century was led by merchants from Barcelona, Pisa, Amalfi, Florence, Venice, Genoa and Marseilles, giving rise to a rich and powerful merchant class, who needed protection for their ships travelling in the Mediterranean. Their vessels carried gold, silver, silks, perfumes, spices and wheat from regions such as Egypt, Persia and India, and were usually escorted by warships manned by the Knights of St John, operating from their base in Rhodes (and later Malta). Also, merchant ships carrying timber, tin, iron, furs, cloth and raw materials from west to east were protected at sea by the knights. However, as trade grew, the tribute system fell away and Barbary corsairs increased attacks on Christian merchant ships.

The Barbary Coast (*Maghrib*) on the Northern coast of Africa, extends from the western border of Egypt to the Atlantic Ocean. The term 'Barbary' is derived from the word 'barbarian', a reflection of how Western powers viewed Muslim regions, although they practised slavery themselves. Islamic corsairs terrorised seafaring traders in the Mediterranean Sea and the Atlantic Ocean as far as Iceland, between the 16th and 19th centuries, even taking slaves from English and Irish ports. Muslims were finally expelled from Spain to the North African coast in 1492, and founded states that were ruled as part of the Ottoman Empire, based in Constantinople (Istanbul). The corsairs' initial motive was to defend Muslim North Africa from the Christians of Europe, leading retaliatory raids against Spain, which eventually expanded to piracy against all European nations. Apart from religious justification, the corsairs were a welcome addition to Ottoman naval defences.

Barbary corsairs now received financial and manpower support from the Ottoman sultans to carry out warfare against their enemies, much as European privateers were operating. A 'Letter of Marque' was given by sultans to corsairs, authorising private parties to raid and capture merchant shipping of an enemy nation. The local State leaders in North Africa were loyal to the Ottoman ruler in Constantinople/Istanbul and assisted the corsairs, giving a tribute from their takings to the sultan. The local ruler was in turn supported by booty and slaves captured in corsair raids, which gave him incentive to approve their attacks. Barbary corsairs typically sailed in loose flotillas, targeting enemies both on land and sea. Merchant ships were captured and Christian captives were sold into slavery, ransomed or used to row the corsair galleys. Ships would very often surrender out of terror. Many Christian slaves converted to Islam and became corsairs, called 'renegades'. Moorish galleys were fast, shallow-draft vessels, easy to manoeuvre in low water and estuaries, often disguised as merchant ships and flying false colours. European nations made repeated attempts to defeat the corsairs, including expeditions by the Holy Roman Emperor Charles V in 1541 and by the British, Dutch, and Americans in the early 19th century.

The great slave markets of Algiers and Tunis and were full of Christians for sale. Some were sailors, but many more men, women and children were captured from coastal raids across Europe. In 1630, of the 32,000 slaves for sale, approximately 3,000 were English. In 1631, the value of 100 slaves was estimated to be about £2,500 (worth £6 million or $8 million today), depressed because of a glut of slaves at that time. In 1645, a raiding party of Turks landed at Penzance and elsewhere on the coast of Cornwall and took 240 men, women and children. In 1646, Parliament sent Edmund Cason to Algiers to negotiate with

Pasha Yusuf for the release of English slaves. He paid an average of £30 a man (women fetched a higher price), but after having ransomed 250 captives, ran out of funds. Over the next eight years, until he died in Algiers, he saved most of the rest. The Barbary pirates provoked the United States' first wars in the Middle East, compelling the US to build a navy. The Barbary Wars with the United States ended in 1815 after a naval expedition ordered by President Madison defeated the Barbary powers, ending three decades of American tribute payments. Some 700 Americans had been held hostage over the course of 30 years. In 1816, a combined British and Dutch fleet bombarded Algiers until it was rubble, to stop slavery. Piracy based in Algiers continued, although weakened, until the French captured the city in 1830.

The Barbarossa (red beard) brothers – Aruj (Oruç) Reis (*c*.1470–1518) and Khizr Reis (*c*.1480–1546)

The brothers were originally possibly Christians, born on the Greek island of Lesbos to a retired Janissary soldier Yaqub, who had been granted land on the island, and the widow of a Christian priest. Of four

Italian woodcut of Barbarossa, *c*.1535 by unknown artist. Courtesy of Rijksmuseum.

sons, Aruj was the eldest and Khizr the youngest or second youngest. Their father Yaqub had become a potter and, with a boat of his own, traded his wares across the Mediterranean. Aruj helped with the boat, while Khizr assisted with the pottery. Aruj claimed to have helped ferry Jews and Muslims out of Spain after the Spanish conquest in 1492. Aruj began his pirate career by attacking Aegean ships from Lesbos, but was captured by the Knights of Rhodes and sent to be a galley slave. After two years he was bought by an Egyptian emir, and was reunited with his brother Khizr in the great port of Alexandria. Another version of his early life is that Aruj was returning from a trading expedition to Tripoli when he and his brother Ilyas were attacked by a galley of the Knights Hospitaller. Ilyas was killed, and Aruj wounded. Their father's boat was taken, and Aruj was held prisoner and detained in Bodrum Castle for nearly three years. Upon learning the location, his brother Khizr went to Bodrum and managed to help his brother escape. They were soon both called *reis,* meaning captain.

Aruj (also known as Aruz or Baba Oruç, Father Oruç) and Khizr now began operating out of Alexandria with ships provided by the local ruler. Together the brothers captured the galleys of Pope Julius II, and in about 1505 moved their operations to the western Mediterranean, where they acquired gold, commanded eight galleons, and began to acquire property and slaves. They flooded their new base of Djerba with plunder. Other Muslim corsairs began to follow the Barbarossa brothers, as they acquired other bases along the Barbary Coast and built several strong fortresses, to defend the ports of Algiers, Tripoli and Tunis. The Barbarossa brothers paid the Sultan of Tunis one-fifth of their booty to use Tunis as their headquarters. Some time afterwards, they moved to the port of Djidjelli near Algiers, after a disagreement with the Sultan of Tunis. They carried out more attacks on the Spanish, raiding coastal towns and forts. In 1508 Aruj, now feared everywhere as *Barbarossa,* captured 23 merchant ships and 4,100 Christian slaves. Fear of him was so great that coastal villages and whole towns moved inland from the coast for security.

By 1510, Aruj was incredibly wealthy, and he and Khizr owned eight well-built galleons, vast property and hundreds of slaves. By 1512, Aruj alone commanded 12 galleys and 1,000 men at arms. However, in 1512, Aruj had his left arm shot away by a Spanish cannon, while leading the charge against the Spanish fort outside Bougie. He was rushed to Tunis for surgical treatment, while Khizr brought 11 ships back to port. Khizr captured a Genoese ship laden with jewellery and other treasures, angering Louis XII of France, who had jurisdiction over Genoa. The Genoese Senate immediately dispatched a squadron of 12 large galleys to kill the Barbarossa brothers.

Aruj now took advantage of local dissent towards the policies of the Sultan of Algiers, who had failed to respond to the Spanish threat. He therefore took the port and killed the sultan, proclaiming himself as sultan in 1516. After two years of conflict with areas still controlled by the Spanish, and many violent clashes with Crusader knights and Spanish soldiers, the red-bearded Aruj was killed while trying to escape a siege of the town of Tlemcan. Khizr assumed control and began dyeing his brown beard red, like his brother, to maintain the mystique of a powerful ruler, becoming the new 'Barbarossa' of the history books.

Khizr, or *Khayrad'din* (the Gift of God, as he was soon called) vowed vengeance, and led attacks upon entire fleets of ships, taking Tunisian ports. Barbarossa's fleet captured a number of Spanish ships returning from the Americas full of gold. His corsairs also raided coastal Spain, Italy, and France, carrying off booty and Christians to be sold as slaves. In 1522, Barbarossa's ships assisted in the Ottoman conquest of the island of Rhodes, which had been a stronghold for the Knights of St John. In autumn 1529, Barbarossa helped an additional 70,000 Moors to flee from Andalusia, where the Spanish Inquisition was trying to convert Moslems. Also in 1529, he was commissioned by the Sultan of Turkey to send troops to drive the Spanish out of Algiers. Barbarossa recaptured Algiers in that year, expelled the Spanish, and placed Algiers under the authority of the Ottoman Sultan, Emperor Suleiman I. In 1534, Khizr's ships sailed up the River Tiber, causing panic in Rome.

In 1538 Pope Paul III organised a Holy League, consisting of the Papal States, Spain, the Knights of Malta (expelled from Rhodes 16 years earlier), and the Republics of Genoa and Venice. They assembled a fleet of 157 galleys under Andrea Doria, to smash Barbarossa and the Ottoman fleet. Barbarossa had only 122 galleys when the two fleets met off Preveza on 28 September. Barbarossa took the offensive and crashed through Doria's attempt at encirclement. The Ottomans sank 10 ships, captured 36, and burned 3, without losing a single ship. They also captured around 3,000 sailors, at a cost of 400 dead and 800 wounded. Algerian corsairs were now to dominate the Mediterranean, with Ottoman protection, for three centuries. Barbarossa took his captured ships and prisoners to Topkapi Palace,

Istanbul, to meet Sultan Suleiman the Magnificent. The emperor needed a great naval commander, as his inexperienced navy was not able to compete properly with the better ships of the seasoned Genoese and Venetian fleets. They had trouble just protecting their own territorial waters, which prevented the further expansion of the Turkish/Ottoman Empire.

Khizr was now universally known in the Islamic world as *Khayrad'din* (the Gift of God) and the Sultan summoned him to his court. Suleiman appointed him *Beylerbey* or 'Governor of Governors' of Ottoman North Africa, and gave him the governorship of Rhodes. He also made Khayrad'din *Kaptan Pasha* (Lord High Admiral) of the Ottoman naval fleet. Khayrad'din reorganised the dockyard system, rebuilt the fleet and improved the quality of the sailors. His new fleet of war galleys each had 50 long oars, with cannon on the foredecks. They were built similarly to today's racing shells, with the length being eight times the beam, and very fast. Over the next few years Khayrad'din would conquer and sack Christian forts in the Aegean, the Ionian Sea and loot the Italian coastline. With the resources of the Ottoman Empire, as Sultan of Algiers he was able both to defend his territory and sack Christian areas such as Nice and Majorca. Venice sued for peace in October 1540. By the time Khayrad'din Barbarossa retired to his palace in Istanbul in 1545, the Ottomans controlled the Mediterranean from the Black Sea to the Atlantic coast of Morocco, and did so until the Battle of Lepanto in 1571. He never returned to North Africa and his kingdom of Algiers. He remained in Constantinople and in 1546, at the age of 63, after appointing his son to rule Algiers, passed away. Suleiman the Magnificent built Barbarossa a tomb of grey granite alongside the Bosphorus, engraved in Arabic 'Dead is the Captain of the Sea'; his victory at Preveza is marked by a holiday in Turkey, where he is a national hero, and is considered one of the greatest men in the history of the Ottoman Empire.

Sayyida (*c.*1485–after 1452) – *Hakima Tatwan al-Hurra*, the 'Undisputed Leader of the Pirates in the Western Mediterranean'

She was born to a prominent Muslim family in the Moorish kingdom of Granada, Spain, but in 1492 Ferdinand and Isabella of Spain conquered Muslim Granada. The Spanish armies of Castile and Aragon murdered and enslaved up to 100,000 Muslims, and forced another 20,000 to flee to North Africa. As refugees, her family settled in Chaouen, Morocco. In a marriage arranged when she was a child, she now wed the much older Abu al-Hasan al-Mandri, the Governor of Tétouan on the Moroccan coast. They jointly ruled the city, which had been destroyed in 1490. The couple rebuilt the high walls surrounding the city and the Grand Mosque. Then in 1515, her husband died. Sayyida now declared herself Governor of Tétouan (*Hakima Tatwan*), obtained the title of *al-Hurra* (a noble lady who is free and independent).

She and her husband had refortified Tétouan, not only for defence, but to launch a *jihad* (holy war), to regain Granada and then the rest of Spain from the Catholics. The success of the Barbarossa brothers, sailing out of Algiers, led to Sayyida entering an alliance with them, some time before 1520. She knew that a stronger force was needed to attack the infidels, and thus assembled a great corsair fleet, attacking both Spanish and Portuguese shipping routes in the Mediterranean. Later realising that it was impossible to retake Granada, she used captured booty and money from slavery and ransoms to make Tétouan a wealthy, strongly fortified city; as a result the Old City of Tétouan is now a UNESCO World Heritage site. Families who had been expelled from Spain were given money to prosper once more, and she was a popular ruler. For 20 years, her ships dominated the Western Mediterranean, while the Barbarossas held the East. In Spain and Portugal, she is mentioned in official State papers as 'lady-ruler', and was the 'undisputed leader of the pirates in the Western Mediterranean', according to Fatima Mernissi in *The Forgotten Queens of Islam*.

In 1541, Sayyida married King Ahmed al-Wattasi of Morocco. He took the unprecedented step of leaving Fez, and travelled to Tétouan for the wedding. This was the only time that any Moroccan king had left the capital to be married. Sayyida carried on ruling as Governor of Tétouan, supervising raids on Spanish ports such as Gibraltar, and organising hostage negotiations. However, around 1542 she was probably deposed by her stepson, a son of King Ahmed, after 30 years of governing Tétouan. She probably died in poverty, but there are no records of her later life or death.

Turgut Reis (1485–1565) – Dragut Rais, 'the Drawn Sword of Islam'

Truly the sea was his element
— Luis del Marmol Carvajal (1520–1600)

Probably of Greek descent, he was born in Anatolia (Turkey) and went to sea as a corsair aged 12, rising in service under the Barbarossa brothers, becoming one of the outstanding commanders of his day. When Aruj Reis was killed in 1518, his younger brother Khizr Barbarossa assumed leadership of the corsair fleet of about 65 ships. Barbarossa promoted Turgut to the position of *reis* (captain or admiral) and made him his lieutenant. Turgut and Barbarossa remained trusted comrades for almost 30 years, until Barbarossa's death in 1546. Sultan Suleiman had come to power in 1521 and his imperial plans included the conquest of Rhodes, to get rid of the Knights of St John, whose fleet protected Christian shipping. Muslim merchants suffered heavy losses if they refused to pay the Knights of St John a tribute for the protection and safe passage of their ships, and the Knights enjoyed a virtual monopoly over commercial sea routes and ports in the eastern Mediterranean. Suleiman determined to end their monopoly, and in December 1522 after a six-month siege and violent fighting, conquered the island of Rhodes. The Knights were now expelled from Rhodes, Bodrum and other towns in the Aegean Sea, so made arrangements with the Holy Roman Emperor Charles V to move to Malta. In return, the Knights would provide safety and protection for Spanish holdings in Libya, in particular at that time, Tripoli.

The Knights of Malta were now closer to the Sultan's North African ports of Algiers, Tripoli and Tunis, constantly fighting Turgut and his corsairs. In 1533 Khizr Barbarossa sailed to Istanbul with Turgut Reis, and from 1534, with Barbarossa as Grand Admiral of the Ottoman Navy, they transformed the fleet and shipyards. Turgut played a major role in Barbarossa's great victory of Preveza in September 1538, against the joint naval forces of Spain and Venice. After a joint campaign in June 1540, Salih Reis and Turgut Reis brought their fleet to Corsica to careen several ships, but were captured and taken prisoner by Genoese soldiers. Turgut Reis first served as a galley slave in Andrea Doria's flagship, and was then imprisoned in a Genoese dungeon. It took his friend Barbarossa four years and a huge ransom to have Turgut and Salih released. Having been humiliated and often lashed, Turgut Reis was vengeful, now killing without mercy, as when he captured Mahdia in Tunisia from the Spanish in 1544. Turgut also raided the coast of Italy, massacred the inhabitants, burned villages, and seized captives. He came to be known in the Christians of the Mediterranean coasts as 'The Sword of Islam'.

Barbarossa died in 1546, but Turgut continued attacking merchant shipping and sacking coastal towns. The Maltese Knights of St John, Genoese, Venetians and Spanish were equally attacking Muslim shipping and ports, irrespective of the season or the weather conditions. In early 1551 Admiral Andrea Doria cornered Turgut on the eastern side of the Kantara causeway, between Djerba Island and the Tunisian mainland, but Turgut secretly cut a channel to the other side, enabling his ships to break out into the open seas. With Grand Admiral Sinan Pasha, he next attacked Malta and Gozo, but with insufficient manpower they turned their focus to Tripoli in Libya, and took it. From 1554 Piyale Pasha, the new Grand Admiral, worked closely with Turgut, being determined to learn the craft of seamanship from the best possible expert. With Turgut Reis and Salih Reis, Piyale now commanded a large fleet to capture the islands of Elba and Corsica in 1554. Turgut Reis was promoted to *Beylerbey* (Chief Governor) of Tripoli. In June 1558 Piyale Pasha and Turgut Reis joined their fleets for an attack on Italian and Spanish towns. During the next three months, they captured and sacked Messina, Reggio Calabria, Amalfi, Salerno, Massa Lubrense, Cantone, Sorrento, Torre del Greco, Tuscany, Piombino and the Aeolian Islands. In September they pillaged Minorcan ports, then both admirals returned to Constantinople with ships full of booty and slaves.

Their fierce attacks upon Italy and Spain forced the formation of a Holy League between Spain, Venice, Genoa, the Papal States and the Knights of Malta, for a counter-attack. The Holy League fleet of 120 ships sailed out from Messina in March 1560, making for Turgut's main naval base on the island of Djerba. Spies informed Piyale Pasha at Constantinople of the forthcoming attack and he assembled a fleet to head for Djerba, joining Turgut Reis, who had moved his ships out to sea to safety. In March 1560, the Holy League captured Djerba and prepared for battle against the incoming Ottoman fleets. However, in May 1560, with superior power and better tactics, Turgut and Piyale destroyed the Christian fleet, taking as many as 5,000 prisoners.

Since their arrival in 1530, the Knights of St John had turned Malta into a naval base from where they attacked Islamic shipping. The island's position in the centre of the Mediterranean made it strategically crucial, especially as the Ottoman Turks increased their assaults into the western Mediterranean throughout the 16th century. In 1563, Sultan Suleiman ordered the conquest of Malta and the total extinction of the Knights. Turgut was Beylerbey of Tripoli, Admiral of the Mediterranean fleet and the admiral most familiar with the seas surrounding Malta, but his advice was not sought during the preparation for the campaign. The Sultan's force of 200 ships and about 40,000 men reached Malta on 18 May 1565, and on 2 June Turgut Reis joined with 15 ships carrying about

2,000 men. On 17 June while directing his own men in the bombardment of Fort St Elmo, he suffered a mortal head wound from debris when a cannon shot struck nearby. Aged 80, he died on the island six days later. Uluç Ali Reis took his body to Tripoli, where Turgut was buried in the grounds of Dragut Mosque. The Ottomans were unsuccessful, and their fleet sailed home on 7 September 1565 with only 6,000 men surviving. Turgut Reis had spent almost 70 years at sea, sacking more than 80 cities, towns and islands, capturing hundreds of ships, killing an unknown number of people and taking more than 50,000 prisoners as slaves.

He is still remembered at Cullera, Valencia, where the Dragut Rais museum commemorates his attack in 1550. His statue is in a cave downstairs, where he is said to have kept his hostages before taking them to the slave market in Algiers. In the coastal towns of Liguria and of Vieste, Italy, annual festivals include visits to the location of *La Chianca Amara* (the bitter stone) near Vieste Cathedral where Dragut Rais in July 1554 ordered the beheading of almost everyone that he could not carry away as slaves. In Mallorca, Pollenca's *Fiesta La Patrona* re-enacts the 1550 clash between local hero Joan Mas and invading Barbary pirates led by Dragut (Turgut) Rais. Villagers dress up in pyjamas and face paint before staging battles on the streets with swords and sticks.

Uluj Ali (1519–21 June 1587) – Giovanni Dionigi Galeni, also known as Kılıç Ali Paşa, Farta, the Christian Saracen Pirate

His Arabic nickname was *farta*, scurvied, caused by the disease picked up by sailors from lack of Vitamin C; if not fatal, it causes red spots on the skin. Giovanni was born in Le Castella, Calabria, Italy, and taken prisoner by Ottoman pirates on 29 April 1536, at the age of 17. He was captured by Ali Ahmed, one of the Barbarossa's Ottoman corsairs, and put to work as a galley slave, permanently chained by one foot under his seat. There were five prisoners to a bench, all pulling a single oar, and each half-naked. If heading into battle, iron bracelets were clapped over the wrist of each rower, so there was no chance of resistance or escape. They were regularly whipped, usually with a wet rope that had been dipped in the sea, to give added pain from the salt getting into bloody wheals. (The Christians also used Muslim galley slaves in the same manner). Giovanni took part in the Battle of Preveza in the Ionian Sea off Greece in 1538, where Barbarossa's Ottoman fleet defeated ships of the Holy League sent by the Pope. After a few years on the oars, Giovanni renounced his Christian faith in order to kill

Uluj Ali leading Ottoman troops to Tunis, 1569.

a Turk who had slapped him, thus avoiding the death penalty under Islamic Law. By 1541 the 'renegade' was becoming known as Uluj Ali (Ucciali to Italians), and serving in the fleet led by the great Admiral Turgut Reis, the Bey of Tripoli. Uluj Ali's father had been a sailor, and his knowledge of the seas allowed him to rise quickly, gaining enough prize money and goods to buy a share in an Algerian brigantine. Soon he was the owner and captain of a galiot, and then a galley, earning fame for his bravery.

Uluj Ali also impressed the admiral Piyale Pasha, and in 1550, owing to his successes in the Mediterranean, Uluj Ali was rewarded by Piyale Pasha with the administration of the island of Samos. In 1560, he served Turgut Reis and Piyale Pasha during the Battle of Djerba, when a Christian Alliance fleet was defeated in a few hours. Uluj Ali was made the Chief Governor of Alexandria in 1565 and participated in the Siege of Malta in that year. He was now known as Uluç Ali Reis, *reis* meaning captain or admiral. Piyale Pasha appointed Uluj Ali to become Turgut Reis's successor as Bey of Tripoli, when Turgut Reis was killed during the Maltese siege. Uluj was appointed Pasha of Tripoli by Sultan Suleiman I, and known as Uluç Ali Paşa. His fleet made constant raids, taking slaves from Sicily, Naples and his birthplace of Calabria.

In 1568, Sultan Selim II appointed Uluj Ali to become Pasha and Beylerbey of Algiers. In 1569 with an army of 5,000 men, Uluj Ali attacked and captured Tunis, whose sultan had been restored by the Spanish. In 1570 he sailed to Istanbul to request more ships and men to evict the Spaniards from North Africa, but came across five Maltese ships and captured four of them. The Maltese admiral escaped, but returning to Malta in disgrace was strangled, placed in a sack and thrown in the harbour. Uluj Ali returned to Algiers to celebrate, but in early 1571 he was faced with a mutiny of his Janissaries. They wanted their overdue wages; Uluj Ali put to sea, leaving the mutinous soldiers behind.

With each campaign on land or sea, one-fifth of the slaves captured became the property of the Great Sultan at Constantinople/Istanbul. The most attractive girls were also sent to his current harem, which consisted of about 300 young women. Most were replaced by younger girls as they aged. Apart from the thousands of slaves he acquired, there were also 'tribute boys'. Every four years men scoured the Turkish Empire to select the most promising boys from non-Moslem families and train them for royal service. These agents were 'a body of officials more skilled in judging boys than trained horse-dealers are in judging colts'. The boys were trained to be the Sultan's personal and loyal slaves, rising in government. The most intelligent became diplomats and advisors, while the strongest became soldiers in the élite corps of infantry, the Janissaries. This 'Praetorian Guard' was formed almost entirely of tribute boys or slaves, well paid, highly trained in military arts, swearing celibacy, and with absolute obedience to the Sultan.

Uluj Ali joined the great Ottoman fleet of Ali Pasha, commanding the left squadron of ships on 7 October 1571 in the disastrous Battle of Lepanto. Uluj Ali outmanoeuvred his direct opponent, Admiral Andrea Doria, but when he realised the day was lost, managed to gather up the remaining ships of the Ottoman fleet and sailed into Constantinople with 87 vessels. Perhaps 50,000 Turks died, 256 Turkish vessels were captured or sunk and 15,000 Christian galley slaves were liberated.

Uluj had captured the great flag of the Maltese Knights from their flagship and presented it to the Sultan, who awarded him the honorary title of *Kılıç* (Sword). In the same month as the battle, Uluj Ali was appointed Kabudan Pasha (Grand Admiral) and Beylerbey of the Isles (of the Mediterranean). He was now known as Kılıç Ali Pasha. With Piyale Pasha, he began rebuilding the Ottoman fleet with heavier ships modelled on the Venetian *galleasses*, and heavier artillery for the galleys. In 1572, now Kapudan Pasha (commander-in-chief of the Ottoman navy), he sailed with 250 galleys and other ships to seek vengeance for Lepanto, but the Christian fleet stayed anchored in an inlet, refusing to give battle. In 1573 he campaigned along the coasts of Italy, but Tunis was now recaptured by the Christians. Uluj Ali took his fleet and a large army and recaptured Tunis in 1574. In 1576 he again raided Calabria and in 1578 ended another mutiny of the Janissaries in Algiers. Aged about 65, in 1584 he commanded an expedition to Crimea, and in 1585 sailed from Alexandria to put down anti-Ottoman risings in Lebanon and Syria. He died in Istanbul, and is buried at the Kılıç Ali Paşa Mosque, which he had built in 1580. The greatest of all the Ottoman admirals along with Barbarossa, he was called Uchali in *Don Quixote de la Mancha*, and known everywhere as Ali Pasha.

Koca Murat Reis (*c.*1540–1609) – Murat Reis the Elder

Born in Albania or Rhodes, he was a young boy when Kari Ali Reis captured him in 1546, and he adopted the Muslim name Murat. After Kari's death in 1565, he took over as admiral of Kari's fleet. On his first cruise he shipwrecked his flagship off Sicily, but a few weeks later his smaller ships captured a prize, using it to continue their expedition. More ships were taken off the Spanish coast, and he returned to Algiers with three ships and slaves to sell. Murat developed the tactic of using smaller galiots, which lowered their masts and concealed themselves behind larger galleys, so that enemy ships underestimated his force. Through the 1570s, his reputation grew through land and sea attacks on Spanish and Italian ports and shipping. In 1570 Murat Reis, commanding 25 galleys, was ordered to clear the seas between Crete, Rhodes and Cyprus, to prepare for the taking of Cyprus. He then blocked Venetian ships sailing from Crete to assist Venetian-held Cyprus, which fell to the Ottomans.

Murat next captured two powerful galleasses, which were taking the Viceroy of Sicily home to Spain in 1574, incurring the enmity of Philip II. The viceroy and his entourage were ransomed for an exorbitant amount, and Philip put a price on the head of Murat Reis. To show his personal approval, the Sultan of Algiers named Murat 'Captain of the Sea' in 1574, but the Ottoman Emperor withheld his approval of the title for 20 years. In 1578 Murat captured a flotilla from France carrying even more in silver and gold coins than the previous ransom taken from Philip II. In 1580 Murat captured the papal flagship and in 1581 alone, he took more than a million ducats in gold and silver (said to be the equivalent to the annual salary of 40,000 tradesmen). In 1585 Murat commanded the first Moorish expedition into the Atlantic Ocean, taking several of the Canary Islands and sacking Lanzarote.

Although outnumbered, in 1595 Murat captured three Sicilian galleasses, while destroying a larger fleet of Knights of Malta warships. For the last 31 years of his life, he helped to crush piracy in the Aegean Sea while raiding Christian cities in the Adriatic. He was also ordered to protect the profitable trade routes between Anatolia and Egypt from being attacked by the Venetians, French and Knights of Malta. His daring attacks upon Southern Italy and captures of Spanish warships around the mid-1590s led to his being given command of ever-larger Ottoman naval fleets. This allowed him to completely control the Eastern Mediterranean by the early 17th century. In 1609, Murat heard that there was a joint French-Maltese fleet of 10 galleys, including the famous 90-gun *Galeona Rossa*, off Cyprus, and sailed to engage them. He severely damaged and took the *Galeona Rossa*, with 6 out of 10 Christian galleys being captured, along with 160 cannons, 500 men and 2,000 muskets. Murat Reis was seriously injured during the battle and possibly died or retired at this time. There is a Murat Reis Mosque in Rhodes, where he was buried in accordance with his will, and his tomb became a popular shrine for Ottoman sailors in the following centuries, visiting it for blessings before setting sail.

Three decades later, a Murat Reis was killed in 1638 during the siege of Vlore, the largest city in Albania. It is almost impossible to believe that this is the same Murat still fighting, aged 98, and they are probably a father and son/grandson of the same name.

There was yet another Murat Reis who joined the fleet of Turgut Reis, possibly being captured. This Murat also sailed with Piri Reis and with Barbarossa to be received by Sultan Suleiman, being involved in the building of a new war fleet on the Golden Horn. He took part in the Battle of Preveza in 1538, preventing the ships of the Holy League from landing, fought in the main sea battle alongside Turgut Reis, and later was rewarded with the post of Commander of the Ottoman Indian Ocean Fleet by Suleiman in 1552. He was now known as Hint Kaptanı (Captain of the Indian Ocean), succeeding Piri Reis. This Murat's fleet used the ports of Basra and Aden in the Persian Gulf, with its main base being at Suez on the Red Sea. From Basra, he sailed with 18 galleys to the Indian Ocean to fight a Portuguese fleet of 25 galleys from Goa. After heavy losses on both sides, both fleets retired to their home ports for repairs at nightfall, and Sultan Suleiman dismissed Murat Reis from his post for his failure. Murat again joined Turgut Reis, until Turgut was killed at Malta in 1565. Another Murat Reis (the Younger) – Jan Janszoon van Haarlem – is described later in this volume.

Siemen Danziger (*c.*1579–*c.*1615) – Ivan de Veenboer, 'Simon the Dancer', Simon Simonson, Suleiman Reis, *Delli Reis* (Captain Devil), 'Captain Crazy'

Born in Dordrecht, Netherlands, his birth name was Ivan de Veenboer, and like Murat Reis, he was known by a variety of names, including Simon Reis, Siemen Danziger, Zymen Danseker, Deli Kapitan, Simon de Danser, and Simon Simonson. Like his contemporary renegado and ally John Ward (Yusuf Reis), he commanded corsair squadrons from Tunis and Algiers. Simon probably served as a privateer for Holland against Spain in the Eighty Years' War, or Dutch War of Independence, receiving a letter of commission in 1606, and settled in Marseilles. In 1607, he stole a small boat with other privateers, and immediately attacked and took a larger ship. With John Ward, they sailed to Algiers. Ward sailed on to Tunis and made that his base of operations. A contemporary ballad relates how they argued about spoils, and the second part of the *Sea-man's Song of Ward and Dansekar the Dutchman* reads:

English Ward and Dansekar
Begin greatly now to jar

About the true dividing of their goods;
Both ships and soldiers gather head,
Dansekar from Ward is fled:
So full of pride and malice are their bloods.
Ward doth only promise
To keep about rich Tunis,
And be commander of those Turkish seas;
But valiant Dutch-land Dansekar
Doth hover near unto Algier,
And there his threat'ning colours now displays.
These pyrates thus divided,
By God is sure provided
In secret sort to work each other's woe;
Such wicked courses cannot stand,
The Divel thus puts in his hand,
And God will give them soon an overthrow.

The Pasha of Algiers welcomed Simon as an addition to his corsairs, and he was 'made welcome as an enemy of the Spaniards', becoming a leading captain. Simon specialised in taking mainly Spanish ships and prisoners to Algiers, and his fleet grew as he incorporated captured ships. He took more than 40 ships in a two-year period after 'turning Turk', and lived in an opulent palace. An experienced shipbuilder, Simon taught the Muslim captains how to sail foreign prize ships, all of which were incorporated into his corsair fleet. The shipyards in Algiers were used to modify these captured merchant ships into warships. With such a huge fleet to support with booty, Simon began attacking ships of any nation, making trading in the Mediterranean increasingly difficult. Simon even led the corsairs through the Strait of Gibraltar into the Atlantic, to seek Spanish treasure fleets and possibly raided as far north as Iceland. *The Ballad of Simon the Dutchman* has the lines:

...He trusteth not his country-men,
He shews the right condition of a thief.
At Tunis in Barbary
Now he buildeth stately
A gallant palace and a royal place,
Decked with delights most trim,
Fitter for a prince than him,
The which at last will prove to his disgrace.
To make the world to wonder,

This captain is commander
Of four-and-twenty ships of sayl,
To bring in treasure from the sea
Into the markets every day:
The which the Turks do buy up without fail.
His name and state so mounteth,
These countrey-men accounteth
Him equal to the nobles of that land;
But these his honours we shall find
Shortly blown up with the wind,
Or prove like letters written in the sand...

A French fleet, assisted by eight Spanish galleys, sought to kill him, but Simon escaped because of a sudden storm, enabling him to sail in shallower waters near the coast. His pursuers, with a greater draft, could not follow for fear of grounding. Then an English squadron, and another fleet of eight Spanish ships were also sent after him. Knowing that his life was greatly at risk because of the attacks on him by three dedicated naval squadrons, in 1609 he fled from Algiers with his possessions. Simon next took a Spanish galleon off Valencia, allowing Jesuit priests on board to go free, with a message for Henri IV of France. Simon wanted to return to his wife and children in Marseilles, and to be pardoned for his crimes. After seizing four warships and booty, killing 150 Algerian Turks and stealing two large brass cannons belonging to the Algerian government, Simon was reunited with his family shortly after arriving in Marseilles on 17 November, 1609. He took with him the four captured warships and a fortune put at half a million crowns. He was officially welcomed by the Duke of Guise, and Simon gave him 'a present of some Turks, who were at once sent to the galleys' and some captured Spanish gold from the ships he had taken.

Simon stayed in Marseilles for a year, and in 1610 planned to raid the city of Algiers, in return for a full pardon. He asked permission and support from the king. The French authorities refused, but granted him permission to lead an expedition against his former allies, the Barbary corsairs. Simon returned to Marseilles from the voyage in early 1611. In 1615 Louis XIII asked Simon to negotiate the release of captured French ships, held by the new Dey, Yusuf, who controlled Tunis and its great slave market. The Turkish militia of Tunis was the strongest army in the region, with 9,000 élite infantry troops, the Janissaries, and regiments of irregular cavalry. There were also more than 200 galleys with marines and corsairs in the port. The famous

'Captain Devil' invited the Dey of Tunis aboard his flagship for a feast. In return for his hospitality he was invited to dinner next day at Yusuf Dey's fortress. As he stepped through the door he was seized by Janissaries and made to kneel before the Dey, who shouted he had committed terrible crimes against the Moors. A Janissary stepped forward to cut off Simon's head.

John Ward (*c.*1553–1622) – 'Jack' Ward, 'Birdy' Ward, Yusuf Reis, the Original Jack Sparrow

Probably born in the coastal village of Faversham, Kent, Ward worked on fishing boats, and after the failed Armada invasion of 1588 went privateering against Spanish ships with a Letter of Marque. In 1602 John Ward may have been jailed for plundering a Danish ship in the Caribbean. James I succeeded to the Crown in 1603, and ended the Spanish wars, rescinding all the English privateers' letters of marque. Ward does not initially seem to have turned to piracy, but worked as a fisherman out of Plymouth. In 1603, Ward was unwillingly impressed into the King's Navy in the Channel Fleet, and hated the harsh discipline, terrible food and low pay on the *Lyon's Whelp*. Hearing that a small 25-ton barque, said to be full of a rich man's treasure, was moored alongside his ship in Portsmouth Harbour, he convinced 30 other macontents to desert with him. They overpowered her guard, sailing away at night, and Ward's new comrades elected him captain. They were able to capture two larger ships, the first, the *Violet*, off the Isle of Wight, and then a French six-gun merchant ship off the Scilly Isles. He immediately renamed her *Little John*, playing upon the 'Robin Hood' element to attract public sympathy. The three ships set sail for the Barbary Coast, with Ward transferring to the French ship.

From 1604 many English and Dutch sailors, including Richard Bishop and Anthony Johnson, were attracted to join the successful Ward at Salé, Morocco, and sell their booty there. In August 1606 Ward arranged with Kara Osman, the commander of the local Janissaries, to use Tunis as a base of operations. In return, Osman would have first refusal on all captured goods. The Dey of Tunis had built the city's prosperity by hosting Barbary corsairs, as they paid duty on the prize ships, treasures and slaves they brought in to sell. In 1606, the Dey welcomed Ward as a new corsair, and Ward offered to join the Islamic campaign against the enemies of England, the Catholic nations of the Mediterranean. He was circumcised, accepting Islam along with his entire crew, and changed his name to Yusuf Reis. According to a French report of 1606, Ward was in command of over

500 Muslim and Christian volunteers. Richard Bishop of Yarmouth was his first lieutenant, Captain Samson was in charge of prizes, and James Procter of Southampton was his master gunner.

Ward next married an Italian woman, an Islamic convert captured from Palermo, called Jessimina the Sicilian, while he continued to send money to his English wife. Two years later, Ward took a 32-gun warship and renamed it the *Gift*, capturing several merchantmen loaded with precious spices and silks. Over the years, Ward often flew Flemish colours as a disguise to capture English and Venetian ships, including the huge Venetian 1,500-ton *Reinera e Soderina*, which he turned into a man-of-war. Its treasure alone amounted to more than 2,000,000 ducats. With his profits, Ward built a palace in Tunis where he held court with great extravagance. It was reported that 'His diet was sumptuous. Swearing, drinking, dicing and the utmost enormities were commonplace. An English sailor who saw Ward in 1608 in Tunis called him: "very short with little hair, and that quite white, bald in front; swarthy face and beard. Speaks little and almost always swearing. Drunk from morn till night... The habits of a thorough salt. A fool and an idiot out of his trade."'

Returning to Tunis from pillaging in June 1607, Ward was told that the *Reinera e Soderina* was rotting and had begun to sink. Ward transferred with his favoured officers to a French prize, renaming her the *Reinera e Soderina*. She later sank off Greece with 250 Muslim and 150 English pirates drowning. Thus Ward lost his new flagship, and two more of his ships were taken by a Venetian fleet a few weeks later. Many were angered at the Moorish losses, but the Dey of Tunis offered Ward sanctuary. However, Ward was unsure of his reception and wrote to James I asking for a pardon. It was refused, so he sailed to Tunis, where he was granted protection.

The expulsion of the Moriscos (Spanish Moslems), from Spain in 1609 led 'at once to the rise of Sallee as a pirate port, and its launch upon its sinister career'. (Corbett). Ward was now said to have rescued thousands of Spanish Jews and Muslims fleeing their expulsion from Spain. Ward and Simon the Dancer are also credited with teaching Barbary corsairs to use well-armed, square-rigged ships of northern Europe, with which they now terrorised the Mediterranean. From Ward, Simon and others, the seamen of the Barbary States learnt much about seamanship and shipbuilding. Captain John Smith (of Pocahontas fame) wrote that before Ward and Danseker, 'the Moors scarce knew how to sail a ship... those were the first that taught the Moors to be men of war.' On the deaths of their leaders, Smith wrote (in *The true travels, adventures, and observations of Captaine Iohn Smith, in Europe, Asia, Affrica, and America*) that

> ...[the European pirates in Barbary] became so disjointed, disordered, debauched and miserable, that the Turks and Moors began to command them as slaves, and force them to instruct them in their best skill, which many an accursed renegado or Christian turned Turk did, till they have made those Sallee men or Moors of Barbary so powerful as they be to the terror of all the Straits, and many times they take purchase in the main ocean, yea, sometimes even in the narrow seas. He [Ward] was called 'the great English pirate... it is said that he was the first that put the Turks in a way to turn pirates at sea like himself.'

Ward continued raiding Mediterranean shipping, commanding a whole fleet of corsairs, with a Venetian 60-gun flagship. By the second decade of the seventeenth century, Ward was master of the central Mediterranean. Edward Coxere wrote that Ward 'always had a Turkish habit on, he was to drink water and no wine, and wore little irons under his Turk's shoes like horseshoes.' Thus Ward may have curtailed his alcohol consumption after his conversion to Islam, in public at least. However, the contemporary ballad, *The Sea-Man's Song of Captain Ward,* relates his drunken behaviour:

> ...This wicked-gotten treasure
> Doth him but little pleasure;
> The land consumes what they have got by sea,
> In drunkenness and letchery,
> Filthy sins of sodomy,
> Their evil-gotten goods do waste away.
> Such as live by thieving
> Have seldome-times good ending,
> As by the deeds of Captain Ward is shown:
> Being drunk amongst his drabs,
> His nearest friend he sometimes stabs;
> Such wickednesse within his heart is grown...

The Scottish traveller William Lithgow visited Ward in 1616, describing his home as 'a fair palace beautified with rich marble and alabaster stones. With whom I found domestics, some fifteen circumcised English renegades, whose lives and countenances were both alike. Old Ward their master was placable and diverse times in my ten days staying there I dined and supped with him.' Ward had profited well from piracy, retiring to his Tunis palace to live a life of opulence until 1622, enjoying his hobby of hatching chickens from an incubator, when aged 70 he reportedly died of plague.

One version of his story is that 'Captain Jack Birdy' was so obsessed with birds during his time in Tunisia that the locals would call him Jack Asfur, *asfur* being Arabic for sparrow, hence 'Captain Jack Sparrow' of the *Pirates of the Caribbean* series of films. Ward's fame was widespread as the most notorious pirate of his day, becoming the hero of several popular ballads, two 1609 'black letter chapbooks' (small cheap popular pamphlets printed in black ink) and a 1612 play. The contemporary play was *A Christian Turn'd Turk* by Robert Daborne, and one of the characters is Simon Dansiker, Simon the Dancer.

An old ballad, *The Famous Sea-Fight between Captain Ward and the Rainbow,* has these lines from Ward to King James I:

Strike up, you lusty gallants, with musick and sound of drum,
For we have descryed a rover, upon the sea is come;
His name is Captain Ward, right well it doth appear,
There has not been such a rover found out this thousand year.
For he hath sent unto our king, the sixth of January,
Desiring that he might come in, with all his company:
'And if your king will let me come till I my tale have told,
I will bestow for my ransome full thirty tun of gold.'
'O nay! O nay!' then said our king, 'O nay! this may not be,
To yield to such a rover my self will not agree;
He hath deceivd the French-man, likewise the King of Spain,
And how can he be true to me that hath been false to twain?
... 'Go tell the King of England, go tell him this from me,
If he reign king of all the land, I will reign king at sea.'...

Another version, Ward the Pirate, is also known in America:

Come all you gallant seamen bold, all you that march to drum,
Let's go and look for Captain Ward, far out on the sea he roams.
For he is the biggest robber that ever you did hear;
And there's not been such a robber found in above this hundred year.
Now a ship it was sailing from the east and going to the west,
Loaded with silks and satins and velvets of the best.
But in meeting there with Captain Ward, it was a sad meeting:

For he robbed them of their wealth and their store and bid them tell their king...

Sir Francis Verney (1584–6 September 1615), the Nobleman Pirate
The only son of Sir Edmund Verney, he was born at Pendley Manor, Hertfordshire, and was related to a total of seven royal families. He had a younger half-brother, Edmund (1590–1642).* Aged 15, Francis was married to his stepsister, Ursula St Barbe, to cement their families' fortunes. Unfortunately, alterations to Sir Edmund's will, to the detriment of Francis, were passed by a private Act of Parliament before his father Edmund died in 1600. Francis was sent to Trinity College, Oxford, where he accrued huge debts of around £3,000 a year (around £600,000 today). He left Oxford and also left his wife, legally separating from Ursula upon reaching adulthood, and providing her £50 a year for the rest of her life. Coming of age, Sir Francis was able to challenge his stepmother in court over the changes in his inheritance, and appealed to the House of Commons, that they had unjustly deprived him of his rights, while he was still a minor. Francis Verney lost the case and sold his estates to pay off his debts. He journeyed abroad, including making a pilgrimage to Jerusalem, and dissipated the rest of his fortune. He returned briefly to England in 1608 to tidy up his legal affairs, and in family tradition joined his relatives the Giffards in Morocco, who were in a small army of English volunteers fighting for a claimant to its throne. After his relatives the Giffards were killed in 1607, many of their followers were said to have become pirates, and Verney took refuge with another relative, Captain Richard Giffard of the *Fortune*, commanding a pirate fleet. Verney is mentioned among his officers, but Tinniswood believes that Verney was a prisoner of Florence from 1607–1610.

Soon Sir Francis was 'making havoc of his own countrymen, and carrying into Algiers prizes belonging to the merchants of Poole and Plymouth', according to an English ambassador. In December 1610, the Venetian ambassador in Tunis accused Verney and John Ward of 'turning Turk', but this may have referred to their adoption of local

---

* Francis Verney's half-brother Sir Edmund Verney accompanied Prince Charles and the Duke of Buckingham on the mission to Madrid in 1623, and became Knight-Marshal to King Charles I. When the Civil War broke out, the royal standard was entrusted to Edmund Verney at Nottingham, and while defending it he was killed at the Battle of Edgehill in 1642. Edmund's younger son, another Sir Edmund (1616–1649), was killed by Oliver Cromwell's soldiers at the sack of Drogheda.

costume. The Tunisian corsair fleet was commanded by Ward, with Verney said to be his lieutenant. It included Jan Janszoon van Haarlem (Murat Reis the Younger); Simon Danseker (Simon the Dancer); Richard Bishop and Kara Osman, commander of the Janissaries of Tunis, who probably supplied the soldiers on each ship. Verney took a Marseilles ship carrying wine to James I, and the king assigned a warship to escort merchant vessels in response. Verney was now captured by a Sicilian privateer, and spent two years as a galley slave until ransomed by an English Jesuit.

Verney was granted his freedom on the condition that he converted to Catholicism, which he did. In dire poverty, Verney spent the rest of his life in Sicily, being forced to enlist as a common soldier to survive. The Scottish traveller William Lithgow found him in 'extremest calamity and sickness' at the pauper's hospital of St Mary of Pity in Messina, and was with him during his final days. Among Verney's few personal effects were a turban, slippers, silk tunics, and the pilgrim's staff signifying his trip to Jerusalem. When his wife Ursula remarried in 1619, she was described as 'widow to him that turned Turk'.

Usta Murad ibn Abdallah (1570–June 1640) – Usta Murad (Murat, Morat), Dey of Tunis

The son of Francesco di Rio, he was born in the port of Levanto, Liguria, 40 miles southwest of Genoa, and was probably captured by Barbary corsairs and sold to Kara Osman Dey, the Dey of Tunis who previously had been a cobbler in Turkey. When di Rio converted to Islam, he took the name Usta Murad (Murat, Morat), becoming a corsair. By 1594 he was known to the French as the Islamic pirate Mourad. His activities at sea led him to great popularity with the Dey of Tunis and, by 1600, Usta had entered his inner circle. In 1610 the dying Dey promoted Yusuf Uthman as the next Dey, instead of any of his sons, and in 1615. Yusuf Dey appointed Usta to the command of the galleys at the corsair harbour of Bizerte. With six great galleys and many smaller ships, Usta constantly attacked European coastlines and shipping, gaining power and incomes for Tunis. He also prevented Maltese, Florentine and other Christian privateers raiding the African coast. Still commanding the fleet, in 1628 Usta was appointed Supreme Commander of the army in a short war against Algeria. Defeated by greater numbers, he did not lose prestige, and used his acquired wealth to build up his own fleet of corsairs.

He created relationships with powerful families in Tunisia, and was joined by his father Francesco, who acted as an intermediary to release

Ligurian slaves. Usta's brothers maintained his developing business relations with Marseilles, Livorno and Genoa, and the family acquired huge wealth. With Yusuf Dey nearing death, Hammuda Pasha II Bey orchestrated the election of Usta Murat as commander of the Ottoman militia in Tunis and tried to make him the new Dey. Usta Murat had been a friend of the pasha's father Hammuda I Bey and, according to European sources, claimed he had captured about 900 ships, and more than 20,000 prisoners, to be sold as slaves at market in Tunis. At Yusuf Dey's death in 1637, thanks to Hammuda Pasha II, Usta Murat was proclaimed as Dey by all but Mami, one of Yusuf Dey's most powerful *mamluks* (white bodyguards). Usta Murat exiled him to Zaghouan, where Mami was murdered. Taking power as the first non-Turkish Dey, Usta immediately closed many wine shops in Tunis, and terminated the sale of flour, semolina and wheat to the French who lived in the Bastion.

He standardised the price, size and quality of loaves, and removed the huge piles of rubbish from the Sea Gates. He founded Porto Farina (now Ghar el Melh) in 1638. Also in 1638, 8 Algerian galleons came to Tunis, to sail alongside eight Tunisian galleons to support the Grand Sultan in his war with Crete. However, they were cornered by a Venetian fleet, and abandoned their ships, burning them along with their chained Christian slaves. The crews made their way overland to Istanbul and were given new galleons to return home by the Sultan. In the same year, the Ottomans took Baghdad, and Usta ordered seven days of celebration in Tunis. He built a vast palace and mausoleum before his death in 1640, and his descendants have always been among the greatest families of Tunis.

Claes Gerritszoon Compaen (1587–25 February 1660) – Claas Compaan, Klaas Kompaan, the Dutch Barbary Corsair

Born at Oostzaan, North Holland, his father may have been a nobleman who rebelled against Spanish rule. Going to sea at an early age, Compaen became a successful merchant, trading along the Slave Coast of Guinea. Compaen used his profits to refit his ships as privateers to fight the Spanish. He took several Spanish ships, including a 200-ton, 17-gun vessel with a crew of 80 men, but some were later released by Dutch authorities, much to his annoyance. About 1621, he sailed off with a Letter of Marque from the Dutch Admiralty, leaving the Admiralty to pay a debt of 8,000 guilders still owed for his ship. He took a fishing boat, and the cargo of another ship, before taking on an extra 50 crew in Vlissingen, and turning to full piracy. Compaen sold his captured loot in England and along the Barbary Coast and, in 1625, began using Clare in Ireland as his base of operations. Having sacked some English ships, he was now forced to only trade with the Barbary Coast. Sailing the English Channel, Irish Sea, Mediterranean and West Africa, Compaen sold captured ships and cargoes at Salé, Mogador and Saffi in Morocco, becoming one of the Barbary corsairs.

If there was an argument among crew members, the two men had to fight inside a circle of pirates until one surrendered. The loser had to pay 100 guilders to the ship's doctor before he would help him, and the number of fights on board decreased dramatically. Compaen sometimes moored under a false flag next to a merchant ship, and began a friendly conversation with the captain before taking the ship by surprise. Taking about 350 ships in his career, Compaen traded at Salé with the son of the Dutch privateer Simon the Dancer (*see* above). Simon the Dancer the Younger drove a hard bargain, and once Compaen gave him a ship with cargo valued at 95,000 guilders, and only received 5,000 guilders worth of gunpowder, fuses and ammunition in return. Thus Compaen instead began dealing directly with Simon's rival, Jan Janszoon (Murat Reis the Younger, *q.v.*). As a result Simon the Younger despatched a fleet to attack Compaen while at port, but the Dutchman was warned and defeated the Moorish fleet.

In 1626 Compaen wished to return home and sought a pardon, but on 5 July came across two Dutch East Indian Company ships, which had separated from the main fleet off Sierra Leone. Possibly owing to pressure from his crew, Compaen ordered his four privateers to attack, but his flagship suffered severe damage from the *Hollandia* under Captain Wybrant Schram, and 70 of his crew were killed. With his flagship disabled, Compaen was forced to allow the *Hollandia* and *Grootebroek* to sail from the port of Sierra Leone on to Batavia, but gained notoriety as 'the most notorious Dutch pirate'. Sailing along the Spanish coast, he also encountered the privateer Collaert of Duinkerken (Dunkirk), but managed to escape. Around 1627 he sailed back to Salé with a number of prizes, and was told he had been granted a pardon in the Netherlands. He left Salé just four days before a Dutch fleet arrived to capture him for his attacks on the East Indiamen in 1626. Leaving some of his pirates in Ireland, he received his pardon at The Hague, but died 'remorseful', and in 'bitter poverty' in Oostzaan, North Holland, in 1660.

Jan Janszoon (*c.*1575–*c.*1642) – Murat Reis the Younger, the Salé Rover, Ancestor of Winston Churchill, Humphrey Bogart and Jacqueline Kennedy

He was also known as Jan Jansen, Jan Jansz or Janz or Janse, Matthias Rais, Morato Arraez, Morat Ariaz, Caid Morato, Matthew Rice, John Barber, and Captain John. Jan Janszoon was born in the port of Haarlem in the Netherlands, and married Soutgen Cave in 1595. They had two children, Edward and Lysbeth. In 1600, Jan Janszoon sailed from Haarlem as a privateer, being given a licence to attack Spanish shipping during the Eighty Years' War of Dutch Independence (1568–1648). However, Janszoon ignored the terms of his licence and instead sailed to the Barbary Coast, from where he could attack ships of any foreign state, using whatever flag served his purpose. He had abandoned his Dutch family and married again in 1600, and had more children. In 1618, Janszoon was captured by Barbary corsairs at Lanzarote in the Canary Islands, and was taken to the Algiers slave market. There he 'turned Turk', i.e. became a Muslim 'renegado'. Europeans at the time usually referred to all Muslims as 'Turks', such was the power of the Ottoman Empire with its capital at Constantinople (now Istanbul). After Janszoon's conversion, he sailed with another renegade, a Dutchman named De Veenboer, who was now known as Suleiman Reis and had sailed with 'Simon the Dancer'. Suleiman Reis was killed in 1619, and Algiers concluded peace with some European nations. Janszoon, now known as Murat Reis, sailed to the port of Salé near Rabat in Morocco, joining the notorious Salé Rovers. He was known as Murat the Younger to distinguish him from another corsair, Murat Reis the Elder (*q.v.*).

The Salé Rovers declared their port to be an independent republic, free from the Great Sultan's rule, and formed a government of 14 pirate leaders. They elected Murat the Younger as president, soon to be elected their Grand Admiral. Murat became one of the most feared of the corsairs, attacking Spanish and Italian ships and raiding Christian settlements along the Mediterranean. Under his leadership, Salé thrived and he became incredibly wealthy. In 1622, he sailed up the English Channel. Murat understood the sailing characteristics of European-built ships, and began moving into European waters. In January 1622, his crew consisted of 24 'Turks and Moors', 18 Moriscos, 8 Dutch renegadoes, a Spanish renegado named Juan Rodelgas, and 13 Dutch slaves who refused to abandon Christianity. Late in the year, in the English Channel, their food supplies ran out and Murat docked under the Moroccan flag in the Dutch Republic at Veere.

He sought help in Holland, as the Sultan of Morocco had recently signed a treaty with the Netherlands. Murat claimed diplomatic privileges as Admiral of Morocco, and his first visitors were his first wife and their son and daughter, Edward and Lysbeth, sent by the Dutch authorities. A contemporary witness wrote that she 'came on board to bid him leave the ship; the parents of the crew did the same but they could not succeed in bringing them to do this as they [the Dutch renegadoes] were too much bitten of the Spaniards and too much hankering after booty.' He left Holland with new Dutch volunteers, which angered the Hollanders, who needed men to fight the Spanish, and Murat soon fought a ship flying the Dutch flag. She changed to her true colours, now flying the Spanish flag, and after a bloody battle with many dead and injured, Murat had to break off ther fight. Sultan Moulay Zidan al-Nasir appointed Murat as Governor of Salé in 1624, giving his daughter as Murat's third wife. This position added to Murat's wealth, since he received a percentage of any prizes taken, plus fees from ships that anchored in the harbour. He also took a share of money paid to pilots for guiding ships into port, and a share from each deal in trading plunder.

In 1626, 15 galliots sailed into the Atlantic under Murat, to raid the coasts of Portugal, Spain, and France. Ekin writes:

> They very deliberately, even at noonday, and indeed just when they please, leap ashore and walk on without the least dread, and advance into the country, ten, twelve or fifteen leagues or more ... and infinite numbers of souls – men, women, children, and infants at the breast – [are] dragged away to a wretched captivity.

He next captured Lundy Island in the Bristol Channel in 1627. Murat held it for five years, using it as a base for raiding expeditions and taking slaves. A captured Dane offered to guide Murat to the North Seas in exchange for his freedom. Murat sailed with three ships of corsairs from Algiers and Salé, on a 5,000-mile round voyage, reaching Iceland in June 1627. It was reported that the pirates 'killed people, cursed and beat them, and did all that was evil', which included raping women in Reykjavik. He led Barbary Rovers on two raids on Iceland, taking hundreds of slaves. As they were leaving the sacked Grindavík, by flying a false flag they managed to trick and capture a Danish ship but the only booty they acquired was salted fish and hides.

His second raid began on 4 July, capturing livestock, stealing silver and other goods, capturing 344 and killing 34 Icelanders. Murat next landed at Heimaey, where 30 men were slain before they surrendered. Murat sailed for home, taking with him more than 400 men, women, and children to sell into slavery. This event was known in Iceland as the *Tyrkjaránið* (the Turkish Raid). Tunniswood relates that 'Icelanders made it legal to kill any Turk on sight; the law remained on the books until its repeal three-and-a-half centuries later. Even today, liturgy used in Iceland contains a prayer asking God to protect them from "the terror of the Turk".'

The pirates also sank a Danish merchant ship and captured an English fishing smack. On 16 July 1627 they arrived at Vestmannaeyjar. One minister was killed, and the other, Ólafur Egilsson, was taken to Algiers. He was later sent back to Copenhagen to ask for a heavy ransom from the King of Denmark to free his Icelandic subjects.

However, back in Salé, the political climate in Morocco had worsened, and towards the end of 1627, in secrecy, Murat relocated his family and pirates back to semi-independent Algiers. Murat Reis had become one of the most feared of the corsairs, attacking Spanish and Italian ships and raiding Christian settlements along the Mediterranean. In 1631, Murat took 'nine Portingales [Portuguese], three Pallicians [Galicians, from Northern Spain], and seventeen Frenchmen' in the Atlantic. In June, his fleet operated in the waters between Ireland and Land's End. At this time, Denehy reports on Murat calling him Captain Matthew Rice: '…a Dutch renegado, in a ship of three hundred tons, twenty-four pieces of ordnance, and two hundred men, and another ship of one hundred tons, eighty men, and twelve iron pieces, … took a ship of Dartmouth of sixty tons, wherein one Edward Fawlett was master, with nine men therein; they took therewith her masts, cordage, and other necessaries, with all the men, and sunk the hull, as they had done to two French ships before.' The Roman Catholic Fawlett gave him information on Irish harbours for his freedom, pointing out Kinsale and the Protestant port of Baltimore, whose residents had settled on lands confiscated from the Catholics, as likely targets.

A captured fisherman, James Hackett, persuaded them not to attack Kinsale as it was too strongly defended for Murat's 230 men. Instead, Murat sacked Baltimore on 20 June, helped by Captain Fawlett and, as a result 99 residents of Baltimore were taken prisoner, including William Gunter's wife and seven sons. The corsairs attacked some other houses, and took 109 prisoners (22 men, 33 women, and 54 children) to join those 24 sailors from a Falmouth barque and some fishermen already imprisoned below decks. The 109 Irish victims were noted as arriving in Algiers on 28 July by the English consul. Only two of the Baltimore residents managed to return home. The survivors had fled to Skibbereen, and Baltimore was almost deserted for generations. A Baltimore pub name, the Algiers Inn, remembers the raid. Fawlett and Hackett had been released by Murat and were imprisoned, but Captain Fawlett was let free upon lying that he only acted under duress. The luckless, and lower class, Hackett was hanged on a high cliff, facing the sea.

Sailing from Malta, a fleet of the Knights from the Order of St John surprised Murat in 1635, near the Tunisian coast. Outnumbered, Murat and most of his crew were taken to dungeons in Malta, where his health deteriorated over the course of five years in chains. In 1640, the Dey of Tunis planned a corsair attack, which managed to rescue the survivors. Murat was honoured upon his return to the Barbary States, and was made Governor of Oualidia, a great fortress near Saffi in Morocco. In December 1640, his daughter Lysbeth Janszoon van Haarlem visited him and stayed with her father until August 1641, when she returned to Holland. It appears that Murat's health had been broken in prison and he may have died around this time. In addition to his first Dutch wife, Murat also married a woman thought to have been named Margrietje, around 1600. She may have been a Dutch woman captured by the corsairs. Their children were named Anthony Jansen van Salee, Abraham Jansen van Salee, Phillip Janz van Salee and Cornelis Jansen van Salee. His eldest sons Anthony and Abraham, by his second wife, possibly became Barbary pirates for a while, but later sailed to New Amsterdam (New York) and took the surname of Van Salee. Anthony Jansen van Salee purchased 200 acres on Long Island, which the locals referred to as 'Turk's Plantation' and was possibly the very first settler in Brooklyn, becoming a major landowner in the early days of New York City. His descendants in the USA include Humphrey Bogart, members of the Vanderbilt family, Jackie Kennedy and her children with John F. Kennedy. In the UK, the Spencer-Churchills including the Dukes of Marlborough and Winston Churchill, are related to the Salé Rover.

The Elizabethan Adventurers

To add the famous John Hawkins and Richard Grenville and many others would take up too much space in this book, and I must apologise for omitting them, but I have included some lesser known privateers who are nevertheless extremely interesting. One would have also wished to add the Cavalier princes Rupert and Maurice, generals and privateers in the English Civil War, as Maurice was captured by the Spanish and left to rot for years in a Caribbean prison, while his brother Rupert desperately searched for him.

Sir Francis Drake (*c.*1540–28 January 1596) – Circumnavigator, The Man who Singed the King of Spain's Beard
Born in Tavistock, Devon, the oldest of twelve sons, he was apprenticed on a trade ship aged just twelve. He inherited the ship in his teens, on the death of its master. Sailing with his second cousin John Hawkins, Drake began travelling to the Americas, carrying slaves, raiding foreign ships and ports, and capturing gold, silver and other loot. In 1568, Spanish ships ambushed Drake, Hawkins and Blondel (*q.v.*) at San Juan de Ulúa, Mexico. They just escaped, losing four ships and with great losses of men and booty, and swore vengeance upon Spain. From 1570 onwards, Drake led repeated raids against Spanish treasure ships and colonies in the New World, many without an official privateer's commission. The Spanish called him '*El Draque*' (the dragon), and Philip II is said to have offered a sum of 20,000 ducats for Drake's head, which would amount to around £5 million today.

In 1572 Drake planned to raid Panama for Spanish treasure, and with just two ships and 73 men took Nombre de Dios, a port on the Atlantic coast. His men noticed that Drake was bleeding badly and

An Elizabethan galleon, as sailed by Drake and Hawkins.

Francis Drake.
Courtesy of
Rijksmuseum.

insisted on withdrawing to save his life. Drake stayed in the area for almost a year, raiding Spanish shipping. In 1573, he joined the French buccaneer Guillaume Le Testu (*q.v.*) in an inland attack on a mule train, taking about 20 tons of silver and gold. Le Testu had been wounded, was captured and later beheaded. The privateers dragged as much gold and silver as they could carry across 18 miles of jungle, to where they had left their boats on the coast, but the boats had vanished. Spanish soldiers were close behind them, so Drake ordered that about 15 tons of treasure be buried on the beach, and built a raft. With two volunteers he sailed 10 miles along the coast to where he had left his flagship. His men asked him how the raid had gone. He looked at the ground, seemingly saddened, then pulled a necklace of Spanish gold from around his neck and shouted 'Our voyage is made, lads!' On 9 August 1573, Drake returned to Plymouth with at least 20,000 British pounds worth of loot (today worth about £58 million in labour value terms).

In late 1577 Elizabeth I sponsored Drake's voyage to circumnavigate the world in the *Pelican*, with 164 men and four other vessels. There was a secret agreement with Queen Elizabeth that he would also raid Spanish shipping. Arriving in South America, Drake ordered that two ships be destroyed as they were unseaworthy. Storms wrecked another ship, with another forced to return to England. By October 1578 just 58 were men left, all on the *Pelican*, which Drake renamed the *Golden Hind*. Drake now discovered that Tierra del Fuego, south of the Magellan Strait, was not part of the southern continent as had been believed, but a group of islands. This meant that ships could avoid the Magellan Strait and sail between the Atlantic and Pacific around the safer Cape Horn route. (Guillaume le Testu [*q.v.*] seems to have told him this.) Upon entering the Pacific, Drake spent months plundering unsuspecting galleons, and ports along the coasts of Peru and Chile. In March 1579 he took the Spanish treasure ship *Nuestra Señora de la Concepción* with a dozen chests of coins, 80 pounds of gold and 26 tons of silver.

In June 1579 he sailed the up the west coast of North America, perhaps as far as Canada, before returning to present-day California. Drake claimed the land, naming it 'Nova Albion' on behalf of Queen Elizabeth. In July 1579, he crossed the Pacific, sailed around the Cape of Good Hope in South Africa, and re-entered the Atlantic Ocean. On 26 September 1580 Drake returned to Plymouth, after a successful circumnavigation of more than 36,000 miles, bringing home all sorts of treasure. According to one account, his financial backers received a return of £47 for each pound they had invested.

Elizabeth I knighted Drake on board the *Golden Hind*. Elected as an MP, Drake took occasional breaks from his political duties to conduct more raids against the Spanish at Santa Domingo, Cartagena and St Augustine, Florida. Partially because of Drake's pillaging, in 1586 King Philip ordered a fleet to be constructed to carry troops to invade England. In 1587 Drake led his fleet to attack and destroy 30–40 Spanish ships and thousands of tons of supplies in Cadiz and Corunna. His 'singeing of the King of Spain's beard', as Francis Bacon called it, may have delayed the Armada's launch by more than a year. In 1588, Drake was one of three vice admirals of Howard's English fleet that defeated the Spanish Armada, the others being Hawkins and Grenville, taking the Spanish flagship *Rosario*. After the defeat of the Armada, Drake attempted to take control of the Spanish-held Azores, but the expedition ended in disaster after he lost 20 vessels and about 12,000 men. In 1595, his attack on San Juan, Puerto Rico was beaten off, as well as a second raid on Panama. Drake contracted dysentery and died at sea off Portobello. Drake's cousin, John Hawkins, died at the same time during this expedition. Drake's body was cased in full armour, sealed inside a lead coffin and buried at sea a few miles off the coastline.

Sir Anthony Sherley (1565–1635/7) – The Luckless Privateer and Adventurer who wrote Shakespeare's Plays?

Oxford-educated, and born into a wealthy family, Sherley and his two brothers were forced by family bankruptcy to make their own way in the world. Aged 26, in 1591 Sherley went to Normandy in the army of the Earl of Essex to assist Henri IV, and was knighted by the French for his bravery. However, in 1593 he was imprisoned in England until he renounced his foreign title. Sherley desperately needed money and influence, so married a cousin of the Earl of Essex, but found his wife was not to his liking. Using his relationship with the Earl of Essex, Sherley acquired funding for an expedition to capture the Portuguese island of São Thomé off the coast of Africa. In 1596, he gathered 8 ships carrying 400 soldiers, but the expedition was struck by disease early in the voyage. With fewer men, he instead sailed north to take Santiago in the Cape Verde Islands, but there was not much treasure. With even fewer men, owing to more sickness and disease, Captain Sherley now sailed his privateer fleet across the Atlantic to sack Santa Marta in Colombia. He then raided Santiago de la Vega in Jamaica, which until 1655 was held by Spain, but acquired little booty from all three raids.

Off Jamaica, Sherley met with the privateers William Parker and Michael Geare, who joined him with their ships to attack Trujillo, Honduras, but were beaten off. They did capture Puerto Caballos but there was again little booty, so Captain Geare sailed off. Sherley and Parker now tried to march across the jungles and mountains of Guatemala to the Pacific and surprise Spanish coastal settlements, but failed and instead sailed with their few remaining men – most had been lost to disease – through the Strait of Magellan. Sherley's men lost faith in their unlucky captain and mutinied, leaving him one ship in which to return to England.

Sherley had accrued incredible debts from his unsuccessful privateering expedition, and desperately needed funds. Towards the end of 1597, he led a group of volunteers to Italy, to fight in a dispute over the possession of Ferrara. However, the disagreement between England and Italy had been settled by the time he reached Venice in 1598. The unemployed Sherley again used his close relationship with the Earl of Essex to raise enough money to sail to Persia. He planned to establish diplomatic relations (without the consent of the English Crown) with the new Shah, Abbas the Great, to promote trade between England and Persia, by which he would profit. Any alliance would also strengthen the Persians against the increasing power and expansion of the Ottoman Turks. With his younger brother Sir Robert (*see* below), Sherley travelled to Persia in 1598, via Constantinople and Aleppo, and was well received by the Shah. From December 1599 to May 1600, it is reported that with 5,000 horses they trained the Persian army according to methods of the English militia, and also retrained its artillery. When Anthony Shirley left Persia, Robert remained in Persia with 14 other Englishmen.

The Shah had made Anthony a *Mirza* (Prince), granting him trading and other rights. Abbas the Great made Anthony Sherley his ambassador not only for trade, but to gain allies against the Ottoman Empire. It was originally intended only to be a mission to Madrid, but Sherley had persuaded the Shah to expand the trade mission into a far grander project, involving negotiations with the Holy Roman Emperor, the Pope ('father of the Christian princes'), Queen Elizabeth of England, and the kings of France, Spain, Poland and Scotland, in order to form an anti-Ottoman alliance. The Shah decided to send three groups on the mission, one led by Sherley, one by the Persian ambassador Hussain Ali Beg, and one by a Portuguese Augustinian ambassador, Nicolau de Melo.

In April 1598 they set off via the Caspian Sea to Russia, avoiding Ottoman territories and ships, but Sherley had violent disagreements with Father de Melo, and twice tried to kill him before they reached Moscow. He also had bitter disagreements with Ali Beg, and the mission's members were imprisoned for five months before Sherley and his embassy was allowed to leave the city, leaving behind Father de Melo and Brother Nicolau de Santo Agostinho. The pair were imprisoned in icy cells on an island near the Arctic Circle, and Nicolau was publicly beheaded in 1605. De Melo was whipped and beaten, but later allowed to return to Persia, where he was burnt to death in 1615, *in odium fidei*.

As the Shah's representative, Sherley visited Prague, Rome and other Christian cities, trying to increase trade between Europe and Persia. However, he was known to have stolen the Shah's gifts intended for European royalty. Two members of his expedition returned to London, and published the pamphlet *The True Report of Sir Anthony Shirley's Journey*. The Shakespearian actor Wille Kemp met Sherley in Rome, which led to two references to '*the Soph*' (Shah) in *Twelfth Night* (1601–02). However, the government would not allow Sherley to return to England, and he remained in Venice.

Sherley finally returned to England in 1603, but his plans were condemned and he was forbidden to return to Persia. His imprisonment in 1603 by James I caused the House of Commons to assert one of its privileges, the freedom of its members from arrest, in the document *The Form of Apology and Satisfaction*. Leaving England again, Sherley travelled between royal courts, allegedly defrauding nobles to fund schemes and expeditions. Details of his life are confusing, but Anthony Sherley entered the service of Spain in 1604, and for a time Sherley was in prison in Venice. In 1605, he travelled to Prague, and from there the Holy Roman Emperor Rudolph II sent him on a mission to Morocco, and then to Lisbon and Madrid. Sherley was appointed a Count of the Holy Roman Empire. The king of Spain then appointed Sherley as Admiral of a Spanish fleet to serve in the Levant (the Near East), but he only led an unsuccessful invasion of Mitylene on the island of Lesbos, and was therefore deprived of his command. Despite this, Sherley was appointed to be an agent for the Spanish in 1607. In this capacity, he wrote to the Barbary corsairs Simonson and Ward (*q.v.*), trying to get them to attack the ships of the Ottoman Empire. In 1609, Sherley assembled a fleet in Sicily, ostensibly to join a Spanish attack on Tunis. Instead he reneged and attacked European merchantmen, looting Greek Islands. After making excuses for his failure to support the attack on Tunis, he lost any influence in the Spanish court. He stayed in Spain, trying to regain favour but died in poverty there in 1635 or 1637.

He wrote an account of his adventurous life:

Sir Anthony Sherley: his Relation of his Travels into Persia – The dangers, and distresses, which befell him in his passage, both by sea and land, and his strange and unexpected deliverances. His magnificent entertainement in Persia, his honourable imployment there – hence, as embassadour to the princes of Christendome, the cause of his disapointment therein, with his advice to his brother, Sir Robert Sherley, also, a true relation of the great magnificence, valour, prudence, justice, temperance, and other manifold vertues of Abas, now King of Persia, with his great conquests, whereby he hath inlarged his dominions. Penned by Sr. Antony Sherley, and recommended to his brother, Sr. Robert Sherley, being now in prosecution of the like honourable imployment. (1613).

There are at least five other accounts of his adventures in Persia.

In 1888 the Reverend Scott Surtees made a case for Anthony Sherley writing or contributing to Shakespeare's plays, part of which reads:

His mother's name was Anne, daughter of Sir Thomas Kempe, and had three sons – Thomas, Anthony, and Robert. 'No three persons of one family ever experienced adventures at the same time so uncommon or so interesting' ... Sir Anthony married a first cousin of the Earl of Essex, 'who had oftentimes to befriend him.' He was sent on embassies to every quarter of the known world. Was ofttimes in communication with Burleigh. We hear of him most in Italy, 'sent by Emperor of Germany as ambassador to Morocco'; 'hired horses to pass the Alpes'; writes to Anthony Bacon, a friend of Essex. It appears that he wrote many letters at this period to his patron Earl of Essex, Mr. Anthony Bacon, and Mr. Secretary Cecil [Burleigh]. He is found everywhere, sometimes employed as ambassador, sometimes on special missions, sometimes in questionable ventures. Milan, Venice, where at one time he seems to have resided for several years, Rome, Persia, Cyprus, Antioch, Syracuse, Prague, Arabia, Tripoli, Aleppo, Bagdad, Constantinople, Portugal, Spain. Sir Anthony appears (Annals of the Shirley Family) with his brother Sir Robert to have always been in debt and difficulty, 'sometimes like to starve for want of bread,' profuse and extravagant when money was to be had, utterly careless how it was obtained. Mention is made of 'Henry Sherley, kinsman of Mr. James Sherley, the play-wright, and who did also excel him in that faculty.' Henry Sherley was the author of the following plays never printed: Spanish Duke of Lerna, Duke of Guise, Gasaldo the country lover. Sir Anthony was ever aiming to get reinstated at Court, and if he had been known to have been mixed up with these plays, it would have been fatal to his chance with Elizabeth. Clearly he had something to do with Will Kempe, a member of Alleyn's company, who acted the prominent parts in *Two Gentlemen of Verona, Merchant of Venice,* etc.

Was not 'Will Kempe' the go-between the manager and the author? Was it not necessary, in order to keep the secret, that the MSS. should not pass from hand to hand, or be entrusted even to the ambassador's bag? Lansdowne MSS. 1608, Milan, Sir Anthony Sherley to his sister, Lady Tracy, 'you will say, I should have written; it is true, but there are such intercepting of my poor papers that before God I dare commit nothing to paper, and now less than ever.' The extraordinary capacity and knowledge of languages and familiarity with places and scenery by Sir Anthony Sherley, especially in Italy, were clearly unequalled. What share had he in what may be a joint-stock company for the production of these plays? It is now acknowledged that many of the plays are translated from Italian plays and other novels. Did he bring this grist to the mill, find novels and stories, translate them, and forward them by his trusted kinsman Kempe to others to ship-shape them and fit them for the stage? May not the name of Sherley have oozed out amongst 'the playwrights,' and thence 'Henry Sherley, who excelled in that faculty,' been spoken of as the man who wrote them. Sir Anthony keeps up his friendship with Anthony Bacon, whom no doubt he knew in earlier days at Court. How fond they all were of the name of Anthony. A greater knowledge of men and manners and languages and the leading men and courtiers of the day or such a master of travel existed not in his time. Strange also is it that 'The Travailes of the three English Brothers, Sir Thomas, Sir Anthony, and Mr. Robert Sherley,' should be presented on the stage by this same company of which Kempe was a member. How were they acquainted with them?

The link between the privateer-adventurer-fraudster Sherley and Shakespeare's plays needs more research, outside the scope of this volume.

Sir Thomas Sherley (1564–*c.*1634) – the Privateer with Eighteen Children

The eldest son of Sir Thomas Sherley, of Wiston, Sussex, and brother of Sir Anthony and Sir Robert, he suffered the same financial difficulties. The brothers had six sisters, all of whom died in infancy, and only Robert achieved real success, in training the Persian army to defeat the Turks. Thomas was educated at Oxford University, and aged 20 was elected MP for Steyning in 1584. The next year he served with his father and brother Anthony in the Low Countries, and fought in Ireland, where he was knighted by its Lord-Deputy in 1589. He then attended the court of Queen Elizabeth and secretly married one of her maids of honour, Frances Vavasour, in 1591. For this act he was committed to the Marshalsea Prison until 1592.

In 1593 Sherley was again elected MP for Steyning, and served as a captain in the Low Countries once more. However, like his brothers, he began to suffer problems arising from their father's deteriorating financial circumstances. Sherley needed a substantial income, so handed over his company of troops at Flushing to his brother-in-law, and instead organised a privateering expedition to attack Spanish shipping. In summer 1598 in the English Channel he captured four 'hulks' sailing out of Lübeck, which were supposedly carrying Spanish merchandise. He may have made some of his attacks from the Queen's ship *Foresight*, which he is known to have captained from 1599. One ship that Sherley took had been returning from San Domingo laden with sugar; it was valued at £4,700. In April 1600, Sherley offered the Earl of Nottingham £600 for his tenth share in two prize ships, which he brought into Plymouth. In 1600 Sherley appeared before the Admiralty Court for seizing a ship from Hamburg, which was carrying some Dutch cargo. His creditors also sought payment, and in July 1600 supporters of Sir Richard Weston broke into Sherley's father's house at Blackfriars. They demanded payment, threatening both father and son. In 1601 his father needed the borough seat of Steyning for its income, so Thomas gave him the seat, becoming MP for Hastings instead.

At the end of 1602 he returned to privateering, equipping two ships and first pillaged 'two poor hamlets of two dozen houses in Portugal'. Sailing to the Levant, he intended to raid the Ottoman Empire of Mehmed III. Sherley was given financial help by the Duke of Tuscany at Florence, acting for Rudolf II, the Holy Roman Emperor. Sherley attacked the island of Kea (Zea in the Cyclades) in January 1603, but was taken by the Ottoman Turks and put in prison in Constantinople. James I appealed to the Sultan to release him, but he was not freed until December 1605, after a ransom of $1,100 had been paid. He sailed to Naples, where he was described in August 1606, as living 'like a gallant'. From there he sent intelligence to Cecil (Lord Burleigh). At the end of 1606 he returned to England, where he wrote an unpublished *'Discourse of the Turks'*, but the Levant Company took action against him for infringement of their trading rights. It was said that he had 'overbusied himself with the traffic of Constantinople, to have brought it to Venice and to the Florentine territories'.* This action led to Sherley in September 1607 being imprisoned in the Tower of London. In 1611 he was declared insolvent, and in 1612 his bankrupt father's death increased his financial problems. Sherley had three sons and four daughters by his first marriage. A second marriage may have been to relieve his debts, but it also brought him five more sons, six more daughters and more problems. To educate and maintain eight sons and ten daughters and introduce them into society was far more than he could afford. He sold his house at Wiston, now in a ruinous state, and retired to the Isle of Wight where he died six years later.

Peter Easton (*fl.*1602–1620) – 'the Notorious Pirate Easton', 'the Arch-Pirate'

Known to be a superb navigator and excellent gun layer, he was the most successful English pirate of his day. The first permanent English settlement in North America was founded in 1607 at Jamestown, Virginia, and the second in 1610 was Jamestown in Cuper's Cove (now Cupids), Conception Bay, Newfoundland. Easton was in Queen Elizabeth's navy, sent to protect the important Newfoundland fishing fleet in 1602, but the pro-Catholic James I succeeded her in 1603 and negotiated peace in the Treaty of London in 1604. The new king ordered all ships that had been attacking the Spanish to return to England, but Easton and his crew, and some other captains, refused to abandon the war. They had not been paid and knew that they would be unemployed with the end of war, so turned to piracy. By 1610, he was known as the 'Notorious Pirate Easton', commanding 40 ships and possibly 5,000 pirates around the English Channel and across the Atlantic.

---

* Sherley, Thomas – entry in *The Dictionary of National Biography*, Smith, Elder & Co., London 1885.

An aside here about the fascinating Maarten Tromp. In 1610, the 12-year-old Tromp was with his sea captain father on a voyage to Guinea, when attacked by Peter Easton leading a fleet of seven ships. Tromp's father was killed by a cannonball, and sources relate that the boy shouted to the crew 'Won't you avenge my father's death?' Easton sold Tromp in the Salé slave market, but two years later Easton regretted his act and ordered Tromp's freedom. At sea again, Tromp was taken in 1621 off Tunis by Barbary corsairs and kept as a slave, but impressed John Ward and the Bey of Tunis at sea with his navigation and gunnery skills. He was kept as a slave until the age of 24. By then he had so impressed the Bey he freed him. In 1622 Tromp was a lieutenant in the Dutch navy, and was the flag captain of Piet Heyn (*q.v.*) during the 1629 battle with Ostend privateers when Heyn was killed. From 1629, as a captain, he successfully fought the Dunkirkers (*q.v.*). In 1633 Tromp led the Dutch fleet that sailed to fight the Spanish fleet near Dunkirk. However, England and France, allies of the Dutch, had joined Spain in a secret alliance. The Spanish aimed to damage the Dutch sails and rigging, while English and French ships attacked Tromp from the rear. Tromp and a few ships managed to escape and in 1637 he was promoted from captain to the *de facto* supreme commander of the Dutch fleet, blockading Dunkirk. In 1639, Tromp defeated a large Spanish fleet of 95 warships in the Battle of the Downs, signalling the end of Spanish naval power. Tromp appears to be the first fleet commander to deliberately use the 'line of battle' strategy. In the First Anglo-Dutch War (1652–1653), Tromp commanded the Dutch in the battles of Dover, Dungeness, Portland, the Gabbard and Scheveningen. In the last, he was killed by a sharpshooter in the rigging of William Penn's ship. His acting flag captain kept up Dutch morale by not lowering Tromp's standard, pretending Tromp was still alive.

Back to the 'Notorious Pirate Easton'. Bristol merchants complained to the Lord High Admiral, Lord Howard of Effingham, who sent a fleet to take Easton. Howard had commanded the English against the Spanish Armada in 1588, but Easton captured his ships, with about $100,000, and 500 captives were recruited to his fleet. James I sent another, stronger, fleet, under Captain Henry Mainwaring (*see* next entry).

Alerted to a strong fleet being assembled, Easton assembled his 10 best ships and crews and sailed for Newfoundland. They settled at Harbour Grace, just south of Mosquito, to build a fortified base to carry on their operations. Easton arrived in 1612 'with ten sayle of good ships well furnished and very rich', and began to raid coastal harbours from Ferryland to Trinity Bay. Another account is that in the spring of 1612 he arrived with just four ships in bad condition, and began raiding the fishing fleet in Trinity and Conception Bays for men and supplies. Easton later demanded tributes from all English fishing boats on the Grand Banks for not attacking them, and began trading in captured ships and goods. Many of the hard-worked local fishermen willingly joined his crews, while others were impressed into service. Harold Horwood claims Easton set up another fort on Kelly's Island, on the far shore of Conception Bay, said to be named after another pirate, and there were legends of buried treasure. However, Easton's main targets for bounty were Spanish colonies in the Caribbean and treasure ships.

By this time, from his fortified base at Harbour Grace, he had also taken two ships, 100 men, and provisions. Easton had plundered 30 English vessels at St John's, and raided French and Portuguese ships at Ferryland. The Scottish Company complained to James I about damage to their plantations and fishing boats in Newfoundland caused by Easton in 1612, to the amount of £20,400. The first English colony in Newfoundland, Cupids Cove, was just a few miles south of Easton's fort, and depended on Easton for protection from raiding Basques and others nationalities. He captured the king's representative and leader of the English fishing fleet, Captain Richard Whitbourne, keeping him prisoner for 11 weeks, trying to make him join his fleet. Whitbourne refused and was then released, but only on condition that he would strongly petition James I for a pardon for Easton. Whitbourne arrived in England and found that a pardon had already been granted to Easton in February 1612, but he had never received it. Whitbourne wrote that Easton, 'with a longing desire and full expectation to be called home, lost that hope by too much delaying of time by him who carried the pardon.'

When Whitbourne left, Easton moved his main base in July 1612 to St John's and then the more easily defensible Ferryland on the southern shore of the Avalon Peninsula. He again fortified the harbour and continued to attack the shipping lanes. Towards the end of August 1612, he seems to have sailed to intercept the Spanish treasure *flota*, which would have left the Caribbean in July or early August. Easton left Newfoundland with 9 ships, 500 men, 100 cannon and £10,400 worth of goods taken from English fishermen. Henry Crout tells us that he had also captured about 30 French vessels. Easton took his fleet to the Azores and ambushed the Spanish fleet, taking 4 ships. In September 1612, sailing the *San Sebastian*, one of the richest prizes ever captured by a pirate, back to Harbour Grace, he was faced with European warships. Sent to protect the French and Basque fishing fleets, they had taken his other fort at Harbour Grace. Seeing his fleet entering Conception Bay, they attacked Easton, but he defeated the Basques, wrecking their flagship *St Malo* on an islet before retaking the fort. In legend, 47 of the pirates who died that day are buried in a graveyard at Bear Cove, near the mouth of Harbour Grace. Easton's pardon had still not reached him in March 1613, so he sailed into Villefranche, Savoy, a pirate 'freeport'. With a reputed £2 million of gold, Easton was welcomed by the impoverished Duke of Savoy.

He soon captured three Spanish treasure ships off the Strait of Gibraltar in about 1615. It was 'the largest pirate heist in world history at that time,' according to Jason Crummey, author of *Pirates of Newfoundland*, the equivalent of $50 million today. Easton then fought for Algiers against Spain, amassing an even greater fortune. Another royal pardon was issued, and a Captain Roger Middleton was commissioned to deliver the pardon to Easton on the Barbary Coast. At Villefranche, Easton had bought a palace, set up a warehouse for his booty, was living in luxury, and became the 'Master of Ordinance' for the Duke of Savoy, remaining in his service until 1620. One of the world's wealthiest men, Easton married a noblewoman and bought the title of Marquis of Savoy from the duke. In Harbour Grace, the old customs house is now a museum with a room dedicated to Easton, with models of his fort and one of his ships, *Happy Adventure*.

Sir Henry Mainwaring (1587–May 1653) – Privateer, Barbary Corsair, Royalist, Author and Pirate Hunter

The second son of Sir George Mainwaring was born at Ightfield, Shropshire, and educated at Brasenose College, Oxford, where he obtained his degree at the age of 15. He was admitted to the Inner Temple to study law in November 1604, and probably served in the Low Countries in the Eighty Years' War against Spain, acquiring nautical and military experience. As a skilful seaman, he was commissioned in 1611–1612 by the Lord High Admiral to command a fleet and capture the Bristol Channel pirates led by Peter Easton (*see* preceding entry), but Easton had crossed the Atlantic. In 1612 Mainwaring bought a small ship for £700, planning to accompany Sir Thomas Sherley to

Persia to fight the Turks, but was prevented from sailing by the efforts of the Spanish ambassador, who feared that the fleet would be used against Spanish interests. The angered Mainwaring fitted out another vessel, the *Nightingale* of Chichester, pretending he wanted to trade in West Africa. Mainwaring now sailed off without the king's permission and began to attack Spanish shipping in the West Indies, captaining the 160-ton *Resistance*.

He returned to the Mediterranean and made La Mamora (modern day Mehdya/Mehdia), on the west coast of Morocco, his headquarters. As a leading Barbary corsair, he quickly assembled a private fleet of 30–40 ships, and by summer 1613 had taken goods worth approximately £3,500 from ships trading to Spain. He took care not to attack British ships, or those carrying British cargo, and made full restitution if it happened by mistake. He also negotiated the release of all Christians enslaved by the corsairs of Salé (Rabat), Morocco.

The Venetian ambassador wrote that Mainwaring had no equal when it came to nautical skill, 'for fighting his ship, for his mode of boarding and for resisting the enemy'. Jean Chevalier of Jersey, who knew Mainwaring during the English Civil War, wrote that he

> ...had been a terrible pirate in the flower of his youth, consorting with the King of Morocco, and carrying into his ports all prizes captured by him from English, French, Spaniards, and Flemings, indiscriminately. By such corsair-like pursuits he contrived to amass immense riches in gold and silver, and owned a large fleet of galleys, which was for a long time the terror of all traders navigating the Straits.' His attacks on Spanish ships became such a problem that Philip III sent the Duke of Medina as an emissary to Mainwaring, informing him 'If you will deliver up Mamora to the King of Spain, his Majesty in return for this gracious favour will be pleased to bestow on you a free pardon and a considerable sum of money.' Mainwaring would be permitted to keep his ships and plunder, and offered 'a high command in the Spanish royal fleet.' Mainwaring also wrote 'The Duke of Savoy sent me my pardon. The Duke of Florence sent me my pardon... The Dey of Tunis ... swore that if I would stay with him he would divide his estate equally with me, and never urge me to turn Turk, but give me leave to depart whensoever it should please your Majesty [James I of England] to be so gracious as to pardon me.

In June 1614, Mainwaring took eight ships to Newfoundland, ostensibly to protect English fishermen from attacks of Spanish-controlled Flemish warships. He instead raided the harbours, taking with him, when he left Newfoundland in mid-September, carpenters, ammunition, 10,000 fish from a French vessel at Harbour Grace, and 400 men. However, in his absence the Spanish had captured Marmora, and he changed his headquarters to Villefranche (Villafranca). The Duke of Savoy, at war with Spain, had declared it to be a free port, and pirates such as Peter Easton, Mainwaring's former prey, had settled there. Mainwaring lost one ship to the Spanish in January 1615. However, in six weeks, his six remaining ships plundered 500,000 crowns from the Spanish, and Philip III issued letters of marque to any of his subjects who wanted to attack Mainwaring and ordered a fleet of five royal warships to hunt down Mainwaring. In July 1615, they battled his three vessels, and the Spanish fleet only managed to escape complete destruction by slipping away during the night, fleeing to Lisbon for safety. According to Mainwaring, Philip III again offered to pardon and give him an annual allowance of 20,000 ducats if he served as 'General of that squadron'. The Savoy-Spain war ended, and James I was trying to arrange a marriage between Prince Charles and the daughter of Philip III, so the king told Mainwaring to accept a free pardon for his piracy, or James would send a fleet to destroy him. Mainwaring's ships were impounded at Dover and he was pardoned in June 1616.

He was knighted in 1618, elected MP for Dover in 1621, and ended his naval career as a vice-admiral in 1639. In 1618, he wrote for James I, *Of the Beginnings, Practices, and Suppression of Pirates*, which 'affords to the student of English history a vivid picture of piracy as it flourished during the early part of the 17th century.' Between 1619 and 1623 he also wrote the superb *Seaman's Dictionary*, the first work in English on seamanship and nautical terms. He was outlawed for debt in June 1641, but apparently avoided arrest. In 1642 the English Civil War broke out, and because he was a Royalist, in November he was forced to resign as master of Trinity House. Mainwaring had joined Charles I at Oxford during the Civil War. The king was captured in 1645, and Mainwaring accompanied Prince Charles to Jersey, where he lived in poverty, and served with the royalist fleet in 1648. In January 1649, Parliament executed Charles I, and the news reached Mainwaring and Prince Charles in The Hague four days later. The exiled Royalists believed Charles II's 'only chance of regaining the throne depended on what measure of success attended his efforts on the sea'. However, Prince Rupert's failings at sea convinced Mainwaring that the new king's cause was lost. Two years later, exhausted and feeling his age, Mainwaring returned to England in dire straits. In November 1651, his entire property consisted of 'a horse and wearing apparel to the value of £8.' For siding with Charles I and Charles II, he was fined £1 6s. 8d and given six weeks to pay. Someone paid the sum for him on 18 December 1651. Mainwaring died intestate, at the age of 66, and was buried on 15 May 1653, in the same cemetery as his wife Fortune. No tombstone marks his grave in St Giles's Church, Camberwell.

Christopher Newport (29 December 1561–August 1617) – the One-armed Privateer responsible for the Success of the Virginia Colony

Born at the port of Harwich, England, Christopher's father was a shipmaster. In 1580 the 29-year-old Newport is noted as deserting the *Minion* of London at Bahia, Brazil. The next record of him is in 1587, as master's mate on John Watts' privateer *Drake*, in Francis Drake's great attack on the Spanish port city of Cádiz (the raid known as 'the singeing of the King of Spain's beard'). By 1589 Newport was captaining the *ma* of London, but by 1590–91 was again sailing under the command of John Watts, being promoted to captain the *Little John*. From 1592–95 Newport was captain of the *Golden Dragon*, and began activities in the Caribbean. In 1592 he commanded a flotilla of privateers attacking Spanish towns across the Caribbean. Puerto Caballos in Honduras was seen as being vulnerable, and was taken and sacked by Newport in 1592. Newport lost his right arm while attacking two Spanish treasure ships off Cuba. Returning home, off the Azores he helped capture the treasure-laden *Madre de Dios* and sailed it back to England.

In 1595 Newport married again (his first wife had died), and he became the owner of one-sixth of the heavily armed ship *Neptune*, which he captained to raid Spanish settlements in the Caribbean. Newport also took part in the Barbary Coast trade. The year 1604 brought an end to his lucrative privateering career, as a peace agreement was signed between England and Spain, and he began captaining merchant ships to the Caribbean. In 1606 Newport was made a master in the Royal Navy, and the Virginia Company of London gave him command of its first fleet to sail to Virginia. On 20 December 1606, three ships carrying 104 settlers set sail from London to Virginia. Christopher Newport captained the *Susan Constant*, Bartholomew Gosnold the *Godspeed*, and John Ratcliffe the *Discovery*. In May

1607 Newport, Captain John Smith and others explored the James River, making friendly contact with four local tribes, but while they were away the new English settlement of Jamestown was attacked with two colonists killed and 10 wounded.

On 22 June 1607 Newport sailed back to England, carrying a letter to the Virginia Company. It vastly exaggerated the new colony's commercial opportunities to attract greater investment and more settlers. His return to Jamestown with fresh supplies in 1608 possibly saved John Smith ('Admiral of New England') from being hanged. He and John Smith visited Powhatan, the major local chief, and Newport gave him a suit of clothing, a hat, and a greyhound. In April 1608 Newport sailed the *John and Francis* back to London, returning to Virginia in October with the first female settlers, again giving Powhatan various gifts and a decorated crown. In December Newport returned to London, and in 1609 captained one of nine ships, with 600 passengers, livestock and provisions to last a year, for Virginia. The fleet's mission was to save the starving colony, but in July a hurricane blew the fleet apart. Newport's ship was destroyed on a Bermudan reef, leaving the crew and passengers stranded until they were able to construct new vessels. They managed to return to Jamestown nearly a year after the shipwreck. With few provisions, only 60 settlers in Jamestown had survived the harsh winter and, in September 1610, Newport returned to England. In May 1611 Newport sailed to Jamestown for the last time, returning to England in October 1611. In 1612 Newport now assumed his Royal Navy post (given in 1606) and began service with the East India Company, sailing to Persia (Iran) aboard the *Expedition* of London in early 1613, and to India in 1615. Making his third voyage with the company, as commander of the *Hope*, on 15 August 1617 Newport arrived in Banten, Java, and died soon afterwards. Between 1606 and 1611, Newport had led a total of five voyages between Virginia and England, bringing supplies and additional settlers back to the fledgling colony, and without his continuing efforts the history of the United States of America might have been completely different.

The Dunkirkers – 1568–1712

In the Eighty Years' War of Independence from the Habsburg Empire (1568–1648), the Hollanders (Dutch) suffered constant problems from Spanish privateers ('Dunkirkers') based at Dunkirk, then held by the Spanish Hapsburgs. The Dutch tried to blockade the Dunkirkers from reaching the open seas, but in winter this defence was very difficult to maintain. In 1587 the United Provinces of Holland declared the Dunkirk privateers to be pirates, and ordered Dutch naval captains to swear an oath to throw all prisoners from Dunkirk privateers into the North Sea. The practice was known as *voetenspoelen*, 'washing the feet', and in winter would be a quick death. There were several major battles, during one of which Admiral Piet Heyn, a Dutch hero, was killed in 1629. It was only in 1646, when the French captured Dunkirk with Dutch naval support that Dunkirker attacks almost ceased. However, in 1652, the Spanish recaptured Dunkirk and the privateers once more became a major threat. The Dunkirkers almost wiped out English trade after England fought Spain from 1654, until Dunkirk was taken again, by a Franco-English force in 1658. The Dunkirkers then based themselves mainly at Ostend. From 1672, France and the Dutch Republic were at war and privateering on behalf of France resumed at Dunkirk, lasting intermittently until 1712.

Pieter Pietersen Heyn (25 November 1577–18 June 1629) – Piet Hein, Galley Slave and Admiral

Born in Rotterdam, the son of a sea captain, Pieter Pietersen Heyn was captured by the Spanish as a teenager, and was a galley slave probably from 1598. In 1602, he gained his freedom after being traded for Spanish prisoners. In 1603 he was again taken, off Cuba, and was a prisoner for another four years. In 1607 Heyn joined the Dutch East India Company, sailing to Asian markets, becoming a captain in 1612. In 1618, captaining the *Neptunus*, the Venetians pressed him and his ship into their service, but in 1621 he escaped overland back to the Netherlands. From 1621, following the end of the 12-year peace treaty with Spain, Heyn became renowned in the continuing struggle against privateers from the port of Dunkirk, then still part of the Habsburg Empire.

In 1623, Heyn was appointed vice-admiral of the new Dutch West Indian Company, sailing for Bahia (Salvador) on the coast of Brazil in December, with a fleet of 26 privateers. In 1624, his fleet bombarded the heavily defended port and castle, and he despatched 60 men to capture the ships moored in the harbour. He then sent 14 ships to capture the city, and Bahia was captured after parts of its walls were destroyed. Some Portuguese ships, not knowing the port had been taken, unsuspectingly sailed into Bahia and were captured with ease. Heyn then sent four ships home, loaded with sugar, tobacco and hides. In August 1624 Heyn crossed the Atlantic to Africa, with seven ships, making for Sao Paulo de Loanda in Angola. He had been ordered to capture this important slave-trading port. He attacked a Portuguese fleet in the Bay of Loanda (Luanda) but failed to capture any ships, becoming stuck in shallows and facing cannon fire from the seaward enemy fleet. Returning to Bahia, he found it had been recaptured, and after fighting a strong Portuguese fleet, returned to the United Provinces of Holland to recruit more men and ships.

He now recrossed the Atlantic to take merchant shipping at the city-port of Vitória, Brazil, but was forced again to retreat to Holland. However, the Dutch West India Company gave him command of a new squadron in 1626. In the next year his fortunes changed, and Heyn took more than 30 fully-laden Portuguese and Spanish ships around Salvador. 1628 saw Heyn take the Silver Fleet, aided by the pirate Moses Henriques (*see* following entry). Part of Heyn's fleet had returned to the Netherlands carrying booty, and it was believed he had left with most of his privateers, so it was safe for treasure galleons to leave Mexico and Venezuela. However, Heyn had assembled a fleet of 31 heavily armed privateers. He waited with part of his fleet off northern Cuba, and after seeing the Spanish *flota* sailing from Mexico, sent part of his fleet to the east of Cuba to prevent their escape back to Spanish-held ports. The lighter, quicker, more manoeuvrable Dutch ships now easily stopped the Spanish escaping into the harbour of Havana. The capture of the Silver Fleet made Heyn a hero upon his return home in 1629. However, disputes over payments, and the sale and distribution of the silver, caused Heyn to resign his Dutch West India Company commission.

He was appointed Lieutenant-Admiral of Holland and West Frisia in 1629, becoming commander of the confederate Dutch fleet, taking as his flag captain the great Maarten Tromp (*see* Peter Easton entry). Heyn was given a commission from the Prince of Orange (*Prins van Oranje*) to take up privateering once again and to form a blockade at the Spanish privateer port of Dunkirk. His flotilla intercepted three privateers from Ostend, and Heyn sailed his flagship between two enemy ships to give them both simultaneous broadsides. He was hit in the left shoulder by a cannonball and was killed, aged 41, and was buried at the Oude Kerk in Delft.

Moses Cohen Henriques *(fl.*1628–1654) – The Sephardic Jewish Pirate

A Dutchman of Portuguese Sephardic Jewish origins, Moses Cohen Henriques helped Admiral Piet Heyn (Hein) of the Dutch West India Company capture the Spanish treasure armada in 1628. During the Eighty Years' War between the Dutch Republic and Hapsburg Spain Henriques participated in the Battle of Matanzas Bay, Cuba. A fleet of privateers met at Blanquilla, an island in the Aves Archipelago, 180 miles northwest of Caracas, Venezuela, to plan the attack. However, a Dutch cabin boy became lost on the island, the privateers sailed without him, and he was taken by the Spanish, revealing the impending attack. A fleet of Spanish treasure ships from Venezuela was intended to rendezvous with a fleet from Mexico, but now stayed in port. However, the Mexican fleet of 16 ships was uninformed and was attacked at night by Heyn, Henriques and others. One great galleon was taken by surprise, and nine smaller ships surrendered, the crews being promised their lives. Two small merchant ships tried to escape, but were captured by the faster privateer sloops, and four galleons were trapped off the coast in the Bay of Matanzas, unable to escape. The Dutch did not fire cannon, not wishing to sink precious cargoes, but after some musket volleys the Spanish realised their hopeless position and surrendered.

In excess of 11,500,000 guilders worth of gold, silver, indigo and cochineal was looted, without a single casualty on either side. Heyn took the ships and their cargoes and set ashore all the crews with enough supplies to reach Havana. Henriques next led a Jewish settlement in Brazil; it comprised mainly Sephardic Jews, who had fled the Inquisition in Portugal and Spain to the religious freedom of the Netherlands. Much of northern Brazil was then ruled by the Dutch, particularly around Recife, where the first synagogue in the Americas was set up in 1636. Dutch privateers had sacked Bahia in 1604, and from 1630 to 1654, the Dutch founded Dutch Brazil permanently along the north-eastern coastline, accessible to Europe. However, the Dutch West India colonists were subject to constant attacks by the Portuguese. Henriques was said to have established his own pirate island off the coast, but the Portuguese recaptured northern Brazil in 1654, and Henriques escaped to join Henry Morgan (*q.v.*) as a close advisor.

Jacob Collaert (*c.*1600–1637) – Collaert of Duinkerken

The Fleming served the Hapsburg Empire as a Dunkirker, a privateer fighting the Dutch. One of his greatest enemies was Claes Compaan (*q.v.*), whom he almost captured off Spain in 1626. Collaert was then created Vice Admiral with the 'Royal Squadron' serving Spain from Dunkirk, from 1633 to 1637. Dunkirk was under a Dutch blockade from early 1635, but on 14 August 1635 Collaert broke out with a fleet of 21 ships.

On 17 August, Collaert found a Dutch herring fleet of 160 boats, protected by just one 39-gun man-of-war. She was crippled by cannon

Jacob Collaert.
Courtesy of
Rijksmuseum.

fire and Collaert destroyed 74 fishing boats. On 19 August, his privateers forced six men-of-war escorts to flee, before sinking or burning 50 herring boats near Dogger Bank. Of the captured fishermen, Collaert placed 150 of the old, young and wounded on a merchant ship to return to the United Provinces, while the others were kept for ransom. In 1635 alone, Collaert's destruction of Dutch herring boats cost the port of Flushing more than 2,000,000 guilders in lost revenues.

Two Dutch naval fleets, with a total of 20 warships, were sent to take Collaert, who managed to damage 4 before escaping in bad weather back to Dunkirk in September, with 975 captive fishermen. In 1636, sailing with two other privateers, he was captured near Dieppe and died of an illness in captivity at La Coruña, Spain, the following year. His son was also a Dunkirker captain.

Admiral Jean Bart (21 October 1650–27 April 1702) – Jean Baert, the Most Successful Dunkirker

Born Jean Baert, the son of a Dunkirker, as a young man he served under Admiral de Ruyter in the Dutch Navy. However, on the outbreak of war in 1672 between the United Provinces and France, he entered French service as a Dunkirk privateer. Unable to become an officer in the French Navy owing to his humble background, he held an irregular privateering commission but was so successful against the Dutch Navy and merchant shipping that he was made a lieutenant in 1679. Once, with just six ships, he broke the Dutch blockade to escort a convoy of grain ships into safety in Dunkirk harbour. His fame was such that Louis XIV sent him to the Mediterranean on a special mission, where he again gained distinction.

In 1689, during the Nine Years' War (1688–1697) between France and, basically, the rest of Europe, Bart was captured by the English and imprisoned in Plymouth. However, after three days he escaped with 20 other sailors, stealing a small boat and rowing to Brittany. In 1691 he again broke the Dunkirk blockade, battling an allied merchant fleet, and then burnt a Scottish castle and four villages.

On 29 June 1694 he saved Paris from starvation by taking a great convoy of Dutch grain ships, and was raised to the nobility in the following year. On 17 June 1696, as the admiral commanding 7 French warships and 2 small privateers, Bart attacked 5 Dutch warships, which were escorting a convoy of 112 merchant vessels. His 7 ships were all frigates, including his flagship the 54-gun *Maure*; *Adroit*, 44 cannon; *Mignon*, 44 cannon; *Jersey*, 40 cannon; *Comte*, 40 cannon; *Alcyon*,

Jean Baert/Bart.

38 cannon; and *Milfort*, 36 cannon. He also commanded 2 long boats, the fire ship *Tigre* and 2 privateers, the 8-gun *Lamberley* and the 6-gun *Bonne Espérance*.

At the Battle of Dogger Bank, Jean Bart on the *Maure* attacked the 44-gun Dutch flagship, the *Raadhuis van Haarlem*. After three hours of fighting its captain was killed and she surrendered, followed by the other four Dutch warships. The *Maure* lost 15 sailors and 16 were wounded. Bart burnt 4 of the Dutch warships, keeping the 38-gun *Comte de Solnis*, and captured and burned 25 of the 112 merchant ships, only breaking away when Admiral John Benbow's squadron of 18 English warships approached. He sailed towards Denmark, staying there until he thought it safe to try to return to Dunkirk. Bart's squadron later slipped through the allied blockade, with 1,200 prisoners, on 27 September 1696.

With the 1697 Peace of Ryswick, Bart's active service in the French Navy ended; he had captured 386 ships and sunk or burned many more. Jean Bart died of pleurisy and was buried in the Église St-Éloi, Dunkirk. His oldest son, François-Cornil Baert, became a vice-admiral. About 30 French naval ships have been named *Jean Bart* over the last 300 years.

Isaac Rochussen (1631–1710) – The Flushing *Kaper*

Also known as Isaac Rockesen, this Dutch privateer fought in the second and third Anglo-Dutch Wars (1665–1667 and 1672–74). Born at the great port of Flushing (now Vlissingen) in the Netherlands, he was active from the 1650s to the 1670s, usually captaining the *Eendracht* (*Concord*). Rochussen achieved European fame on 7 July 1672, taking the heavily armed and richly laden East India merchantman *Falcon* after a long pitched battle off the Isles of Scilly. He wanted to take the damaged *Falcon* to Amsterdam but was afraid of it being retaken in the English Channel, and there may have been unfavourable winds, so instead he sailed the *Eendracht* and *Falcon* all the way past Ireland, Scotland and England to the North Sea. He first stopped to reprovision in Bergen in Norway, then Hamburg in Germany, staying at each port for weeks. The circular voyage home took him five months, arriving in Amsterdam in December 1672.

The *Falcon* and her tremendous cargo were sold for 350,000 guilders, the highest amount paid for a captured vessel at the time. The Zeelander privateers sold another 29 vessels around this time for 812,000 guilders, an average of 28,000 guilders per ship, so the *Falcon* was worth more than twelve times the average prize. However, a large quantity of the jewels and diamonds taken did not appear at the sale, having been embezzled. There were several lawsuits against Rochussen, stating he had sold valuables at Bergen and Hamburg, and one Jewish diamond merchant in Amsterdam claimed he had two bags of diamonds on the *Falcon*, which had disappeared. Rochussen should also have brought the *Falcon* not to Amsterdam for sale, but to Vlissingen or the Zeeland Admiralty in Middelburg. However, as a national hero of the new Dutch Republic, nothing came of Rochussen's misdemeanours, and he received a gold medal for the capture. The *Falcon* was soon afterwards referred to by the Dutch as the *Gouden Valk* (*Golden Falcon*). Using his share of the prize money (and probably some of his stolen loot), the privateer set himself up as a merchant at Vlissingen, and financed privateers including his son in the Nine Years' War (1698-1697). His son inherited a thriving business, and Rochussen's descendants profited from his fame, riches and prestige.

Sir Lars Gathenhielm (1689–1718) and Ingela Gathenhielm (1692–1729) – The Swedish Privateer and the 'Shipping Queen'

They are included under Dunkirkers as they traded stolen goods there. Born Lars Andersson Gathe (and also known as Lasse i Gatan),

Lars was one of the nine children of the sea captain Anders Börjesson Gathe, and is said to have been illiterate. From Onsala, on the coast of Halland County, Sweden, he met his wife Ingela when they were children, as she lived on the neighbouring farm. He married Ingela Olofsdotter Hammar in 1711, and they had five children.

Sweden was involved in the Great Northern War of 1700–1721. Peter the Great of Russia, Augustus the Great of Saxony-Poland and Charles V of Denmark attacked the Swedish Empire, and after several victories Charles XII of Sweden marched towards Moscow in 1709. The Swedes were initially successful, but the Russian 'scorched earth' policy, and the 'Great Frost' of 1708–09, left no resources for its army in the Russian winter. Charles XII's Swedish army had shrunk to 24,000 men by the time it was destroyed at the Battle of Poltava. In May 1709, Charles fled with his surviving 543 men to the protection of the Ottoman Turks. After the battle, Russia kept its new possessions in the Baltic and Ingria, and consolidated its hold over Poland and Ukraine, and Denmark re-entered the war. Seeing a weakened Sweden, Britain and Prussia copied Denmark and also warred with Sweden.

In exile in Turkey, in June 1710 Charles XII tried to protect Swedish shipping routes from pirates and Russian, Danish and other enemies, and he appointed Lars Gathe as a privateer in the Swedish Navy. Gathe now had royal permission to attack and plunder ships of enemy nations on the Baltic Sea, selling any loot at Dunkerque and becoming extremely wealthy. Gathe took many ships with his galleon *Lilla Jägaren* (Little Hunter), and he recruited many men from his home town of Onsala as sailors, as he used the captured vessels to build a great privateer fleet. Lars had a hip injury, which made him dependent on crutches, so more and more he operated his privateers from land at Gothenburg. Gathe was accused of also attacking Swedish vessels, but was protected by the king. Lars Gathe and his brother Christian were ennobled by the king in 1715, given the new family surname of Gathenhielm.

In 1718 Lars Gathenhielm died of tuberculosis, aged only 29, and his wife Ingela took over and expanded his business empire and privateering enterprises, until her own death 11 years later. She had actively worked with him throughout his life, and Ingela came to be called the 'Shipping Queen'. She stopped attacking Danish ships after the 1720 peace treaty, and Russian ships in 1721. She remarried but was buried with Lars in Onsala Church. Their white sarcophagi lie next to each other, each with the skull and crossbones carved on it.

Chinese Pirates

Wang Zhi *(fl.1540s)* – **Wufeng, the 'Japanese Dwarf Bandit'**
Although born in Huangshan City, China, he was one of the most notable leaders of the feared Japanese pirates called *wako* (*wokou* in Japanese, and *waegu* in Korean). The name translates as 'dwarf bandit', and the early *wokou* originally contained a number of nationalities raiding the coastlines of China, Japan and Korea. However, later they were said to be about 70% Chinese and 30% Japanese. For more than a millennium they had plagued the coastline, with a Korean monument of 404CE recording that *wokou* (Japanese dwarf bandits) had crossed the sea and were defeated by Gwanggaeto the Great.

Japanese *Wokou* pirates pillaging on the China coast during the Ming dynasty.

Being a pirate, smuggler and a trader, Wang Zhi arrived in Japan in the 1540s, operating out of the archipelago of the Goto Islands, near Nagasaki in the East China Sea. Portuguese traders were shipwrecked off the coast of Japan in 1543, and Wang Zhi captained a junk that rescued some, this being the first contact between Europe and Japan. Using the name of Wufeng, Wang Zhi acted as their interpreter in Japan, probably using language picked up during his control of a great smuggling syndicate. His men constantly raided China, but Wang Zhi said he never participated, calling himself a mere *hai-shang* (sea merchant). However, when he was captured, he was beheaded by the Chinese. Luckily for him, he was not operating in the previous century. In 1405 twenty captured *wokou* were sent to China, where they were boiled in a cauldron in Ningbo.

Zheng Zhilong (1604–1661) – Nicholas Iquan Gaspard, 'Commander of the Largest Pirate Army in World History', Turncoat and Father of Koxinga

Zheng was born in Nan'an, Fujian, the province on the south-east coast of China, opposite Taiwan. He was the son of a middle-ranking financial official, and left home as a teenager aboard a merchant ship. He may have fled after being caught attempting a liaison with his stepmother. Zheng travelled to Macau to stay with his uncle, and was there baptised as a Catholic, Nicholas Gaspard.

At the request of his uncle, he took cargo to Lin Dan, known as 'Captain China' in Nagasaki, Japan. Lin Dan became his mentor and arranged for Zheng to work as an interpreter for the Dutch, as he had learned Portuguese in Macau, and the Dutch merchants had some knowledge of that important trading language. In 1622, Dutch forces took over the Pescadores Archipelago, and Li Dan sent Zheng to the Pescadores, off the Taiwan Strait, as a translator in peace negotiations. Before leaving Japan, Zheng married Tagawa Matsu, but he had left Japan before she gave birth to the famous Zheng Chenggong (Koxinga, *q.v.*) in 1624.

Li Dan (Captain China) died in 1623, and Zheng inherited his fleet of ships. Zheng soon became a highly successful pirate under Dutch patronage; they provided more ships and weapons in exchange for a percentage of the booty. With the assistance of Zheng's Chinese pirates, they were attempting to monopolise trade routes to Japan.

In 1625, Zheng Zhilong founded the Shibazhi, a collective of 18 well-known Chinese pirate captains, which won a series of battles against Ming Dynasty fleets. By 1627 Zheng commanded 400 junks and perhaps 20,000 men, and in 1628 won a comprehensive victory against the Ming Southern fleet. The Emperor now offered him a post, and Zheng was appointed a navy major-general. Zheng and his new wife resettled on an island off the coast of Fujian, where on behalf of the Emperor he operated a large pirate fleet of more than 800 ships between Japan and Vietnam. Zheng was appointed Admiral of the Coastal Seas, and in October 1633 defeated an alliance of junks under a renegade Shibazhi pirate and Dutch East India ships, in the Battle of Liaoluo Bay. Now incredibly wealthy, he became a great landlord.

The invading Manchu had almost overrun the Ming armies, and Jiangyin held out against about 10,000 Qing Han Chinese troops for 83 days. When the city wall was breached on 9 October 1645, the Manchu-Mongol-Han Chinese Qing army was ordered to 'fill the city with corpses before you sheathe your swords', and massacred the entire population, killing between 74,000 and 100,000 people. After the city's capture, Zheng became commander-in-chief of the retreating Ming imperial forces, and was ordered to defend the newly established capital of Fuzhou. However, in 1646, he secretly defected to the Manchus, leaving passes unguarded, allowing the Manchu army to capture Fuzhou. The traitorous Zheng was greatly rewarded and created a Count of the Second Rank by the new Qing Dynasty government. However, his son Koxinga remained loyal to the Ming Dynasty and continued to fight the Qing, so Zheng was placed in chains for 15 years. He was executed in 1661 because of Koxinga's continued resistance.

'Koxinga' (1623–1662) – Zheng Chenggong, Zhèng Chénggōng Miào, Kuo-hsing Yeh, 'Lord of the Imperial Surname', Last Defender of the Ming Dynasty

This adopted son of the last Chinese Ming Emperor is a national hero in three nations – Japan, China and Taiwan – and is the only pirate ever to be worshipped as a living God of War. He was the son of the Chinese warlord pirate, Zheng Zhilong (*see* above) and a Japanese mother.

She herself is of great interest. Tagawa Matsu (1601–1646), lived most of her life in the coastal town of Hirado, in the Nagasaki region of Japan, then later migrated to China to join her husband Zheng Zhilong. In legend she was said to have given birth to Koxinga during a journey with her husband, when she was picking up seashells on the Senli Beach, Hirado. The stone beside which she gave birth still exists, known as the Koxinga Child Birth Stone Tablet, almost 3 feet tall and 10 feet wide, submerged during high tides. Tagawa

Matsu raised Koxinga in Japan by herself until he was seven, and in 1630 she was reunited with Koxinga by moving to Quanzhou, Fujian. In 1646, when Koxinga was away, the city was invaded by the Manchu. Koxinga immediately returned to Quanzhou, only to discover that his mother had hanged herself in a refusal to surrender to the Manchus. Some people say she was raped and killed by the Manchus. In Koxinga Memorial Temple in Tainan, Taiwan, Tagawa Matsu's ancestral tablet is placed in a chamber called the Shrine of Queen Dowager Weng, her posthumous title based on Koxinga having become Prince-King of Yanping Prefecture in the Southern Ming Empire.

From early youth Koxinga (his Portuguese name) was inspired with a hatred of the Manchu invaders. He was born in Nagasaki, Japan, and one legend is that he trained as a samurai as young as six years old. In his mid-teens he was called back to China by his father to take part in his successful pirate fleet. His father also operated in the black market silk trade with the Dutch and British East India Companies, at this time making more than 100,000 silver taels a year (about 4.5 tons of silver). Koxinga then left piracy to study government administration at Nanking University, but Manchuria took Beijing in

Koxinga.

1644, smashing the Ming armies, hanging the Emperor and declaring a new Imperial Dynasty, the Qing. The Emperor's only surviving son fled to Koxinga's father, Zheng Zhilong. Koxinga's Ming loyalists fought against a majority Han Chinese Bannermen Qing army when it attacked Nanjing. Koxinga became so successful in his raids along the China coast that the Qing Emperor ordered the inhabitants of more than 80 ports to migrate 10 miles inland, after first destroying their homes. This massive depopulation policy was carried out in order to deprive Koxinga's Ming loyalists of resources.

Koxinga was symbolically adopted by the childless Emperor, given an imperial sword, a seal with the words 'Great Rebel-Quelling General' on it, and the title Koxinga. (Koxinga is a Portuguese approximation of Guóxìngyé, a title meaning 'Lord of the Imperial Surname'.) He was successful in the field for six months, until his father betrayed the Emperor, surrendering Fukien to the Qing army, composed of Manchus, Han Chinese and Mongols. Koxinga's father had been promised that he could keep his position and title if he would give up the Ming Emperor. The Qing Emperor initially rewarded Zheng, but because of his son's continued fighting, his officers dismantled Zheng's pirate fleet, drowned the Emperor in a well, and dragged Zheng to Beijing in chains, to rot in a dungeon for 15 years before his execution. Koxinga was an outlaw, and his Emperor was dead. His father had commanded the 'largest pirate army in world history', but all Koxinga had left were about a dozen of his closest commanders, hidden in a small Confucian temple in the mountains. He now ceremonially burned the scholar's robes he wore at Nanking University, swearing that he would only wear full plate armour until the Qing were thrown out of China back to Manchuria, and the Ming Dynasty was restored.

Koxinga headed for the only remaining outpost of Ming resistance, Xiamen province, to rebuild an army. He carried out a series of campaigns over the next 15 years, and built a fleet of more than 3,000 warships to attack Qing coastal settlements, raiding their shipping to finance his operations. He also carried on his father's black market silk trade to fund his armies. On land, he attacked towns and forts, leading from the front and personally beheading any of his officers who ordered their troops to retreat. Koxinga continued to build up his forces and, in 1659, with supplies and food running short, launched a full-scale assault to re-take the former Imperial Capital of Nanjing. He sailed up the Yangtze River, took the outer walls, but some of his soldiers raided the city's alcohol supplies and stopped fighting, allowing the Qing the opportunity to charge and destroy them, with flaming arrows and fire boats. In a horrendous defeat, Koxinga's army of 170,000 troops was reduced to just 15,000.

Koxinga retreated to Fujian Province. Pressured by Qing fleets and with too few followers to defeat the Qing, in April 1661 Koxinga loaded 25,000 loyal citizens on a fleet of 800 warships and sailed across the 100-mile Taiwan Strait, landing his remaining 15,000 soldiers on the shores of Taiwan. He besieged the Dutch-controlled Fort Zeelandia. After nine months, he expelled the Dutch, taking the fort's commander's daughter as his concubine, and declared himself King of Formosa (Taiwan). This was the first Chinese-controlled government of Taiwan, and Koxinga built up its infrastructure, continuing his trading with Japan, Southeast Asia, and Britain. After his death from malaria in 1662, only six months after taking Taiwan, he received official canonisation. Gosse noted that 'The direct descendant of Koxinga, the pirate, is one of the very few hereditary nobles in China.' His pirate kingdom on Taiwan lasted until 1683 before falling to Manchu Qing forces from mainland China, with 60,000 troops and 200 ships.

Ching Yi (1765–1807) – Zhèng Yī, Commander of the Red Flag Fleet, and one of a Notorious Threesome

Known in the west as Cheng or Ching I, Zhèng Yī sailed out of Canton (now Guangdong) and terrorised the South China Sea, helped by some government officials who wished to interfere with the Vietnamese succession. He was supposedly homosexual, in love with a young captive, Cheung Po Tsai, whom he adopted as his son. However, in 1801 Ching Yi sought the assistance of the famed prostitute and Cantonese brothel owner Shih Yang, who had access to the secrets of the rich and powerful, through indiscreet disclosures in 'pillow talk'. Ching Yi proposed marriage to the madam, supposedly offering a formal contract, granting Shih Yang 50 per cent of his profits. Thus young Cheung Po Tsai became her stepson, but at the same time shared Ching Yi's bed. Shih Yang became known as Ching Yi Sao (wife of Ching Yi), and 'participated fully in her husband's piracy'. His wife Ching Yi Sao helped Ching Yi gather Cantonese pirate fleets into an alliance and develop a huge fleet of nearly 150,000 pirates, and possibly about 1,800 vessels (many of them small, however). By 1804, they were known as the Red Flag Fleet. Ching Yi was probably thrown overboard off Vietnam by his wife's followers, drowning on 16 November 1807.

His feared wife Ching Yi Sao became known as Ching (or Cheng) Shih (Ching's Widow). She now forced her husband's lover Cheung Po Tsai to marry her, while taking full command of the fleet.

Madame Ching (1775–1844) – Shi Xianggu, Ching Shih (Ching's Widow), a Madame from a Brothel who became a Pirate Commander and Married her Adopted Bisexual Son

She was born Shi Xianggu, in Canton. Some believe that she was captured by pirates, but it is more likely that Ching Yi (*see* above) came to an agreement with her. Upon the death (probably murder) of her husband Ching Yi in 1807, Ching Shih worked to take leadership of the Red Flag Fleet. To prevent her rivals fighting her, she won the support of powerful members of her husband's family, Cheng Po-yang and Cheng Ch'i. By diplomacy, the 32-year-old former prostitute soon personally commanded 20,000–40,000 pirates manning more than 300 junks, upon which also sailed women and children. The naval fleet, commanded by her subordinates, additionally had about 1,500 boats with possibly 180,000 followers in coalition. With this great force to control, Madame Ching needed someone loyal to assist her, but also accepted by her pirates. She chose her late husband's lover, Cheung Po Tsai, and they later married, with Ching Shih giving birth to Cheung's son before 1810. Their fleet generally preyed on ships belonging to the British, Portuguese and the Chinese Qing dynasty. She was described by Victor Luis Borges as 'a lady pirate who operated in Asian waters, all the way from the Yellow Sea to the rivers of the Annam coast'. The fleet itself had a constitutional-monarch-style government, with Madame Ching as queen; a council, whose members she selected; and a prime ministerial position, held by her lover/husband Cheung Po.

The fleet under their joint command established control over many coastal villages, in some cases even imposing levies and taxes on settlements. According to Robert Antony, Ching Shih 'robbed towns, markets, and villages, from Macau to Canton'. The pirates' income came from raiding wealthy towns, and/or collecting money as a 'protection' fee, which gained the town a defence from pirates. The money went into pirate stores, but much subsequently found its way back into the poor towns, where Madame Ching employed a huge network of spies – farmers, tailors and suchlike – who kept her empire afloat. Accounts from eyewitnesses to her raids are horrifying. The Chinese Navy in 1808 embarked on a mission to take Madame Ching. Admiral Kwo-Lang led the fleet into battle against Cheung Po's Red

Squadron, but the pirates took 63 of the navy's ships. Captives were offered a choice of joining the pirates or being nailed to the deck and beaten. Ellms states that Admiral Kwo-Lang committed suicide out of fear of being captured. Next, the government tried to starve the pirates out by cutting off their supply ships, but failed as Madame Ching's vast network of peasants on land fed the pirates.

However, the Admiral of Madame Ching's Green Squadron was jealous of Cheung Pao and lost a battle against him. He appealed to the government of Macao for amnesty, which was granted. Madame Ching now also decided to seek an amnesty, but would not bow to any official. Thus it was proposed that the Governor of Macao would perform a marriage between her and Cheung Pao in 1810, which would require the bride and groom to bow to thank the registrar, a rule that would satisfy the governor's wish. She surrendered her ships, kept all of her money, and became a private citizen of China once again. Cheung Po was allowed to keep his fleet and became a government official. All but 376 of the pirates under her command kept their loot and retired or joined the Chinese Navy. She now opened gambling houses, ran cartels of smugglers and smuggled opium. She died in her sleep, aged 69. In 2007, in *Pirates of the Caribbean: At World's End* she was portrayed as Mistress Ching, one of the nine Pirate Lords. In the same film, her husband Cheung Po Tsai became Sao Feng.

The Pirate Code of Madame Ching

Neumann translated *The History of Pirates Who Infested the China Sea* and claims that it was Cheung Po Tsai who issued the code, but Yung-Lun Yüan says that Cheung issued his own code of three regulations for his own fleet. The code was very strict and harshly enforced, to instil discipline in his Red Flag Fleet.

(1) Anyone giving their own orders (that did not come directly from Ching Shih), or disobeying the orders of a superior officer was to be beheaded on the spot.

(2) No one was to steal from the public fund or from any villagers that supplied the pirates.

(3) All loot was to be presented for inspection by the group of pirates who had seized it. The booty was then registered by the purser, to be distributed by the leader of the fleet or squadron involved. The original seizer received 20 per cent, with the rest placed into the

public fund (which provided living expenses, food and bought resources for the pirates).

(4) Any actual money, e.g. coinage, was given to the fleet or squadron leader, who gave a small amount back to the original seizer. The rest was used to purchase supplies for less successful ships.*

Philip Maughan relates that the punishment for a first-time offence of holding back treasure was a severe whipping of the back. However, for large amounts of withheld booty or subsequent offences there was the death penalty.

There were other parts of the code, where transgressions were punished with clapping in irons, flogging or quartering. Deserters had their ears chopped off, then were paraded around their squadron. There were also rules for female captives. Pirates who raped female captives were put to death. Women were normally released or ransomed (men were impressed into service or ransomed), but pirates tended to make their most beautiful prisoners their concubines or wives. If a pirate took a wife he had to be faithful to her. However, if a pirate had consensual sex with a captive, he was beheaded, and the woman had cannonballs attached to her legs and was then thrown over the side of the boat.

Rape was explicitly prohibited: 'No one shall satisfy [their] lust with captured women in the villages or public places. On board, the permission of the squadron leader must be obtained for this purpose, and the act performed inside, in the ship's hold.' Those who disobeyed, or employed the use of force against a woman without permission, were executed on the spot. In typical pirate practice of the period, captured women were hung off the side of the ship by their hair.

Cheung Po Tsai (c.1794–1826) – The Pirate who Married his Lover's Wife, 'Steadiest of the Steady'

The son of a Tanka (sea gypsy) fisherman, Cheung was 15 when he was captured by Ching Yi (*see* above) and impressed into piracy. They became lovers. Cheung rose rapidly through the pirate ranks, being adopted by Ching Yi to give him the rights of a son and heir. He was appointed as a fleet commander, earning respect from the pirates. Cheung married Ching Yi's widow, Madame Ching, running the pirate confederacy the Red Flag Fleet, and they had a child. In 1810 they began to lose control

---

* Yüan, Yung-Lun and Neumann, Karl Friedrich *History of the Pirates who Infested the China Sea, from 1807 to 1810*, Leopold Classic Library, 2015.

of the great fleet, which they had broken into six squadrons. He was the commander of the red squadron, and each squadron had its own flag, as well as its own commander with a title such as Mealtime of the Frog, or Knife in the Neck. Cheung was called 'Steadiest of the Steady'. The Qing Emperor Jiaqing offered them full pardons to leave piracy, and Cheung Po was appointed as a commander in the Imperial Fleet. Now known as Cheung Po Tsai, the Emperor apointed him as his admiral to wipe out his former Red Flag Fleet. He died in his late 30s of an unknown cause, possibly poisoned by his former pirate comrades.

Chui A-poo (d.1851) – Xú Yàbǎo, the Opium War Victim

In 1799 Emperor Jiaqing banned the use of opium, and merchants who dealt in it were classified as smugglers. However, the British East India Company (EIC) wished to trade their opium to China, because tea, silk, and porcelain were incredibly sought-after in Europe. The Chinese government, however, now restricted foreign trade, opening only the port of Canton (Guangzhou) to foreigners. The British had virtually no exports of interest to the Chinese, except opium, so the EIC had to pay cash for such profitable luxuries. Over half a century, the EIC paid £27,000,000 for imports, but only exported £9,000,000 worth of goods. To compensate for the imbalance, the captains of the EIC smuggled in opium, bribing corrupt Chinese officials, while merchants illicitly sold the drug in exchange for silver. By 1838 nearly 40,000 chests of opium were imported annually into China, causing an epidemic of drug addiction. Britain turned a blind eye to Chinese anti-opium edicts, and war broke out. However, Chinese junks proved no match against British steam warships. More than 20,000 Chinese died in the Chinese Navy compared to 69 Britons and the First Opium War ended in 1842 with the Treaty of Nanking, which forced the Chinese to open five ports to foreign trade. Incredibly, China also had to pay compensation for lost earnings from the opium trade, plus the cost of the war, and give Hong Kong to the British. The humiliating defeat, depressed economy, government corruption and shattered navy meant that piracy became rife in the region.

The Qing Chinese, Chui A-poo, commanded a fleet of more than 50 pirate junks in the South China Sea, sharing notoriety in the area at this time with Shap 'ng-Tsai, whom he served as a lieutenant. Many junks were fitted with small cannon and other weapons and were called war junks or armed junks by Western navies, which began entering the region more frequently in the 18th century. English, American and French warships fought several naval battles with war junks in the

19th century, during the Opium Wars. Chui A-poo is said to have commanded in excess of 500 junks in his pirate career, based in Bias Bay, now called Daya Bay, northeast of Hong Kong in Guangdong Province. It is now home to six nuclear reactors. At Bias Bay, Chui A-poo kept his arsenal and built war junks. In February 1849, Chui A-poo fled from Hong Kong after killing two Britons who had insulted him. One of his wounded pirates was captured, and informed the Royal Navy that he worked in a dockyard owned by Chui A-poo, who 'was the head man of the pirates … that Hong-maou-kop was his country; his younger brother is named Chee-sam, and is also a pirate chief; they both belonged to Shap 'ng-Tsai's fleet, and were implicated in the murders of Da Costa and Dwyer.'

The people of Hong Kong pressured the Royal Navy to capture Chui A-poo, and make the seas safe. At the time he commanded about 1,800 pirates on 27 war junks. Commander John Hay captained the 12-gun brig HMS *Columbine*, with 80 crew and 20 marines, and was assisted by the P&O steamer *Canton* under Lieutenant Bridges; they headed for Bias Bay. The village had been burned by the pirates, who then fled to Tysami and also burned that village.

On 29 September 1849, Hay spotted a squadron of Chui A-poo's fleet heading southwest in two lines of seven large junks. In becalmed conditions, his steamships easily caught up with the 14 junks, and 3 were abandoned while another exploded. Chui A-poo's pirates suffered 250 casualties and more than 200 cannon were destroyed or captured and taken back to Hong Kong. In what was known as the Battle of Tysami, 10 junks escaped back to their base at Bias Bay, to be joined by another 13 vessels, so Hay sent for reinforcements, with Commander John Willcox bringing the 6-gun sloop HMS *Fury* to take part in the action. Trapped by 3 ships, the pirates at this time fled further into Bias Bay, and were forced into the small Pinghoi Creek, where the remaining 23 junks, each displacing an average of 500 tons and with 12–18 cannon (mostly made in England), were destroyed before the pirate base was burned. More than 400 pirates were killed and Chui was seriously wounded, either then or during the next month, but he managed to escape with his commodore Shap 'ng-Tsai and 1,400 others.

A bounty of $500 had been offered after the murder of the two officers in Hong Kong. Chiu A-poo continued his piratical attacks until a few of his own men betrayed him to the British in 1851 and handed him over. He was sentenced to lifelong imprisonment in Tasmania, but hanged himself in his cell before he was due to sail.

Shap 'ng-Tsai (*fl.*1845–1859) – 'Fifteenth Son'

His real name was Chin Chay-mee, nicknamed Shap 'ng-Tsai (fifteenth son), and he led a pirate fleet which sailed the coastal waters of Guangdong and Fujian Provinces. Shap may have been a Triad member. His main base of operation was at Tien-pai (now Diancheng), 175 miles west of Hong Kong. Coastal villages and traders paid Shap 'ng-Tsai protection money so they would not be attacked. Chinese naval ships that pursued him were captured, and their officers taken captive and held for ransom. The Chinese government offered him a pardon and the rank of officer in the navy but he would not accept. He seized junks, killed or ransomed men, sold children into slavery, raided and burned villages, stole goods, and either sold captive women or forced them to become prostitutes. According to Scott, five Chinese navy war junks 'were chased by [Shap's] six pirate boats, which boarded them, put their crews to death, and carried the commanders ... on shore, where a fire was kindled, and the unfortunate officers were burnt alive.' His network of spies supplied information on the treaty ports, and his commanders frequently sailed to Hong Kong, where local chandlers provided them with arms, ammunition, and information while fencing their plunder.

By the end of the 1840s, Shap 'ng-Tsai's fleet numbered more than 70 vessels, and some of his men were Europeans. According *The China Mail* in October 1849, his 'band has mustered in such force on the coast of Hainan and in the Gulf of Tonquin, as to set the authorities at defiance; and recently at Tien-pahk, an important salt mart, after capturing upwards of forty junks, the pirate chief entered the town in great state, and took possession of it, levying tribute from the inhabitants, and raising the amount of blackmail assessed from the salt junks from 30 to 120 dollars.' Shap 'ng-Tsai was blamed for sinking an American ship and three British ships carrying opium in spring of 1849. A squadron of British ships sailed to Tien-pai and found 100 captured ships being held for ransom, but failed to find his main pirate fleet.

The Royal Navy had almost captured Shap 'ng-Tsai at the Battle of Tysami and Pinghoi Creek with his lieutenant Chiu A-poo (*see* above). General Wang, a mandarin, headed the Chinese squadron of eight naval junks that now sailed with Hay, and tracked Shap 'ng-Tsai to his new hideout north of Haiphong on the Red River, Vietnam, in October 1849. Shap had 64 armed junks with 3,150 men and 1,250 guns, with his flagship having 120 men and 42 guns. To block their escape, Hay positioned part of his force to obstruct the mouth of the river, and the Royal Navy suffered only one fatality, while killing about 1,800 pirates and capturing or sinking perhaps 58 vessels. Shap 'ng-Tsai escaped the battle with 6 smaller junks and 400 men. Shap 'ng-Tsai had previously refused an earlier offer of a pardon from the Qing government, but now he accepted a renewed offer, being pardoned and becoming an officer in the imperial navy. His duties included hunting pirates and smugglers. The British now established the China Station at Hong Kong, and the presence of the Royal Navy and its steam warships ensured the pirates never again posed a serious threat to commerce.

The Buccaneers of the
Caribbean

English and French sailors began to settle on Hispaniola around 1630, being termed *boucaniers* (buccaneers) because they hunted wild pigs and smoked their meat on wooden *boucan* frames. The Spanish tried to force the buccaneers out by removing their food supply, sending hunters to slaughter the plentiful pigs which roamed the island. With their livelihood and food sources disappearing, vengeful buccaneers turned to piracy to survive, many moving to Tortuga, off Haiti (then part of Hispaniola). Thus from 1630 French and British pirates sailed from Tortuga, and from 1655, British pirates operated from Jamaica as their main base. Because of continuing wars in Europe, the great nations could not send sufficient military and naval reinforcements to their colonies, so monarchs and governors issued 'letters of marque', or 'letters of commission', which allowed private ships to attack ships from rival nations. These vessels effectively acted as a private naval presence across the seas, and when buccaneers and pirates were commissioned as mercenaries, they were called privateers (or corsairs in the Mediterranean). Crews were not paid, but they received agreed portions of the value of any cargo they captured. Many strayed into piracy, especially after letters of marque were withheld, or peace left them without employment. Most of the spoils of privateers in the West Indies came not from capturing other ships, but from raiding Spanish settlements, taking slaves and prisoners, and accepting ransoms to return captives or not burn towns.

The 7,000 islands in the Caribbean are now home to 28 nations, but around 1650–1725 were mainly possessed by Spain, with a few small outposts belonging to the other great trading nations of France, England, the Netherlands, Denmark and Portugal. The 'Triangular

Trade' had developed, with goods and money going to East Africa in exchange for slaves, then the slaves being exchanged in the Americas for sugar, spices, logwoods (for dyes) and silver, for return to Europe. Using the prevailing winds and currents, all ships at some stage had to pass through the Caribbean Islands, a notorious 'choke point' where pirates and privateers could raid ships, hide, and exchange their booty. It was the region through which the great treasure fleets of the Spanish and Portuguese would sail and be attacked.

Admiral Cornelis Corneliszoon Jol (1597–31 October 1641) – *El Pirata* (Spanish*), Houtebeen* (Pegleg, Dutch), *Pie de Palo* (Wooden Leg, Spanish) *Perna de Pau* (Wooden Leg, Portuguese)

Born in the port of Scheveninghen, The Hague, Cornelis Corneliszoon Jol was 29 when he joined the Dutch West India Company. He became an admiral, admired for his 'courage and prudence, his integrity, resoluteness and tenacity of purpose'. During the Eighty Years' War between the Dutch Republic and Spain, Jol acted as a corsair, attacking Spanish and Portuguese ships across the Spanish Main and the Caribbean.

Cornelis Jol captained a squadron of seven ships in the Battle of the Downs – painted *c.*1639 by Reinier Nooms.

Losing a leg in battle, he was one of the earliest documented privateers to adopt a wooden leg. With Diego el Mulato, Jol took 10 ships in 1633 to sack Campeche, on Mexico's Yucatán Peninsula. He took Santiago de Cuba on 3 August 1635, by hoisting Spanish flags and having his crew dress up as Spanish monks, to enable him to enter the harbour. After hours of battle, he sacked ships, looted the city, and sailed away with much plunder. However, later in that year Jol was captured off Dunkirk by 'Dunkirk privateers', raiders of commercial shipping in the service of the Spanish, but released about six months later.

Jol sailed the Atlantic nine times to attack the Spanish and Portuguese, across the Caribbean and along the coast of Brazil. In an early voyage he captured the archipelago of Fernando de Noronha, 220 miles off the coast of Brazil, which stayed a part of 'Dutch Brazil' until 1654. In 1638 he sailed to capture the Spanish treasure fleet off Cuba, but his captains refused to fight, jealous of his fast promotion to admiral above their prior claims.

In 1639 Jol commanded seven ships at the Battle of the Downs, sailing the *Jupiter* in the decisive Dutch victory over the Spanish. In 1640, he attempted again to intercept the Spanish treasure armada off Havana but in a hurricane, four of his ships were wrecked. He generally used Dutch Curaçao as his base when attacking the Spanish. Jol sailed from Brazil for the coast of Africa in 1640, taking Luanda (Angola) and the island of Sao Tomé from the Portuguese. However, there Jol contracted malaria and died on 31 October 1641.

Pierre le Picard (1624–*c.*1690) – One of the first buccaneers to raid shipping on both the Caribbean and Pacific coasts

Like Vauquelin, he is first recorded as one of the captains in l'Olonnais' 1666–67 expedition from Tortuga, which attacked Maracaibo, Gibraltar, Puerto Cabello and San Pedro. He commanded 40 men in a brigantine, and with Vauquelin, encouraged other captains to desert the fleet after a disagreement with l'Olonnais. After privateering unsuccessfully with Vauquelin, he joined up with Henry Morgan (*q.v.*), either at Port Royal or Tortuga, captaining 90 men on the 10-gun *St Pierre*. Le Picard piloted Morgan to his successful attack on Maracaibo in 1669, just three years after he had sacked it alongside l'Olonnais. Le Picard then took his *St Pierre* to join Morgan's march across the isthmus to loot Panama. There are reports of le Picard dying around 1679, but in 1682 Henry Morgan, now in an official capacity as Lieutenant-Governor of Jamaica, wrote that le Picard was privateering against English and Spanish shipping off Jamaica.

He is almost definitely the 'Captain le Picard' recorded on the 1685 expedition to replicate Morgan's crossing the Isthmus of Panama, to plunder Spanish settlements and intercept the Spanish Pacific fleet.

It seems that at the same time, several other privateers had decided to try to take the same treasure fleet, planning to meet along the Pacific coast. Captains Edward Davis, Charles Swan and Peter Harris were already waiting in the Pacific, and joined by captains François Grogniet and L'Escuyer with 200 French *filibustiers* (privateers) and 60 Englishmen. Swan gave them a recently captured ship, and in return Grogniet issued privateering commissions from Petit Goâve. On 3 March, yet another group of 180 privateers under Captain Townley joined the fleet. They were next joined by captains le Picard, Rose and Desmarais and 264 mainly French pirates, who had crossed the isthmus. Captain William Knight now sailed in, giving a combined fleet of 3 large ships, 7–8 smaller ones and perhaps 1,000 men. However, they were taken by surprise, missing the great opportunity of attacking the *flota*, leading to arguments between the captains. Some ships sailed off, but le Picard came to lead the remaining buccaneers, spending the next six months in small boats raiding up and down the coast of Panama, and sacking Nicoya in Costa Rica. Disease took a toll, and with only 250 men it was difficult for le Picard to recross the isthmus, because of hostility from native peoples and a heavier Spanish presence.

Panama was now too powerfully guarded to attempt its capture. In late January, Grogniet suggested that they should instead attack and loot the city of Guayaquil, which they did in April 1687. Le Picard, Grogniet and the English Captain George Hout only had four cannon left, with one *galiot* (a small type of galley) and a few barks, piraguas and canoes. With Hout's men, and Edward Davis rejoining, their force consisted of just 300 pirates. Guided by a fugitive mulatto, they attacked in three groups, sustaining casualties of only 9 dead and 12 wounded. At the head of '50 lost children', the name given to those who formed the first wave of attacks, le Picard led the eight-hour assault. However, much treasure and valuables had been hidden in the jungle, and the pirates therefore asked for ransoms not to kill citizens or burn the city. Grogniet died of wounds on 2 May, and four severed heads were sent to the authorities to express the pirates' dissatisfaction at the delay in payment (the captives drew lots for who was to die). They also sent a message saying that 50 heads would be sent next, if the ransom was further postponed, but the Spanish informed them that it was impossible and the pirates had to be satisfied with just

42,000 pesos and 100 sacks of flour. Meanwhile the Spanish had been preparing to attack them, and sent three ships on 27 May. After a short, inconclusive battle, Davis and le Picard decided to split their plunder, and le Picard led his men north.

He decided to recross the Isthmus of Panama by the shortest route, rather than the better-defended Spanish trails. Leading 260 men, three years after setting out, after many more difficulties and deaths, in 1688 he completed the return. Sailing back across the Caribbean to Saint-Domingue, he looted the city of Segovia, but received bad news. Peace had returned to Europe, meaning that he could not obtain any more privateering commissions. It seems that le Picard decided to retire near Acadia in New France, south-eastern Canada. He now commanded a small squadron during King William's War and attacked the English colonies of Rhode Island and Providence Plantation in 1690. However, owing to heavy losses the French were forced to retreat. He may have been preparing to attack Newport, Rhode Island, when his former privateer comrade Thomas Paine forced him to withdraw.

Bartolomeu Português (*c.*1635–*c.*1669/1692) – Bartolomeo *el Portuguese*, Bartholomew the Portuguese, '*Pirata desventurado*' (the Hapless Pirate)

Supposedly a devout Catholic, his birthplace is unknown, but he formulated one of the earliest pirate codes, a set of 'articles' of behaviour, which all the crew agreed to and signed. Bartolomeu arrived in the West Indies in the early 1660s, seemingly robbing settlements and ships along the coast of Mexico from 1662, then operating between Jamaica and Cuba, having captured a small 4-gun sloop, which he manned with 30 crew. About 1663, off Cape Corrientes on the western coast of Cuba, he spotted a Spanish galleon sailing from Maracaibo and Cartagena (both in Venezuela), and bound for Havana (Cuba) and Hispaniola (now Haiti and the Dominican Republic). She had 20 cannon and around 70 sailors and passengers, and Bartolomeu immediately attacked her, failing in his first attempt at boarding. After a brutal second attack, he managed to take the vessel, but 10 of his 30-man crew were killed and 4 injured. Despite his casualties, Bartolomeu spared the lives of prisoners, transferring them to a rowboat bound for Havana.

The cargo was 120,000 pounds of cacao beans, but the ship fortunately also held 70,000 pieces of eight. (A piece of eight was a Spanish silver dollar, worth 8 reales, and was the first currency universally accepted by the Western nations, so could be used anywhere). Bartolomeu wished to return to his base at Port Royal, Jamaica, but was driven back by storms to Cuba, heading for safety in calmer waters off Cape San Antonio. However, Bartolomeu was surprised by three Spanish warships, which took their booty and imprisoned the crew. Another sudden tropical storm now forced the four ships to head for San Francisco de Campeche in southeast 'New Spain' (now Campeche City, Mexico). Traders and local magistrates discovered that the Portuguese was among the prisoners, and decided to hang him the next day. He was imprisoned on the ship he had captured, separate from his crew, at anchor outside the port of San Francisco. Knowing his fate next morning, at nightfall he managed to break his chains and stabbed the only sentry with a stolen knife. However, he could not swim, so Bartolomeu wrapped two large earthenware wine storage jars with oilskins to make a crude raft, and paddled with makeshift oars for the shoreline.

For three days he remained hidden in the alligator-ridden mangrove swamps, and then followed the coast at night, feeding on crustaceans and fruit. To cross rivers, he made rafts with pieces of wood, tied with lianas. After two incredibly difficult weeks, travelling through 120 miles of rainforest, Bartolomeu reached the Gulf of Triste (Triste is an island near Veracruz) on the east of the Yucatán Peninsula. This was a popular rendezvous for pirates operating out of Jamaica, and he was found by an English privateer who took him back to Port Royal. After a short rest, Bartolomeu took a boat and 20 volunteers to recapture his stolen treasure. Eight days later they arrived in San Francisco de Campeche, and captured the same boat that had served as his prison, and sailed off with its cargo, which was now only 600 kg of cocoa, but with 700 gold coins. They sailed for Jamaica, but a storm wrecked the ship on the Isle of Pines, southeast of Cuba. The pirates escaped in a canoe to Jamaica and Bartolomeu led another expedition but was not heard of again, apart from Exquemelin writing that he: 'made several and very violent attacks on the Spaniards without gaining much profit from marauding, for I saw him dying in the greatest wretchedness in the world.' Known as *pirata desventurado* – the hapless pirate – it is said that he was sick and destitute, begging in front of the taverns, dying in 1669 in Jamaica. However, he may have died in the 1692 Port Royal earthquake.

Nikolaas van Hoorn (1635–24 June 1683) – 'Colonel' Nicolaes van Hoorn

Born in Flushing, Zeeland (the Netherlands), Van Hoorn is first recorded in Dutch merchant shipping records in 1655. In 1659 he bought his own ship and began privateering. He looted a French ship in the Caribbean, and the French sent pirate hunters after him in 1663, so for a time he no longer sought French prizes. Discovering that Spanish treasure galleons were at San Juan harbour in Puerto Rico, Van Hoorn approached its Spanish governor, complaining about his problems with the French and his need for Spanish protection. The governor therefore allowed Van Hoorn to protect the armada as it left Puerto Rico, but as soon as it sailéd past the Antilles, Van Hoorn took over the Spanish galleons, with treasure estimated as 2,000,000 livres (*c.*$20 million today). He swiftly sailed to England, as both France and Spain now wanted to capture him. In 1666 he gained a French commission to capture Spanish ships and became even wealthier.

After the May 1668 Treaty of Aix-la-Chapelle, which ended the 'War of Devolution' between France and Spain, he was expected to refrain from privateering, but carried on his 'career'. Probably through his French wife, he had a connection with the Governor of Cayenne, French Guiana, and received a commission as 'Colonel' van Hoorn in 1681 to supply slaves. He now sailed from France to buy an old 400-ton naval ship *Mary and Martha* in London, which he renamed the *St Nicholas*. With 120 crew and 40 cannon, he sailed for Cadiz with another 12-gun 160-ton ship under his command. After stealing four brass *pedreros* (cannon) from Cadiz, off Lanzarote, he whipped to death an English crew member, Nicolas Browne, for no cause whatsoever. Men began deserting his increasingly brutal rule wherever he stopped for supplies.

Off Guinea he took two Dutch merchant ships, and 'seized a canoe that came from Cape Coast with goods for Negroes, killing three of the Negroes in the said canoe.'* Trading his stolen goods, Van Hoorn took on board about 100 slaves, and later his two ships captured another 600 black people by flying English colours. He then burned all the houses and destroyed stores of corn, palm oil and rice that the natives had stored in the countryside. Next he seized 4 canoes with about 20 blacks, one of whom he shot out of hand. Sailing to Cayenne, he put ashore 6 English captives, bought a house and left 80 slaves with his wife's brother-in-law. He sold about 300 surviving slaves at Santo Domingo, where its President confiscated Van Hoorn's four stolen brass *pedreros*, and ordered him to sail away in December 1682.

---

* *The Nefarious Exploits of Nicolaes Van Hoorn*, crommelin.org/history/Biographies/1647/Daniel/1681VanHoorn/VanHoorn

In January 1683, Van Hoorn, seeking revenge for the loss of his cannon, sailed to Petit-Goâve, whose Governor Jacques de Pouncey gave him a privateering commission against the Spanish. De Pouncey also authorised around 280 men from the colony to sail with Van Hoorn, giving him as lieutenant the famous privateer Captain Michele de Grammont. In April 1683, Van Hoorn took two great Spanish ships in the Gulf of Honduras and sailed them to Bonaco Island, earning the enmity of Laurens de Graaf (*q.v.*). De Graaf had been waiting for the galleons to be laden before attacking them. De Graaf then reluctantly accepted Van Hoorn joining him, Grammont (*q.v.*) and others in the great raid upon Veracruz, Mexico. The pirates took 4,000 prisoners with them back to the Isla de Sacrificios to be ransomed back to the Spanish governor, who refused to do so, presumably because he had no money left. The angered Van Hoorn ordered the execution of 12 prisoners, and was said to have sent their heads in response. Because of this, De Graaf challenged Van Hoorn to a duel, inflicting a flesh wound that turned gangrenous, which resulted in his death. He was buried near the northern coast of Yucatán, near Cayo de Mujeres, on a small island called Loggerhead Key.

Michel de Grammont (1645–October 1686) – The Pirate Chevalier

The Chevalier de Grammont was a noble, born in Paris, but forced to leave France after killing his sister's suitor in a duel. He sailed to Saint-Domingue (Haiti), and was given a ship and a French privateering commission. Around 1470 Grammont captured a Dutch merchant fleet worth about 400,000 livres (about $4 million today). He set out again but ran aground on a reef, and now relocated to the pirate haven of Tortuga. There he bought and outfitted a larger ship and took on another crew to attack Spanish shipping. When the Franco-Dutch War began in 1678, De Grammont joined with the Comte d'Estrées to raid Dutch Curaçao, but in June 1678 their entire fleet of 17 ships was wrecked on the Las Aves Archipelago. Only 6 ships were salvaged, and Grammont commanded this reduced fleet with 700 men, sailing through Lake Maracaibo to take Maracaibo, Gibraltar and other smaller settlements in Venezuela. His men penetrated as far inland as Trujillo, and remained in Spanish territory for six months, constantly gathering plunder and ransoms. The buccaneers in a night attack then took the port of La Guaira, Venezuela, but were quickly forced to retreat before a larger Spanish force.

In June 1680, with Captain William Wright and Thomas Paine (*q.v.*) and just 50 men, he captured Cumana, Venezuela, which was defended by 2,000 soldiers, and 17 ships with 328 guns. De Grammont was injured in a sword fight, and returned to the Las Aves islands to recover. He then commanded eight ships and in 1682 was asked by the Governor of Petit-Goâve, Haiti, to join Captain van Hoorn and attack Spanish shipping. On 17 May 1683, Laurens de Graaf, De Grammont, Van Hoorn, Michiel Andrieszoon (*q.v.*) and Yankey Willems (*q.v.*) sacked the treasure port of Vera Cruz (Veracruz), Mexico. When Van Hoorn was wounded in a duel and placed in chains by De Graaf, Grammont took command of Van Hoorn's *St Nicolas* and renamed her *Le Hardi*. In July 1685, De Grammont and De Graaf sacked Campeche, Mexico, and after two months of plundering the city, De Grammont sent a demand for ransom to the governor, who refused. De Grammont began to execute prisoners, but De Graaf, as at Vera Cruz with van Hoorn, stopped the executions and they parted company. De Grammont next raided settlements in Spanish Florida, including the Mocama mission and St Augustine. He was reported in April 1686 sailing in the northeast direction off St Augustine, and his flagship *Le Hardi* was reported lost in a storm off the Azores in October 1686.

Chevalier Laurens Cornelis Boudewijn de Graaf (*c.*1653–24 May 1704) – Laurencillo, El Griffe (the Devil), de Graff, le Sieur de Baldran, Scourge of the West, 'the Great Pirate of Petit Goâve'

De Graaf was born in Dordrecht, the Dutch Republic (now the Netherlands), reportedly captured by Spanish slave traders as a child or young man, and taken to the Canary Islands to work on a plantation. In the early 1670s, De Graaf either escaped or was freed, and married his first wife François Petronilla de Guzmán in 1674 in the Canary Islands. He may have learned to sail on Spanish ships, but began his known nautical career not long after marrying De Guzmán, sailing 'on the account', from around 1675 or 1676 as the captain of a French privateer.

One of his first recorded attacks was a terrible assault on Campeche in March 1672. It had suffered several attacks but De Graaf's looting was possibly the worst. He set fire to a partly-built frigate and totally sacked the town. When an unsuspecting merchant ship sailed into the harbour, he took more than 120,000 pesos' worth of silver and other cargo. In the 1670s, De Graaf captured a number of vessels, converting each in turn to join his fleet. Following a typical privateering pattern,

De Graaf would capture a larger ship, and then use that vessel to capture a larger one again. Given a letter of marque by the French governor of what is now Haiti, in autumn 1679, De Graaf attacked part of the *Armada de Barlovento* (the 'Windward Fleet' of 50 ships, which patrolled its overseas possessions for Spain), capturing a 28-gun frigate which he renamed the *Tigre*; it became his flagship.

The Spanish wanted revenge for the loss of the frigate and the *Armada de Barlovento* was given orders to take De Graaf. During a brief stay in Cuba, he was informed of the threat. However, instead of escaping, he sailed to find the Spanish. In 1682, after a battle of several hours, the 30-gun warship *Princesa* surrendered, having lost 50 men to De Graaf's 9 sailors. De Graaf put the seriously wounded captain of the *Princesa* ashore, with his own surgeon and a servant to care for him. The *Princesa* itself carried the entire payroll for the Spanish colonies in Puerto Rico and Santo Domingo, approximately another 120,000 pesos in silver. After sharing out the prize monies, De Graaf retired to Petit-Goâve, 40 miles south-west of Port-au-Prince, Haiti, to refit his ships. De Graaf now made the *Princesa* his new flagship, renaming it the *Francesca*, and sailed the Caribbean, causing such disruption that Henry Morgan sent his Jamaica Station frigate *Norwich* in pursuit of De Graaf, but failed to find him.

Next De Graaf sailed the Gulf of Honduras, and spotted two unladen Spanish galleons. (He could tell that they were not carrying cargo by their depth in the sea). De Graaf decided to wait for them to be loaded with booty, and retired to Bonaco Island near St Eustatius to careen. However, Nicholas van Hoorn attacked the ships and took them to Bonaco. He proposed to join forces with de Graaf, and was initially turned away by the angered de Graaf. At this time Michel de Grammont and de Graaf decided they needed van Hoorn to attack the treasure port of Vera Cruz in Mexico, so their joint forces amounted to 1,300 men, 5 large vessels and 8 smaller ones. De Grammont took the lead, with de Graaf and Van Hoorn as his lieutenants.

Vera Cruz was protected by at least 700 soldiers, plus 300 soldiers manning its fort, San Juan de Ulúa. The Spanish were expecting the great Plate Armada to arrive, and did not suspect anything when the two captured Spanish galleons, followed by other ships, anchored on the evening of 18 May, 1683. De Graaf and the pirate known as Yankey Willems landed in secrecy with a small group, took over the town's fortifications and battled its militia. Simultaneously, Van Hoorn approached from the landward side. Vera Cruz citizens were rounded up and 5,000 of them were packed into the *Catedral de la Asunción*, in high temperatures, with no food or water, for three-and-a-half days. Some climbed to the top of its bell tower to jump to their deaths. The governor himself was taken, and a payment of 70,000 pieces of eight (*reales*, the currency of the time) was required to secure his release. The wealthiest citizens were also abducted for ransom, along with 30 of the prettiest young women that the pirates could find, and taken to de Graaf's base, in Laguna de Términos. After two days of terror, the powerful Spanish *Flota de Indias* (the West Indies Treasure Fleet, also called the silver fleet or plate fleet), appeared on the horizon, so the privateers swiftly packed their booty and hostages, and relocated to a small island in the Gulf, Los Sacrificios.

From there, Grammont, De Graaf and Van Hoorn demanded ransoms from the Spanish warships. However, the warships fired on the island, while the privateers were taking food from their own ships to feed their prisoners. In retaliation, Van Hoorn lined up some hostages and beheaded them, against De Graaf's wishes. Van Hoorn questioned his courage and Exquemelin writes that they agreed a duel, not a fight to the death but a French version, to settle honour. De Graaf struck Van Hoorn on the wrist. Van Hoorn was then said to be *port en coupe* (carrying a blow), and the duel ended with De Graaf upholding his honour. Unfortunately for Van Hoorn, the wound turned gangrenous and he expired a fortnight later. He was buried, according to Exquemelin, at Cay Logrette on Sacrifice Island.

After receiving ransoms, the privateers abandoned the female captives, who were left without food or water for five days before they were rescued. The fleet sailed away, slipping past the Spanish to land around the peninsula on Isla Mujeres. There the spoils were divided, with each man receiving 800 pieces of eight. In late November 1683, De Graaf with Andrieszoon, Yankey Willems and a fleet of seven ships arrived off Cartagena. The Spanish governor had escaped and commandeered 3 slave-trading vessels, the 40-gun *San Francisco*, the 34-gun *Paz* and a smaller 28-gun galiot. On Christmas Eve 1683, 800 Spanish troops and sailors set out in the 3 ships to fight the pirates, but the *San Francisco* was grounded and the other 2 ships were captured. A total of 90 Spaniards were killed, compared to only 20 pirates. De Graaf re-equipped the *San Francisco* as his new flagship and named her *Neptune,* now carrying 42 guns. Andrieszoon took the *Paz* and renamed her *Mutine*, and Willems was given command of the *Francesca*. The group released a large number of Spanish prisoners on

Christmas Day, and sent them ashore with a note for Governor Estrada, thanking him for the Christmas presents. The pirates then proceeded to blockade Cartagena for a month, taking any ships sailing into the port.

Several nations, including Spain and England, now wished to enlist De Graaf into their own privateering fleets. He accepted the English offer, but sent only one captured Spanish ship, laden with sugar, to the English colony in Jamaica. In January 1684 an English naval convoy, headed by the 48-gun *Ruby*, gave a note for De Graaf from his wife, offering a Spanish pardon and commission. De Graaf ignored the note, not trusting the Spanish to keep their promises, and invited English officers to board his vessels and trade with his men. Soon after, De Graaf left for Petit-Goâve and remained there for the summer of 1684. In September 1684, De Graaf set sail from Isla Mujeres in his flagship *Neptune*. He gathered another fleet and with De Grammont led yet another raid on Campeche, Mexico, with 12 ships and 10,000 men, on 6 July 1685. However, the Spanish had been warned, and De Graaf was met by a fleet of five Spanish warships. Exquemelin called De Graaf the bravest of his crew, as he sailed through the centre of the armada, firing both port and starboard broadsides. De Graaf was wounded but would not leave the deck, supervising the cannon. At nightfall, to his surprise, the Spanish left the action, and Campeche was taken.

However, after witnessing the protracted battle off Campeche, many of the richer Spanish had fled the town, leaving little plunder and few valuable prisoners to ransom. After two months, the disillusioned privateers began to burn the town and execute prisoners. De Graaf halted the slaughter and left Campeche in September 1685, carrying away captives for ransom. The fleet now separated, and De Graaf set sail aboard the *Neptune*, laden with treasure. He was accompanied by Pierre Bott (Blot). The Dutch captains encountered two Spanish warships off Yucatán.

One of the Spanish ships fired 1,600 rounds, and the *Neptune* took 14 hits broadside, but De Graaf refused to surrender, and escaped with 'only a couple of spars shot away, even though he was being attacked from both sides within musket range.' Both privateers jettisoned valuables and guns to lighten their ships, but Bott's ship was captured and he was taken prisoner. A steady wind helped De Graaf escape to Isla de Pinos, south of Cuba, to recuperate, repair and resupply.

In February 1686, the Spanish raided De Graaf's plantation in Haiti. In retaliation, he raided Tihosuco, but returning to Petit-Goâve he wrecked his ship while chasing a Spanish barque. However, he managed to take the barque using only his ship's long boat. A Mexican military officer named Robles reported seeing 'Lorencillo' in Isla Mujeres between 8 June and 13 June 1686, '*que estaba muy malo*', ('in a very bad state'), so he may have been wounded. Off Cuba in 1687, De Graaf fought the Cuban *costa garda* (Coast Guard), and a Biscayan frigate, before returning to Saint-Domingue (Haiti), where he now defended the harbour at Petit-Goâve against Spanish forces from Cuba. In December 1689, he captured some ships off English-held Jamaica, and blockaded the Jamaican coast for more than six months before leaving. Off the Cayman Islands, De Graaf next took an English sloop.

In 1689, François Petronilla de Guzmán formally divorced De Graaf. He had returned to France, receiving a hero's welcome for all of the wealth diverted from the Caribbean into his patron country. De Graaf was given the position of Governor of Cap François (now called Cap Haitien), a French colony in Haiti. After another land raid at Tihosuco, De Graaf settled on Saint-Domingue, buying a plantation and becoming a French citizen. De Graaf was appointed to the local militia and defended Saint-Domingue from 1691 to 1695 during the war against England.

In Haiti in March 1693, De Graaf met his second wife, Marie Anne le Long, known as Marie Dieu-le-Vent (Marie, God Wills it), after her catchphrase. After De Graaf had publicly insulted her, she pointed a pistol and demanded an apology. He asked her to marry him and she accepted, being pregnant with their daughter at the time. Marie often sailed out privateering with him, being called a 'lioness'. In 1693, De Graaf spent the summer attacking Jamaica in several raids, being given the title *Chevalier* in reward. The English retaliated in May 1695 with an attack on his home at Cap François, capturing his wife with their two young daughters, but De Graaf paid the ransom to get them back. De Graaf died in Saint-Domingue's Quartier Morin in 1704, leaving an estate worth approximately 200,000 *livres* to his wife and daughters. Some sources relate he died at Biloxi, Mississippi, having helped to set up a French outpost there. In legend he was killed by a cannon ball.

Exquemelin called Laurens de Graaf 'the great pirate of Petit Goâve, writing: 'To resolve, to attempt and to accomplish, these are all the same thing to him.' He also named him the 'greatest artillerist' of his day. Handsome, blond and around 6 feet 3 inches tall, De Graaf always carried a trumpet and violin, played for his crew, and could recite Shakespeare in Dutch and Spanish. The replica pirate ship *Lorencillo* sails around Campeche Bay most evenings.

In Vera Cruz it is said that the Mexican folksong, *La Bamba*, dates from his attacks. When De Graaf and his men were arriving to attack Veracruz, the news spread across the countryside, and the tolling of the chapel bell at the nearby Hacienda Malibrán summoned workers and their families. The hacienda owner Doña Beatriz del Real thought the workers would not be able to fight back, because they were not *marineros*, and her foreman Malanga replied repeatedly that although they were not *marineros*, they would now have to become soldiers to defend themselves. They prepared their defences, and then learned that the pirates had already passed about 10 miles to the north, and proceeded to celebrate. In folklore a visiting musician named El Guaruso, from nearby Tlalixcoyan wrote *La Bamba* about the brave villagers who were prepared to take a stand, and who said '*No soy marinero*'. The phrase '*Soy Capitan!*' is said to represent their confidence and courage. *Bambolear* means swinging or swaying, and a *bambollero* or *bambollera* is a man or woman who likes to boast, (e.g., 'I'm not a sailor, I'm a captain!'). *Bamba* is a word of African origin, which means party or celebration. *Bambarria* means to try to prevent something after it has already happened, referring to the authorities who fortified Vera Cruz after the attack. *La Bamba* began as a wedding song, performed while the bride and groom danced over a ribbon, tying it into a bow. The citizens trapped in the church climbed the bell tower ladder to escape the pirates and the heat, shouting '*arriba y arriba*', which means faster and faster, and the tempo speeds up.

> *Para bailar la bamba/ Se necesita una poca de gracia,/ Una poca de gracia para mi para ti./ Arriba y arriba y arriba y arriba,/ Por ti sere. Por ti sere./ Yo no soy marinero. Soy capitan.*
>
> To dance la bamba/ You need a little prayer/ A little prayer for me and for you/ Up & up and Up & up! [faster & faster up the ladder]/ I'll be there for you I'll be there for you/ I'm not a sailor, I'm a Captain!

The second verse is about the desperate Veracruzanos climbing up a long ladder, then a short ladder, to leap to their deaths from the bell tower of the *Catedral de la Asunción*:

> *Para subir al cielo/ Se necesita/ Una escalera grande/ Y otra chiquita/ Ay arriba y arriba y arriba y arriba/ Arriba iré*
>
> To go up to heaven/ You need a big ladder/ And another small one/ And up and up and up and up/ Up I'll go.

Anne *Dieu-Le-Veut* (1654 or 28 August 1661–11 January 1710) – 'the Lioness'

A Breton or Norman, born Marie-Anne or Marianne, she was possibly deported to the French island of Tortuga as a criminal, arriving when Bertrand d'Ogeron de la Bouere was governor, either between 1665–1668 or 1669–1675. Another source relates Anne arriving in the early 1680s, possibly among the hundreds of women shipped to Saint-Domingue (Haiti) in 1685 to marry into the local French male population. The colony had a population of about 7,000, and only one in six were female. Among the population of pure European descent, only one in ten was a woman. Anne was pursued by the former *filibustier* Pierre Lelong, who had left Tortuga and founded Cap François in 1670. In 1684 or 1688, she married Lelong, who was killed on 15 July 1690, leaving her with a daughter Marie Marguerite Yvonne Lelong (1688–1774). In 1691, Anne married Joseph Chérel, who died in June 1693, leaving her with a son Jean-François Chérel (1692–1732). In March 1693, she met and married the successful privateer Laurens de Graaf. In legend, she challenged De Graaf to a duel to avenge the death of her late husband. De Graaf unsheathed his sword, and Anne drew her pistol, and De Graaf wisely then said he would not fight a woman. They married on 28 July 1693, and had two children, Marie Catherine de Graaf (1692 or 1694–1743), and a son who died as a child in 1705.

Anne was regarded as a good luck charm, supposedly actively participating in De Graaf's piracy and fighting by his side. She was described as brave, stern and ruthless, and became known as Anne *Dieu-Le-Veut* (God Wills It) from the frequency with which she used the phrase. In 1693, De Graaf raided Jamaica, being given the title of *Chevalier*, the post of Major Lieutenant and a privateering commission from Île-à-Vache, the buccaneer island just off Haiti. To retaliate, the English attacked in May 1695 and took Anne and her children, keeping them as hostages for three years, despite attempts to release them. In 1698, she was released, and we do not know much about her final years. Some report that she and her husband settled in Louisiana or Mississippi. One legend is that as they attacked a Spanish ship, a cannonball killed De Graaf, and Anne took his place as captain, but with her crew she was captured and taken to Vera Cruz and then Cartagena to be judged. When the French Secretary of the Marine heard of this, he wrote to Louis XIV, asking him to make the King of Spain intervene on her behalf. Anne was freed, but she was never heard of again. We do not know for sure whether she actually did follow a pirating career, but De Graaf left her and their daughter Marie-Catherine a huge estate, and a sugar plantation with at least 120 slaves.

Some associate Jacquotte Delahaye sailing with Anne *Dieu-Le-Veut*. Delahaye was the daughter of a French father and a Haitian mother, reportedly born in Saint-Domingue. Her mother is said to have died giving birth to a mildly mentally handicapped son, who was left in Delahaye's care after her father died, possibly murdered. According to tradition, with no money Jacquotte Delahaye then became a pirate in the Caribbean, to support herself and her young brother. To escape her pursuers, she faked her own death and took on a male alias, disguising herself as a man for many years. Upon her return to piracy, she became known as 'back from the dead red' because of her striking red hair. From her ship the *Red Ribbon*, she was said to have led a gang of hundreds of pirates, and with their help took over a small Caribbean island, which was called a 'freebooter republic'. Several years later, she was said to have died defending it.

Charles François d'Angennes (5 December 1648–before 2 April 1691) – Marquis de Maintenon, the Noble Privateer

Charles François was the oldest son of Louis d'Angennes de Rochefort de Salvert, 'Marquis de Maintenon et de Meslay', and he inherited the title of Marquis de Maintenon. Born in Chartres, the marquis sailed from Toulon in 1669, and arrived in the Antilles, where he served on the king's ship *La Sybille*. The marquis commanded it from 1672–1673, after the death of the Sieur de Lau. In 1674, preferring a life in the French Navy to living in France, Charles d'Angennes sold his castle and title to the king's mistress, Françoise d'Aubigné, after the king had given her 200,000 *livres* for 'services rendered'. (As 'Madame de Maintenon' in 1683 or 1684 she became the second wife of Louis XIV of France.) In 1673, returning from an attack on Curaçao with Governor-General Baas, d'Angennes was sent to attack English ships moored in the Bay of Irois, Saint-Domingue. D'Angennes returned to France that year, returned to the Antilles in 1674, and then sailed back to France where, in Paris, he was commissioned to return to the Caribbean.

At Nantes in October 1675, he captained the frigate *Fontaine d'Or*, armed with 24 cannons, and sailed to raise a fleet of 10 ships and 800 privateers, in 1676 at Saint-Domingue. His fleet attacked and seized Margarita Island, Venezuela, in early 1677, and Nueva Valencia on the coast of Cumaná, taking much booty. D'Angennes may have also attacked Trinidad. He sailed to unload the *Fontaine d'Or* at Petit-Goâve, but his crew scuttled her in May 1677, to avoid the frigate falling into the hands of a Dutch squadron, which was threatening the port.

From 1679 to 1685, the marquis was governor of the small island of Marie-Galante, between Guadeloupe and Dominica. In 1681, he sailed from France in command of the king's ship *La Sorcière* to establish commercial relations in the West Indies with the Spanish colonies, having obtained the monopoly on French trade with Spanish Venezuela. In this role, he turned to hunting down his former privateer captains in the region, and confiscated the commissions relating to Saint-Domingue. In 1685 he was dismissed from his post at Marie-Galante, as he had only resided there a few months in a period of five years. He lived the rest of his life at Martinique with his wife and four children.

Michiel Andrieszoon (*fl.*1683–1684) – De Graaf's Lieutenant

We do not know how the Dutchman arrived in the West Indies, but eventually he commanded his own ship, the *Tigre,* with a crew of 300 buccaneers and 30–36 guns. Andrieszoon was De Graaf's lieutenant in the great meeting of buccaneers at Petit Goâve in February 1683, which planned the attack on Vera Cruz. In a barque and a sloop, with 500 men, they sailed to the Bay of Honduras and began capturing Spanish ships, while they waited for everyone to assemble. At dawn on 17 May 1683, the buccaneers, led by Andrieszoon, Grammont, Van Hoorn, De Graaf and Yankey Williams, invaded the city and captured the Spanish garrison and most of the citizens, whom they ransomed. In November 1683 Andrieszoon was with De Graaf, Captain Yankey and François le Sage attacking Cartagena and blockading the city. Viceroy Juan de Pando Estrada organised three Spanish warships to destroy the pirates. On 23 December the 40-gun *San Francisco*, the 34-gun *Paz*, and a 28-gun galiot, with 800 Spanish soldiers left Cartagena but were out-sailed by the smaller ships of the buccaneers. The *San Francisco* ran aground early in the engagement, and the *Paz* was taken after four hours. Yankey Williams captured the galiot, with only 20 buccaneers and 90 soldiers being killed in the fighting. Andrieszoon and the buccaneers kept up the blockade of Cartagena for another three to four weeks, while De Graaf refloated the *San Francisco* for his new flagship. The Spanish soldiers were released to the governor of Cartagena, with a note thanking the Spanish for the Christmas present of the three ships.

Roche Braziliano (c.1630–c.1671) – Roche Brasileiro, Gerrit Gerritszoon, Rock the Brazilian, Le Roc, Roque Brasiliano, the Cruellest Buccaneer

Born Gerrit Gerritszoon in Groningen, the Netherlands, he was made famous by Exquemelin. Along with l'Olonnais (*q.v.*) and Montbars (*q.v.*), he was one of the cruellest pirates. 'Rock the Brazilian' was probably in the Dutch Brazil colony (New Holland) until 1654, when the Portuguese forced the settlers out. Serving as a merchant crew member, he quarrelled with his captain, stole the ship's boat, deserted with other men and began a life of piracy. Next he took a Spanish galleon sailing from Mexico, carrying gold and silver. He sailed it to Port Royal, Jamaica. This seems to have been the base of his operations, but we have no record of Rock for some time, except that he was taken by the Spanish and imprisoned in Campeche, Mexico. Somehow he forged a letter, supposedly sent by other pirates, threatening vengeance if he was not freed. The city would be burnt and all its occupants killed. Perhaps the plan worked, with the Spanish believing that these fictitious pirates were on their way to rescue him, as Rock was not executed in Campeche, but sent to Spain for trial. However, Rock escaped his Spanish prison before his trial and impending hanging, and managed to return to Port Royal. Rock now

ROCK. BRASILIANO

Rock the Brazilian, from *The Buccaneers of America*.

bought a ship from l'Olonnais, and began sailing alongside Henry Morgan. Renowned for his tortures of captives, Rock would shoot anyone who would not drink with him. On one occasion, two Spanish farmers refused to hand over their pigs, so he roasted them alive on wooden spits. He also enjoyed chopping off the limbs of Spanish captives. (The above atrocities are detailed by Exquemelin; his various accounts of the buccaneers of the time when he sailed with Morgan were written to sell copies. The account varied according to the language into which it was translated. See this author's *The Illustrated Pirate Diaries* for more information.)

Returning to invade Campeche again in 1669, Rock's ship ran aground, with possibly only 30 men escaping, and with just a few muskets and little powder between them. The survivors headed for 'Sad Gulf' (Golfo de Triste), where Dalzeel (*q.v.*) and Bartolomeu Português (*q.v.*) had also sought refuge and rescue. They may have rested at Punta Coca Beach in Isla Holbox, on the Yucatán Peninsula, hoping for rescue, before being caught by Spanish cavalry on the mainland. There was a running battle as they tried to escape, and some may have taken to sea in stolen Indian *piraguas* (canoes). Rock managed to capture a small local ship, and used it to take a Spanish merchant vessel loaded with merchandise and silver. He then returned to Jamaica, but there is no record of his death, and after 1671, Rock was never seen again. If he was captured or killed, the Spanish would probably have recorded it, so he may have died in a storm; or of sickness; or of drink; or in his sleep.

Moïse Vauquelin (*fl.*1650–1670) – Moses Vanclein, the Norman Chart Maker

Originally from Normandy, he joined the fleet that l'Olonnais (*see* next entry) assembled at Tortuga, which looted Spanish settlements for the next two years. Captain Vauquelin was present with l'Olonnais at the 1666 raids on Maracaibo and Gibraltar, and on Puerto de Caballos and San Pedro in 1667. Shortly after a Spanish ship was taken off the coast of the Yucatán Peninsula, Vauquelin, Pierre le Picard and others argued with l'Olonnais, who wished to attack Guatemala, leading to the breaking up of the fleet. With Le Picard, Vauquelin privateered for a few months, and they captured Veraguas in Costa Rica. However, they collected only a few pounds of gold, so attempted to cross the isthmus to attack Natá, on the Pacific coast. But the Spanish had gathered troops in large numbers, and the pirates failed and were driven back to the seas (recorded by Exquemelin). The two separated and Vauquelin may have lost his ship, but joined fellow-privateer, the Chevalier du Plessis, later that year. When Du Plessis died, Vauquelin was elected as his successor and took a Spanish galleon, carrying a large cargo of cacao, off Havana. In 1670, at the request of the Vice-Admiral of France, Jean d'Estrées, Vauquelin and the privateer Philippe Bequel charted their explorations of the Honduran and Yucatán coastline.

Jean-David Nau (*c.*1630/35–1668) – François l'Olonnais, 'the Flail of the Spaniards', eaten by cannibals

Born at Les Sables d'Olonne, on the Vendëe coast of France, he was renowned for his cruelty to the Spanish. As a young man, he was sold to a master who took him to the West Indies, and from 1650 to 1660 he lived as an indentured servant on the French colony of Martinique. This device enabled poor Europeans to leave for the Americas and work for an employer to pay off the cost of the voyage through hard labour for a specific number of years. When the contract was fulfilled, and many did not survive it, the worker could leave that employer and look for a better post. Some indentured servants worked with African slaves and endured the same treatment. Many escaped their harsh conditions and turned to piracy. Some historians believe that l'Olonnais was so abused in his indentured service that he lost his sanity and began to hate humanity. One favoured punishment of some plantation owners was to force a slave to defecate into the mouth of another. L'Olonnais may well have fled his indenture.

Whatever the circumstances, in 1660 l'Olonnais joined the buccaneers in Saint-Domingue (now Haiti, the French portion of Hispaniola) but was hunted down by Spaniards and escaped to the isle of Tortuga. He began robbing and killing any Spaniard he could find. In 1625 French settlers had established an outpost on Tortuga off Haiti, and became known as *boucaniers*, or buccaneers, from their cooking methods. They were joined by runaway indentured servants, escaped African slaves, and pirates, and lived mainly by hunting, becoming excellent marksmen. The Spanish tried to drive them out, hunting them through the dense forest, and the buccaneers developed a hatred for the Spanish. Some took to outright piracy, and others joined French, Dutch or English privateering commissions to attack the Spanish. Tortuga became a haven for these pirates and privateers, from where they could easily ambush Spanish treasure ships.

Soon after l'Olonnais arrived at Tortuga, Governor La Place gave him a small 10-gun ship to command, and in the Mona Passage, between

FRANCIS LOLONOIS.

Francois l'Olonnais, from *The Buccaneers of America*.

the east coast of Hispaniola and Puerto Rico, l'Olonnais attacked a large Spanish trading vessel. After a long fight, she was captured. Whenever he took a ship, he seems to have almost always killed all its crew and passengers. He soon acquired such a reputation for cruelty to Spanish prisoners and ships that they fought against him to the last man rather than be captured. L'Olonnais also became one of the first buccaneers to organise overland attacks on Spanish settlements.

In 1663 his ship was wrecked in a storm near Campeche on the Yucatán Peninsula. His crew survived, but they were all slaughtered by Spanish soldiers, incensed by l'Olonnais' actions. Only l'Olonnais managed to escape, by hiding under his dead companions, smothered with their blood and pretending to be dead. Dressing himself in a Spanish uniform, he released some slaves at Campeche and they escaped in canoes. (However, according to another account, there was fighting at Campeche, l'Olonnais being shipwrecked near the town in 1666 or 1667 with a small band of followers, being chased by Spanish soldiers but escaping with some of his crew). Rowing to Tortuga he took a small ship, killing all its crew except one man, who was sent to tell the Governor of Havana that l'Olonnais had survived, and was seeking vengeance. At Tortuga the governor gave him another ship, and off Cuba l'Olonnais surprised and took a Spanish ship of 10 guns and 90 men, which had been expressly ordered to take him. He killed all the crew, including a black sailor, who confessed under torture that he had been recruited to hang l'Olonnais when the Spanish captured him. Another version of this story is that l'Olonnais was sailing near Cayo Largo, off the southern coast of Florida. There was a Spanish *costa garda* (patrol boat) in the harbour, to protect local fishermen and shipping. In the night, the buccaneers boarded the Spanish ship, killing its soldiers, sending a single survivor back to shore with a message for the Governor of Cuba: 'I shall never henceforward give quarter [show mercy] to any Spaniard whatsoever; and I have great hopes I shall execute on your own person the very same punishment I have done upon them you sent against me. Thus I have retaliated [sic] the kindness you designed to me and my companions.' This was because he found on the *costa garda* an executioner, with instructions to hang any pirates that were captured.

In 1666, with Michel de Basco (Michel Basque), and Montbars 'the Exterminator' (*q.v.*), l'Olonnais assembled more than 600 buccaneers and 8 ships to attack Maracaibo and Gibraltar in Venezuela. The Gulf of Venezuela narrows just outside Maracaibo, leading to the great inland sea of Lake Maracaibo. On the way to Maracaibo, they took more ships, including a large 40-gun Spanish galleon loaded with cocoa and 300,000 silver talers (talers were silver coins used across Europe). She was carrying the payroll for Spanish troops in the Americas. L'Olonnais was to send his booty back to Tortuga, selling any merchandise at a profit and refitting the captured Spanish ships for his own use. Maracaibo is located on the coast of the great

Lake Maracaibo, connected by a narrow channel to the Atlantic. The buccaneers landed out of range of its fort's 16 cannon, and attacked the 'impregnable' fort and city from its less defended landward side. Spanish soldiers and its 4,000 inhabitants fiercely defended the city, but it was taken. The residents had fled, and the buccaneers found little treasure in the empty city.

While the pirates were finding citizens hiding in the jungle, taking them for ransom and torturing them to find out if they had hidden valuables, l'Olonnais discovered that a Spanish force was approaching. He quickly gathered 380 men, and ambushed and killed 500 Spanish soldiers near Gibraltar. His losses were only 40 killed and 30 wounded. The pirates now marched to Gibraltar, a city on Lake Maracaibo's opposite shore that was guarded by a strong fort. After a fierce battle, l'Olonnais entered the town, and captives were raped, tortured and murdered, with part of the town burnt. He demanded, and received, a ransom of 10,000 pieces of eight (Spanish dollars), to spare the city from total destruction. Returning to Maracaibo, l'Olonnais again sought citizens who had hidden in the jungle, torturing them to find out where they had hidden any valuables before killing them. He demanded another 20,000 pieces of eight as ransom not to destroy the town. With the booty from this expedition, l'Olonnais was welcomed back to Tortuga as a hero. He had seized treasure worth an estimated 260,000 pieces of eight, 100,000 crowns and much silver and gold from the churches.

L'Olonnais was now known as 'the flail of the Spaniards', and in common with other pirates, always tortured prisoners to force them to reveal the hiding places of their monies and possessions. He was noted as being crueller than most, taking pleasure in the torture, and 'having tormented any persons and they not confessing, he would instantly cut them to pieces with his hanger [sword] and pull on [out] their tongues.' After slicing a victim to pieces, he would lick the blood off his sword or dagger. Other barbarous acts included 'burning with matches and suchlike torments, to cut a man to pieces, first some flesh, then a hand, then an arm, a leg, sometimes tying a cord about his head and with a stick twisting it until his eyes shoot out, which is called woolding.'

In 1667/68 l'Olonnais planned another great raid, upon the eastern coast of Nicaragua, gathering 700 buccaneers and 6 ships. They sailed to Cape Gracia a Dios, but the flotilla was driven by storm and currents into the Gulf of Honduras. There he decided to take small towns along the coast, waiting until the bad weather abated to continue the expedition. Landing in canoes, the pirates attacked small turtle-fishing villages, earning the hatred of Indians as well as the Spanish. He next landed near the small port of Puerto Caballos (present-day Puerto Cortés) on the northern coast of Honduras. After capturing the town, as well as Spanish merchant ships in its harbour, l'Olonnais marched with 300 men 30 miles inland to the region's capital, San Pedro Sula, forcing two captured soldiers to act as his guides. However, they were ambushed and l'Olonnais accused the soldiers of deliberately misleading him. Exquemelin tells us that he sliced open the chest of one prisoner, ripped out the beating heart, and chewed on it before forcing it into the other man's face. The terrified prisoner immediately suggested a new route, which led the buccaneers safely to San Pedro.

L'Olonnais and his men drove out the defending troops and then spent several days plundering the town, but most people had already fled, hiding their belongings in the jungle. Without much treasure l'Olonnais set fire to the town and headed back to the coast, losing many of his men to disease. Both Puerto Caballos and San Pedro were poorer settlements, and there was not much treasure, so l'Olonnais now asked his men to wait for a Spanish treasure ship. He knew of its imminent arrival from having tortured prisoners. His fleet waited off Puerto Caballos for the expected ship, but it arrived three months late, with 41 cannon and 130 men. The buccaneers took it using only four canoes, but there was no gold and silver, only paper and steel, and most of its precious cargo had already been landed in a nearby port. Two of his senior followers now left after arguing with l'Olonnais, who wished to attack Nicaragua and Guatemala. Some of the disaffected pirates left with their newly elected captain, Moses Vauquelin (*q.v.*), to operate from Tortuga. Captain Pierre le Picard (*q.v.*) left with more men to plunder the Caribbean, initially with Vauquelin. L'Olonnais was left with one ship but still had 300–400 men, so he burnt Puerto Caballos and sailed into the Gulf of Honduras.

L'Olonnais still wanted to raid Nicaragua, his original target in the 1667 venture, and sailed south from Honduras, but ran aground on a sandbank on the treacherous Mosquito Coast. Removing the ship's guns and rigging, he attempted to refloat the ship but failed. The survivors made a camp on the shore and then divided into two groups. One group began building a smaller boat from the wreckage of their ship. The other, led by l'Olonnais, hacked its way along the San Juan River to the town of Solentiname, but the Spanish had been warned by local Indians and ambushed the party. L'Olonnais and the survivors were barely able to escape back to their camp. For the next six months l'Olonnais' remaining 150 men had to defend themselves against incessant attacks by Indians. Having built enough small flat-bottomed boats for all his men, l'Olonnais now headed for the relative safety of the Gulf of Darien, east of Panama. With little protection from the weather, and without food or water, the starving pirates soon became exhausted and weak. They reached as far as the mouth of Rio San Juan, leading to Lake Nicaragua, but were repelled from landing by Indians and Spaniards, so continued to sail along the coast of the Gulf of Darien. Landing for food and fresh water on the Panama coast, l'Olonnais and some of his men reached a small native village that would be easy to attack. However, Indians surrounded the buccaneers, killing most of them with poisoned arrows and hacking l'Olonnais to pieces. Only one man survived, to relate the cannibalising of l'Olonnais, in Exquemelin's words: 'They chopped him to pieces, roasted, and ate him.' In another story, the Indians burned the pieces of l'Olonnais' body and scattered his ashes, to destroy any trace of his existence.

Daniel Montbars (*c.*1645–*c.*1707) – 'Montbars the Destroyer', 'The Exterminator'

Philip Gosse records:

> MONTBARS, THE EXTERMINATOR – A native of Languedoc. He joined the buccaneers after reading a book which recorded the cruelty of the Spaniards to the American natives, and this story inspired him with such a hatred of all Spaniards that he determined to go to the West Indies, throw in his lot with the buccaneers, and to devote his whole life and energies to punishing the Spaniards. He carried out his resolve most thoroughly, and treated all Spaniards who came into his power with such cruelty that he became known all up and down the Spanish Main as the Exterminator. Eventually Montbars became a notorious and successful buccaneer or pirate chief, having his headquarters at St. Bartholomew, one of the Virgin Islands, to which he used to bring all his prisoners and spoils taken out of Spanish ships and towns.

Montbars may have come from one of the best families of the Languedoc region of France, sailing to the Caribbean in a merchant ship captained by his uncle. Raised as a gentleman, he may have developed his hatred of the Spanish by reading the account by the missionary Bartolomé de las Casas, of the cruelties inflicted by the *conquistadores* on Native Indians in their American conquests. (Known as the 'Defender of the Indians', las Casas crossed the Atlantic ten times in all, and his 1552 *Brief Relation of the Destruction of the Indies* is a terrifying account of Spanish cruelty). Montbars seems to have had a pathological hatred of Spaniards, learning as a young boy how to shoot well, in order to kill the enemies of his country. On arriving in the West Indies, Montbars is said to have served under his uncle in an attack on a Spanish ship, leading the boarding party and looting 30,000 bales of cotton, 2,000 bales of silk, and a casket of diamonds. He joined pirates from Hispaniola (now Haiti and the Dominican Republic), to attack Spanish towns, and they killed Spanish cavalry in an ambush. Some Indians impressed into Spanish service joined them. Returning to their ships, the Indians and pirates insisted on serving under Montbars, so his uncle gave him the captured Spanish ship, and they searched for more Spanish ships to attack.

Some days later, they were attacked by four larger ships, the first of the great Silver Plate Armada sailing to rendezvous off Havana before crossing to Spain. Montbars' uncle, old and unwell, directed his ship from an armchair, and after three hours of battle, sank his two opponents but his ship was also badly damaged and sank. Montbars sank one of the Spanish ships and boarded the last. After his uncle's death, he sailed to Tortuga to join the buccaneers. Smith, in 1835, described one of his attacks on a Spanish galleon: 'Montbars led the way to the decks of the enemy, where he carried injury and death; and when submission terminated the contest, his only pleasure seemed to be to contemplate, not the treasures of the vessel, but the number of dead and dying Spaniards, against whom he had vowed a deep and eternal hatred, which he maintained the whole of his life.'

He regularly tortured and killed all Spanish captives. Cordingley describes Montbars' favourite torture as cutting open the abdomen, extracting one end of the large intestine and nailing it to a post, then forcing the man to 'dance to his death by beating his backside with a burning log.' It may have been in revenge for the Spanish Inquisition practising similar tortures, or perhaps it was an anti-Catholic vengeance for their tortures of Cathars in the Languedoc.

Montbars raided Spanish settlements on Cuba, Puerto Rico, the Antilles and the coasts of Mexico and Honduras. He was on the l'Olonnais expedition which looted and set fire to Maracaibo,

Gibraltar, Puerto Ceballos and San Pedro in 1666–67, and destroyed numerous forts and settlements. He took Cartagena and Vera Cruz, and throughout the Spanish Main became known as Montbars the Exterminator, perhaps a name he had given himself. He never gave quarter to his enemies, preferring to torture them to death. 'The Exterminator' may have been lost at sea in 1707, and reportedly buried a fortune near Anse du Gouverneur or Anse de Grand Saline on St Bart's, dying before he could return for it.

Daniel Montbars as imagined for a cigarette card series, 'Pirates of the Spanish Main', issued *c.* 1888. Quite a fine-boned, delicate-looking 'Exterminator'.

The Indian Ocean Pirates

For Europeans, the Indian Ocean was the source of expensive spices, silks and precious gems. The Spanish and the Portuguese founded East India Companies in 1587, and in 1595 the Dutch initially achieved almost a monopoly with the Dutch East India Company. England began trading in 1600 with its own East India Company, followed in 1664 by the French with the *Compagnie Française des Indes Orientales*. There were similar companies run by the Danes, Swedish, Austrian and Americans. The Swedish East India Company alone sent 132 expeditions to Java and Whampoa in Canton China, using 37 different vessels. The soon-dominant rich English trade with India attracted French corsairs carrying *lettres de marque*, who made the islands of Mauritius and Réunion rich. From 1794 to 1810 there were about 110 of these French privateers, making around 193 known privateering voyages around the Indian Ocean. Famous French privateers included the three brothers Robert, Nicolas and Noël Surcouf of Mauritius, and the three Hodoul brothers, Jean-François, Bathélémy and Antoine of Seychelles. 'Pirate Rounders', also known as the 'Red Sea Men', now left the Caribbean to round the Cape of Good Hope, also to attack the rich East Indies trade. The greatest prizes sailed in the Indian Ocean and pirates often based themselves in havens along the coast of Madagascar, raiding the ships of the various East India Companies. All of the 'pirate rounders' are interconnected, either sailing with each other or serving each other. 'Black Bart' Roberts, the most successful pirate of all time, was involved in Red Sea and Indian Ocean piracy, before being elected to succeed Howell Davies off the Slave Coast of Africa.

Henry Every (1659–*c*.1699) – Long Ben, the 'Arch Pirate', the 'King of Pirates'

Also known as Henry Evory, Henry Avery, John Avery, Long Ben and Benjamin Bridgeman, he was celebrated in plays, poems and books. He was the main character in Daniel Defoe's *The King of Pirates*, published a year after *Robinson Crusoe*, and the model for Defoe's hero in *Life, Adventures, and Pyracies, of the Famous Captain Singleton* (1720). From Newton Ferrers, Devon, Every may have been in the Royal Navy during the 1671 bombardment of the pirate haven of Algiers, and in 1689 was promoted from midshipman to one of the three master's mates on the 64-gun HMS *Rupert*, in the Nine Years' War against France (1688–1697). Captain Wheeler transferred to the 90-gun HMS *Albemarle* in June 1690 and invited Every to join him, but Every was discharged later that year. He then sailed for the Governor of Bermuda, Cadwallader Jones, in the illicit slave trade along the African Guinea coast from 1690–1693. In 1693, Captain Thomas Phillips of the *Hannibal*, sent by the Royal Africa Company on a slaving mission to Guinea, wrote: 'I have no where upon the coast met the negroes so shy as here, which makes me fancy they have had tricks play'd them by such blades as Long Ben, alias Avery, who have seiz'd them and carry'd them away'. Every lured potential slave traders onto his ship by flying friendly English colours, then seized the slave traders along with their slaves, and chained them in his ship's hold. In August 1693, Every was first mate on the 46-gun Bristol privateer *Charles II* on the 'Spanish Expedition', requested by Spain to attack French shipping off 'New Spain' (Mexico). After the crews had not been paid for six months, Every led a mutiny in 1694.

Captain Gibson was an alcoholic, sleeping heavily in harbour at La Coruña, Spain, when Every and about 25 other crew members set sail in the *Charles II* for Madagascar, to begin his career of pure piracy. Every had invited non-conspirators to join his crew. According to Ellms, Every told Captain Gibson: 'If you have a mind to make one of us, we will receive you; and if you turn sober, and attend to business, perhaps in time I may make you one of my lieutenants; if not, here's a boat, and you shall be set on shore.' The captain was set ashore with several other sailors, but the surgeon was pressed into pirate service. All the men now left on board the *Charles II* elected Every as their new captain. He soon sacked three English ships off the Cape Verde Islands, then took a French privateer near Johanna Island. It was laden with treasure taken from Moorish ships. At Johanna, Every wrote a letter, reported in the English press:

To All English Commanders. Let this satisfy that I was riding here at this instant in the *Fancy*, man-of-war, formerly the *Charles* of the Spanish expedition who departed from La Coruna 7th May 1694, being then and now a ship of 46 guns, 150 men, and bound to seek our fortunes. I have never yet wronged any English or Dutch, or ever intend whilst I am commander. Wherefore as I commonly speak with all ships I desire whoever comes to the perusal of this to take this signal, that if you or any whom you may inform are desirous to know what we are at a distance, then make your ancient [ship's flag] up in a ball or bundle and hoist him at the mizzen peak, the mizzen being furled. I shall answer with the same, and never molest you, for my men are hungry, stout, and resolute, and should they exceed my desire I cannot help myself. As yet an Englishman's friend, here are 160 odd French armed men at Mohilla who waits the opportunity of getting any ship, take care of yourselves. At Johanna, 18th February 1695 – Henry Every.

Sailing in the *Fancy* to the Arabian coast, Every was joined by five other pirate vessels, and in 1695 attacked the Great Moghul's ships *Gang-i-Sawai* and its escort *Fateh Mohamed*. The *Fateh Mohamed* gave up almost immediately, having been weakened by Thomas Tew's attack (*see* next entry), during which he died. The ship was carrying about £50,000–£60,000 in coins and treasure. The massive 62-gun *Gang-i-Sawai* ('*Exceeding Treasure*') had 600 passengers, but carried 400–500 musketeers, so had sailed with only the one escort. Fortunately for Every, one of the *Gang-i-Sawai's* cannon exploded on her first broadside, causing casualties, and then one of Every's cannon broke the Indian ship's mainmast. She surrendered after a two-hour pitched battle on deck, and the pirates proceeded to beat, torture and rape her passengers in anger over their dead and injured. The treasure included 500,000 pieces of silver and gold, pearls, jewels and a saddle set with rubies, intended as a gift for the Great Moghul. When the pirates finished looting both ships they set them adrift with their sails and rigging destroyed, but kept the surviving women.

The pirate ships eventually made port at Surat, but the women were either thrown overboard or taken ashore at Réunion, where the pirates distributed their booty. It may have been the richest pirate prize in history. Estimates of plunder were £325,000 to £600,000, of which each pirate's share was more than £1,000, with Every receiving two shares as captain. Every captured at least 11 vessels by September 1695, including the Emperor Aurangzeb's *Gang-i-Sawai*. He also took the *Rampura*, a Cambay trader carrying 1,700,000 rupees. Every's fleet then dispersed, with Every sailing to the Danish island of St Thomas in the Caribbean (now part of the US Virgin Islands). There he sold off some of his valuable cargo. Sailing to the Bahamas, he presented the governor with the *Fancy,* and gifts and bribes worth about £7,000. Because of Every's raid, the Great Moghul ceased all trading with the East India Company until it paid massive compensation, and placed a massive reward of £500 a head on each of Every's crew, and £1,000 for Every. Suddenly they were wanted by pirate hunters across the Caribbean and were no longer safe in any of the British colonies.

Every altered his name to Benjamin Bridgeman, bought a small sloop and sailed for obscurity in Ireland. Later, 24 of the crew were arrested in England, of whom 6 were hanged. Every had disappeared, however. Some sources state that he tried to sell off his share of the treasure, mostly diamonds, was cheated by merchants and died in poverty. In October 1781 the Collector of Customs at St Ives, Cornwall, was told by a descendant of Every's that his 'father had told him that Captain Every, after wandering about in great poverty and distress, had died in Barnstaple, and was buried as a pauper'. It was possibly the most lucrative pirating raid ever, taking up to $400 million in today's money. His incredible success led many men to turn to piracy in the Indian Ocean and Red Sea.

Thomas Tew (*fl.*1682–1695) – The Rhode Island Pirate

Tew came from a good Rhode Island family, and was in Bermuda in 1692 'with gold in his pockets'. A king's counsellor wrote that during Tew's stay in Bermuda 'it was a thing notoriously known to everyone that he had before then been a pirate,' and a sailor who had known him well testified that Tew 'had been a rambling [i.e. pirating]'. He probably had also served as a privateer in the war with France. He was seen in Newport, Rhode Island, in 1694 by a traveller who had known Tew in Jamaica twelve years earlier, so it appears his career began around 1682. During the 1690s Tew pirated in the Red Sea, operating from Bermuda, Rhode Island and New York, bringing Madagascar trade into New York warehouses.

In Bermuda, Tew purchased a share in the 70-ton sloop *Amity* and received a privateering commission from its governor to attack the French at Gorée on the River Gambia in West Africa. He was sailing alongside Captain George Drew's privateer sloop but in a storm, Drew's ship sprung her mast and the *Amity* lost sight of her. Defoe tells us that Tew now asked his 60-man crew to turn to outright piracy, and they elected a quartermaster to represent them. Tew told them that attacking

Thomas Tew.

a French factory or colony would bring little treasure, and the crew shouted 'A gold chain, or a wooden leg, we'll stand by you!' He now sailed around the Cape of Good Hope to the Red Sea, to reprovision at Madagascar. In late 1693 Tew sighted a 'tall vessel', a large Arab dhow bound from India to the Ottoman Empire. She was manned not only by a large crew but also 300 soldiers. Tew told his men that this was their opportunity to strike for fortune, and that Arabs lacked courage. He took the ship with little resistance and no pirate casualties, and was told by prisoners that the ship was a part of a convoy leading six merchant vessels. The booty is said to have been worth £100,000 in gold and silver alone, plus ivory, spices, precious stones, and silk. Tew wanted to attack the rest of the fleet, but the quartermaster and most of the crew voted against him. The *Amity* sailed to St Mary's Island (Île Sainte-Marie) off Madagascar, to divide the treasure, and Tew careened the ship. The 45 pirates shared between £1,200 and £3,000 per man, with Tew himself claiming about £8,000. Tew then returned to Newport, Rhode Island, after 15 months, having sailed 22,000 miles.

Tew arrived at Newport in April 1694, and paid off the owners of the *Amity*, who made fourteen times the value of the ship. Tew sold the *Amity*, and spent several months ashore, receiving a pardon. He next took his family to New York, where he met Governor Benjamin Fletcher, who was encouraging pirates to bring their loot to the town. Tew bought a letter of marque from Fletcher for £300, and returned to Newport to build a new *Amity*. Tew sailed off in November 1694, with the pirates Thomas Wake and William Want, and reprovisioned at Madagascar, before sailing to the Red Sea. Between June and September 1695, Tew was sailing with Henry Every (*q.v.*) and others when they sighted two great Indian ships, and Tew attacked the escort *Fateh Mohamed*, but it was well-armed and prepared to defend itself. It belonged to the Great Moghul, and 'a shot carried away the rim of Tew's belly, who held his bowels with his hands for some space. When he dropped, it struck such terror to his men that they suffered themselves to be taken without further resistance'. Many of Tew's pirates were executed immediately, but the *Fateh Mohamed* was soon taken by Henry Every. William III mentioned Tew as a specially 'wicked and ill-disposed person' in his Royal Warrant granted to Captain Kidd to hunt the now deceased Tew down.

Alexander Dalzeel (*c.*1662–5 December 1715) – The Fourth Time Unlucky Captain

Born in Port Patrick, Scotland, Dalzeel went to sea aged 12, on his uncle's ship in the Baltic trade. After six successful voyages, by the age of 23 he was captain of his own ship, trading with Hamburg. With a reputation for dishonesty, Dalzeel arrived in Madagascar in 1685, and joined the pirate Henry Every. In August 1694, Every came across the *Ganj-i-Sawai*, carrying the daughter of the Great Moghul, part of a 25-ship convoy. Every had formed a temporary alliance with four other pirates to attack the convoy. It was travelling from what is now Saudi Arabia to India, and chasing the ship through the night, Dalzeel was the first to board her. After a great battle, the heavily outnumbered pirates took the *Ganj-i-Sawai* and £500,000 worth of loot. Every gave Dalzeel his own ship within his fleet, and Every had gained enough treasure to retire with his captured concubines. He was said to have named Dalzeel as his successor, and the Scot left the Indian Ocean for the Caribbean.

In the West Indies, Dalzeel was unsuccessful, and provisions were running out when the pirates spotted a well-armed Spanish war galleon, probably separated from its escorts. Dalzeel gave orders to close in on her, but the Spanish captain paid little attention to Dalzeel's small ship, retiring to his cabin to play cards. As his ship approached the galleon, Dalzeel ordered a hole to be drilled in the side of his own vessel, so that his crew would be forced to fight to the death. Caught off guard and with their captain missing, the Spanish were quickly overcome. Dalzeel took his prize to Jamaica, and en route attacked a fleet of 12 Spanish pearl ships. However, a Spanish man-of-war escort intervened, and attacked Dalzeel. Dalzeel had only 22 crew left alive, and in exchange for surrendering, the pirates were not to be forced into slavery or hard labour. The Spanish captain did not wish to lose the Spanish galleon or the £100,000 in pearls that Dalzeel had captured. Thus Dalzeel's prize ship and booty were taken, and the pirates were put ashore.

Finding his way to Jamaica, Dalzeel began outfitting another ship with four small guns and 30 men, and headed for the Cabo de Corriente, Cuba. He attacked a 20-gun vessel from Cartagena and Maracaibo, but was then captured by a Spanish *costa garda*, one of a naval patrol of three ships. The pirates were sentenced to be hanged at sea, but according to Alexander Smith Dalzeel secretly purchased a dagger and killed his guard. Being a non-swimmer, he made it to the Mexican shore, using two great earthenware storage jars as floats. Dalzeel hid in the trunk of a tree in the forest for three days, avoiding search parties. He then struggled, starving, overland for two weeks, fashioning makeshift rafts to cross rivers, to the coastline of Golfo

Triste, 40 leagues from Campeche. Alert readers will have noticed the suspicious similarity of this story to that of Bartolomeu Português: it seems Captain Smith has sexed up the dossier here. Dalzeel came across a group of pirates that he knew from Jamaica, and asked for a small boat and 20 men, to take the *costa garda* which he knew would be anchored in Campeche, and rescue his men. The *costa garda* believed that Dalzeel's men were intending to trade contraband, and allowed him to board. He promptly took the unsuspecting crew unawares, released his crew and made off with his booty in the captured ship. Captain Dalzeel now headed once more for Jamaica to fence his loot, but near the Isle of Pines, off Cuba, a great storm wrecked the *costa garda* and he and his crew were forced to escape in a longboat.

Managing to reach Jamaica again, Dalzeel sailed to France and was appointed captain of a privateer to fight in the War of the Spanish Succession. He enjoyed much success, taking English and allied ships before his third capture in 1712. After spending 12 months in heavy irons in the squalid Marshalsea prison in Southwark, Dalzeel was convicted of high treason against Great Britain, and sentenced to be hanged, drawn and quartered, the normal punishment for treason. However, because of the influence of the Earl of Mar, Dalzeel somehow received a royal pardon. Upon his release, he sailed for French waters, where he turned pirate again. Sailing near Havre de Grace, he took a French ship. He then had the captured crew's necks tied to their heels and threw them overboard to watch them drown. He sailed with the cargo to sell it in Scotland and was arrested there. Sent to the Marshalsea, and then Newgate, he was tried again by the High Court of the Admiralty, condemned for murder and piracy, and hanged at Execution Dock, Wapping on 5 December 1715, aged 53.

William Kidd (*c.*1645–23 May 1701) – 'The Most Unfortunate Pirate Ever to Sail the High Seas'

Strangely, Kidd has become one of the most well-known pirates, but only took one major ship. The son of a seaman, born in the port of Greenock, Scotland, it was his bad luck to be sailing as a privateer/pirate when rules changed, and he was outlawed. Kidd captained the merchant ship *Antigua* and in the 1680s emigrated to New York, where he married the 20-year-old Sarah Bradley Cox Oort. Already twice widowed, she was extremely wealthy, with much property and they had two children. Kidd could have retired, but during the Nine Years' War (1688–1697), he was a privateer captain, initially with

William Kidd by
the celebrated pirate
illustrator Howard Pyle.

Robert Culliford (*see* next entry). In 1689, in the *Blessed William*, they were sent to pillage French settlements in the West Indies, and defend American and English trade routes to the Caribbean. However, in 1690 he was abandoned at Antigua by the crew, and replaced as captain by William Mason. In 1695, Kidd was asked to return to England, to receive a royal commission as a privateer. He met many prominent citizens, including the new governor of New York and Massachusetts, Sir George Bellomont, who formed a consortium to fund his voyage. Kidd acquired two commissions, to hunt pirates in the Indian Ocean and to capture French ships. Their cargo would potentially bring vast profits to his backers, and in February 1696 Kidd left Deptford with 150 crew in the 287-ton, 34-gun *Adventure Galley*.

However, his best men were soon taken by two Royal Navy ships, which were forcibly impressing experienced sailors. Kidd was forced to sail back to New York to recruit a new crew, but they were mostly hardened smugglers and unemployed former pirates, and they wished to attack any vessel in their new warship. On 6 September 1696, Kidd

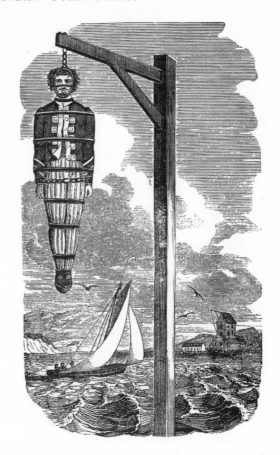

William Kidd hanging in chains.

left New York for the Indian Ocean, and arguing between him and new crew members broke out almost immediately. A number of his men died of disease, and when Kidd found few French ships to attack, he faced pressure from his increasingly quarrelsome crew. In early 1697, Kidd sailed toward Madagascar, a great gathering point for many pirates such as his former partner, the famed Robert Culliford. There were next a few failed attacks upon French ships, and his crew was angered when Kidd fled from potential prizes that seemed well armed. Often hoisting French colours, Kidd captured a few small Indian merchant ships, but used all his captured booty to repair the *Adventure Galley* in the Laccadive Islands. Some sailors now deserted, and the rest pressured Kidd because of his evasiveness. In one of many arguments, Kidd was in a furious rage when faced with his mutinous crew, and struck his ship's gunner, William Moore, with an iron-bound bucket, breaking his skull. Moore died within twenty-four hours, but the mutiny ended.

A group of Armenian merchants had hired the 350-ton *Quedagh Merchant*, owned by an Indian, assisted by a local English East India Company representative. It was captained by John Wright, sailing with two Dutch first mates, a French gunner, more than 90 Indian sailors, and 30 Armenian merchants. She was loaded with sugar, opium, silk, muslin, saltpetre and iron, worth a rumoured £70,000. She had been granted safe passage around the tip of India by the French East India Company. On 30 January 1698, Captain Kidd hoisted a French flag and took it. As the voyage had been promised safe passage by the French, this technically made his seizure a legal capture. However, Kidd discovered that an agent for the English East India Company had brokered the voyage, and looting the ship could cause trouble back in England, so Kidd asked the crew to vote on whether to take the ship and its cargo, or sell it back to the Armenians. The *Adventure Galley*, *Quedagh Merchant*, and *Rouparelle*, another ship captured by Kidd and renamed *November*, now set sail for Cochin, to sell some of the goods to finance the voyage back to England. After selling much of the cargo for gold, Kidd arrived at St Mary's Island aboard *Adventure Galley*, and spotted the *Mocha*, belonging to the pirate Robert Culliford.

Kidd called for his men to fight against his former fellow privateer Culliford, but the crew, without pay for two years, voted 100 to 15 to join Culliford. They began to off-load the treasure from the *Quedagh Merchant*. Culliford's men stripped all three ships of anything of value, and sank *November*, leaving Kidd with two ships and a skeleton crew. Kidd moved everything left of value to the *Quedagh Merchant*, renamed it *Adventure Prize* and sailed for the Caribbean en route to New York. At Anguilla in April 1699 he discovered he was now a wanted pirate. With *Adventure Prize* leaking, Kidd bought a sloop, *St Antonio*, and headed north to convince one of his backers, Governor Richard Bellomont, that he was innocent. *Adventure Prize* was left in a small lagoon on Santa Catalina. Kidd sailed for Boston, stopping along the way to bury booty on Gardiners Island and Block Island. Some of the booty on Gardiners Island was later recovered. His friend the privateer Thomas Paine (*q.v.*) was arrested for having gold bars, but claimed they were his own as they had been given as a gift by Kidd, and managed to escape imprisonment.

Bellomont, himself an investor in Kidd's voyage, had Kidd arrested upon 7 July 1699 in Boston. Imprisoned in New York, Kidd would not reveal the location of *Adventure Prize*, believing that the treasure aboard the ship could be used as barter to free him. However, the men Kidd had entrusted with his ship looted it, and then set it ablaze. Kidd was sent to England aboard the frigate *Advice* in February 1700. On 16 April 1700, 'the notorious pyratt' was examined before the Lords of Admiralty and committed to Newgate. Later in April there was a rumour that jewels found on Kidd's ship had been valued at £30,000 (perhaps equivalent to some £10 million today). The 'pirate's' connections with the English élite and government officials caused a sensation. His trial, only recently found to have been explicitly rigged against Kidd, started on 8 May and ended the next day. Kidd was found guilty of the murder of one of his crew and guilty of multiple acts of piracy. Kidd's final statement in court was: 'My Lords ... I am the innocentest of them all, only I have been sworn against by perjured persons.'

Nine members of his crew were in the dock with him on piracy charges, and he and eight of his crew were hanged on 23 May 1701. To the chaplain's disapproval, Kidd was drunk. The first rope put around this neck broke, so he had to be strung up a second time. His corpse was placed in a gibbet at Tilbury Point on the mouth of the Thames, and left to rot. After his death, his legend grew, especially the stories of buried treasure. Captain Kidd's 'treasure chest' was held in the Customs House, Queen's Square, Bristol, for many years but vanished over a century ago. Authors such as Robert Louis Stevenson in *Treasure Island* and Edgar Allan Poe in *The Gold Bug* may have used the tale of Kidd's buried treasure.

Robert Culliford (1664/1666–after 1702) – 'Cutlass' Culliford

Born in East Looe, Cornwall, Culliford served with William Kidd aboard the French privateer *Sainte Rose* in 1689, with just six other Britons in the crew. After the Nine Years' War broke out between France and other countries, including England, the English crew mutinied, taking the ship and renaming it the *Blessed William*, with Kidd in command. They attacked, looted and burned the island of Marie-Galante in the West Indies. However, in February 1690, Culliford and Samuel Burgess (*q.v.*) mutinied against Kidd and the pirates elected William Mason (or May) as captain. In the West Indies they ransacked towns and ships, selling their booty in New York, where the acting governor gave Mason a letter of marque. Mason and Culliford next sacked two towns in French Canada, and Mason gave a captured French frigate, *L'Esperance*, to Culliford. He renamed it the *Horne Frigate*, and their booty was sent in two ketches to New York, but they were in turn taken by French privateers. Culliford and Mason returned to New York on the captured French *Jacob*. Culliford next sailed to India in 1692, where the pirates managed to survive by robbing the local population. Culliford and 17 other pirates were captured and he spent four years in a Gujarati gaol.

In spring 1696, Culliford and some pirates escaped and managed to reach Bombay (now Mumbai, British from 1661 as part of Charles II's marriage settlement with Catherine of Braganza). They signed aboard the East India Company ketch *Josiah*, but in Madras they mutinied, took over the ship and made for the Bay of Bengal. One version of this event is that Culliford argued with Mason, when careening the vessel in the Nicobar Islands, and left the *Josiah*. The other tale is that the original crew retook the ship, and marooned Culliford in the Nicobar Islands, where he was discovered by Ralph Stout, captaining the *Mocha*. Culliford became captain of the *Mocha* when Stout was killed in 1697, and chased the English East Indiaman *Dorill* in the Straits of Malacca. When the *Dorill's* cannon shot down the *Mocha's* main mast, Culliford managed to sail to St Mary's Island off Madagascar. Repairing his ship, he took some small merchant vessels and looted a French ship with £2,000-worth of cargo. Sailing in consort, Culliford next took a Moorish 200-ton ship laden with rice, and then a Portuguese vessel carrying gold and silk to the value of £12,000, before returning to St Mary's Island. One story is that Culliford would order his men to load their cannon with china dishes, as pottery shards would shred the sails of the ships he attacked. Culliford's surgeon was aptly named Jon Death.

William Kidd wanted to capture Culliford, but Kidd's crew mutinied and most joined Culliford. Soon after leaving St Mary's Island, Culliford joined forces with Dirk Chivers (*see* next entry), and they took the *Great Mohammed* in the Red Sea in September 1698. It was said to have carried £130,000 in gold coins. The pirates returned to St Mary's Island, and each pirate made more than £700. Chivers and Culliford took another ship in February 1699. Four British warships arrived at the island, and the pirates were offered a royal pardon to give up piracy. However, George Booth (*q.v.*) and Nathaniel North (*q.v.*) disbelieved the offer, and escaped to continue pirating. Chivers and Culliford accepted but Culliford was arrested, and granted bail in August 1700. However, 'one day in the streets of London he [Culliford] recognized and denounced another pirate called Burgess,'* who was taken to the Marshalsea Prison. His pardon was ruled invalid, but Culliford was saved from hanging for his piracy of the *Great Mohammed*, as he was needed to turn King's Evidence in the trial of Samuel Burgess. Burgess had previously sailed with Culliford. Culliford had enjoyed a 'close relationship', possibly non-platonic, with another pirate, John Swann. All of Culliford's men were hanged, but Culliford was granted a pardon and released in April 1702. Following the trial, he disappears, but may have joined the navy.

Dirk Chivers *(fl.*1690s) – The Man Credited with making St Mary's Island a Pirate Haven

Chivers probably came from the Republic of the United Netherlands, but some say he came from Hamburg. He may have sailed on the pirate *Batchelor's Delight* from 1688 to 1692, and was first mate in the 90-ton Rhode Island privateer *Portsmouth Adventure* from January 1694. Captained by Joseph Farrell, the privateers helped Henry Every take two ships, but when they returned to Rhode Island, the *Portsmouth Adventure* was wrecked on a reef in a storm off Mayotte. (The island is in the Comoros Islands, between Mozambique and Madagascar.) Some crew joined Captain Every, but Chivers and others made it to Réunion and joined Captain Robert Glover's 200-ton privateer *Resolution*. She was a French ship taken from Barbary corsairs, formerly called an Algerine galley, which now held 20 guns and 110 pirates. *Resolution* had little success pirating on the Red Sea, and Chivers was a ringleader in a mutiny. In 1696 the pirates imprisoned Captain Glover and 24 of his loyal crew aboard a captured Arab vessel, the *Rajapura*. The pirates elected Chivers as their new captain and renamed the *Resolution* as the *Soldado*.

Successful throughout the Indian Ocean, Chivers now sailed the *Soldado* in consort with Captain John Hoar in the *Charming Mary*, and a privateer belonging to the New York pirate merchant Frederick Philipse, taking two East India merchant vessels. The three ships took more rich prizes, among them the East Indiaman *Ruparel*. Her captain, Sawbridge, suggested that the captured ships and passengers could be ransomed in Aden. The Governor of Aden refused to give a ransom, and a shot was heard from the shore, signifying that no ransom would be paid. The pirates then looted two ships of anything

---

* Gosse, Philip, *The Pirates' Who's Who*, Burt, Franklin, NY 1924.

usable and burnt them, before sailing for St Mary's Island (Île Sainte-Marie) off Madagascar. A story from the time is that a captured Captain Sawbridge kept complaining about his conditions in captivity, so his lips were stitched shut with a sail needle.

The pirate captains now had four captured prizes, and on 23 November 1696 sailed into Calcutta (Calicut) harbour to try to ransom them. They fired a broadside into a ship in the harbour to announce their arrival, spreading panic, and pirates in longboats captured another four ships, including one belonging to the East India Company and one of the Moghul Emperor's merchantmen. In response, the Indian authorities arrested all local representatives of the East India Company. Chivers wanted £10,000 sterling, or he would burn all the ships in the port, but the governor would only pay £5,000. In the night Chivers moved his prizes to deeper water, and the next morning the negotiator asked Chivers to take pity on the white captives ashore. Chivers responded with: 'We acknowledge no country, having sold our own, and as we are sure to be hanged if taken, we shall have no scruple in murdering and destroying if our demands are not granted in full.' Meanwhile Calcutta's governor had sent messages to native pirates, and when these arrived in 10 ships, Chivers and Hoar sailed away to St Mary's Island. Chivers overwintered to careen his ships, while Hoar sailed into the Red Sea.

Chivers now linked up with Culliford's *Mocha* for 'happy plundering', and divided their booty in the Maldives, then sailed to the Strait of Malacca. The slave trader Adam Baldridge reported:

> June 9th 1697. Arrived Captain Chivers, commander. [He] had met with a mossoon [monsoon] and lost all the masts, and put into Madagascar about ten leagues to the Northward of Antogil Bay and there masted and fitted his ship. Whilst there took the brigantine Amity, captain Glover for her water casks, sails, rigging and masts, and then turned the hull adrift to run upon a reef and be lost. Captain Glover promised to forgive them what was past, if they would let him have his ship again, and go home to America with him, but they [Chiver's crew] would not, except he would go into the Indies with them. September 25th set sail for the Indies.

In April 1698, Chivers took the English *Sedgwick*. The ship had been chased by William Kidd for three days a few days previously, out-rowing him in a flat calm. Chivers negotiated with Captain Watts not to destroy the ship.

Her cargo of pepper not being to their liking, they dismissed the ship after they had taken out of her two courses, her sheet anchor and cable, cordage, pitch, tar, and other stores which they required. Though some of the Pirates were mightily taken with the build of the Sedgwick, saying she would make a fine Pirate cruiser, Capt. Watts in the end prevailed on them to give him back his ship by merry management of a bowl of punch which caused them to say 'He is an honest old fellow, let him go with his ship.'

It seems that Captain Watts now agreed to begin to supply rum for Chivers to trade for slaves and other goods. At the end of June 1698 Chivers took another prize off Madras with a cargo of sugar, which he wanted to exchange for saltpetre to make gunpowder.

Chivers had again joined with the notable pirate captains Robert Culliford and Nathaniel North by September 1698, and on 23 September they captured the *Great Mohammed* treasure ship, probably worth around £130,000. The gold coins and ingots aboard possibly amounted to more than £100,000, with each man receiving a share worth £700–£800. The Indian owner complained that: 'The villaines turned adrift in the ship boats, without Oars, sail or Provisions, 150 of the pilgrims, whom the Tide carried to Bassen. The women passengers, about 60, were kept aboard, and inhumanely abused them. To avoid such indignity five stabbed themselves [to death].' The *Soldado* was becoming unseaworthy and badly affected by the teredos worm, and Chivers transferred his cannon to *Great Mohammed*. Now leading 200 pirates, he renamed her *New Soldado*.

Possibly returning to St Mary's, they met another pirate ship, the *Pelican*, with a Portuguese prize laden with cloth and wine. The legend is that the excited pirates, flushed with loot, bought two barrels of wine for 100,000 pieces of eight, before taking another ship on 10 November 1698, before returning to St Mary's on 12 December. However, in September 1699 Chivers was forced to sink the *New Soldado* to block the harbour of St Mary's when English men-of-war arrived. Chivers and Culliford took the royal pardon offered to those who would give up piracy, and the now wealthy Chivers returned to Holland aboard a merchant ship, the *Vine*. Another version is that he wished to return to New York and paid $100 for a passage in Samuel Burgess's *Margaret*. However, when the *Margaret* arrived in December 1699, en route from Cape Town, she was captured by the East Indiaman *Loyal Merchant*. *Margaret* was taken to Bombay so Chivers took passage on the merchantman *Vine* to North America.

Samuel Burgess (*c.*1650–1716) – the New York 'Pirate Rounder'

He was born in New York City. With Culliford, Mason and Kidd, Burgess seized the *Blessed William* in 1689. In 1690 the privateers attacked the French in the Gulf of St Laurence, taking seven ships, and Burgess was promoted to quarter-master. In 1690 Burgess sailed to Madagascar, taking a ship and raiding a Portuguese settlement in the Cape Verde Islands. However, he was left behind by his ship, as the crew were suspicious of his behaviour. After six months the *Blessed William*, under a new captain, Edward Coates, took him back on board. Coates had succeeded William Mason as captain, possibly having killed him. (Coates probably had also previously removed Burgess from the captaincy of a ship.)

By June 1692 the pirates had taken four ships in the Red Sea, with each man receiving £800. (The annual pay of a mariner at this time was about £20–£25). The pirates returned to St Mary's Island, and bought provisions from Adam Baldridge, the agent of Frederick Philipse on the island. In April 1693 Burgess returned to New York City with £800, and sought out Philipse, New York's wealthiest 'pirate merchant'. Burgess now bought a splendid house, working in illegal trading for Philipse. Backed by Philipse, Burgess sailed to Madagascar in 1695, profitably trading guns, ammunition, food, clothing and essential supplies to pirates, in exchange for gold and slaves. Pirates who wished to secretly return to America would pay him 100 pieces of eight.

However, in September 1699, captaining the *Margaret*, Burgess was prevented from entering the pirate haven of St Mary's Island, off Madagascar, by a blockading English fleet. He and his crew were offered a pardon for 'piratical activities' and several of Burgess's crew accepted, using some of their loot to buy their passage home with the fleet. Instead, Burgess sailed to Cape Town, and around December 1699 the suspicious Captain Lowth of the East India Company accused Burgess of piracy, seizing the *Margaret*, along with Burgess' slaves, booty and gold. Lowth took £17,000 and 80 slaves. Some of the goods would have been taken from British ships by the Madagascar 'pirate rounders' and Burgess could not prove that they were not pirated goods.

Captain Lowth sailed the ship to Bombay, so the owners of the *Margaret* made claims against the East India Company to retrieve it. Burgess was taken to London in 1701 and accused of piracy. Captain Culliford testified against Burgess in exchange for his own pardon, and Burgess was convicted. However he was pardoned on the grounds that he had already received a pardon from a Governor of New York. Burgess next briefly served under William Dampier (*q.v.*) on a privateering expedition. He sold his house in New York, settled in London and became first mate on the *Neptune*, sailing to Madagascar to trade liquor for slaves. When a hurricane wrecked John Halsey's pirate flotilla in 1708, Burgess helped Halsey seize the *Neptune*, being made quartermaster. However, in 1709 Halsey died of fever, and Burgess was removed from the quartermaster's post by Halsey's men.

He returned to Madagascar with £1,200 to become a slave trader with David Williams. By 1715, he had decided to leave Madagascar aboard a slaver, but Williams asked him to appease a local ruler in an argument concerning prizes. However, Burgess was poisoned by the chief and died.

Edward Coates (*fl.*1690s) – Captain of Samuel Burgess and Robert Culliford

He served as an American privateer in the Nine Years' War (called King William's War in the USA), and in 1689 served on *Jacob* under the command of William Mason. Mason had briefly sailed with Kidd, Culliford and Burgess. Mason was commissioned in New York to raid French settlements and vessels along the coast of French Canada – 'to war as in his wisdom should seem fit.'* Finding it difficult to locate French ships, Mason instead raided English shipping, making so much that each crew member received up to 1,800 pieces of eight. Suspected of retaining a portion of the crew's shares, in the Indian Ocean Mason disappeared after stopping at an uninhabited island. Coates had probably murdered Mason, and took command of the 16-gun *Nassau*.

He sailed to the pirate haven of St Mary's Island, Madagascar, in October 1692, and was in New York in April 1693. There he arranged a pardon for his crew's piracy with Governor Fletcher, as well as an assurance that the New York authorities would not interfere with his future operations. Coates gave Fletcher's wife silks, cashmere shawls and jewels, and gave Fletcher $1,800 for himself and other colonial officials. In 1694, Coates sailed to the Red Sea, with Samuel Burgess and Robert Culliford as his quartermasters. Several years later he was taken and executed.

---

* Nash, J. Robert, entry for Edward Coates in *Encyclopedia of World Crime*, Crimebooks 1990.

John Halsey (d.1708) – the Ancestor of Admiral 'Bill' Halsey (1882–1959)

The Boston-born Halsey captained the privateer brigantine *Charles*, carrying 10 cannon in Queen Anne's War, attacking French fishing fleets in Newfoundland, before sailing to the Azores and fighting Spanish shipping in 1705. With his privateer's letter of marque due to expire in 1706, he sailed for Madagascar to take up piracy. Taking on water and supplies at Augustine Bay, Halsey came across several shipwrecked sailors, survivors from the 700-ton 52-gun HMS *Degrave*, which had been wrecked there five years earlier. Halsey took them on as crew, and sailed to the Red Sea to loot the Great Moghul's Indian treasure ships. In late 1706, a huge Dutch ship was seen, and Halsey refused to attack a European nation friendly to England. The crew thus elected to relieve him and the gunner from their posts, accusing them of cowardice. As the *Charles* closed with its 'easy victim', it proved to be well armed and fired a broadside, which injured the helmsman, destroyed one of the swivel guns and ripped apart the topsail. Some of the *Charles's* crew fled into the hold, and others managed to sail the *Charles* out of cannon range. Halsey gained respect for his wisdom in not wishing to attack, and was re-elected captain.

Halsey took two coastal trading ships off the Nicobar Islands in February 1707, and sailed to the Straits of Malacca. However, morale was very low after the Dutch incident and the men were unwilling to follow orders. Halsey decided to return to Madagascar and took on a more committed crew, with Nathaniel North as his new quartermaster. Sailing to Mocha, Halsey entered the Red Sea in August 1707, and faced an English naval flotilla of 5 ships with 62 guns. Probably to counter the previous accusations of cowardice, Halsey attacked, forcing the English to flee and taking two ships, with £50,000 in coins and a fortune in trading goods. Sailing the *Charles* back to Madagascar in January 1708, his fleet was soon after virtually destroyed in a hurricane, and Halsey died of a fever. Some of Halsey's crew joined Christopher Condent and gave Condent advice on how to take Indian and Arab shipping. Johnson (Daniel Defoe) wrote:

> He was brave in his Person, courteous to all his Prisoners, lived beloved, and died regretted by his own People. His Grave was made in a garden of watermelons, and fenced in with Palisades to prevent his being rooted up by wild Hogs.

His descendant, Admiral William Halsey, was Commander of the US Third Fleet in the Second World War. Delayed by a storm from reaching Pearl Harbor on the USS *Enterprise*, he entered the port the day after the attack and surveyed the wreckage of the Pacific Fleet, remarking: 'Before we're through with them, the Japanese language will be spoken only in Hell.' After the cessation of hostilities, Halsey, still cautious of Japanese *kamikaze* attacks, ordered the Third Fleet to maintain a protective air cover with this communiqué: 'Cessation of hostilities. – War is over. – If any Japanese airplanes appear, shoot them down in a friendly way.'

George Booth (d.1700) – the Captain who Sailed with Four Pirate Captains

George Booth led a crew that included the later pirate captains Thomas Howard, Nathaniel North, Thomas White and John Bowen, and was one of the first European pirates in the Red Sea and Indian Ocean. Booth initially served with Nathaniel North, operating out of Jamaica as a privateer in the Nine Years' War. He was a gunner on the *Pelican*, and then on the *Dolphin*, when she was trapped at St Mary's Island by four English men-of-war in September 1699. Some pirates accepted the offer of a pardon, but Booth, North and others refused and burnt the *Dolphin* with any incriminating evidence. They escaped to Madagascar at night in the ship's longboat. The pirates now assumed the role of 'traders' who wished to trade slaves for alcohol and other goods, and by this means trapped and took a French merchant ship. Nearing land, they spotted a French ship out of Martinique, carrying alcohol to trade for slaves at Ambonavoula, Madagascar. Booth captained the pirates, and he took 10 men aboard with money, ostensibly to buy liquor. Captain Fourgette checked each man coming aboard for arms, but Booth's men managed to smuggle four pistols aboard. The 20 French crew had their small arms ready in the awning should any fighting break out. Three men went down below to eat at the captain's table, while Booth stood near the awning and gave a signal by firing at a Frenchman. With the pirates wielding handspikes, the French on deck were overcome. Fourgette's pistol failed to fire and he tried to attack the pirates with a silver fork, but was easily subdued. The French ship was taken as prize and Fourgette and his crew were placed with provisions on Madagascar, where Booth took on the survivors of the *Dolphin* to bring his complement to 80 pirates.

At Methelage, Booth joined with captains White and Bowen and came across a large English slaver, the 450-ton *Speaker,* formerly a French warship, off north-west Madagascar in April 1699. A young sailor, Hugh Man, aboard the *Speaker* had been bribed £100 to wet the priming on his ship's cannon, so when attacked it could not fire. She was quickly taken as a prize and sailed to St Augustine where more pirates joined. Booth fitted the *Speaker* out with 54 guns, 260 men including 20 blacks, and White was elected quartermaster. Booth was again elected captain, and they sailed the short distance to Madagascar to fit out the ship for more pirating. They then sailed for Zanzibar for supplies and goods, arriving in late 1700. At 'Zanguebar' the pirates celebrated, while Booth accepted an invitation from the local governor. However, Booth and 20 of his entourage were killed by the governor's men, while others managed to escape. They elected John Bowen as their new captain and made for the Red Sea where a Moorish ship was taken, earning the pirates £500 a man.

John Bowen (d.1705) – the Creole Captain

Born on Bermuda, and thought to be of Creole origin, John Bowen was on an English ship when it was captured by French pirates and forced to sail to Madagascar. However, the vessel ran aground on a reef near the island. In the confusion, Bowen and others took a longboat and sailed approximately 45 miles to St Augustine. After about 18 months, Bowen took up piracy, becoming George Reed's sailing master, and they took a large Indian ship. After splitting the loot at Madagascar, we next find Bowen sailing with George Booth, and in April 1699 they took the 450-ton, 50-gun *Speaker*. At this time Thomas Howard joined the ship, which Booth made his new flagship. Bowen was elected captain in 1700 when Booth was killed by Arabs on Zanzibar.

Bowen next attacked a fleet of 13 Moorish traders, taking one with cargo worth about £100,000. The *Speaker* continued taking ships off the Malabar Coast, and in November 1701 took Captain Conway's East Indiaman off the port of Callequilon (Callicoon). Bowen sold the captured ship in three shares to merchants at Callequilon.

After Bowen also sold the East Indiaman's cargo, in late 1701, the *Speaker* was sailing for Madagascar when it was wrecked on St Thomas's Reef, off Mauritius. Bowen and the survivors were treated well by the French governor, and bought a sloop, fitting it out as the pirate brigantine *Content*. Bowen presented the governor with gifts and sailed to Madagascar's east coast, to fortify and use as a pirate haven, which they named Fort Maratan. In early 1702 Bowen captured Captain Drummond's *Speedy Return* and an old brigantine that Drummond was intending to convert to a 'blackbird' (slave ship). Bowen took both ships, and soon after burned the brigantine at Augustine Bay, after she was damaged on rocks. The *Content* also ran aground, but Bowen's new ship, the *Speedy Return* was safely anchored off the Mascarene Islands. At Augustine Bay Bowen examined the *Content,* found it to be rotten, and burnt it. Bowen now searched for other pirates to form a convoy and around Christmas 1702 found his former comrade Thomas Howard captaining the *Prosperous* at Mayotte.

Operating from the port, they plundered the Indian Ocean, and between March and July 1703 sacked the English East Indiaman *Pembroke*, near the Comoros Islands. In August 1703 Bowen and Howard attacked two Indian ships in the Red Sea, capturing the largest one. At Rajapura, Bowen and Howard found that their ships were unsound and burned the *Speedy Return* and the *Prosperous*, using a captured prize as their new ship, calling her *Defiant*. With 160 pirates and 56 guns, the powerful *Defiant* was off the Malabar Coast when she once again plundered the *Pembroke* of its new cargo. They shared the £70,000 loot, amounting to approximately £500 per man, at Rajapura, on the coast of Gujarat, and Bowen and 40 other pirates left for a civilian life on the French island of Bourbon (later called Réunion). Thomas Howard married there, but others wanted to return home. Within six months Bowen died of colic and was buried on the island. 'On March 13, 1705, a sudden attack of colic carried him off, before he had time to utter a single word,' and a local priest refused to bury Bowen as he was considered a heretic, so 'a simple grave in the underbrush was Bowen's final resting place.' In the 2007 volume *X marks the spot: the Archaeology of Piracy*, author Patrick Lizé relates the story of Mauritius and the wreck of the *Speaker*, 'the first pirate ship to be investigated archaeologically'. Nathaniel North now captained, but soon lost, the *Defiant*.

Thomas White (d.1708) – the Reluctant Pirate

Charles Ellms devotes a chapter in *The Pirates Own Book* to White, born in Plymouth, England. White served aboard a man-of-war, moved to Barbados, married, and eventually captained a merchant brigantine, *Marygold*. He made two voyages to the African Guinea

Coast, but around 1698 on his third trip, with some other ships, was taken by French corsairs. His ship was now used by the pirates, and he with other captains and useful men were taken aboard for their use as sea 'artists'. Ellms writes: 'I beg leave to take notice of their barbarity to the English prisoners, for they would set them up as a butt or mark to shoot at; several of whom were thus murdered in cold blood, by way of diversion.' They were going to use White as target practice, but a French pirate had become friendly with White and saved him, being himself shot and killed by mistake. The drunken crew then ran their ship aground off Madagascar, and White escaped to the shore in the longboat with Captain Boreman, Captain John Bowen and some of their crews. They stole a native boat and were welcomed at St Augustine Bay, 10 miles away, by a local chief. After 18 months, tiring of provisioning them, the chief placed them on a passing pirate ship captained by William Read. White was now 'forced' to become a pirate in Read's crew of about 40 men.

Read's expanded crew was fairly successful in the Indian Ocean and the Red Sea, his 60-ton brigantine taking a 200-ton 'grab' (a one-masted ship) in the Persian Gulf. Desperately searching for treasure, they threw all the bales of cargo overboard, including one that they later discovered contained gold. Captain Read died, succeeded by Captain James, and the brigantine being rotten they sailed to Mayotte. There they took the masts from the brigantine, and fitted them on the grab. After staying on the island for the six-month monsoon season, they then sailed for Madagascar. White stayed in Methelage, becoming friendly with the local king, then signed on as a quartermaster on the pirate Thomas Howard's *Prosperous*. Howard's ship, with Bowens', took several rich prizes in 1703. Most of the crews retired in India or on Mauritius, but White and the remainder of the crew sailed to Madagascar under Nathaniel North. North then abandoned White with 30 other members of the crew who had gone ashore for provisions.

In 1704, White refitted a small abandoned ship, was elected captain and plundered several Indian ships and a Portuguese merchantman in the Red Sea. In August 1706, two English ships were taken and the pirates earned around £1,200. In 1707 White joined the pirate John Halsey as his quartermaster and took part in all of his voyages. In early 1708, the now alcoholic White died at Madagascar after becoming ill with the flux 'which in about five or six months ended his days.' White provided for a son whom he had had with a native woman and asked that the three guardians chosen for the boy, all of different nationalities, ensured that he was put aboard an English ship, bound for England to be educated and 'be brought up in the Christian religion.' White was buried with the full ceremonies of the Church of England, his sword and pistols carried on his coffin, and three English and one French volley fired over his grave.

Thomas Howard (*fl.*1698–1703) – 'a Morose Ill Natur'd Fellow'

It is thought that Howard arrived in Jamaica to seek his fortune in 1698, after squandering his inheritance. Penniless, with some others, Howard stole a small canoe, then a small boat, and the pirates upgraded their vessel with each prize until they possessed a 24-gun ship. Howard was elected quartermaster, and for the remainder of 1698, they attacked settlements and shipping on the North American Atlantic seaboard, before following the trade winds and currents to Africa. After raiding the west coast of Africa, they sailed to Madagascar in 1699. Approaching the island, the pirates spotted a ship aground on a reef, which they took and refloated. However, after hunting for food, the crew abandoned Howard on Madagascar, sailing into the Indian Ocean. An alternative version of this story is that Howard's ship was stranded, and while the pirates were trying to dislodge her, Howard sailed off with treasure in the ship's longboat. It would make his marooning more plausible. Howard was rescued by George Booth in early 1701 and, after Booth's death at Zanzibar, sailed under John Bowen. Howard was later stranded on the *Speaker*, wrecked on St Augustine's reef, and settled on Mauritius for a time.

There, he recruited pirates and around Christmas 1702 was captain of the 36-gun ship *Prosperous*, meeting John Bowen again at the port of Mayotta (Mayotte). Joining forces, they seized the East Indiaman *Pembroke* in March 1703, off Johanna Island in the Comoros Islands. Bowen left to career his *Speedy Return*, but rejoined Howard in August 1703 in the Red Sea. They took two Indian ships worth about £70,000. The pirates took the better of the great ships as their new flagship, and the crews of Howard and Bowen merged. Bowen was elected captain of the 56-gun ship renamed the *Defiant*, and sailed to the port of Rajapura to divide the treasure. The now wealthy Howard remained in Rajapura when Bowen left, and married a local woman. Charles Johnson (Defoe) writes: 'Howard married a Woman of the Country, and being a morose ill natur'd Fellow, and using her ill, he was murder'd by her Relations.'

Nathaniel North (*fl.*1689–1709) – The Pirate who served alongside Dirk Chivers, Robert Culliford, Samuel Inless, George Booth, John Halsey and John Bowen

Born in Bermuda, and probably a Creole, Nathaniel North was said to have sailed on a privateer in 1689, in the Nine Years' War (1688–1697). However, he was then forcibly impressed by the Royal Navy and escaped to Jamaica to return to privateering. Again taken by the Navy, he jumped overboard and swam ashore. In 1696, he was aboard the privateer that captured the 18-gun *Pelican* off Newfoundland. With a letter of marque to attack the French in West Africa, instead the *Pelican* sailed to Madagascar, chasing Arab and Indian ships. Failing, the pirates raided villages in the Comoros Islands. Upon returning to Madagascar, the experienced North was elected quartermaster, and the *Pelican* allied with Robert Culliford and Dirk Chivers to take the *Great Mohammed* in September 1698. Chivers and Culliford refused to equally share the booty, claiming that the *Pelican* had not fully taken part in the battle. The *Pelican* set sail for the coast of India, and seized three small ships, keeping one and renaming her *Dolphin*. The *Pelican* and *Dolphin* were damaged in a hurricane, forcing them back to Madagascar for repairs, and when their treasure was divided, each of the pirates received about £700.

North now sailed as quartermaster under Samuel Inless, the newly elected captain of the *Dolphin*. They took a large Danish ship in 1699, sailing to St Mary's Island to divide their loot, with each share amounting to £400. There, Inless was forced to burn the *Dolphin*, rather than surrender to four English warships. Several men accepted a pardon, but North fled to Madagascar with George Booth and others in the ship's longboat. The longboat was said to be overturned during a storm, with some of the pirates swimming to shore but losing all their possessions.

In 1701, North began raiding settlements on the Comoros Islands, and held the Sultan of Mayotte for ransom. He served as a quartermaster alongside George Booth from 1701 until late 1703, until Booth was killed, when he sailed under John Bowen. North was elected captain of the brigantine *Defiant* after Bowen retired at Mauritius in 1703, and frequently intervened in the native wars, to gain slaves and women. In 1707 we find North serving as a quartermaster in James Halsey's frigate *Charles*, which took two English ships. Halsey took one, and returned to Madagascar, leaving North as captain of the *Charles*. However, North was wrecked on a reef soon after, and returned to

Madagascar, living with the King of Maratan. In 1709 North settled in Ambonavoula, Madagascar, where he traded with Mauritius and acquired slaves from Johanna. North commanded a pirate base at Ambonavoula, where he died some time after 1709, apparently murdered in his bed by irate natives, with whom he and his gang of pirates were at war.

David Williams (*fl.*1698–1709) – the Welsh Captain Tortured to Death

The son of a Welsh farmer, David Williams was recorded as being a morose character, who 'knew as little of the sea or of ships as he did of the Arts of natural Philosophy'.* A seaman on a merchant ship bound for India, probably the *Mary*, an East Indiaman out of Bristol, he was accidentally left on Madagascar. Williams found employment in fighting for native chiefs in an inter-tribal battle. He fought so well that he was befriended by the king, but a short time later this tribe was wiped out and Williams was taken prisoner. The king of this next tribe, knowing of Williams' reputation, made him leader of his army, but Williams was again captured, by another king named Dempaino. He was now made commander-in-chief of an army of 6,000 men, and supplied with slaves, expensive clothing and all his needs.

Escaping, he sailed on the Rhode Island privateer *Pelican* in 1698, and then joined the *Mocha* under Robert Culliford, possibly around May 1698, when the pirate was at St Mary's Island, off Madagascar. Culliford took £2,000 in cash from a French ship there, to add to his previous record of other European, Indonesian and Chinese captures, and also took on scores of the crew of his former captain, William Kidd. Culliford now sailed off in the *Mocha*, with Dirk Chivers' *Soldado* and the *Pelican*. Chivers and Culliford plundered the *Great Mohamed* in the Red Sea in September 1698. There was £130,000 in cash, each crewman receiving £700. Another prize was taken, and the ships sailed to St Mary's in February 1699.

In September 1699, the crew of the *Mocha* split up at Madagascar, sinking the *Soldado* when British warships arrived. All of the 24 pirates who took the offer of a pardon seem to have been hanged in London, except for Culliford and Chivers. Culliford was kept alive to testify against Samuel Burgess. At Madagascar, Williams had not trusted the pardon offer, and instead helped George Booth take a French ship.

* Gosse, Philip, *The Pirates' Who's Who*, Burt, Franklin, NY 1924.

Booth's *Dolphin* was trapped at St Mary's Island in 1699, and burned, but her crew escaped to Madagascar. They then joined up with John Bowen, and Williams sailed on the *Speaker* until it was wrecked in 1701. He returned to Madagascar, and joined Thomas Howard's *Prosperous* in 1702. However, he was accidentally left behind yet again when Howard attacked a Dutch trader on the island. According to Gosse, and details are entangled here, Williams was next captured by the Dutch pirate Ort van Tyle, who was sailing out of New York. Van Tyle was an associate of the Welsh pirate Captain James, and they both roamed the coasts off Madagascar and the Indian Ocean. He put his prisoners to work on his Madagascar plantation as slaves, and David Williams worked there for six months before making his escape to a friendly tribe in the neighbourhood. He lived with Prince Rebaiharang's tribe for a year, then joined a Dutchman named Pro, who had a small settlement on the island. Williams was arrested by a naval frigate, HMS *Severn*, in November 1703, but escaped with Pro, taking a boat from the Comoros Islands in February 1704. The *Severn* and the *Scarborough* had been sent at the request of the East India Company on a 'search and destroy' mission against the pirates infesting the waters around Madagascar.

Williams now joined Thomas White's pirates at Methelage, in Madagascar, and became Captain White's quartermaster in 1704. White had been captured with John Bowen back in 1698, and had been Thomas Howard's quartermaster. Williams was present when several more ships were taken in the Red Sea, as White sailed in consort with Captain Halsey, before dying of fever. White had married a local woman of Methelage, and died in her arms in 1708, reportedly of 'excessive drinking and other irregularities'. A Bostonian, Halsey had a commission to raid French and Spanish shipping in 1704, but turned from privateer to pirate in 1705, taking the 10-gun *Charles* to Madagascar. In 1706, he was deposed by pirate council for cowardice, when he refused to attack a large Dutch ship. However, when the Dutch ship attacked the *Charles*, he was quickly reinstated as captain. Williams became John Halsey's quartermaster in 1707, making a fortune. Two coastal merchant ships were taken in February 1707 at the Nicobar Islands. At Mocha, in the Red sea, in August 1707, the pirates attacked a fleet of five British ships, with a total of 62 guns.

The fleet scattered, but Halsey took two of the vessels, with £50,000 worth of cash and cargo. In January 1708, the *Greyhound* and *Neptune* arrived at Madagascar to trade alcohol and other provisions, but a hurricane wrecked Halsey's pirate ships and their prizes. With the assistance of Samuel Burgess, first mate on the Scottish ship *Neptune* and a former privateer, the pirates now took over the *Neptune* and plundered the *Greyhound*. (Culliford had testified against Burgess in his London trial, but Burgess was mysteriously pardoned in 1702). Halsey became captain of the *Neptune*, and Burgess made quartermaster as his reward. On Halsey's death from fever in 1708, Burgess was voted out as quartermaster, and Williams became the captain of the *Neptune*. However, another hurricane wrecked the ship before he could leave Madagascar. Undeterred, Williams and 10 pirates fitted out a small sloop and sailed for Mascarenas Island. Missing the island, they sailed around Madagascar to Methelage, where Williams laid up the boat for a year, dealing in slaves with Burgess and others.

The local king, annoyed by Williams's irrational outbursts of temper, ordered him to leave, but prevailing winds meant that Williams could not reach his intended destination on the north of the island but was forced into the port of Boyne, just a few miles from Methelage, and still within the king's realm. Boyne was noted for its Arab trade, and Williams anchored offshore, intending to see its Arab Governor. He took a canoe inshore and asked for directions to Kings Town, but an ambush had been laid. Defoe states that his 13-year pirate career came to an end in 1709:

When they had left the Boyne, Williams and Meyeurs, a Frenchman, who also came ashore in the canoe, went to buy some Samsams, which are agate beads; and as they were looking over these goods, a number of the Governor's Men came about them, seized them both and immediately dispatched Meyeurs, Williams they bound, and tortured almost a whole day, by throwing hot Ashes on his Head and in his Face, and putting little Boys to beat him with Sticks; he offered the Governor $2,000 for his life, but he answered he'd have both that and the money too; and accordingly when he was near expiring, they made an end of him with lances.

Williams' former friend and benefactor, King Dempaino, revenged his death by sacking the Arab town and executing its chief with lances.

Christopher Condent (*fl.*1718–1720) – 'Billy One-Hand'
Also known as William, Edmond, or John, Christopher Condent's surname was also spelt Congdon, Condell or Connor, and he was born in Plymouth, Devon. He appears to have been a quartermaster

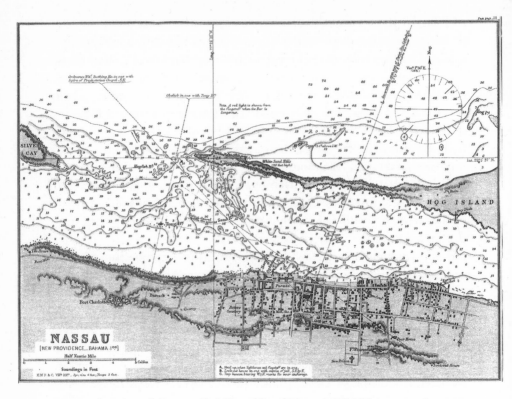

Nassau, location of the so-called 'Republic of Pirates' 1706-18.

on a 'New York merchant' ship, and was at New Providence Island, Nassau, when Woodes Rogers arrived in 1718 offering royal pardons to English pirates. Condent's anonymous captain almost immediately sailed off aboard his 'merchant' vessel, a 12-gun sloop, to cross the Atlantic. A Native American member of the crew had been mistreated, and threatened to blow up the ship, locking himself in the powder magazine. Condent jumped into the hold through a hatch, and was shot in the arm by the Indian, but shot the Indian in the face with his pistol. It may be from his incident that a disability gave rise to his nickname of 'Billy One-Hand'. The rest of the crew hacked the body to pieces, and it is reported that the gunner removed the heart from his chest cavity, cooked it and served it for supper. The crew then captured a merchant ship called the *Duke of York*. There seems to have been an argument, and Condent took captaincy of the new prize. He sailed toward the Cape Verde Islands and took a Portuguese ship carrying wine.

Sailing to the Isle of Mayotte in the Comoros, he took the whole salt fleet, consisting of 20 sailing ships, and now decided to administer justice to the officers of the ships. If any crewman of the ships had any complaint against the officers' treatment of them, the officers were whipped and their wounds soaked with vinegar. Taking what provisions and valuables he wished and augmenting his crew with forced men, Condent departed for St Jago and captured a Dutch privateer, renaming the sloop the *Fiery Dragon* (also called by some the *Flying Dragon*), and taking it as his personal flagship. The pirates headed next to the coast of Brazil, where they took several Portuguese prizes. Condent specialised in torturing their crews, slitting off their noses and ears. Condent usually pretended to be a friendly English merchant ship to sail close to his victims.

The next ship taken was the *Wright* galley, commanded by John Spelt of Plymouth. Condent kept the *Wright* for some time as a consort. They took another Portuguese merchant and a Dutch East Indiaman of 26 guns, before making for the Island of Ferdinando and careening his three ships. Condent now freed Captain Spelt and several of the forced men, giving Spelt some cargo from the Portuguese ship. After a failed attempt to take a 70-gun Portuguese man-of-war, during which Condent's sailing skills helped the pirates escape, they took another Portuguese ship and turned for the Gold Coast. Off the Guinea coast the pirates captured the *Indian Queen* and came across a 44-gun Dutch ship and the English *Fame* in Loango Bay, scaring them both into beaching. Salvaging the Dutch ship, Condent then headed for the East Indies taking an Ostend East Indiaman and Dutch East Indiaman before setting course for Madagascar and St Mary's Island.

Condent sailed to the Indian Ocean, to the island of Johanna near Madagascar. There he took on some former crew of the pirate John Halsey, who had died in 1716. Their experience helped him learn trading routes in the Indian Ocean and the Red Sea. Condent began taking East Indiamen, now using the nearby pirate haven of St Mary's Island as his base from April 1719. His greatest prize was a galley carrying the Viceroy of Goa, taken around October 1720 off the coast of Bombay. It was a huge treasure-filled Arab ship worth about £150,000. Because of its tremendous value, Condent ordered the crew not to abuse any of the captives – there was an increased Royal Navy presence in the area, and he did not wish to anger the British East India Company even further. Gosse writes that Condent took the ship to Zanzibar where 'they plundered her of a large amount of money.' Returning to St Mary's Island, Captain Condent divided the loot, giving each pirate up to £3,000. Some settled on Madagascar, but Condent and about 20 others petitioned the French Governor of Mauritius (or Réunion), for a pardon. The governor agreed if the pirates broke up their ship on arrival. Condent married the governor's sister-in-law, and Gosse writes, 'A few years later, the captain and his wife left the island and sailed to France, settling at St Malo, where Condent drove a considerable trade as a merchant.'

St Mary's Island (Île Sainte-Marie) was a pirate haven, as it was near the routes sailed by richly-laden ships returning from the East Indies. It possesses many bays and inlets, protected from storms, had abundant fruit and was situated in relatively quiet waters. Condent, Kidd, Culliford, Levasseur, Every, Tew and Abraham lived on the Île aux Forbans, an islet in the bay of Sainte Marie's main town, Ambodifotatra. It is thought that several pirate vessels still lie in the Baie des Forbans, one of which may be Condent's *Fiery Dragon*.

Benjamin Johnson (*fl.*1750–60) – 'the Brahmin Bashaw'

Philip Gosse in 1924 wrote *The Pirates' Who's Who: Giving Particulars of the Lives and Deaths of the Pirates and Buccaneers*, and along with Defoe's work, stimulated an interest in pirates that has lasted until this day. His entry on Benjamin Johnson is typical:

> Benjamin Johnson tortured many of his victims until they died. When he attacked the town of Busrah [Basra in Iraq], he slew the sheik and most of the residents before returning to the Sultan of Ormus with the hold of his ship laden with diamonds, pearls, and gold. At an island on the edge of the Persian Gulf, he slaughtered 2,000 priests; all but one out of 700 dancing girls had their noses cut off and their upper lips split. He spared the most beautiful one this ordeal only to abduct her. He also stole treasure amounting to 5,000,000 rupees. On the way home, he plundered an East Indiaman from England and killed her crew. At some point, he decided he no longer wished to serve the Sultan of Ormus. Stealing his master's fastest ship, into which he stowed enormous wealth amounting to £800,000, he sailed to Constantinople, where he became a bashaw [pasha]. Although many lost their lives by his hand, he lived a long life and died naturally.
>
> When a lad he had served as a midshipman in an East Indiaman, the *Asia*, but having been caught red-handed robbing the purser

of brandy and wine, he was flogged and sent to serve as a sailor before the mast. In 1750, while in the Red Sea, he deserted his ship and entered the service of the Sultan of Ormus. Finding Johnson to be a clever sailor, the Sultan appointed him admiral of his pirate fleet of fourteen vessels. The young admiral became a convert to Brahminism, and was ceremoniously blessed by the arch-priests of the Temple. Amongst his crew Johnson had some two hundred other Englishmen, who also became followers of Brahmin, each of whom was allowed, when in port, a dancing girl from the Temple. Johnson proved a most capable and bloodthirsty pirate, playing havoc with the shipping of the Red Sea, taking also several towns on the coast, and putting to death his prisoners, often after cruel tortures. His boldest exploit was to attack the fortified town of Busrah. This he did, putting the Sheik and most of the inhabitants to death, and taking back to his master, the Sultan, vast plunder of diamonds, pearls, and gold.

On another occasion Johnson landed his crews on the Island of Omalee, at the entrance to the Persian Gulf, a favourite place of pilgrimage, and raided the temples of the Indian God Buddha. Putting to death all the two thousand priests, he cut off the noses and slit the upper lips of seven hundred dancing girls, only sparing a few of the best looking ones, whom he carried away with him along with plunder worth half a million rupees. On their way back to the Red Sea the pirates met with an English East Indiaman, which they took and plundered, and Johnson, remembering his previous sufferings in the same service, murdered the whole crew. Shortly afterwards Johnson and ten of his English officers contrived to run away from their master, the Sultan, in his best and fastest lateen vessel, with an enormous booty. Sailing up to the head of the Persian Gulf, Johnson managed to reach Constantinople with his share of the plunder, worth £800,000. With this as an introduction, he was hospitably received, and was made a bashaw, and at the end of a long life of splendour died a natural death.

Amaro Rodríguez Felipe y Tejera Machado (3 May 1678–14 October 1747) – Amaro Pargo, 'the Spanish equivalent of Francis Drake'

Amaro Pargo (his family name) was born to a wealthy family in San Cristóbal de La Laguna, Tenerife, and three of his sisters became nuns. In 1701 he was second lieutenant on the king of Spain's galley *Ave María*, sailing between the Caribbean and Cadiz, when it was attacked by pirates. Pargo asked his captain to pretend to surrender, but to

Amargo Pargo.

begin fighting upon a given signal, and the pirates were beaten. The captain, in gratitude for his advice, requested that Pargo be given his own ship, and with it he began operating in the slave trade from Africa to South America. King Philip V now gave him a letter of marque to enable him to attack unfriendly shipping. From 1703 to 1705, Pargo is recorded as captain and master of the frigates *Ave María* and *Las Ánimas* in the Spanish *Flota de Indias* (the West Indies Treasure Fleet, also called the silver fleet or plate fleet.) In this great convoy he is known to have sailed between Tenerife and Havana, and he began building up his own fleet of privateers.

Pargo also used his ships to sell his own brandy and wine in Havana and Guyana, while constantly attacking and looting any English or Dutch ships he encountered. He is said to have fought Blackbeard, and boarding a great ship from Jamaica fought her captain with sabres and pistols. The duel ended with the captain seriously wounded and Pargo with only a cut on his fingers. Pargo also fought Barbary corsairs in the waters off the Canary Islands. In January 1725, in Madrid, for the loot he had brought into the kingdom, and his services to Spain, Philip V raised Pargo to the nobility as a *hidalgo* (a noble without a hereditary title). The king also made him a *'señor de soga y cuchillo'*, a title giving him the authority to punish, even with the death penalty. In addition, he was declared a 'gentleman' in 1725 and obtained a certification of nobility and royal arms in 1727. As a privateer, he protected the treasure route between the Caribbean and Cadiz, attacking foreign ships, and was regarded as 'the Spanish equivalent of Francis Drake'. One of the most important men in 18th-century Spain, Pargo was also an excellent businessman, noted for his aid to the poor and for many religious donations.

Pargo became the richest man in the Canary Islands, and died in his home town of Laguna, Tenerife, being buried with great ceremony in the family tomb in Santo Domingo de Guzman Convent. His marble headstone shows the family shield, and a skull and crossbones with a winking right eye. In his will Pargo described a carved chest that he kept in his ship's cabin. He stated that it contained gold, silver, pearls, precious stones, jewellery, rare porcelain, silks and paintings, all itemised in a book wrapped in parchment and marked with the letter 'D'. Both the chest and book are missing, and one of his houses, in Machado, Rosario, Tenerife, was ransacked by treasure hunters. It has been suggested that his booty is in the Cave of San Mateo, Punta del Hidalgo, in the northeast of Tenerife. His tomb was exhumed by Ubisoft Montreal, for input into their pirate video game series *Assassins' Creed*, and a supervisor of the company claimed that Pargo was 'a character who in his time had the same reputation and popularity as Blackbeard or Francis Drake'.

James (John) Plantain (*fl.*1715–1728) – 'The King of Ranter Bay'

The author Clement Downing served on a variety of ships in the Indian Ocean as an officer in the British Navy, working for the East India Company, and from 1721 was a lieutenant on the sloop *Emilia*, sailing in consort with the *Hunter* in the Indian Ocean. In his *A Compendious History of the Indian Wars; with an Account of the Rise, Progress, Strength, and Forces of Angria the Pyrate* (1737), he tells us that Bart Roberts (*q.v.*) sailed with Edward England (*q.v.*) and James Plantain. During his ship's efforts to counter piracy, Downing landed at the pirate settlement at 'Ranter Bay', Rantabe, a riverine harbour in north-east Madagascar. The pirate leader, John Plantain from Chocolate-Hole, Jamaica, called himself the 'King of Ranter Bay', virtually ruling over all of Madagascar. It seems he went to sea aged 13, fell in with Rhode Island pirates, and sailed with Edward England's pirate flotilla when it parted from Roberts (recounted in the section upon Roberts). England captured the East India Company ship *Cassandra* from Captain James Macrae in 1720 and after looting the ship the pirates sailed to Madagascar and divided their plunder. Plantain and a number of others remained behind, and he moved to Rantabe, befriending Malagasy natives and using slaves to build a settlement and heavily defended 'castle' on the cliffs.

Hundreds of pirates came to support Plantain, and he subjugated rival leaders or kings until the entire island paid tribute to him. He organised local Malagasays to make war against their neighbours, using firearms to decide battles. Plantain and his allies traded with passing ships of all nations, offering food, water, supplies, and slaves in exchange for guns, gunpowder, shot and clothes. Plantain and his men took multiple Malagasay wives. A naval squadron visited Madagascar in 1722 looking for England, John Taylor and Olivier Levasseur. Plantain told them that most pirates had left, inviting the officers to visit his settlement. England himself was present, ill and near death, having been deposed from command by the brutal Taylor for being too kind to the *Cassandra's* Captain. Downing relates:

News of the Indian Seas being incumbered with Pyrates of our Nation, so far alarmed the Court of Directors, as to petition the Crown to grant a Squadron of Men of War to be sent thither to suppress them, who for near two Years continued to infest those Parts... They made the Island of Madagascar their Rendezvous, where they committed all manner of Enormities, and every one did as his own vicious Heart directed him... Plantain, James Adair, and Hans Burgen, the Dane, had fortified themselves very strongly at Ranter-Bay; and taken possession of a large Tract of Country. Plantain having the most Money of them all, called himself King of Ranter-Bay, and the Natives commonly sing Songs in praise of Plantain. He brought great Numbers of the Inhabitants to be subject to him, and seem'd to govern them arbitrarily; tho' he paid his Soldiers very much to their Satisfaction. He would frequently send Parties of Men into other Dominions, and seize the Inhabitants Cattle. He took upon him to make War, and to extort Tribute from several of the petty Kings and his Neighbours, and to increase his own Dominions...

This Plantain's House was built in as commodious a manner as the Nature of the Place would admit; and for his further State and Recreation, he took a great many Wives and Servants, whom he kept in great Subjection; and after the English manner, called them Moll, Kate, Sue or Pegg. These Women were dressed in the richest Silks, and some of them had Diamond Necklaces... The chief Weapon used by the Natives is the Lance, which they are very dexterous in throwing. But Plantain had got some hundreds of Firelocks, which he distributed among his Subjects, and had learned them to exercise in a pretty regular manner. He also had great Store of Powder and Ball, and a good Magazine provided with all manner of Necessaries. He was a Man of undaunted Courage ... these Pyrates live in a most wicked profligate manner, and would often ramble from Place to Place, and sometimes have the Misfortune of meeting some of the Natives, who would put them to lingering Deaths, by tying their Arms to a Tree, and putting lighted Matches between their Fingers; that they served two of his Ship-Mates in the like manner, and would stand and laugh at them during the time of their Agonies. This I think was a just Retaliation to the Pyrates for the inhuman Barbarities they are guilty of...

The Wars between Plantain and these petty Princes were carried on for near two Years; when Plantain having got the better of them, put several of his Enemies to Death in a most barbarous manner... King Dick, and all that belong'd to him, were taken by Plantain; however the Lady on whose account these Wars were begun, prov'd to be with Child by one of the Englishmen which Plantain had murder'd. This so much inrag'd him, that he ordered King Dick to be put to the same cruel Death as the English and Dutchmen had suffered... After he had destroy'd King Dick, and King Kelly, he established two Kings in their stead, leaving them to rebuild and make good what he had demolished. They were also tributary to him, and sent him in every Month, a certain number of Cattle of all sorts that the Places afforded; and they were to keep the Lands in good order, and to pay him Tribute for all sorts of Grain, Sugar-Canes, &c...

Plantain was resolved that he would now make himself King of Madagascar, and govern there with absolute Power and Authority. He kept now near 1000 Slaves, which he employed constantly on the Fortifications of his Castle; and had he acted as Capt. Avery did, would certainly have made a very strong Place of his chief Residence; for Capt. Avery only took to the Island of St. Mary, and seldom or ever troubled the Inhabitants of Madagascar for any thing except Supplies of Provision... Plantain now arrived near Port Dolphin, being resolved to make an end of the War that Summer: In his March he destroy'd several Towns ... putting Men, Women and Children to the Sword...

In 1728 a rebellion threatened his rule and he was forced to flee for his life with his favoured wife, sailing for India in 1728 and serving in the Maratha navy under Conajee Angria (*q.v.*) His ultimate fate is unknown.

Conajee (Kanhoji) Angria (August 1669–4 July 1729) – the Rebel Sarkhel (Admiral)

Also known as Kanhoji Angré, Angria was commander of the Rajah of Mahratta's fleet in 1698, with the title of *Darya-Sáranga*, operating mainly off the 240 miles of coast between Bombay and Vingorla (Vengurla). He came to virtually control this strip of coast as well as up to 40 miles inland. From about 1702 he turned to piracy and in 1704

Kanhoji Angria, courtesy of Pratishkhedekar.

he is described as a 'Rebel Independent of the Rajah Sivajee'. The East India Company ordered Angria to cease his activities. Angria responded that their ships were not his targets, but for the next quarter century he was successful in looting both European and Indian ships, with his warships equipped with up to 40 cannon. In particular, he targeted British ships, holding captives for ransom. In 1707 his fleet attacked the frigate *Bombay*, which was blown up after a brief fight. In about 1710, he was operating from the fortress of Severndroog on the island of Vijayadurg, and extorting protection money from nearly all ships using Bombay. In 1710 Angria took over the Karanja and Kolaba islands near Bombay as his new bases. In 1711 the directors of the East India Company were informed that Angria could take any ship except the largest European ones – 'along the coast from Surat to Dabul he takes all private merchant vessels he meets.' In 1712 he captured two British ships near Karwar. One vessel was an 'armed yacht', with the East India Company's Governor of Bombay aboard. The Company paid a £3,750 ransom for him, as well as agreeing a truce to stop attacks on British merchants.

Angria now attacked Indian vessels trading with Bombay, but in January 1716 the new Governor of Bombay, Charles Boone, was ordered to end Angria's activities, and Angria resumed his raids on English shipping. For the next five years, English fleets failed to take Angria, or his fortifications, and he carried on seizing ships of all nationalities. Angria even blockaded Bombay's harbour, and the Company now paid him £8,750 to agree a peace. The Company's ships were technologically and militarily superior, but could not out-manoeuvre Angria's small, lightweight, faster vessels. Furthermore, their large ships could not pursue the lighter vessels into shoals or shallow estuaries. Again, Angria only stopped pirating for a few months, and beat off the Company's specially built new gunships near Gheriah and Deoghar. By 1721 the situation was so bad that England sent four naval men-of-war carrying 6,000 soldiers, under Commodore Thomas Matthews, to kill Angria at Kolaba Island. However, Angria gave a joint English and Portuguese fleet a humiliating defeat. In December 1723 Commodore Matthews returned to England and was arrested and convicted of trading with Angria's pirates, who now had about 26 fortified bases. Angria's manpower had grown and grown with his successes, with many of his ships having Dutch captains, and hundreds of out-of-work European joined his fleets. The undefeated Angria continued to harass British, Dutch, Portuguese and Indian shipping until his death, aged almost 60, and his pirate empire passed to his two sons, Manajee and Sumbhajee Angria.

Sumbhajee Angria (*fl.*1729–1746), and Toolaji Angria (fl.1743–1756) – the Nose-Slitter

Sumbhajee had taken control of most of his father's empire within six years of his death, allowing his brother Manajee just a small region around Kolaba, south of Bombay. The brothers continued their father's success throughout the 1730s, despite an increased British naval presence and the armed escort of merchant ships. In 1736 Sumbhajee's men plundered the *Derby*, heading for Bombay with all the gold needed for the East India Company to conduct business for the following year. Sumbhajee deployed nine of his ships to attack from the rear, thereby eliminating the possibility of the larger British ship using her guns to fire broadsides. In 1738 Sumbhajee held off an attack by a Dutch fleet including seven men-of-war. In 1740 with 40 to 50 ships and 2,000 men, he tried to seize his brother Manajee's smaller territory, but the East India Company sent a fleet to counter his attack. Sumbhajee's half-brother Toolaji took over in 1743, three years before Sumbhajee's death.

Toolaji was initially successful, but the East India Company formed an alliance with the local Mahratta (Maratha) tribes. A British chronicler wrote that around 1754 Angria no longer remitted his annual tribute to the Maratha state and that instead he 'slit the noses' of the Maratha ambassadors who came to collect it, and sent them back empty-handed. Eventually only a joint Anglo-Maratha force of more than 10,000 troops and 100 vessels was able to finish off the Angria dynasty. Britain began a campaign of successful attacks, destroying all pirate bases until Severndroog and then Bancoote fell to a joint force led by Commodore William James in 1755. James's expert navigational skills around the Indian coastline had led to the successful attack on Severndroog. Another joint assault was carried out in 1756 against Geriah. The Maratha and the East India Company forces converged on the fortress that had once been described as 'impenetrable'. Toolaji surrendered to the Maratha force of 9,000 soldiers, leaving his brother-in-law to defend the fort. Commodore Charles Watson and Colonel Robert Clive (who later commanded at Plassey), commanded 1,350 troops on land and sea. After a night and day of bombardment, Geriah surrendered and was occupied by Clive's men. Toolaji was placed in prison and his fleet destroyed, ending half-a-century of Angrian success.

The Brethren of the Coast

The 'brethren' were a loose coalition of pirates and privateers operating across the Caribbean, Atlantic and the Western coast of the Americas. Sometimes called buccaneers, they were mainly composed of British, Dutch and French Protestant sailors, often operating under letters of marque against the Spanish. Generally based at Tortuga and Port Royal, Jamaica, they operated under rules of behaviour generally codified by Henry Morgan.

William Jackson (*fl.*1639–1643) – Temporary King of Kingston
English buccaneers used Providence Island off the coast of Nicaragua as a base from 1629, and Robert Rich, the Earl of Warwick, formed the Providence Company. In 1631 Captain Anthony Hilton was appointed its first governor, and Tortuga then came under the protection of the Company. In 1634–35 Spaniards invaded and massacred most of the English settlers and buccaneers in Tortuga. In 1637 the Dutch offered to buy (New) Providence for £70,000, but Charles I blocked its sale. In that year Nathaniel Butler replaced Hilton as governor, and in 1638 Spaniards raided again, and slaves revolted in 1639. Spaniards led by Francisco Diaz de Pimienta attacked yet again in 1641, and only a few English escaped to the Mosquito (Miskito) Coast.

William Jackson had been a privateer in the service of the short-lived Providence Island Company from 1639 until the island was lost in 1641. Using Guanaja and Roatan as his bases, in 1641 he took a Spanish slave ship at Trujillo, accepting a ransom for the return of her 8,000 pounds of indigo, 2,000 pieces of eight and two gold chains. In that year he returned to England, selling indigo and sugar to buy supplies for another privateering expedition. Jackson accepted a three-year letter of marque from the Earl of Warwick, Parliament's Admiral of the Fleet, and in 1642 commanded a fleet including captains Samuel Axe, William Rous and Lewis Morris. The Earl of Warwick wanted a punitive strike on the Spanish for their wiping out his colony on Providence.

Commodore William Jackson, in his 350-ton 30-gun flagship *Charles*, sailed into Barbados on 27 September 1642, with Samuel Axe captaining the 240-ton 20-gun *Valentine* and John Newcombe commanding the 140-ton 16-gun *Dolphin*. Jackson recruited 650 men from Barbados and 250 from St Kitts to attack Spanish colonies at Margarita, Puerto Cabello, and Maracaibo. At Margarita Island they were repelled but took a ship. On 14 December, his fleet of five ships and three pinnaces approached La Guairia, but suffering heavy fire from the fort, sailed away. Puerto Cabello was taken by 140 troops and plundered, with six guns being taken. At Dutch Curaçao, they then took on board a pilot who had been on the successful 1641 Dutch invasion of Maracaibo. In December 1642, William Jackson managed to cross the great sandbar, but his bigger ships could not advance across it and pass into Lake Maracaibo. He left his flagship with 120 men in the open sea, and took more than 1,000 men across the shoals, giving the Spanish ample warning to gather 250 musketeers. He circled around them with two groups of 400 men in the evening, and they fled, and Maracaibo was taken on 27 December 1642.

As a result of these delays, Jackson only managed to take some tobacco, hides and sugar, and Maracaibo's residents gave 10,000 pesos for him not to set fire to the city. After sending out foraging parties, Jackson moved to Gibraltar, also on Lake Maracaibo in modern-day Venezuela; but the Governor of Mérida, Felix Fernandez de Guzman, had manned it, and Jackson chose not to attack but to forage for provisions. Then the Venezuelan Governor Fernandez de Fuenmayor arrived in Maracaibo with 400 Spanish troops, 150 natives and guns to find it deserted, and wrote to Jackson, requesting him to withdraw from Spanish waters or to fight. The English chose to sail and were planning to attack Cartagena de Indias, but instead headed for Jamaica.

On 25 March, 1643, his fleet anchored in the harbour of present-day Kingston in the Spanish Colony of Santiago (now Jamaica), and Jackson led 500 privateers against its capital St Jago de la Vega. After heavy fighting, in which he lost 40 men, he took the town. For sparing it from being burnt, Jackson received a ransom from the Spaniards of 200 cattle, 10,000 pounds of cassava bread, and 7,000 pieces of eight. The privateers were so impressed by the beauty of the island, that in one night alone 23 of them deserted to the Spaniards. In May Jackson took a Spanish frigate and on 28 July took Trujillo unopposed, quitting it on 23 September. In October, Captain Wollmer and many of his men were taken by 'cannibals' at Bocas del Dragon and never seen again, and in November Jackson torched the deserted town of Veragua. On 24 November, desperate for provisions, his fleet raided Tolú, Colombia, and took much booty while its inhabitants fled. At Cuba in January, Samuel Axe (*see* next entry) rejoined the fleet. After taking several towns on the coast of the Gulf of Mexico, Jackson returned to England in 1645.

Samuel Axe (fl.1629–1643) – The Defender of New Providence

This English privateer was in Dutch service in the early 17th century, and then sailed to the new colony of (New) Providence in the Caribbean. Captain Axe, a fortifications expert, helped to build Warwick Fort and the town of New Westminster in 1629, and in 1630 a royal patent issued the charter for the Providence Island Company. In 1630 the first settlers arrived at the Puritan colony from Bermuda, with Phillip Bell and Daniel Elfrith, who had been appointed governor and admiral. Axe argued with Elfrith, possibly over the capture of Spanish and Portuguese slavers, and with Abraham Blauvelt (*q.v.*) and Sussex Cammock, left Providence and sailed for Honduras in 1633. He sent the company a 'plan' of the Miskito Coast in 1634. Despite still being employed by the Providence Island Company, in 1635 Axe took Dutch letters of marque. His acts of privateering might have spurred the Spanish into attacking New Providence in July 1635, and he returned to the island to help defend it. Gregorio de Castellar y Mantilla anchored his fleet off New Westminster harbour and demanded the island's surrender, but was beaten off. In response to this, and the Spanish wiping out the English colony at Tortuga earlier that year, Charles I altered his policy and its governor was allowed to issue letters of marque to attack Spain and protect the colony.

'Captain Ax' was documented selling three slaves in New Netherland (New York) in 1636, and also in that year reported to the Providence Company that grass could grow a finger's length in a single night on the island, trying to encourage more settlers. He had been asked to return to Providence to assist against Spanish attacks in 1636, and did so only on condition that Elfrith left the island. In March 1638, Axe's *Relation of the Isle of Providence* noted that if it grew its own provisions the island could maintain 1,500 men, giving a list of the crops and livestock that prospered in the conditions. Like Henry Morgan, Axe viewed it as a base from which not only to plunder Spanish possessions in the New World, but actually to conquer the Spanish and Portuguese and take their riches.

From 1636 to 1641, he privateered across the Caribbean, taking a ship filled with gold, silver, jewels, indigo and cochineal back to England in May 1640. On 29 March 1641 Axe was congratulated by the company for his 'spirited defence' of the island. When Providence was retaken by the Spanish in 1641, the Providence Island Company was dissolved. Axe escaped to St Kitts, and as a vice-admiral, sailed in William Jackson's privateering expedition (*see* above entry) across the Caribbean from 1642 to 1645, attacking Jamaica in 1643. Axe was given a prize on Jackson's expedition to Maracaibo which he named the *Maracaibo*.

Abraham Blauvelt (*fl.*1630–1663) – Map-Maker and Founder of Bluefields

Also recorded as Abraham Blewfields or Bluefields, the Dutch corsair mapped the Atlantic coasts of Honduras and Nicaragua in the early 1630s. The Bluefield River, Bluefields Harbour and Bluefields Town in Nicaragua are named after him. The privateer was in the service of the Dutch West India Company, but sailed to England to look for assistance to establish a colony in the Rama Indian (*see* William Williams' entry) lands at Bluefields. Blauvelt was next known to be captaining his own privateer from 1644, attacking Spanish shipping and using Bluefields Bay in Jamaica, also named after him, as his base. He took his loot to New Amsterdam (now New York), but in 1648 the Peace of Westphalia was agreed between the Spanish and Dutch. Blauvelt was no longer welcome in New Amsterdam because of his reputation, so he sailed to Rhode Island in 1649, where the English were still the enemies of Spain. There he tried to sell off his remaining booty, but its governor instead took one of Blauvelt's prize ships. His crew then began arguing over their shares of the loot, and the wary colonists forced Blauvelt and his men to leave. Blauvelt then captained the French ship *Garse*, before settling back among the Rama Indians, near the Honduras-Nicaragua border of Cape Gracias à Dios.

It is not certain whether at this time Blauvelt used Bluefields Bay again for piracy, but the place, and the Miskito Coast, were a haven for European pirates, with many tactical advantages for attacking Portuguese and Spanish shipping along that coastline and in the Caribbean. They used the Escondido River to rest, careen, repair damage and reprovision. In 1663 Blauvelt heard of Sir Christopher Myngs' plans to organise a raid on the Spanish colony at Campeche Bay in Mexico. With Henry Morgan, he was an active participant in the attack by 14 ships and 1,400 privateers, but may have died then, as he disappears from the records.

Vice-Admiral Sir Christopher Myngs (1620/25–1666) – Henry Morgan's Mentor

Born in Norfolk, England, Myngs (or Mings) joined the Royal Navy as a boy before the English Civil War, and became a captain in Cromwell's Commonwealth Navy. In the First Anglo-Dutch War of 1652–54, captaining the *Elisabeth*, Myngs fought and brought back to port a Dutch convoy, including two men-of-war. He was now given command of the new 52-gun frigate *Marston Moor* in 1655, suppressing an embryonic mutiny with firmness rather than the normal floggings and executions, and in January 1656 became a commander in the naval squadron known as the 'Jamaica Station'. Newly taken by the English from Spain, Jamaica needed defence from Spanish attempts to retake it. Myngs desperately needed assistance, so enlisted local buccaneers as privateers, deciding the best form of defence was attack. Potential Spanish attacks were thus halted by constant raids on Spanish ports and shipping. Myngs and the privateers raided Santa Marta, Venezuela, in May 1656, and he was given full command of the Jamaica Station by January 1657, with instructions to defend Port Royal at all costs.

In October 1658 Myngs narrowly missed taking a Spanish treasure fleet, and sailed on to loot and burn Tolú and Santa Maria in Columbia. Cumana, Puerto Caballos and Coro in Venezuela were plundered and devastated in the following year, and Myngs returned to Jamaica with enormous booty, the attack on Coro alone yielding a large silver shipment. He was spreading terror across the Spanish Main, and the Spanish diverted resources to the defence of their colonies and treasure shipments, instead of concentrating upon taking Jamaica, which now became a haven for pirates of all nationalities. Myngs divided much of the £500,000 treasure between his privateers, instead of

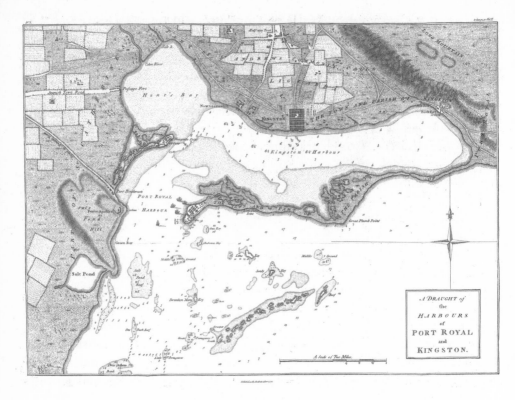

Port Royal, Jamaica, courtesy of the Wellcome Collection.

reserving shares for the Governor of Jamaica and the Commonwealth Government. As a result, he was arrested for embezzlement back in Port Royal, and sent back to England in disgrace in the *Marston Moor* in 1660. However, Charles II had only been restored to the monarchy in 1661 and had no desire to harm a public hero as one of his first acts, and the charges were dropped. By late 1661 Myngs had returned to Port Royal, captaining HMS *Centurion*.

Spain and England were now at peace, but the English carried on using Jamaica as a base to raid Spanish colonies. Charles II's Restoration Government knew that the Spanish were unpopular, and wanted success overseas. His advisors realised that destroying the Spanish infrastructure in the West Indies and the Americas would open up opportunities for England to accrue wealth and influence. Myngs thus promised buccaneers across the Caribbean the opportunity of joining forces for increased plunder. The new Governor of Jamaica agreed, and sacked large numbers of troops, who in their red coats joined Myngs' expeditions. Myngs thus quickly assembled a naval and privateering fleet, destroying the strongly defended port of Santiago de Cuba in October 1662, and capturing six ships. He next commanded a fleet in February 1663, leading eminent privateers such as Edward Mansvelt, Abraham Blauvelt, Henry Morgan and John Morris. It was the largest buccaneer fleet as yet assembled. Approximately 1,400 English, French and Dutch buccaneers captured 14 Spanish ships and 150,000 pesos in treasure at San Francisco de Campeche, Mexico. During the attack Myngs was severely wounded, and he gave Edward Mansvelt charge of his troops.

The Spanish outcry at the raid forced Charles II to forbid further attacks. In 1664 Myngs returned to England to recover from his wounds and in 1665 was promoted to vice-admiral. He fought the Dutch in the Second Anglo-Dutch War at the Battle of Lowestoft in that year, and for his actions was knighted. In June 1666, he was wounded on the *Victory* in the Four Days' Battle, hit twice by musket balls fired by a sharpshooter on the Dutch flagship. 'On the fourth day he was heavily engaged with [Vice-Admiral] De Liefde when he was shot through the throat. He remained standing on deck compressing the wound with his fingers until he fell, shot again through the neck. He died some days later.' The forgotten hero Myngs was described by Samuel Pepys as a 'very stout man, and a man of great parts, and a most excellent tongue among ordinary men.'*

Edward Mansvelt (*fl.*1659–1666) – First Admiral of 'the Brethren of the Coast'

In 1657 the English had beaten off an attack trying to reclaim Jamaica for Spain. The governor Edward D'Oyley desperately needed privateers to help him defend the island and bring in wealth from captured enemy shipping to sustain the new English possession. Also known as Mansveld or Mansfield, the Dutch Captain Mansvelt was given a privateering commission at Port Royal in 1659 by the governor. By 1663 the Governor of Jamaica noted that he had 'eleven frigates and briganteens belonging to Jamaica'. With a total of 740 men and 81 guns, they were now commanded by Sir Thomas Whetstone, with Captains Mansvelt, Swart, Gaye, James, Cooper, Morris, Brenning, Goodler, Blewfield [Blauvelt, *q.v.*] and Herdre. There were also three smaller ships with 100 men and 12 guns, commanded by the Dutch

---

* Royal Museums Greenwich, Flagmen of Lowestoft, prints.rmg.co.uk/products/flagmen-of-lowestoft

Captain Senlove, and four ships with 32 guns from Tortuga, with 258 French privateers, under the command of a Portuguese captain and captains Davis, Buckell and Colstree. Mansvelt fought at Campeche, Mexico, in 1663, taking over command when Myngs was badly injured (*see* above entry).

Jamaica and Tortuga had become real pirate havens for men who attacked Spanish and Portuguese treasure ships and ports. At the end of 1665, Mansvelt led about 200 buccaneers to plunder an unknown Cuban town. As a result, the new Jamaican governor, Sir Thomas Modyford, commissioned him to lead an expedition against the Dutch at Curaçao. Buccaneers were growing in numbers and influence all over the Caribbean and the Spanish Main, but resistance to their attacks strengthened, so it became necessary for them to form themselves into fleets of mixed nationalities under the command of an 'Admiral'. In March 1666, Modyford wrote that 'our Privateers have chosen Capt. Edward Mansveld their Admiral, and a fleet sailed from Jamaica, with privateering commissions, their destination, Curaçao.' However his privateers, many of Dutch them like himself, insisted that the richest prizes were Spanish. According to the contemporary privateer and writer, Exquemelin, instead the fleet plundered the island of Grenada in January 1666, but this is disputed by some historians.

Mansvelt had been elected admiral of a fleet of about 10 ships and 500 men, and sailed to Costa Rica in April 1666 intending to sack the wealthy city of Cartago, several miles inland. However, they were turned back by the Spanish outside the town of Turrialba. Some of his captains departed to return to Tortuga or Jamaica but, with the rest of the fleet, Mansvelt captured the small island of Santa Catalina (St Catherine) in May 1666, and Providence Island. (New Providence, midway between Costa Rica and Jamaica, was now called Providence after being taken by the Spanish, and then confusingly called Old Providence). He wanted to establish a privateering base on the route of the treasure fleets from Portobello. In June 1666 Mansvelt tried to persuade Governor Modyford to send reinforcements to make the island a permanent base for attacks upon the Spanish, but failed to convince him. In August 1666 the Spanish recaptured the island. Exquemelin wrote that Mansvelt now left for Tortuga, but he was probably captured off Cuba, taken to Portobello and executed as a pirate. His second-in-command, Henry Morgan, took over the title of Admiral of the Brethren of the Coast.

Admiral Sir Henry Morgan (c.1635–25 August 1688) – Admiral of the Brethren of the Coast, 'the Sword of England', the Greatest Privateer of All Time

Henry Morgan was a younger son born at Llanrhymney Hall, a mansion and estate to the east of Cardiff. Two of his father's brothers, Edward and Thomas, were opposing colonels in the English Civil War. The eldest brother inherited the estate and the youngest, Henry's father, became a 'gentleman farmer'. Morgan served in Cromwell's 'Western Design' to take Hispaniola in 1654, and when Penn-Venables' unsuccessful expedition instead took Jamaica, he stayed there to seek his fortune. His uncle Colonel Edward Morgan was Lieutenant-Governor of Jamaica, and Henry Morgan married his daughter, Mary. By 1661 Commodore Christopher Myngs had appointed Morgan captain of his first vessel, and Morgan sailed under Myngs in 1663, destroying Santiago de Cuba. Morgan next sailed with John Morris and Captain Jackman in 1665 and they sacked Spanish settlements at Vildemos (on the Tabasco River in the Bay of Campeche, Mexico), Trujillo in Honduras and Granada in

Admiral Sir Henry Morgan.

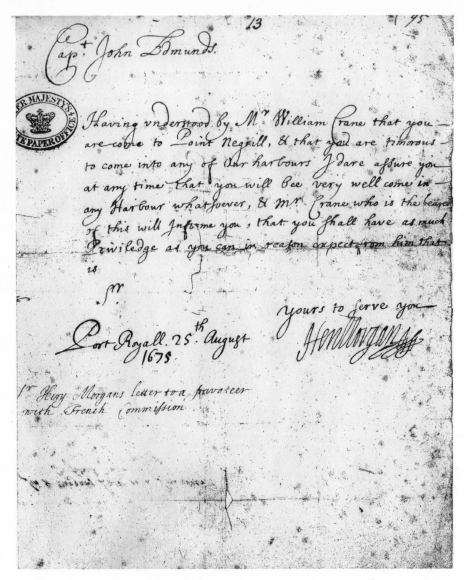

Letter from Henry Morgan to Captain Edmunds, Port Royal Jamaica, 25 August 1675.

Mexico. Lord Windsor, the new Governor of Jamaica, refused to stop his privateers from attacking Spanish ships, believing, like Morgan, that attack was the best form of defence. The pro-Spanish Charles II therefore replaced Windsor with Sir Thomas Modyford, but Modyford again agreed with his friend Morgan, that the only strategy for the English colony to survive, was by weakening the Spanish possessions and shipping that surrounded them. When Morgan returned to Jamaica, Modyford

The Towne of Puerto del Principe taken & sackt

Morgan's attack on Puerto del Principe 1667.

had received letters from Charles II to stop 'piracy' but continued to issue letters of marque to attack Spanish and Dutch shipping.

Modyford now commissioned Edward Mansvelt (*q.v.*) to assemble 15 ships and 500–600 men to attack the Dutch settlement of Curaçao. Morgan had captured several ships off the Mexican coast of Campeche, and was appointed vice-admiral. However, at sea most

Three men-of-war destroyed by Captain Morgan at Lake Maracaibo 1669.

captains decided that Curaçao was not lucrative enough for the risks involved. Many privateers now deserted the expedition, but Mansvelt and Morgan decided to attack Santa Catalina and Providence Island. The Spanish were unprepared and surrendered all their forts, and all but one was destroyed. Privateers remained on the island to gather its wealth, while Morgan and Mansvelt sailed back to Jamaica to gather reinforcements. Modyford appointed his brother, Sir James, as Governor of Providence. Mansfield was captured and killed by the Spanish shortly afterwards, and the privateers elected the impressive Morgan as their new 'Admiral of the Brethren of the Coast'.

With no income except from privateering, it seems that Morgan told Modyford the Spanish were going to attack and capture Jamaica, and his ever-willing friend provided yet another commission, asking Morgan to capture Spaniards in Cuba to interrogate them about the forthcoming 'invasion'. Modyford and Charles II, and the king's brother James as Lord of the Admiralty, took a cut of the profits of any privateering expeditions. However, Morgan had a clause written into his letters of marque that their share would only come from ships taken at sea, not from overland targets, so his men had more loot to share between them.

Morgan assembled 10 ships by sailing to pirate havens and granting commissions, gathering 500 men. He wished to take Havana, but it was too heavily defended, and in 1667 Morgan landed on Cuba to take Puerto Principe. However, a Spanish prisoner that Morgan held hostage escaped, and warned the citizens who quickly deserted the town with their valuables. After searching, only 58,000 pieces of eight were taken, not enough to pay off his Jamaican debts, so Morgan decided to raid the third most important Spanish city in the New World, Porto Bello, well protected by three great Spanish forts. With information from a prisoner, the forts were taken and the city entered. The Spanish counterattacked, but Morgan organised an ambush of the more powerful Spanish fleet in a narrow passage. After two months of sacking and ransoming, his men collected 100,000 pieces of eight and valuables worth another 100,000 pieces of eight. England had sent Modyford HMS *Oxford* to protect Port Royal, and he handed it to Morgan. Attacked by the English authorities, Modyford wrote to them that his commissions were utterly necessary to protect Jamaica, 'proving' his point by giving Morgan another letter of marque.

As many as 900 privateers of all nations, in 11 ships, flocked to join the multilingual and unbeatable Morgan at the Île de Vache off Haiti. His next target, Cartagena, was one of Spain's most defended cities, holding all the gold and silver in transit from Peru to Spain. The captains celebrated the decision, but that night a fuse was accidentally lit on the *Oxford* near the gunpowder stores and the new flagship was blown to oblivion, with several captains dying. Somehow Morgan was rescued from the water and survived. In March 1669 he led 10 ships and 800 men to attack Cartagena. Storms and headwinds meant that his number of crew had dropped to just 500 men, too weak to attack Cartagena, so Maracaibo in Venezuela was selected instead. It was at the inner end of Lake Maracaibo, a huge lake reached through a shallow channel, and protected by a great fort. The fleet could not pass the fort without being destroyed, and Morgan landed to attack it. After several attacks, strangely, it had been abandoned, but a privateer spotted a slow-burning fuse meant to blow up the powder stores, the fort and all the enemy within. Everyone ran away, but Morgan ran towards the fuse and extinguished it. Delays meant that most of the citizens of Maracaibo were able to escape with their valuables into the jungle. Morgan took what he could and set off to attack nearby Gibraltar. After collecting booty and ransoming Gibraltar's residents, Morgan loaded his ships to return to Jamaica. However, the fort had been retaken by the Spanish, and guarding the narrow entrance from Lake Maracaibo to the open ocean were stationed the Spanish men-of-war *Magdalena*, *San Luis* and *Nuestra Señora de Soledad*.

Sending a fireship, Morgan destroyed the *Magdalena*. He captured the *Nuestra Señora de Soledad*, while the *Santa Luisa* was run ashore. Morgan was still unable to cross the channel because of the fort's cannon, but he spent the day in sight of the fort, shifting men in rowboats to the forests onshore. However, they all returned to their ships, hidden on the floor of the boats. The Spanish expected a night attack from inland by all the men who had 'landed', and moved all their cannon from covering the sea passage to the inland side of the fort. That night, Morgan used the tide to drift all his ships through the passage, unnoticed. Afterwards, Morgan returned to Port Royal on 27 May 1669 in his new flagship, *Nuestra Señora de Soledad*. Returning to Jamaica, he was officially reproved but not punished by Modyford, who instead made him commander-in-chief of all the ships of war in Jamaica.

Panama, on the Pacific coast, the richest city in New Spain, had never been taken, and Morgan gathered men to march across the isthmus and sack it. Morgan recaptured the island of Santa Catalina from Spain on 5 December 1670, and on 27 December took the fortress of San Lorenzo, Panama, killing 300 men of the garrison and leaving 23 alive. Morgan left 200 men to guard his ships, and with 1,200 men he advanced through jungle towards the Pacific coast and Panama City. Constantly being ambushed, and suffering sickness, thirst and starvation, by 28 January 1671 the privateers met the Spanish in battle on the plains outside the city. Morgan won the pitched battle against superior forces, and a new city of Panama had to be built after it was set on fire (by the Spanish, not Morgan). The sack of Panama violated a peace treaty, and Morgan was arrested and taken to London in 1672. However, Charles II could not punish his country's greatest hero, known as 'the Sword of England', as his régime was still unstable. His reign had already seen the Great Plague, the Great Fire of London and the Dutch destroying the Royal fleet in the Medway, sailing off with his new flagship. Instead of any punishment, Morgan was fêted across London and knighted in 1674, before returning to Jamaica in 1675 as Lieutenant-Governor.

An account of Morgan's exploits was published by Alexandre Exquemelin, once his confidant, in a Dutch volume entitled *De Americaensche Zee-Roovers* (*History of the Buccaneers of America*). Morgan successfully brought the first libel suit in history against the book's publishers, securing a retraction and damages of £200. This author has translated Exquemelin's account of Morgan's expeditions as *The Illustrated Pirate Diaries – A Remarkable Eye-Witness Account of Henry Morgan and the Buccaneers.* Upon Morgan's death, he was laid in state at the King's House in Port Royal, and all the ships anchored in the harbour fired broadsides in salute. He was buried in Palisadoes cemetery, Port Royal, which sank beneath the sea after the 1692 earthquake. As with 'Black Bart' Roberts, it is almost impossible to do justice to his remarkable career.

John Davis (*fl.*1662–1671) – 'Robert Searle', Henry Morgan's Most Trusted Lieutenant

Probably originally known as Robert Searle, little is known of Davis before he was sailing under Sir Christopher Myngs out of Jamaica. Returning from raiding Santa Marta and Tolú (in today's Colombia), Myngs took four Spanish merchant ships; John Davis took command of the largest, the 60-ton, 8-gun *Cagway*. Davis was its captain in the 1662/63 raid on Santiago de Cuba, again in Myngs' fleet of 12 ships and 1,300 men. Santiago's plunder was taken back to Port Royal. Governor Thomas Modyford had backed the privateers, as his first line of defence against the Spanish, but in early September received a letter from Charles II that 'again strictly commanded [Modyford] not only to forbid the prosecution of such violence for the future, but to inflict condign punishment upon offenders, and to have the entire restitution and satisfaction made to the sufferers.' Davis had taken two rich Spanish ships out of Cuba, anchored them at Port Royal's harbour, and landed boxes of Spanish coinage, in order to assess the king's share. However, Modyford's Jamaican council decided that 'all persons making further attempts of violence upon the Spaniards be looked upon as pirates and rebels, and that Captain Searle's commission be taken from him and his rudder and sails taken ashore for security.' There was a furious argument between Davis and Modyford, as Davis was now prevented from sailing off in the *Cagway* and making any money.

However, Davis was needed at the outbreak of the Second Anglo-Dutch War in 1665, and his ship, sails and rudder were returned to him. Davis then sailed in Colonel Edward Morgan's expedition of nine ships and 650 men to St Eustatius and Sabá in March 1666. Edward Morgan, the corpulent uncle of Henry Morgan, dropped dead, possibly of heatstroke, on arrival at the islands. In 1667, with Captain Stedman, John Davis and 80 men sacked the Dutch island of Tobago and disposed of the loot at Barbados, still distrusting Governor Modyford. In 1668, Davis was at Nassau on New Providence Island in the Bahamas, when the Spanish raided the English colony in retaliation for Henry Morgan's raid on Maracaibo. (Providencia, Providence, New Providence and Old Providence were all names given to an island off Nicaragua, easily confused with this island in the Bahamas). Despite Modyford having again withdrawn all commissions in 1667, Davis led other disgruntled captains to sack the Spanish town of St Augustine in Florida in 1668. There he rescued Henry Woodward, the first English settler of South Carolina, who had been imprisoned by the Spanish. Expecting punishment again from Modyford, as the leader of the raid, Davis refused to sail the *Cagway* into Port Royal and instead anchored off Macary Bay. He was arrested when he went ashore, and was awaiting trial when released to join Morgan's incredible 1671 expedition to take Panama. It may well be that Morgan personally requested Davis' release, being a great friend of Governor Modyford and knowing Davis' quality as a successful captain.

Davis was Morgan's trusted lieutenant, ordered to prevent any Spanish ships from escaping Panama. Having travelled across the isthmus, Davis needed a ship, and discovered a barque lying fast aground, which the Spanish had tried to burn. He quickly made her seaworthy and used her to capture three other ships. He searched for ships hiding in inlets and for loot on offshore islands including Perico, before sailing to the Pearl Islands (Las Islas del Rey). Don Juan Pérez de Guzmán, President of Panama, recorded:

> The English, having got possession of the Relics of our town, found a Bark in the Fasca [harbour], although I had given order that there should be none, yet had they not complied with my command, and when they would have set it on Fire, the Enemy came fast and put it out and with it they did us great damage, for they took three more with it, and made great havoc of all they found in the Islands of Taboga, Otoque, and Las Islas del Rey, taking and bringing from thence many Prisoners.

On Taboga, by accident the privateers captured the seven-man crew of a longboat, sent to fetch water for a Spanish galleon. Davis discovered, by threatening them with torture, that the ship was the 400-ton treasure ship *Santísima Trinidad*. However, he and his men were too drunk to bother taking one of the richest prizes in history. Davis thus earned the hatred of Morgan and his men, who had been busy sacking Panama. Later, according to William Dampier, Davis was killed in a duel with an English logwood cutter in Mexico. The place where this happened, a small islet, the Laguna de Términos at the northern end of Gulf of Campeche, became known as 'Serle's Key.'

Janke Willems (*fl.* 1680–1688) – Captain Yankey, Yankee Williams, 'the Original Yankee'

Also known as Jan Williams, the Dutch 'Captain Yankey' captained a ship in Thomas Paine's 1680 attack on Rio de la Hacha (Paine, *q.v.*). Captain William Wright was also in the raid, and around September 1681 was with Willems as they sailed their ships to Bocas del Toro, taking a Spanish merchant barque carrying tobacco and sugar off the coast of Colombia. Willems took this ship for himself and gave his own to Wright, who burned his own boat. They then sailed for Dutch Curaçao to sell their goods, but its governor refused to allow them to land. Forced to leave, they made for the remote Isla de Aves and the Islas des Roques off Venezuela, where they careened their ships and stayed until February 1682. In 1683, the French privateer Jean Hamlin in *La Trompeuse* was attacking English shipping around Jamaica, and Governor Lynch offered Yankey Williams a free pardon, men, victuals, naturalisation, and £200 if he could catch the French privateer.

In 1683, Captain Yankey joined the 17 May raid on the city of Vera Cruz. With Laurens de Graaf, at night he sailed two captured Spanish galleons into the harbour to land buccaneers on the shore. Most of the Spanish soldiers were sleeping, and the pirates managed to kill all the sentries to allow the rest of the fleet to enter the harbour. Vera Cruz was looted for four days before the privateers retreated when the New Spain Fleet was spotted returning to its home port. After De Graaf had fatally wounded Van Hoorn in a duel and the loot and ransom monies had been shared out, Yankey sailed again with De Graaf, Andrieszoon and François le Sage, plundering Spanish ships off Cartagena in November 1683. De Graaf blockaded Cartagena in 1684 and gave Yankey his flagship after taking three Spanish warships. Willems also attacked Campeche in 1685 in a pirate fleet, and possibly died in the Gulf of Honduras in 1688.

The earliest written definition of 'Yankee' is in the *Oxford English Dictionary*, referring to Captain Yankey Williams. Its origin is probably from the Dutch Janke, a meaning 'little' Jan. Yankee became a generic nickname for Dutch pirates, with the first acknowledgements being Yankee Dutch (1683), Captain Yankey (1684), and Captain John Williams (Yankee) in 1687. The next earliest reference is a 1725 estate inventory, listing a slave named Yankee. The earliest recorded usage of the term for Americans is in a 1758 letter by General James Wolfe, famed from the Battle of Quebec, and used as a pejorative term.

Edward Davis (*fl.*1680–1702) – Circumnavigator, the Earliest Pirate to use Cocos Island as a Safe Haven

Known as a 'gentleman pirate', his later exploits were detailed by William Dampier. He participated in the 1680 expedition led by Bartholomew Sharp and John Coxon, then sailed on a French privateer in the Caribbean under Captain Yankey (*see* above). On Captain Tristian's ship, Davis was in the crew that mutinied at Petit-Goâve, and he is next seen in Virginia selling prizes, where he met Dampier. In August 1683, Davis privateered under John Cook as his navigator or quartermaster. They took the 36-gun *Batchelor's Delight* off Guinea, and rounded Cape Horn for the Pacific in November 1683. In March 1684 they were joined by Captain John Eaton in the *Nicholas* and raided Spanish settlements on the eastern seaboard of South America. Sailing to the Juan Fernandez Islands, they rescued William, a Miskito Indian, who had been accidentally marooned there by Bartholomew Sharp since January 1681. At the Galapagos Islands on 19 July 1684, Captain John Cook died and Davis was elected in his place. After an unsuccessful attack on El Realejo, Nicaragua, he and Captain John Eaton parted company, and further raids in Peru, Chile and Ecuador brought little loot. Davis took some small slavers, and 15 slaves joined his crew.

Off Panama the *Batchelor's Delight* attempted to take Spanish silver ships, and raided coastal settlements in a pirate fleet led by Pierre le Picard (*q.v.*), Francis Grognet and Captain Townley. Sailing south to Ecuador, on 2 October Davis persuaded Captain Charles Swan and Peter Harris to join him in pirating. With their *Cygnet* and some captured vessels, they decided to attack the Peruvian silver fleet off Panama, but were chased off by Spanish warships. After a dispute, Davis and Swan sailed off, and on 1 January 1685 took a packet-boat and discovered the whereabouts of the silver fleet. On 28 May they found it, but much of the cargo had been unloaded. In the indecisive Battle of Panama, the pirates were heavily outnumbered, and captains Swan and Townley left for Mexico. Arriving in November at the Juan Fernández Islands, Davis and Captain Knight divided their spoils, each pirate receiving £1,150, and Knight left.

Davis next raided Sana in March 1686, taking £25,000 in silver and jewels, and kept raiding, with 39 African slaves joining his men.

In other raids he killed priests and officials who would not disclose where there was 'treasure', and the town of Pisco paid £5,000 in ransom to prevent it being burnt. Now with 80 pirates, in February 1687 Davis took £10,000 from Arica, Chile. From prisoners, Davis discovered that a squadron from Peru was being sent against Pierre le Picard (*q.v.*), so he sailed to join le Picard and attack Guayaquil in May 1686. The pirates defeated the Spanish and shared £50,000 in booty. He sailed away on 12 June, reprovisioning at the Galápagos Islands and Juan Fernández Islands. Davis returned to the West Indies in early 1688, then sailed to Philadelphia in May.

Davis, Lionel Wafer and John Hingson were arrested on 22 June 1688 for piracy in Virginia. At his trial four days later, Davis denied everything, stating he had been a resident of Jamaica for seven years. After various submissions, the pirates may have received a royal pardon in exchange for money, but the Council of Virginia ordered the privateers to return to England, and Davis returned in 1690. He successfully undertook actions to have most of his former property and estates returned to him. A royal order in March 1692 gave him most of what he had asked, but £300 was retained by the Crown. Davis is claimed to be the earliest buccaneer to bury treasure, on Cocos Island off Costa Rica, when anchored in Chatham Bay in 1684 and 1702. Men have since searched for chests supposedly containing ingots, pieces of eight and £300,000 in silver bar and plate taken from settlements in Peru and Chile.

Charles Swan (*fl.*1684–1690) – The Captain Almost Eaten by his Crew

Captain Swan was said to have been forced into piracy by his crew, or by Edward Davis, in the 1680s, and he wrote letters to the owners of his ship *Cygnet*, in London, asking them for a pardon from James II. However, at the same time he was looting ships and villages in South America. He burnt Payta in 1684 after not finding much loot, and sailed alongside Edward Davis and Peter Harris, before Davis sailed for Peru. On 25 August 1685 Swan assaulted the silver-mining town of Santa Pecaque, Mexico. He sent 54 men with laden horses back to the anchorage, the famous Basil Ringrose amongst them. However, they were ambushed by Spanish soldiers and the 54 pirates were massacred. Swan returned to the scene, and told William Dampier that they were 'stript, and so cut and mangl'd, that he scarce knew one man.' On 31 March 1686 Swan tried to take a

Manila treasure galleon in the Pacific, but failed and headed for the East Indies. Lacking provisions, 'There was not any occasion to call men to victuals being made ready at noon, all hands were aloft to see the quartermaster share it, wherein he had need to be exact, having so many eyes to observe him. We had two dogs and two cats aboard, they likewise lived on what was given them, and waited with as much eagerness to see it shared as we did.'* A pirate was caught stealing extra rations, and each pirate gave him three lashes across his bare back, beginning with Swan.

Dampier recorded the harrowing details. Crossing nearly 5,000 miles they saw no ships or land until, after 51 days, land was sighted. It was late May. Dampier wrote:

> It was well for Captain Swan that we got sight of it before our provision was spent, of which we had enough for three days more, for, as I was afterwards informed, the men had contrived to kill first Captain Swan and eat him when the victuals was gone, and after him all of us who were accessory in promoting the undertaking this voyage. This made Captain Swan say to me after our arrival at Guam, Ah! Dampier, you would have made them but a poor meal; for I was as lean as the captain was lusty and fleshy.

From Guam, after three weeks the freshly provisioned pirates headed for the Sultanate of Mindanao, which was now out of Spanish control. The pirates spent months living there, but on 14 January 1687 the crew mutinied, forcing Dampier and the surgeon, Henry Coppinger, to accompany them. They left Swan and 36 others behind. Swan had managed to save £5,000 and remained on the island of Mindanao, becoming an officer in its army, but in 1690 tried to flee the island in a passing Dutch ship. He was chased by warriors, who capsized his boat and speared him in the water.

Bartholomew Sharp (c.1650–29 October 1702) and Richard Sawkins (d. May/June 1680) – Leaders of the 'Pacific Adventure'
At his first trial in June 1682, Sharp was described as having been born in the parish of Stepney, around 1650, and of having boasted of being a pirate since a teenager, for some 16 years. Dampier suggests that he was one of William Wright's pirates who plundered Segovia in

---

* Dampier, William, *A New Voyage Round the World* 1697, 1937 reprint, Adam and Charles Black, London.

Bartholomew Sharp's map of South America from his 1680–83 voyages.

Nicaragua in 1675. Sharp next joined other privateer captains in the Gulf of Honduras and on 26 September 1679, they took a Spanish ship loaded with wine, cochineal, cacao, money, silver plate, tortoiseshell and 500 chests of indigo, fencing the goods at Port Royal. In December 1679 a group of captains met at Port Morant, Jamaica, to discuss an expedition. Sharp agreed to join Cornelius Essex, Thomas Maggott, John Coxon, Peter Harris, Edmund Cook and Robert Allison to sack Porto Bello. On 17 January they sailed off and 20 miles out were joined by a pirate brigantine under Jean Rose. They were about to embark upon 'the Pacific Adventure', raiding Spanish settlements on the Pacific coast of South and Central America. The pirate Richard Sawkins had been captured by HMS *Success* and imprisoned in Port Royal awaiting trial for piracy in December 1679. For some reason he was released, as he is then recorded captaining a 16-ton, 1-gun ship with 35 men, joining Sharp's expedition.

In April 1680, seven pirate ships rendezvoused at Golden Island on the north coast of Panama, three of them having recently sacked Porto Bello in 1679 for a large amount of gold. Informed by Indians of a new mining camp on the other side of the isthmus, they left a small force to guard the ships and 331 pirates marched across the isthmus, armed with new French muskets, which were much better than the harquebuses used by the Spanish. Richard Sawkins had been elected to command the expedition, and Darien Indians guided them. William Dampier, Lionel Wafer and Basil Ringrose all wrote accounts of the nine-day crossing through the jungle, to the Gulf of San Miguel and the Pacific Ocean. On 25 April the buccaneers advanced, with 50 Indians in 68 canoes, to the royal mines at Santa Maria. Sawkins led an advance party over the stockade, which killed 26 Spaniards, with only two pirates suffering wounds. There had been a forewarning, however, and three hundredweight of gold was missing, hurried away to Panama City. The Indians killed 50 Spaniard prisoners, and the survivors were tortured to give up a small amount of gold and silver.

On 27 April, command of the expedition was transferred to Coxon, and the angered pirates fired Santa Maria before they rowed to the coast. There they took a bark, which was given to Sharp with 135 men, and then several *piraguas* (dugout canoes with sails). The next day, they took another bark, given to Captain Harris. Sawkins, Harris and Coxon then led 68 men to attack Panama City on 3 May, and came across five large ships and three barks, anchored at the defended port on Perico Island. The 228 Spanish defenders were mainly blacks and mulattoes and they manned the barks. After five hours of fighting, one of the barks sailed off and the other two surrendered. Harris and 20 buccaneers were killed, and the Spanish probably lost more than 100 men. Sawkins was now celebrated for his bravery at the 'Battle of Perico'. Three of the large ships were taken, among them the 400-ton *La Santísima Trinidad*. Renamed *Trinidad*, it was refitted for piracy. (It had actually been the treasure galleon that escaped from John Davis at Panama, in Morgan's 1671 attack). The pirates now controlled all shipping in and out of Panama City, but feared to attack the city itself because of their small numbers. However, most of the city's troops were away fighting natives.

On 5 May the hot-tempered Coxon argued with the other captains and left in a bark with 78 men, to march back across the isthmus. The main reason was Coxon's jealousy of Sawkins' bravery and popularity. Leadership of the expedition reverted to Sawkins. Sawkins' pirates set fire to their prizes, and sailed off in the *Trinidad* and an 80-ton ship. Some time in May, off Taboga, Bartholomew Sharp took a Spanish ship sailing from Lima, Peru, with 51,000 pieces of eight. The pirates then took another two ships, and Sharp and his crew took over a 100-ton bark for themselves. Edmund Cook took an 80-ton bark.

After reprovisioning at Taboga, around 25 May, Sawkins and Sharp sailed to Coiba Island to careen their crafts and use it as a base for attacking shipping. One bark was blown off course and sailed to join up with Coxon, and another was taken by the Spanish. On 22 May or 1 June 1680, Sawkins led 60 men to attack Pueblo Nuevo, south of Veragua. However, three well-fortified breastworks had been newly built by the time of his raid. Although the Spanish were expecting him, Sawkins continued to attack the town and while leading his men was killed by a musket-ball. Returning to Coiba, the pirates took a 100-ton ship loaded with corn. It was renamed *Mayflower*, and Edmund Cook was elected its commander. However, 67 pirates would not serve Bartholomew Sharp and left on a bark, which meant he had 146 men. Sharp still captained the *Trinidad*, but Edmund Cook had been deposed in a mutiny and John Cox now captained the *Mayflower*. Sawkins had been a far more religious man than the roistering, ungodly Sharp, and once threw dice overboard when he saw men gambling on the Sabbath.

Sharp's crew mutinied on New Year's Day 1681. They clapped him in irons and put him down below in the ballast. Sharp had wanted to sail around the Horn back to the Caribbean, having made plenty of money, but other less wealthy buccaneers had grown impatient over his waiting to plunder Arica in Northern Chile. They elected an old pirate and a 'stout seaman,' John Watling, in his place, who began his command by giving orders for the strict keeping of the Sabbath Day, and on 9 January buccaneers observed Sunday as a day apart, the first time since Sawkins' death in June.

An old native was captured but could not give answers about Arica's defences, and Watling wanted to shoot him. Sharp had been released and tried to dissuade him, but the harmless man was killed, whereupon, as recorded by Ringrose, Sharp took a pitcher of water and washed his hands, warning the ship's company that they would certainly now fail to take the town. On 30 January, Watling headed a raid on Arica, but the Spaniards had had three days' warning, and had gathered together 2,000 defenders. A furious attack was made, with great losses on both sides. In one attack, Watling placed 100 of his prisoners in front of his storming party, hoping this would prevent the enemy firing at them. After taking the town, the buccaneers were driven out, owing to the arrival of a number of soldiers from Lima. During the retreat from the town Watling was shot in the liver and died. (It seems he gave his name to Watling Island in the Bahamas, the first part of America that Christopher Columbus ever saw, and a favoured haven for buccaneers.) The rest of the crew now begged Sharp to resume his captaincy in late January, three weeks after his deposition. However, 44 men still refused to serve Sharp, including Dampier and Lionel Wafer, and they took a longboat to shore in Ecuador to recross the isthmus by foot. In April 1681, Captain Cook led another 50 men back across the isthmus.

After these setbacks, the 65 remaining buccaneers led by Sharp went on to capture some small ships and raided Spanish coastal villages. They took the *Rosario*, shooting the captain while boarding, and took her goods and silver before torturing the 24 passengers and the crew to find if there was any more. They turned the *Rosario* adrift with her sails and rigging cut, and took five or six of the crew to the Island of La Plata. There they killed one and tortured another, before trying to take Payta with just 32 men and failing. On 16 May they entered the Gulf of Nicoya, stayed for three weeks careening and reprovisioning, and burnt the town of Esparza. On 8 July, rather than finding a rich haul of treasure on one prize, they found she was loaded with 700 dull grey metal pigs (bars), which they thought were tin. Dejected, Sharp and his pirates decided to cut their losses and head home. They threw 699 bars overboard, saving only one to be cast into musket balls. Sharp and his men elected to return to the Caribbean via the Straits of Magellan, but storms passed the *Trinity* too far south and they became the first Englishmen to sail east around Cape Horn.

When Sharp tried to make harbour at Barbados on 7 February 1782, he found a Royal Navy frigate waiting for him. The Spanish claimed that 25 ships had been destroyed and at least 200 Spaniards killed on the 'Pacific Adventure', with massive damage to ports and fortifications. Sharp had assumed that because England was an enemy of Spain, he would be recognised as a privateer but the English were not at war at the time and arrest warrants had been issued for him because of his piracy. His other piece of bad news was that his men had run out of lead to cast musket balls and had begun using the remaining 'tin bar' captured from the Spanish galleon. In fact, they discovered, it was silver. This meant they had thrown an estimated £150,000's-worth of treasure into the sea, which would be worth about £21,000,000 today. Steering clear of Barbados, the disillusioned Sharp made for Antigua, but was barred from entry. At Nevis, the company broke up and he sailed with some supporters to England.

Sharp reached Plymouth from Nevis in the *White Fox* on 25 March 1682, staying at the Anchor Inn with his fellows. Ringrose and 13 more pirates arrived at Dartmouth from Antigua, in the *Lisbon Merchant*, on 26 March. As soon as news of the pirates' arrival reached London, the Spanish ambassador demanded that they be brought to trial for piracy and the murder of Don Diego López, captain of the *Rosario*. On 9 May 1682, Thomas Camp of Stepney made a written statement, counter-signed by the Secretary of State, stating that the landlord of the Anchor Inn, Plymouth, had told him in the presence of three witnesses that Sharp was lodging at the Anchor, and that he had boasted of being an 'outlyer' (pirate), for about 16 years and robbed all nations, particularly the Spanish. Sharp had apparently said that 'he had lived a wicked Course of Life abroad & thought that he should never dye a Naturall Death, that he came home to sue out his Pardon, which he had no great hopes to obtain, & if he did not, that he would return again to the West Indyes, or Words to that effect.'

In addition, the landlord informed Camp that Sharp had several thousand pounds as well as several portmanteaux of jewels, gold and silver, coined and uncoined. He said that about ten of Sharp's men were now in London. Bartholomew Sharp, Gilbert Dick (aka William Williams), and John Cox were arrested on charges of piracy and the murder of the master of the *Rosario* in July 1681. They were committed to Marshalsea Prison in Southwark, acquitted at Southwark on 10 June, and pardoned and released, to the fury of the Spanish. The reason was that Sharp had been translating an immensely important book of maps (a 'waggoner') taken from the *El Santo Rosario,* which he presented to Charles II, providing a great impetus to English navigation in the South Seas. Sharp also edited his own journals and those of Ringrose. In November 1682 Sharp was given a captain's commission in the Royal Navy and appointed to command the *Bonetta* sloop, but he never took up the commission. His fellow pirate Dick (Williams) said Sharp wasted all his money on good fellowship, and Sharp returned to the Caribbean to take a commission from the Governor of Nevis in January 1684, for Sharp in his own ship to 'take and apprehend savage Indians and pirates'.

On 31 October Sharp captured a ship off Jamaica, which he renamed *Josiah*. He sailed to Bermuda where he became friendly with the governor, who described him as 'very zealous' in the king's service. However, at the end of 1686 Sharp was taken to Nevis to stand trial for piracy, at Jamaica in 1684, and at Campeche on the Yucatán Peninsula in 1686. It was strongly suspected, but could not be proved, that in July 1685 Sharp had joined Grammont and De Graaf in their sacking of Campeche. One of his accusers called Sharp a proclaimed pirate, an absconding debtor, a cattle thief, and a traitor who had sold his services to the French. He complained that when writs had been served on Sharp, he had lit his pipe and 'wiped his breech' with them. Sharp was acquitted on 30 December 1686 by a grand jury, but was brought to trial again on other charges on 12 February 1687, and acquitted by a petty jury. The famous physician Dr Hans Sloane was serving the Duke of Albemarle, Governor of Jamaica from 1687, and in 1688 wrote that 'Captain Sharp, formerly an English Commander in the South Sea' was commander of Anguilla, in the Leeward Islands.

In summer 1699, Rear Admiral Benbow visited St Thomas in the Virgin Islands searching for Captain Kidd, and its Danish governor told him 'that there were not any subjects of England on the Island, Captain Sharp, the noted pirate, only excepted who was confined for misdemeanours, and having some Alliegence to the King of Denmark, could not justifiably be delivered up.' By 1696, Sharp had established himself on the island and by 1700, tried to flee from paying his debts. He was imprisoned, dying there in 1702. An eyewitness account of Sharp's adventures was published in 1684, *The Dangerous Voyage and Bold Assaults of Captain Bartholomew Sharp and Others*, by Basil Ringrose.

Lionel Wafer (1640–1705) – Surgeon, Buccaneer and Author

Wafer wrote that he first went seafaring in 1676/77 aboard Captain Zachary Brown's *Great Ann* of London, bound for Bantam, Indonesia, 'in the Service of the Surgeon of the Ship; but being then very young, I made no great Observations in that Voyage.' Back in London in 1679, he joined a voyage to the West Indies, as a surgeon's mate, to see his brother who worked for Sir Thomas Modyford, the former governor of the island. Wafer deserted his ship in Port Royal and his brother found him a house where he practised as a surgeon for a few months. Wafer was induced by the privateer captains Linch (Lynch) and Edmund Cook to be a surgeon on an expedition to Cartagena. Wafer agreed, as he had not served a full apprenticeship, so probably was not getting many clients and needed money.

In 1699 Lionel Wafer wrote and illustrated his book, *A New Voyage and Description of the Isthmus of America.*

Lionel Wafer's account of his travels.

In 1680, Wafer met William Dampier (*q.v.*) at Cartagena, and they sailed under Bartholomew Sharp. In the 'Pacific Adventure' in January 1681 there was a disastrous attack on Arica, Chile, where Wafer writes, 'we lost a great number of our Men; and every one of our Surgeons was kill'd beside my Self, who was then left to guard the Canoas.' He was then with Dampier and the band of discontented men who left Sharp and tried to cross the Isthmus of Panama. On 5 May 1681, in an accidental ignition of gunpowder, Wafer was badly burned, 'the Flesh being torn away, and my Thigh burnt for a great way above it. I applied to it immediately such Remedies as I had in my knapsack: and being unwilling to be left behind by my companions, I made hard shift to jog on.' He could not keep up with Dampier and the other pirates, and was left with four others on the Isthmus of Darien, Panama, where he stayed with the Cuna Indians. Wafer wrote that he had 'no means to alleviate the Anguish of my Wound [so] the Indians undertook to cure me; and apply'd to my Knee some Herbs, which they first chew'd in their Mouths to the consistency of a Paste, and putting it on a Plantain-Leaf, laid it upon the Sore. This prov'd so effectual, that in about 20 Days use of this Poultess [poultice], which they applied fresh every Day, I was perfectly cured.'

He returned the favour by bleeding a wound of one of Chief Lacenta's wives. His success meant that he 'was taken up into a Hammock, and carried on Men's Shoulders, Lacenta himself making a Speech in my Praise, and commending me as much Superiour to any of their Doctors. Thus I was carried from Plantation to Plantation, and lived in great Splendor and Repute, administring both Physick [medicine] and Phlebotomy [bloodletting] to those that wanted.' For almost a year Wafer gathered information about their culture, and studied the natural history of the isthmus. The following year, Wafer left the Cuna, promising to return and marry the chief's sister, and bring back dogs from England. Wafer and his four companions suffered extreme hardships as they struggled through the dense tropical jungle during the wettest season of the year.

Wafer next reunited with Dampier, and after privateering on the Spanish Main with him until 1688, accepted a pardon and settled in Philadelphia. In 1690 he returned to England and published the brilliant *A New Voyage and Description of the Isthmus of America* (1695), which described his adventures. Wafer's adventures are also recounted by Basil Ringrose in his *Dangerous Voyage and Bold Assaults of Captain Bartholomew Sharp and Others*, and by William Dampier in his *New Voyage Round the World*.

William Dampier (September 1651–March 1715) – The First Three-Times Circumnavigator, Navigator, Hydrographer, Travel Writer, the Man who First gave us the words *avocado, barbecue, breadfruit, cashew, catamaran,* and *chopsticks*

The son of a tenant farmer of East Coker, Somerset, Dampier was orphaned and sailed as a ship's boy from Weymouth to Newfoundland, probably fishing on the Grand Banks. From England, he next sailed to Bantam in Java, and in 1673 may have been impressed into the Royal Navy, as during May and June he sailed in the two Battles of Schooneveld in the Dutch War, under Sir Edward Sprague. Falling extremely ill, Dampier was sent ashore to convalesce, and the next we know of him, he was for a short time the under-manager of a Jamaica estate in 1674. In 1675–76 he made two voyages to the Bay of Campeche, Mexico, and seems to have alternated between working with logwood cutters and privateering. In 1678 he was in England. In 1679, from Jamaica, he joined Bartholomew Sharp's pirates on the 'Pacific Adventure'. Abandoning Sharp in 1681, he crossed the

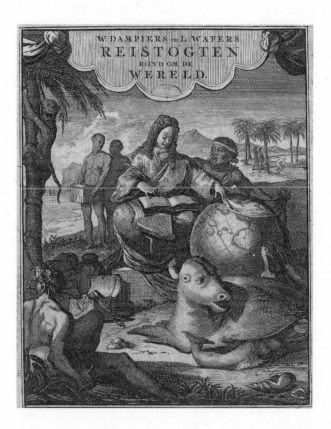

William Dampier
astride the globe,
1717, courtesy of
the Rijksmuseum.

Isthmus of Darien from Panama, leaving a wounded Lionel Wafer with the Cuna Indians. After another privateering expedition across the Spanish Main, Dampier sailed to Virginia to serve under John Cook for a privateering voyage to the South Seas. They sailed in August 1683, touched at the Guinea coast, then proceeded around Cape Horn into the Pacific. Having landed at Juan Fernandez, they then sailed the coast of South America, cruising along Chile and Peru. They took some prizes, and with these they sailed to the Galapagos Islands and to Mexico, where Captain Cook died. The command passed to Edward Davis, who, with several other pirate vessels, English and French, raided the west American shores for the next year, attacking Guayaquil, Puebla Nova, etc.

Dampier left Davis to board Captain Swan's *Cygnet*, and sailed with him along the northern parts of Mexico as far as southern California. Because of little success, Swan proposed to cross the Pacific and return via the East Indies. Sailing from Cape Corrientes on 31 March 1686, they reached Guam in the Ladrones on 20 May, just as the men were preparing to kill and eat their officers. After six months of debauchery in the Philippines, the majority of the crew, including Dampier, left Swan and 36 others in Mindanao. They then sailed the *Cygnet* from 1687 to 1688, from Manila to Pulo Condore, then to China, then the Spice Islands and for three months around New Holland (the Australian mainland). In March 1688 the pirates were off Sumatra, and in May, off the Nicobar Islands. There Dampier was marooned with two other Englishmen, a Portuguese and some Malays. In his memoirs he states that it was at his own request, for the purpose of establishing trade in ambergris. The marooned men managed to navigate a canoe to Sumatra, but Dampier almost died on the voyage. After making voyages to Tongking, Madras, and across the East Indies, it appears that he was made to serve as a gunner in the English fort of Benkulen.

Somehow, Dampier returned to England in 1691, penniless but in possession of his journals. He also had an Indonesian slave known as Prince Jeoly, who became famous for his 'paintings' (tattoos); Dampier exhibited Jeoly in London to make money. Dampier's account of these experiences, published in 1697 and 1699, established him as an authority on the South Seas. The Admiralty thus gave him command of the expedition to explore the Southern Hemisphere, and in January 1699 he sailed off in HMS *Roebuck* with 50 men.

It was a leaking fifth-rate warship, and from January to April 1700 the *Roebuck* was on the north coast of New Guinea, but the poor condition of his ship caused her to founder on the homeward passage, preventing Dampier from discovering the east coast of Australia. His route back to England took the ship to the Dutch port of Batavia on Java and then to the Cape of Good Hope and St Helena. The *Roebuck* was leaking seriously and had to be abandoned at Ascension Island. The men made tents from the sails and five weeks later they were rescued by Royal Navy vessels bound for Barbados. Dampier transferred to another ship and reached England in August 1701. He had managed to save some of his specimens and his journals. As with his other voyages, he was disliked by crew members, who complained about him. His reputation with the Admiralty was harmed when he was found guilty in 1702 of mistreating an officer, and deemed unfit to command any naval vessel. Dampier was fined the total amount of his three years' naval salary. His standing with the scientific community remained high, however, and he gave his many plant specimens to the Royal Society.

Dampier led a privateering expedition to the South Seas in 1703, which ended in failure. During the voyage, in late summer 1704, he was captain of the privateer 26-gun *St George*, with 120 crew, and Thomas Stradling was captaining the consort 16-gun *Cinque Ports*, with 63 crew. Following an argument, Alexander Selkirk (*q.v.*) was marooned at Juan Fernandez, and the expedition again failed. However, Dampier's last voyage, as pilot to Woodes Rogers in the circumnavigation of 1708–11, was successful. Selkirk was rescued from Mas a Tierra in 1709, despite his hatred of Dampier, and a profit of nearly £200,000 was made on the expedition. However, before his prize money was ever paid, Dampier died four years later in London. Dampier's accounts of his voyages are famous, his works setting an entire fashion in travel literature. They were *New Voyage Round the World* (1697); *Voyages and Descriptions* (1699); *Voyage to New Holland* (1703 and 1709); and Dampier's *Vindication of his Voyage in the Ship St George* (1707). Woodes Rogers later wrote *Cruising Voyage Round the World* (1712).

Basil Ringrose (January 1653–19 February 1686) – Navigator, Author, Duellist

Christened on 28 January 1653 at St Martin-in-the-Fields, Westminster, it seems that in 1679 Basil Ringrose sailed to Jamaica. He joined the 'Pacific Adventure' of Sharp, Coxon and Sawkins in early 1680. He accompanied Bartholomew Sharp for almost two years, as outlined in previous entries. Ringrose kept a full and graphic journal, in which he gave descriptions of the various natives and their customs and drew charts and sketches. From various sources, we know that he had some French and Latin, and his Spanish was good enough to act as the buccaneers' interpreter. His knowledge of navigation and pilotage techniques was superior to that of most sailors of his time, as he determined longitude by observing a solar eclipse. He was also supportive of the Indians against the Spanish, as the colonisers practised 'Insupportable crueltyes to these poor natives I hope in due time will reach the allmightyes ear, who will open the hearte of a more christian prince to deliver this people and drive away these Catterpillers from there superbous seats of Lazyness.' On the expedition, he duelled with Sharp's quartermaster, James Chappel, at the Isle of Plate, in August 1681.

After the *Trinity* voyage, Ringrose arrived at Dartmouth on 26 March 1682, prepared his journal for the press, and in 1685 it was published as *The Dangerous Voyage and Bold Assaults of Captain Bartholomew Sharp and Others*, being the second volume of Exquemelin's *History of the Buccaneers*. During this time, Ringrose convinced some London merchants that a ship should be fitted to trade along the western coasts of South America. On 1 October 1683 he sailed as supercargo (managing the trade of the cargo) with 36 crew, on Charles Swan's 16-gun, 180-ton *Cygnet*. She carried a cargo worth £5,000 for barter, but at Valdivia in March 1684, the privateers were driven off by the Spaniards, despite a flag of truce. Of the landing party, two were killed and all the others wounded, save for Ringrose and one other.

They then attempted trading in the Gulf of Nicoya, Costa Rica, but were again unsuccessful. Men began deserting, and Captain Swan, meeting Edward Davis at the Isle of Plate in October 1684, instead decided to join French and English buccaneers 'on the account'. Swan thus threw the greater part of his cargo overboard to lighten his ship, and began piracy, but met with little success in raiding Spanish coastal settlements. On 19 February 1686, Swan and his men landed at the mouth of the Rio Grande de Santiago in Mexico, seeking provisions. Fifteen miles inland, the pirates took the small town of Sentispac (now Santa Pecaque). While transferring maize to horses, to take to their canoes in the river, the Spanish ambushed and killed a quarter of Swan's entire force. Fifty buccaneers died, including Ringrose, with Dampier writing that he was 'my Ingenious Friend Mr. Ringrose... who wrote that Part of the *History of the Buccaneers* which relates to Captain Sharp. He was at this time Cape-Merchant, or Super-Cargo of Captain Swan's Ship. He had no mind to this Voyage; but was necessitated to engage in it or starve.'

William the Mosquito (*fl.*1681–1684), Thomas Stradling (*c.*1683– *c.*1711) and Alexander Selkirk (d.1712) – the Men behind *Robinson Crusoe*

In January 1681, privateers under Captain Watling were scared off the uninhabited Juan Fernandez Island, and in their haste left a Mosquito Indian called William behind. He had been in the woods, hunting for wild goats. On 22 March 1684, privateers under Captain Cook of the *Batchelor's Delight* and Captain Swan of the *Cygnet* came into sight of Juan Fernandez. Some of Cook's men had sailed under Watling, and wanted to send a boat ashore to look for William. William Dampier related in his journals that he went ashore on the boat with another Mosquito (Miskito) Indian named Robin.

> Robin, his countryman, was the first who leaped ashore from the boats, and, running to his brother Mosquito-man, threw himself flat on his face at his feet, who, helping him up and embracing him, fell flat with his face on the ground at Robin's feet, and was by him taken up also. We stood with pleasure to behold the surprise, tenderness, and solemnity of this interview, which was exceedingly affectionate on both sides; and, when their ceremonies were over, we also, that stood gazing at them, drew near, each of us embracing him we had found here, who was overjoyed to see so many of his old friends come hither, as he thought, purposely to fetch him. He was named Will, as the other was Robin; which names were given them by the English, for they have no names among themselves, and they take it as a favour to be named by us, and will complain if we do not appoint them some name when they are with us.

William had seen the buccaneers anchor, and had killed three goats, which he dressed with vegetables, preparing a treat for them when they landed. The Spanish had known that William was on the island for three years and had tried to trap him and find where he was hiding. 'He had built himself a hut, half-a-mile from the sea-shore, which he lined with goats' skins, and slept on his couch or barbecu [wooden hurdle] of sticks, raised about 2 feet from the ground and spread with goats' skins.' The goats were left there by the Spanish to multiply and supply fresh meat (much like the wild hogs and cattle on other

Alexander Selkirk reading his Bible.

islands), and there was fresh water flowing at two places. William had been left on the island with just a musket, knife, a little powder and some shot. Dampier tells us that 'when his ammunition was expended, he contrived by notching his knife to saw the barrel of his gun into small pieces, wherewith he made harpoons, lances, hooks and a long knife, heating the pieces of iron first in the fire, and then hammering them out as he pleased with stones.' Fishing lines were made from the skins of seals laboriously cut into thongs and knotted. He had no clothes left, and wore a goatskin apron around his waist.

The crews reprovisioned with goats, wild vegetables, fish, sea lions and seals, before they weighed anchor on 8 April 1684. It seems that William fits the lifestyle of Daniel Defoe's *Robinson Crusoe* perfectly. Dampier's *Journals* were published in 1697 and 1699, and Defoe's book in 1719. However, most people believe that the Robinson Crusoe story was inspired by Alexander Selkirk, a Scot marooned by a Welsh privateer near the same island. Dampier again features no less than 30 years later, in this alternative version. In late summer 1704, he was captain of the privateer 26-gun *St George*, with 120 crew and Thomas Stradling was captaining the consort 16-gun *Cinque Ports*, with 63 crew. He had replaced its captain, Charles Pickering, who, with several crew, had died of scurvy. As the voyage progressed, opportunities to clean and repair the ships in order to prevent worm damage were lost, and the ships soon began to leak. Relations between the two captains reached the point where they both agreed that on reaching the Bay of Panama, they should divide the spoils and go their separate ways. In September, the *Cinque Ports* desperately needed caulking and put into Mas a Tierra, one of the Juan Fernandez Islands, where its sailing master Alexander Selkirk and its young captain Stradling had a blazing row. Selkirk said that the repairs were not good enough and that the ship would leak badly. He shouted that if Stradling insisted on setting sail in her, he could 'go to the bottom alone'. Stradling was not a seaman, but a 20-year-old 'gentleman' from St Donat's Castle in Glamorganshire. In anger at a lowly seaman disputing his authority, Stradling left Selkirk ashore with his sea chest. Selkirk had thought that other men would join him, forcing Stradling to properly repair the ship, but they rowed off. As the boat pulled away from the beach, Selkirk shouted to Stradling that he had changed his mind. Stradling shouted back that he had not changed his, and Selkirk was marooned.

After leaving Selkirk, Stradling soon discovered that his ship was foundering, as Selkirk had predicted, so he was forced to run it aground near the rocky and barren Malpelo Island, off Colombia. The crew took to rafts, and only 18 sailors survived to reach the South American mainland. A Jesuit priest came across them and handed them over to the Spanish, who threw Stradling and the survivors into dungeons in Lima, Peru, for four terrible years of mistreatment. After a few escape attempts, Stradling was handed over to the captain of a French frigate, who took him to St Malo, Brittany. When interrogated in its castle, he told a story about buried treasure on the Rio Plata, and offered to take a boat there in exchange for a percentage. The relevant minister, Pontchartrain, discounted the story, and in 1710, Stradling was transferred to Dinan, Brittany. He and 17 other prisoners managed to escape by tying their bed sheets together and somehow they got to Jersey in late 1710 or early 1711, after which he disappears.

At first Selkirk expected the ship to return, read copiously from his Bible, prayed for rescue and almost starved, before he realised that there would be no quick rescue. A resourceful man, Selkirk must have known that William had survived there for three years a decade ago, and he set to work. Two grass-covered huts were built and lined with goat-skins, one for living in and one for cooking. He replaced his ragged clothes with goatskin garments, using a nail as a needle and unravelled stockings for thread. He wore out his knife, but made fresh blades from iron barrel hoops left on the island. When his ammunition ran out, he ran down goats on foot to kill them.

On 31 January 1709, William Dampier was sailing under Woodes Rogers after rounding Cape Horn, trying to put into Mas a Tierra for supplies. The privateer ships *Duke* and *Duchess* could not get closer than 12 miles away, because of winds, so it was decided to send a pinnace ashore. The crew were sick, seven had succumbed to scurvy, and fresh water, vegetables, fruit and meat were urgently needed. The pinnace took hours to get to within 3 miles of the island, and at nightfall a huge bonfire was seen on the coast. The pinnace returned to the *Duchess*, thinking that the French or Spanish were on the island. Next morning Captain Rogers could see no enemy ships at either bay on the island, and managed to get closer to the islands before the ship's yawl could be sent out with seven armed men.

It did not return, so Rogers risked sending the pinnace to the island, with chosen musketeers on board. It did not return for hours, and Rogers hoisted signal flags. When the pinnace eventually came back, it was loaded with fresh crayfish and a barefoot, bearded semi-intelligible man dressed in goatskins. He was asked how long he had been there and answered four years and four months – he had kept note of the time by marking wood. He was asked his name and replied with difficulty, Alexander Selkirk, master of the *Cinque Ports*. Dampier then came forward to fill in the details. When Selkirk saw Dampier, the commodore of the ill-fated voyage of the *Cinque Ports* and now the pilot of Woodes Rogers' voyage, Selkirk asked to be put ashore again, but was talked out of it. On Dampier's recommendation Selkirk was made mate aboard Rogers' ship, the *Duke*.

Rogers used this period to help his crew recuperate. Apart from the seven who died, there were another dozen or so suffering from scurvy, of whom two could not be saved. Ashore they found turnips and parsley, planted by previous parties of buccaneers, and there was abundant wild cabbage, flocks of goats, crabs, lobsters and crayfish. Rogers' men pronounced that seal tasted as good as English lamb, and picked their teeth clean with sea lion's whiskers, soon forgetting the horrors of the rounding of Cape Horn. After six weeks, on 14 February, Woodes Rogers continued upon his remarkable circumnavigation of the world. The following year, after the capture of the Spanish treasure ship *Nuestra Senora de la Encarnación Disenganio*, Selkirk was promoted to sail master on the ship, now renamed the *Batchelor*. Woodes Rogers's voyage ended in 1711 with their arrival in the Thames. Both Rogers and Selkirk achieved fame on their return. Selkirk was asked to give evidence in a court case brought against William Dampier by Elizabeth Creswell, the daughter of the owner of the first voyage, for the losses incurred in the 1703 venture. After this, Selkirk sailed on a trading voyage to Bristol, where he was indicted for assault. This charge may have been brought about by supporters of Dampier but Selkirk was kept in confinement for two years. Alexander Selkirk died at sea in 1721. Defoe had read the story of Selkirk in William Dampier's *Voyage Round the World*, and also Woodes Rogers' account, with the same title.

Thomas Paine (1632–1715) – the Rhode Island Buccaneer

Perhaps born in Martha's Vineyard, and a resident of Jamestown, Rhode Island, Thomas Paine went to sea about 1647, and perhaps sailed with l'Olonnais and Henry Morgan. He was a buccaneer captain in Jean Comte d'Estrée's fleet that was wrecked off Las Aves. His small 6-gun ship had a shallow draft, so avoided having its bottom ripped open by the reefs, and Paine probably took aboard many stranded pirates from the larger wrecked ships. He then accompanied de Grammont (*q.v.*) to sack Maracaibo in June 1678, and later that year returned to Las Aves to careen his ship, and probably to salvage any remaining supplies and cannon from the wrecked fleet. He took a Dutch sloop to replace his small ship. Paine raided several Spanish settlements, with William Wright (*q.v.*) and Yankey Willems (*q.v.*), looting Rio de la Hacha (Riohacha, Colombia) in 1680. In June 1680, Paine joined Michel de Grammont and Captain Wright at Blanquilla Island and took Guaira, Caracas and the heavily defended Cumaná, on the Venezuelan coast. Paine and Grammont were part of the rearguard that held off Spanish reinforcements to allow the pirates to depart after looting the town. The pirates returned again to Las Aves, with Paine commanding a small fleet, probably then sailing to Tortuga.

In May 1681 Paine was at Springer's Key in the Samballoes Isles in a 10-gun ship with 100 men, joining forces with other buccaneers to attack Carpenter's River. A storm dispersed the fleet and he was driven to Boca del Toro, where he careened his ship. Aged about 50 in autumn 1682, Paine received a privateering commission from Jamaica's governor Sir Thomas Lynch, to 'seize, kill, and destroy pirates'. In March 1683, Paine joined a privateering fleet led by the French Captain Abraham Bréhal on the *Fortune*, with other captains John Markham, Jeremiah Canoe, George Younge, Conway Woolley, and Jan Corneliszoon. They sailed to raid St Augustine, Florida, with Paine captaining 60 men in an 8-gun barque, the *Pearl*. Bréhal held a French privateering commission obtained from the governor of Saint-Domingue, so the fleet sailed under French flags. On 30 March, a small party of pirates captured five sleeping sentries from a wooden watchtower overlooking Matanzas inlet, and tortured them for details of the town's defences. However, they had been spotted by a Spanish corporal, and preparations were made to fend off their attack. On 31 March, 8 miles from their target, the main body of pirates was ambushed by 40 musketeers, and they fled in boats back to their ships. Regrouping, on 5 April the fleet anchored outside the sandbar protecting direct access to St Augustine, but decided not to attack.

Instead, the force of 300 pirates had to make do with looting some surrounding villages and towns, including Guale and the mission villages of Santa Maria and San Juan del Puerto. At St Simon's Island they looted the church and killed the Indian inhabitants, then careened on the Isla de San Pedro, where they buried their dead, before raiding church missions along the coast to the north. Paine returned with Captain Bréhal and John Markham to New Providence, the Bahamas, but its governor tried to arrest Markham and Paine for violating England's peace agreement with Spain. They therefore sailed off to join Corneliszoon and Woolley to try to salvage a wrecked Spanish treasure galleon, the *Nuestra Senora de las Maravillas*. Paine and Bréhal sailed north to reprovision at Rhode Island, but a visiting governor charged Paine with carrying a counterfeit commission. Bréhal was allowed to leave and Paine was eventually cleared.

Settling back in Rhode Island, Paine was said to have driven Pierre le Picard and his French pirates from Block Island, becoming a celebrated local hero. According to Howard M. Chapin's 1930 book on Paine: 'In July, 1690, Rhode Island was amply rewarded for giving shelter seven years earlier to Captain Thomas Paine. A fleet of French privateers arrived off the coast about July 12. Their commander was Captain Pekar or Picard, who is unquestionably identical with the buccaneer Pierre Le Picard … and with the Captain Picard, whom Sir Thomas Lynch described as a pirate in 1682.' Chapin described the atrocities committed by the alleged pirates and how Paine drove them from Block Island. According to one eyewitness account, 'the pirate Pekar' fled from Block Island saying he 'would as soon fight the devil as Paine'.

Paine now gained fame and fortune, becoming a pillar of Jamestown society. In 1690 he joined his father-in-law as a tax assessor for Jamestown, and in 1692 Paine became captain of the Jamestown Militia. In 1698, Paine built a house at Cajacet (Jamestown) and was admitted as a freeman of the colony, with all voting rights. In 1699, he was visited by the privateer Captain William Kidd, and apparently agreed to store some treasure for him. Because of this incident, and past acts of piracy, dealing in black-market goods and reselling pirate loot, Paine was charged with a number of crimes by the Earl of Bellomont, but was again cleared and went on to help establish Trinity Church in Newport, becoming a prosperous farmer and merchant. He is buried in Paine Cemetery, Jamestown, Newport County, Rhode Island.

William Wright (*c.*1655–after 1682) – The Indentured Servant turned Privateer

It seems that William Wright was an indentured servant in Saint-Domingue in the early 1670s, having possibly been captured as a young man. He took a privateering commission from its French governor in 1675 to raid the Spanish settlement at Segovia, Nicaragua. Wright sailed to the San Blas Islands to gather a crew and then to the Miskito (Mosquito) Coast (now the Atlantic coast of Nicaragua and Costa Rica) where he met John Gret. White, Gret and Jean Bernanos sailed back to the San Blas Islands to form an alliance with local natives to try to take the Spanish town of Chepo. Failing to capture Chepo, Wright left for Petit Goâv, and was next recorded alongside Thomas Paine (*q.v.*), sailing from Cartagena to Caracas. There they took a Spanish ship, despite it being protected by the *Armada de Barlovento*. In May 1680 Wright and Paine were off Isla Blanca, where they were joined by Michel de Grammont to attack La Gauyra, the port of Caracas. They took it, but were forced to retreat upon sighting a Spanish fleet in July. By May 1681 Wright commanded just 40 men in a small 4-gun barque, and planned with other English privateers to rendezvous at the San Blas Islands, and then raid Cartago in Costa Rica. The attack was unsuccessful, as many privateers failed to join the mission at San Andres Island. Wright next looted Spanish ships in the region, then sailed with two French captains to Corn Island. After little success, he left them and joined Yankey Willems (*q.v.*) at Bocas del Toro to sail south along the coast of Columbia. They captured a Spanish merchant ship, and in February 1682 Wright left Captain Yankey, possibly returning to Saint-Domingue.

Captain Greaves (*c.*1649–*c.*1695) – 'Red Legs' Greaves

From 1644 to 1651 Scotland was involved in the Wars of the Three Kingdoms. Greaves' parents were tried for treason for their participation and sold into slavery, along with many other Scottish Royalists and Covenanters. 'Red Legs', a common nickname given to poor whites in the early English colony of Barbados, was born there shortly after his parents were deported to the island. He became an indentured servant but, when his parents died, he was sold to another settler, who was said to have been violent and to have often beaten the teenage Greaves. He escaped, swimming across Carlisle Bay, and stowed away upon a ship about to sail. However, it was a pirate ship under a cruel captain named Hawkins, who was in the habit of torturing women and killing prisoners. Discovered, Greaves was offered a pistol and the ship's articles to sign to join the pirate crew. As the alternative was probably being thrown overboard, he signed and soon was a capable member of the crew.

He hated Captain Hawkins for his brutality and in a fight killed him, then was elected the new captain. Accepting the crew's request, Greaves rewrote his ship's articles, banning cruelty towards prisoners, and abandoning the normal practice of killing merchant captains for resisting boarding. For a decade, he sailed the Caribbean. He refused to attack poor coastal villages. Red Legs never tortured his prisoners, nor robbed the poor, nor maltreated women. In 1675, he captured some Spanish ships and turned his cannon on the coastal forts of Margarita Island, off the coast of Venezuela. He stormed it, and after taking a huge amount of gold and pearls, he left without looting or harming the inhabitants.

Now wealthy, he retired from piracy and became a gentleman farmer on Nevis. However, he was recognised and turned in to authorities by someone who wanted to collect a reward. Guilty of piracy, Greaves was sentenced to be hanged in chains, and imprisoned in the Port Royal dungeon in Jamaica. Luckily, a few days before his execution in 1692, Port Royal was submerged by a *tsunami* after an earthquake, and he was one of the few survivors, being picked up by a whaling ship.

He joined the crew and later became a pirate hunter, gaining a royal pardon for taking a pirate ship that had been raiding whaling fleets. Greaves again retired to a plantation and became known as a philanthropist, donating much of his wealth to various public works before dying of natural causes.

The Golden Age of Piracy

During the 'Golden Age of Piracy', lasting roughly from 1700 to 1725, hundreds of pirate ships plagued the shipping lanes, mainly focussing upon the 'choke point' of the Caribbean and targeting the 'Triangular Trade'. Apart from the opportunities afforded by Spanish and Portuguese treasure ships taking advantage of trade winds and the Gulf Stream to return to Europe, the three-way slave trade had grown rapidly. The trade in black Africans began with Portuguese, and some Spanish, traders taking slaves to the American colonies they had established. British merchants and privateers became involved in the trade later, with the 1713 Treaty of Utrecht giving them the right to sell slaves in the Spanish New World Empire. Thus, perhaps 6 million Africans in the 18th century were taken to the Americas as slaves, more than a third of them in British slave ships known as 'blackbirds'.

British slavers made a three-legged voyage, called the 'triangular trade', using trade winds to carry trade goods, such as guns, trinkets and brandy, to the west coast of Africa to exchange for slaves. Slaves were then packed onto the 'Middle Passage' across the Atlantic to sell in the South and Central America, the West Indies and North America. Ships returned to England with silver, dye-woods, hides, tobacco, spices, rum and sugar. Pirates followed the Triangular Trade ships, striking off the coast of Africa, but sometimes also sailed into the Pacific and Indian Oceans. Their plunder was mainly traded goods that were profitable at the time, but also weapons, cannon, gunpowder, ammunition and food and drink, especially alcohol. Fishing ships were also robbed when merchant ships could not be found, with pirates taking not only fish, but often sails, rigging and nets. Tools were highly sought after. A carpenter's tools, surgeons' knives or navigational items were always taken. Medicines were especially looted, especially mercury to treat syphilis. Blackbeard held Charleston hostage in 1718 and received a chest of medicines in exchange for lifting his blockade.

Pirates had little access to ports where they could repair their ships, and their hard usage meant that they constantly required new sails, ropes, rigging tackle, anchors and the like to maintain their ships. They would often also plunder wood, masts or parts of the ship if necessary, and swap ships if their prize was in better shape. They also needed items such as frying pans, large iron pots called kettles, candles, thimbles, thread, soap, and so on. Pirates rarely knew what they would find on merchant ships, but 'trade goods' at the time included tanned animal hides, spices, sugar, logwood and other rare dyes, cocoa, tobacco, bolts of cloth and cotton. Many pirates had contacts with merchants in places such as Nassau in the Bahamas, or Port Royal, Jamaica, who were only too willing to purchase stolen goods. Most merchant ships had some gold, silver, jewels or coins aboard, and captains could be tortured to reveal the location. Very, very few pirates, such as Kidd, actually buried treasure. They tried to spend any takings immediately upon alcohol and women.

George Lowther (*c.*1680–*c.*1724) – the Captain who Turned Harris to Piracy

The *Gambia Castle* was a slave ship of the Royal Africa Company, captained by Charles Russell, with George Lowther as First (or possibly Second) Mate and about 30 crew. The *Gambia Castle* was taking a contingent of soldiers, commanded by John Massey, to garrison a small fort on the African coast. The *Gambia Castle* arrived at her destination in May 1721. It was Lowther's first voyage on a slaver, with an impressed crew and low morale, in harsh conditions. The crews on slave ships were generally treated extremely badly, with a life expectancy of 18 months, so many preferred the better life of piracy. Anchored off the coast of Gambia, in roasting heat, slaver crews might have to wait for weeks, or even months, until enough 'cargo' could be taken and then brought aboard from the great slave dungeons. Living conditions and food were terrible, and diseases such as scurvy, malaria and dysentery were rife. Captain Russell was disliked by his crew, and the experienced sailor George Lowther was respected. Russell distrusted Lowther, and when a disagreement broke out, he attempted to have Lowther flogged. However, many

George Lowther.

crew members took Lowther's side and defended him, preventing the punishment, causing a split among the crew.

The crew was angry and bored, and incensed by the appalling conditions aboard ship upon reaching Gambia. The slave trade was almost at a stand-still and the ship remained anchored for months. The Governor of the Royal Africa Company in Gambia was ill, and the Company seemed to care little about the crew. To worsen matters, Captain Massey and his soldiers had left their fort, which was in such a poor state of repair that it was uninhabitable. They now set up headquarters on board the overcrowded ship. One night while Captain Russell was ashore, Massey and Lowther decided to set sail without him. Massey had intended to return to England, but Lowther, the crew, and Massey's own soldiers disagreed. Lowther was elected captain and he renamed the *Gambia Castle* as *Delivery*. They attacked many ships off Africa but when Massey wanted to pillage a village on shore, he lost the vote as the risk was thought too great. Lowther was now able to obtain a smaller ship, named the *Happy Delivery*, and Massey took over the *Delivery* with some of his soldiers.

Massey sailed to Jamaica, where he turned himself in to its governor and pleaded for mercy, offering to go and hunt Lowther. Instead, Massey was tried and hanged for piracy. George Lowther had chosen to 'go on the account', and his crew willingly signed his articles of piracy, so Lowther left Africa and sailed to the Carolinas. There he careened the *Happy Delivery*. Ships' wooden hulls were soon fouled with weeds and barnacles, making them slow and difficult to manoeuvre, so they had to be beached (there were no docks), and the marine growth on their hulls cleaned off at regular intervals. Lowther's cruise took the pirates to the Cayman Islands where, as a warning shot, they fired cannon across the bow of the *Greyhound*, captained by Benjamin Edwards. However, Edwards responded with a full broadside. A battle took place before the *Greyhound* was boarded and ransacked. It is said that Lowther beat the entire crew, taking them captive and burning the ship. Another version is that Lowther offered the captives a tankard of rum and gave them the option to join his crew. Charles Harris (*q.v.*) accepted, and became one of his most prominent pirates. By this time, Lowther had acquired a small fleet under his command, and Harris was soon given command of one of the ships. In taking vessels, Lowther had developed the tactic of ramming his ship into another one, probably having strengthened his bow, so that his men could board and loot without the prize sinking.

Lowther was taking shipping off Hispaniola, Puerto Rico and Honduras, and around Christmas 1721 came across a small ship of pirates captained by the vicious Edward Low (*q.v.*), who joined his fleet. Low was made a lieutenant, and together they took several ships in the Bay of Honduras and added to the fleet. On 28 May 1722, Low and Lowther decided to part company. Lowther and his men spent most of 1723 off Newfoundland, then sailed south to the Caribbean. We next hear of the *Happy Delivery* needing another careening, in Guatemala, where Lowther was attacked by natives. He was forced to abandon some crew and ships and set sail quickly. The *Happy Delivery* was no longer seaworthy, so he transferred everything of value to the *Revenge*, his sole remaining ship. Lowther next managed to take a well-stocked brigantine, and replenished his supplies. The *Revenge* was also in need of urgent repair and in October 1723 Lowther decided to careen her on the secluded Venezuelan island of Blanquilla. However, before landing he was spotted by Walter Moore, the pirate-hunter commander of the *Eagle*, a well-armed English sloop. Lowther was able to escape to the island by slipping out of his cabin window with a dozen crewmen, but only four made it to shore. After an extensive search, Lowther's body was said to be found. He had shot himself in the head rather than be taken prisoner. Eleven of this crew were hanged at St Kitts on 22 March 1722.

However, the only known copy of the *Post-Boy* newspaper suggests, on 2 May 1724, that Lowther did not die in 1723:

> The last Letters from S. Christopher [St Kitts] bring Advice, that on the 20th of February, the Eagle Sloop … out from that Island, had brought in thither the Pyrate Sloop she had taken from Lowther, with twenty of the Men that were on board, (Lowther himself and many of the Crew having made their Escape) and it was believed that twelve or thirteen of them would be convicted of Pyracy, and that the others would be clear'd, as being forced into the said Pyrates Service.

Charles Harris (*fl.*1722–1723) – Ned Low's Comrade-in-Arms

Harris was the navigator, *de facto* the most important officer on a ship, and also First Mate on the *Greyhound*, sailing from Honduras to Boston with a huge cargo of logwood. This tree, also known as *bloodwood*, was native to Central America and extremely valuable from the 17th to the 19th centuries for dyeing textiles and paper. It produced, in acidic conditions, a reddish-yellow dye, and gave a very valuable purple colour in alkaline conditions. Bloodwood was also used in medical applications. In January 1722, with Captain Benjamin Edwards commanding, the *Greyhound* was attacked by George Lowther in the *Happy Delivery*. After an hour, Edwards surrendered, and Lowther's pirates were unhappy that there was no gold or valuables on board. Two captives were tied to the mainmast and flogged with whips until their backs bled, trying to get them to disclose any hiding places, and others were badly beaten. Lowther took some of the cargo and the merchant crew aboard the *Happy Delivery*, burned the *Greyhound* and set sail. Lowther was not one of the more brutal pirates, like Spriggs and Low, and was possibly unable to prevent his furious crew from harming the captives, but on his ship he gave the prisoners each a tankard of rum. He showed them his 'pirate code' and asked them to join him. Harris and four others signed Lowther's articles, and the remaining sailors were given a previously captured ship to sail home.

Harris was quickly promoted, being a skilled navigator and capable seaman, and given captaincy of his own ship. For more than a year, he sailed alongside Lowther and Edward Low, capturing ships across the West Indies. In 1722, however, for five months Harris disappeared, possibly careening his ship or lying low in some pirate haven. He then reappears in the sloop *Ranger* off Carolina, with Low in the *Fortune*. They sailed in consort up the Eastern Seaboard of North America, taking many ships, with Low prominent in torturing seamen. Particularly because of Low's brutality, pirate hunters were commissioned to hunt the pirates down, and on 11 July 1723 Captain Solgard in the English man-of-war *Greyhound* located them (*Greyhound* was a popular name for ships). Low and Harris spotted her on the horizon, and thinking she was a large merchant prize, sailed towards the *Greyhound*.

Solgard allowed them to approach within cannon range before firing a broadside; the fight was said to have lasted from 5am until to 4pm the next day. With her sails shot away and masts broken, Harris's *Ranger* was dead in the water, and Low now fled the action in the *Fortune*. Harris and his crew of 48 surrendered; 11 died from wounds, and 30 were sent to Newport, Rhode Island, for trial. Solgard enlisted Harris and seven other pirates to help him find Low, searching over the next few weeks. He was unsuccessful, and Harris stood trial in Newport on charges of piracy and murder. Harris and 25 of his crew were found guilty of piracy and hanged, with Harris being sent to London for hanging and gibbeting at Execution Dock.

His pirate code is as follows, with some spellings modernised:

(i)   The Captain is to have two full Shares; the [Quarter] Master is to have one Share and one Half; The Doctor, Mate, Gunner and Boatswain, one Share and one Quarter.

(ii)   He that shall be found guilty of taking up any Unlawful Weapon on Board the Privateer or any other prize by us taken, so as to Strike or Abuse one another in any regard, shall suffer what Punishment the Captain and the Majority of the Company shall see fit.

(iii)   He that shall be found Guilty of Cowardice in the time of Engagements, shall suffer what Punishment the Captain and the Majority of the Company shall think fit.

(iv)   If any Gold, Jewels, Silver, etc. be found on Board of any Prize or Prizes to the value of a Piece of Eight, & the finder do not deliver it to the Quarter Master in the space of 24 hours he shall suffer what Punishment the Captain and the Majority of the Company shall think fit.

(v)   He that is found Guilty of Gaming, or Defrauding one another to the value of a Ryal [Real] of Plate [Silver], shall suffer what Punishment the Captain and the Majority of the Company shall think fit.

(vi)   He that shall have the Misfortune to lose a Limb in time of Engagement, shall have the Sum of Six hundred pieces of Eight, and remain aboard as long as he shall think fit.

(vii)   Good Quarters to be given when Craved.

(viii)   He that sees a Sail first, shall have the best Pistol or Small Arm aboard of her.

(ix)   He that shall be guilty of Drunkenness in time of Engagement shall suffer what Punishment the Captain and Majority of the Company shall think fit.

(x)   No Snapping of Guns in the Hold.

'Commodore' Edward Low (*c.*1685–*c.*1724/26?) – the Psychopathic Captain

According to Defoe, 'Ned' Low or Loe was born in poverty in Westminster, London, and at an early age was a pickpocket and thief, stealing farthings from other boys, before gambling with the footmen who waited in the lobby of the House of Commons:

> While still quite small one of his elder brothers used to carry little Edward hidden in a basket on his back, and when in a crowd the future pirate would, from above, snatch the hats and even the wigs off the heads of passing citizens and secret them in the basket and so get away with them. The Low family were the originators of this ingenious and fascinating trick, and for a time it was most successful, until the people of the city took to tying on their hats and wigs with bands to prevent their sudden removal. When he grew up, Ned went to Boston and earned an honest living as a rigger, but after a while he tired of this and sailed in a sloop to Honduras to steal log-wood. Here Low quarrelled with his captain, tried to shoot him, and then went off in an open boat with twelve other men, and the very next day they took a small vessel, in which they began their 'war against all the world'. Low soon happened to meet with Captain Lowther, the pirate, and the two agreed to sail in company. This partnership lasted until May 28th, 1722, when they took a prize, a brigantine from Boston, which Low went into with a crew of forty-four men. This vessel they armed with two guns, four swivels, and six

quarter-casks of powder, and saying good-bye to Lowther, sailed off on their own account. A week later a prize fell into their hands, which was the first of several.

His brother Richard Low worked with Edward as a thief and in 1707 was hanged at Tyburn for a burglary in Stepney. Edward Low was also a burglar and in 1710, aged about 25, left for the Americas, travelling around before settling in Boston. In 1714, he married Eliza Marble and had a son, who died while an infant, and then a daughter, Elizabeth, born in late 1719. Eliza Low died in childbirth, leaving Low with his daughter, whom he left behind when he took to sea as a rigger in 1721.

Early in 1722 with another 12 sailors he joined the crew of a sloop sailing for Honduras to collect a cargo of precious hardwoods. Told he would have to wait to eat, he grabbed a loaded musket and shot at the captain, missed and hit another sailor in the throat. A mutiny failed and Low led his 12 fellows (including Francis Spriggs – *see* the next entry) in capturing a small sloop off Rhode Island, with Low killing a crew member. Defoe tells us that Low now decided 'to go in her, make a black Flag, and declare War against all the World.'

Low soon took another Rhode Island sloop, cutting its rigging so that it would take days to return to port and raise the alarm, and then a number of merchant ships, before heading to the Caribbean where, from around Christmas 1721, he acted as lieutenant to George Lowther (*q.v.*) on the *Happy Delivery* and then the *Ranger*. Renowned for his cruelty to prisoners, Low taught Francis Spriggs how to tie a captive's hands with rope between his fingers before setting it alight,

Edward Low's flag was a red skeleton on a black background.

to burn the flesh down to the bone. After more ships were taken, Lowther gave Low a large brigantine, the 6-gun *Rebecca,* in May 1722 and Low almost immediately began sailing on his own account. Harris left Lowther's fleet at the same time.

In June 1722, Low attacked 13 New England fishing ships at anchor in Nova Scotia. The fleet surrendered upon Low telling them that all would be otherwise killed, and he robbed every vessel. Low took the *Fancy,* an 80-ton schooner and armed it with 10 guns, as his new flagship, then sank the rest of the fleet. Many fishermen were forced to join his small crew, including Philip Ashton, who refused to sign Low's articles to become a pirate. After his escape, Ashton wrote of his being beaten and whipped by Low, and kept in chains. He wrote: 'Of all the pyratical crews that were ever heard of, none of the English name came up to this, in barbarity. Their mirth and their anger had much the same effect, for both were usually gratified with the cries and groans of their prisoners; so that they almost as often murdered a man from the excess of good humour, as out of passion and resentment; and the unfortunate could never be assured of safety from them, for danger lurked in their very smiles.'

Low hoisted false colours to approach ships, and carried on taking vessels off Newfoundland before heading east to the Azores. This was part of the 'Triangular Trade', the merchant seaway using prevailing winds and currents from New England/Newfoundland to the Azores/ Europe, then to Brazil, the Caribbean and back up the Atlantic Coast to New England/Newfoundland. He captained a number of ships, usually maintaining a small fleet of three or four. Off the Azores he took a former man-of-war, a narrow-sterned fast ship called a pink, and rearmed and renamed it the *Rose Pink* as his new flagship. On his next capture, of an English vessel, he took two Portuguese passengers and hoisted them up the yard arm, letting them crash down to the deck until they died. Recrossing the Atlantic from the Canaries to Cape Verde and Brazil, bad weather forced him into the Caribbean, where he captured the British *King Sagamore,* and now styled himself 'Commodore' of his fleet. A quarrelsome, illiterate man, Low and his pirate crews captured at least 100 ships during his short career, burning most of them.

East of Surinam, Low lost the *Rose Pink* and nearly all his provisions, owing to his mistake when careening her, and was left with only the newly captured schooner *Squirrel* and the *Fancy,* captained by Charles Harris. At the French island of Grenada, Low hid his men below decks, pretending to be a merchant ship (which carried considerably fewer crew), and asked to be allowed to take on water. A French sloop approached, and was taken, being renamed the *Ranger*. Low gave the *Squirrel* to his quartermaster Spriggs (*q.v.*), who renamed it the *Delight*. Low carried on taking ships, keeping the *Fortune*. It was stripped for refitting for piracy, and Low beat one of its crew severely, cutting off his ear with a cutlass.

Soon after, in January 1723 he took the Portuguese *Nostra Signiora de Victoria*. Her captain allowed a bag containing 11,000 gold moidores (worth then around $18,000) to fall into the sea rather let Low have it. Low, in blind anger, slashed off the captain's lips with his cutlass, broiled them, and forced the Portuguese captain to eat them while still hot. He then murdered the captain and all the crew. There are many tales of Low's brutality, perhaps deliberate propaganda to frighten ships into surrendering, but in a pirate trial, his own men described him as a 'maniac and a brute'. Taking a 34-gun French ship off the Azores, Low is said to have burnt a French cook alive, saying he was a 'greasy fellow who would fry well so the poor man was bound to the main mast and burnt in the ship to the no small derision of Low and his Mirmidons [sic].' When he captured the Spanish galleon *Montcova*, he personally slaughtered 53 officers with his cutlass, and made one Spaniard eat the heart of another before killing him.

With a bounty on his head in the Caribbean, and almost being taken by the *Mermaid* man-of-war, Low and Harris sailed east to terrorise shipping around the Azores, but again naval ships were sent to destroy him, and they sailed the Atlantic for the Carolinas. Defoe writes that in South Carolina '...he he took several prizes, one the Amsterdam Merchant (Captain Willard), belonging to New England, and as Low never missed an opportunity of showing his dislike of all New Englanders, he sent the captain away with both his ears cut off and with various other wounds about his body.' It was reported that after capturing a Nantucket whaler, Low made her commander eat his own sliced off ears, sprinkled with salt, before he killed him. However, the heavily armed HMS *Greyhound* now smashed into his fleet, having been specifically ordered to hunt Low. Low just managed to flee in the *Fancy* with a skeleton crew and £150,000 in gold, leaving Harris in the disabled *Ranger* in a hopeless position, and sailed north intending to return to the Azores. Harris and the *Ranger* were taken, with 25 pirates being hanged near Newport, Rhode Island, with Harris being sent for hanging in chains at Execution Dock, Wapping, London.

At the trial, *The American Weekly Mercury*, 6–13 June 1723, reported:

The Pyrates [were] waiting there for them, took them and Plundered them; they cut and whiped some and others they burnt with Matches between their Fingers to the bone to make them confess where their Money was, they took to the value of a Thousand Pistoles from Passengers and others, they then let them go, but coming on the Coast off of the Capes of Virginia, they were again chased by the same Pyrates who first took them, they did not trouble them again but wished them well Home, they saw at the same time his Consort, a Sloop of eight Guns, with a Ship and a Sloop which were supposed to be Prizes, they were Commanded by one Edward LOW. The Pyrates gave us an account of his taking the Bay of Hondoras from the Spaniards, which had surprised the English and taking them, and putting all the Spaniards to the Sword Excepting two boys, as also burning The King George, and a Snow belonging to New York, and sunk one of the New England Ships, and cut off one the Masters Ears and slit his Nose, all this they confessed themselves.

(A snow carried square rigging on both of her masts with a trysail on her main mast.)

Low next took a whaling vessel 80 miles out at sea, and tortured the captain before shooting him through the head. He set the whaler's crew adrift with no provisions, intending them to starve to death, but they managed to survive and reach Nantucket. He next took a fishing boat off Black Island and decapitated the captain. Low captured another two fishing boats near Rhode Island, but his sickened crew refused to carry out his orders to torture the simple fishermen. Following his defeat by HMS *Greyhound*, Low had now become 'peculiarly cruel' to any captives who were English. *The New York Times* reported that Low's tortures would have 'done credit to the ingenuity of the Spanish Inquisition in its darkest days... Low and his crew became the terror of the Atlantic, and his depredations were committed on every part of the ocean, from the coast of Brazil to the Grand Banks of Newfoundland...' Low was known to severe the ears, lips and noses of prisoners before mixing them into a stew that he later forced them to eat. However, the loss of his wife and his often expressed regret for the two-year-old daughter he left in Boston, meant that he did not press-gang married men into piracy, and also he allowed women to return to port safely.

Instead of making for the Azores, Low seems to have been intent on vengeance for the loss of Harris, and sailed south again, taking a 22-gun French ship and the *Merry Christmas*, a large merchant vessel out of Virginia. Low and his crew certainly practised torture, and Edward Leslie described him as a psychopath with a history filled with 'mutilations, disembowelings, decapitations, and slaughter'. During one torture session, one of Low's own crew accidentally cut Low in the mouth, leaving him scarred and disfigured, an even more terrifying captor. Gosse records:

> It happened that one of the drunken crew, playfully cutting at a prisoner, missed his mark and accidentally slashed Captain Low across his lower jaw, the sword opening his cheek and laying bare his teeth. The surgeon was called, who at once stitched up the wound, but Low found some fault with the operation, as well he might, seeing that 'the surgeon was tollerably drunk' at the time. The surgeon's professional pride was outraged by this criticism of his skill by a layman, and he showed his annoyance in a ready, if unprofessional, manner, by striking 'Low such a blow with his Fists, that broke out all the Stitches, and then bid him sew up his Chops himself and be damned, so that the captain made a very pitiful Figure for some time after.' Low took a large number of prizes, but he was not a sympathetic figure, and the list of his prizes and brutalities soon becomes irksome reading. Low, still in the Fancy, and accompanied by Captain Harris in the Ranger, then sailed back to the West Indies and later to South Carolina, where he took several prizes.

In July 1723, Low's three ships possibly rejoined George Lowther's fleet. Low brutally disciplined one of Spriggs' crew, so Spriggs sailed off secretly one night in his *Delight* around Christmas 1723, with a small, trusted crew. Off the Guinea coast, Low was left with the 34-gun *Merry Christmas* and the *Fancy*, but we are unsure of how he met his demise, possibly in 1724. There are no more reports of him, but Defoe repeated rumours that he had sailed for Brazil or that his ship sank in a storm with the loss of all hands. Robert Ossian and *The Pirates Own Book* state that Low was set adrift without provisions by the crew of the *Merry Christmas*, after Low had murdered a sleeping pirate after an argument; Low was rescued two days later by a French ship, brought to trial, and was hanged in Martinique. Another account is that he was marooned with Francis Spriggs. Low at first used the same flag as Blackbeard, then a red skeleton on a black background. He also had a green silk flag with a yellow figure of a man blowing a trumpet. This 'Green Trumpeter' was hoisted to call his fleet's captains to meetings aboard his flagship.

Francis Spriggs (*c.*1695–1726?) – the Sweating Specialist

This English pirate probably served George Lowther before becoming Edward Low's quartermaster and took a succession of ships with Low, who gave him a 12-gun sloop, the *Squirrel*, which Spriggs renamed the *Delight*. He captained in Low's small fleet until late December 1723, and after a great argument with the maniac Low, secretly sailed off one night. Spriggs adopted the same flag as his previous partner, as he knew it would inspire fear. He sailed from the Guinea Coast back to the Caribbean, and on 28 January 1724 looted Richard Duffie's Rhode Island slave ship. Spriggs next took a Portuguese ship, and after stripping its valuables 'sweated' the captain and crew. A ring of candles was lit around the mainmast and each captive was forced to run around it, attached to the mast by a short rope. A circle of pirates poked and prodded the victim with cutlasses, swords and various sharp instruments, while he tried to dodge the blows. The victim's only option was to run or 'dance' around the mast all the time, sometimes accompanied by the sound of the ship's fiddle. It became Sprigg's trademark torture, combining sadism and amusement. The Portuguese were then put back on their own ship, which was set on fire.

Soon he took a merchant sloop of St Lucia, taking as much of the expensive logwood cargo as could be carried to resell, and throwing the rest into the sea. Sailing off the coast of New England, the *Delight* captured a Rhode Island sloop on 27 March 1724. By early April 1724 Spriggs anchored his small fleet off the coast of Roatan in the Bay of Honduras, and ordered many of his prisoners to be sent ashore. They were freed so that the pirates could appear 'legitimate' privateers, but many of their victims had severe wounds after torture, with some having been forced to eat plates of hot wax. It seems that Spriggs had heard that George I had died and he and his crew were hoping for a pardon from the new king, George II, but that mad first Hanover king of England did not die until 11 June 1727.

Spriggs repaired and careened the *Delight*, and sailed for St Kitts, wishing to destroy the pirate hunter Captain Moor on his sloop *Eagle*, who had recently tried to attack Spriggs's comrade pirate George Lowther. However, instead he came across a French man-of-war and fled towards Bermuda, where a schooner was taken. Returning to St Kitts, a merchant sloop was taken on 4 July 1724. Spriggs is recorded as being increasingly brutal, hoisting captives as high as the main or top sails, and repeatedly dropping them onto the deck below. The victims were badly injured and thrown overboard, or died. He next took a Rhode Island ship carrying several horses, which the pirates tried to ride around the deck. Then they tortured their prisoners apparently because they kept falling off, not having saddles and spurs. After taking a sloop off Port Royal, Jamaica, Spriggs was forced to flee from the English men-of-war HMS *Spence* and HMS *Diamond*, which were too slow to catch up with him. Spriggs took another sloop, and sailing to the Bay of Honduras captured 10 or 12 English merchant ships, before escaping an English man-of-war. He pirated off South Carolina, and then sailed back to the Bay of Honduras, taking another 16 ships, before an English man-of-war chased the *Delight* into the open seas.

We now lose sight of Spriggs, but he may have still been operating on the Eastern Seaboard of the USA and West Indies in April 1725, taking several vessels. There is one account, on 25 June 1726, in the only known original copy of the *Post-Boy* newspaper, which states on its front page that a sloop from the Bay of Honduras was captured by a Spanish vessel, and when the Spanish were captured they were 'put on board the Diamond Man of War, who had taken a Pyrate, commanded by one Cooper, and had a great many Prisoners on board, and was bound to Jamaica with them … [and] that Lowe and Spriggs were both maroon'd, and were got among the Musketoo Indians.' The Miskito Indians lived along the coast from Honduras to Costa Rica and Nicaragua.

Olivier Levasseur (*fl.*1716–17 July 1730) – *la Bouze, la Buze, la Buse* (the Buzzard), *la Bouche* (the Mouth)

Possibly from Calais, Levasseur was a small man with a limp, who sailed from the pirate haven of New Providence in 1716, cruising with another pirate ship commanded by Benjamin Hornigold and later by Samuel Bellamy. With Bellamy and Paul Williams, he captured English and French ships off the Virgin Islands, but their ships were separated by a great storm early in 1717.

In July 1717 Captain John Frost, in a ship of 20 guns and with a crew of 170 men, was chased by Levasseur for 12 hours. Levasseur caught up with Frost at nine in the evening, and to force him to surrender, he fired a broadside of 'double round and cartridges, and a volley of small shot', so each of 10 guns was loaded with two cannon balls and a bag of partridge shot. The terrible bombardment, combined with the firing of muskets and landing of grenades, forced Frost to surrender his wrecked ship. Levasseur left his New Providence base when Woodes Rogers became Governor of the Bahamas in July

1718, although he accepted the King's Pardon. The Buzzard then made for the easier targets along the coast of West Africa.

Edward England (*see* next entry) found few prizes along the coast at this time, because Levasseur had scared away much of the merchant shipping. In spring 1719, Levasseur joined up with Howell Davis (*q.v.*) and Thomas Cocklyn. He bore down to attack Davis, only to see Davis also raise the black flag. The three pirates took the galley *Bird* at Sierra Leone, which was given to the Buzzard to replace his rotting brig, but the three captains argued and parted. Cocklyn, John Taylor and Levasseur joined up with Edward England's pirates and took some merchantmen off the Cape Coast, then sailed to the Portuguese fort at Ouidah, where they took the English *Heroine*, two Portuguese and a French ship. Later in 1719, they all sailed to Madagascar.

In 1720 Levasseur commanded the 250-ton *Indian Queen* with 28 guns and 90 crew. Sailing from the Guinea Coast for the Red Sea, Levasseur was wrecked on Mayotte in the Comoros Islands in 1720. Early in 1721, he met up with Taylor again, when he landed at St Mary's Island to careen, and Taylor gave him command of the *Victory,* which Levasseur renamed *Victorieux*. Off Réunion they took great treasure off a Portuguese carrack, *Virgen del Cabo* (*Vierge du Cap*), and divided the booty back at St Mary's Island. The booty, belonging to the Bishop of Goa and the Viceroy of Portugal, consisted of

> ...bars of gold and silver, dozens of boxes full of golden Guineas, diamonds, pearls, silk, art and religious objects from the Se Cathedral in Goa, including the Flaming Cross of Goa made of pure gold, inlaid with diamonds, rubies and emeralds. It was so heavy, that it required 3 men to carry it over to le Vasseur's ship. The total treasure was estimated at over 2 billion dollars in today's money. When the loot was divided, each pirate received at least £50,000 in golden Guineas (approximately $12,000,000), and 42 diamonds each. Le Vasseur and Taylor split the remaining gold, silver, and other objects, with le Vasseur taking the golden cross.*

During his 14-year pirate career it is said that the Buzzard took spoils estimated to be worth more than £300 million in today's money. Some of the crew were left at St Mary's Island. In 1721 Levasseur in

---

* http://thepirateempire.blogspot.com/2014/05/some-pirates-became-what-they-were-out.html

Le Victorieux, with John Taylor, sailed to the Seychelles and in 1722 plundered the Dutch garrison at Fort Lagoa, Delagoa Bay, Mozambique.

On sailing from the Guinea Coast to the East Indies, the Buzzard seems to have been wrecked off Madagascar, again on the Island of Mayotte. He and about 40 of his men started building a new ship, and the rest of the crew left in canoes and joined pirates led by Captain England at the island of Johanna. Levasseur seems to have retired on the islet of Bel Ombre near Mahé in the Seychelles, and was offered an amnesty by the French government. However, when he realised that he would have to give up his booty, he turned it down. He carried on intermittent piracy, until trapped and captured by the French man-of-war *Méduse,* off Fort Dauphin. He was tried and sentenced to death.

On the scaffold on the French island of Réunion (or Mahé), he flung a coded message into the crowd, crying, 'Find my treasure he who can!' Levasseur was supposed to have hidden treasure on an island in the Indian Ocean. The Buzzard's 'code' seems to have surfaced in the Seychelles, the French islands 1,100 miles north of Réunion, soon after the First World War. Levasseur's clues ended up in the hands of a Mauritian lady called Rose Savy, married to a Seychellois who owned the treasure site. She took a steamboat to Kenya in the 1920s, and then flew to France to have the document authenticated at the national library in Paris. In 1948 Reginald Cruise-Wilkins, a former British army officer, bought the cryptogram for $29, believing that it showed Levasseur's treasure to be buried at Bel Ombre Bay on Mahé, the main island in the Seychelles. He spent the rest of his years searching for the booty, finding what he thought was an 18th-century pirates' graveyard, and dozens of artefacts contemporary with the Buzzard. His son John still believes that $250 million of treasure exists in a network of underwater tunnels.

Edward England (1685–1721) – a 'Partner in All their Vile Actions'

Born in Ireland, and also known as Jasper Seagar and Edward Seegar, he was sailing as a mate from Jamaica to New Providence in the Bahamas, when his sloop was taken by the pirate Christopher Winter. Forced to join the crew for his sailing skills, England was given command of a sloop of his own, and began pirating from a base at Nassau, Bahamas. In 1716 he was in the attack led by Henry Jennings, taking £87,000 in gold and silver from the Spanish salvage camp at

Edward England.

Palma de Ayz, Florida. England was quartermaster on the pirate Henry Vane's sloop *Lark* in March 1718. She was taken by the Royal Navy, but England and others were freed, to tell their Nassau comrades that a pardon was being offered to pirates. Charles Vane (*q.v.*) gave England a captured ship in mid-1718 and when Woodes Rogers took New Providence and offered an amnesty, England instead sailed for Africa. He captured several ships, including the small Bristol slaver snow, the *Cadogan*, with Captain Skinner in command. Skinner's former boatswain recognised him, saying, 'Ah! Captain Skinner is it you, I am much in your debt, and now I shall pay you in your own coin.' Some of the crew, for his past treatment of them, bound Skinner to the windlass and pelted him with glass bottles before shooting him.

England next seized the *Pearl*, swapping her for his sloop, and renaming her *Royal James*. With this more powerful ship, he soon led a fleet. He took Howell Davis on the *Pearl*, who refused to sign pirate articles, which impressed England. Becoming friendly, he gave Davis command of the *Cadogan* to sail away, which led to Davis being classed as a pirate.

England returned to Africa in spring 1719, and his fleet took nine ships between the River Gambia and Cape Coast. They released three after plundering them, burnt four and refitted as pirate ships the *Mercury* and the *Elizabeth and Katherine*. They renamed these *Queen Anne's Revenge* and *Flying King*. Captain Lane was given the *Queen Anne's Revenge* and Robert Sample was given command of the *Flying King*, and they left the fleet to pirate in the Caribbean. England took two more ships, the galley *Peterborough* and the *Victory*, releasing the latter and keeping the former. England next exchanged his flagship the *Royal James* for a more powerful 34-gun Dutch ship, renamed *Fancy* in honour of Henry Every.

Nearing Cape Coast Castle, on the Gold Coast of West Africa (now Ghana), the pirates spied two ships at anchor, the *Whydah* and *John*, but the ships upped anchors and sailed to within covering fire from the fort. Subjected to cannon fire, England instead sailed south to Whydah Roads, but found that another pirate, Olivier Levasseur (*la Buze*) had already taken any booty of value. England needed to careen his ships, and renamed the *Peterborough* as the *Victory*, taking the captaincy and giving John Taylor the *Cassandra*. They spent a few weeks drinking, carousing, mistreating local women and killed a few natives. Fighting then broke out, the pirates burned the local village and set sail for the East Indies, taking supplies in Madagascar in early 1720, then sailing for the Malabar Coast. Olivier Levasseur joined England's fleet in the Indian Ocean. England and the Buzzard took several Indian ships, and a Dutch vessel, which they exchanged and refitted.

At Isla Juanna (Johanna) in the Comoros Islands, England encountered two English vessels and a Dutch ship from Ostend. On 7 August, the *Greenwich* under Captain Kirby, and the *Cassandra* under Captain Macrae, were sailing for Bombay and Surat, and were anchored at the island of Johanna, taking on water. A few days previously, they had received intelligence that the pirate Olivier 'la Buze' had run aground on a reef off Mayotte, losing his ship, and was building a new one. Macrae and Kirby agreed to go in search of him and attack the Buzzard, when two strange sails hove in sight. Macrae and Kirby, in agreement with the Dutch captain of the third ship, prepared to fight the oncoming flotilla, hoping for the handsome reward offered by the East Indian Company for the capture of the pirates. The *Greenwich* and the Ostender, having a better wind than the *Cassandra*, sailed some distance away. Macrae fired shot after shot at the *Greenwich* to make Kirby join him in action, but the captain of the *Greenwich* kept her course, accompanied by the Ostender. Around 3 miles away, they hove to, to watch the battle.

The 380-ton *Cassandra* was a new ship, on her first voyage, and early in the engagement Macrae hit the *Victory* near the waterline, which made England halt his action until he had stopped the leaks. Becalmed, John Taylor launched the *Fancy's* boats and tried to tow her alongside the *Cassandra* to board her. Musket fire held his boats off, and Taylor called off the action. After three hours, the *Victory* had repaired her damage and now again closed upon Macrae's ship. Macrae had lost too many of his crew to fight, and ran his ship aground, intending to save his crew. The *Fancy* drew less water and Taylor wanted to board the *Cassandra*, but also ran aground, within pistol shot. The ships fired at each other until the *Fancy's* depleted crew left their cannon and ran below for small arms. At this moment, the cowardly Captain Kirby set sail in the *Greenwich* for Bombay.

England in the *Victory*, seeing that the *Greenwich* had fled, now sent three ship's boats to reinforce the *Fancy*. Seeing this, the *Cassandra's* crew refused to fight any more, having lost 13 men, with 24 wounded, among them Captain Macrae, struck by a musket ball in the head. Some used the long boat and some swam to shore, leaving on board three wounded men who could not be moved. They were butchered by the pirates. The wounded Macrae led his remaining crew 25 miles inland, reaching a village the following morning. They were almost naked, injured and exhausted, but the natives treated the fugitives well, and refused to surrender them to the pirates, although offered a reward. The *Cassandra* had £75,000 on board in cash. Captain Macrae tried to open communications with the pirates, several of whom had sailed with him. England gave him a promise of safety, and after 10 days, Macrae ventured among the pirates. The *Cassandra* and the *Fancy* had been refloated, and Macrae was entertained on board his own ship, with his own liquor and provisions. Perhaps 90 of the pirates had died in the attack, and Taylor wanted to torture Macrae. During the quarrel a fierce-looking pirate, with a wooden leg and his belt full of pistols, intervened and approached Macrae, who thought his last moment had come. He was surprised when the pirate took him by the hand, and swore with many oaths that he would make mince-meat of the first man that hurt him. He told the assembly that Macrae was an honest fellow, and he had formerly sailed with him. He may have been the model for Long John Silver, 'a man with a terrible pair of whiskers and a wooden leg, being stuck round with pistols.'

Taylor was plied with punch until he agreed that the heavily damaged *Fancy*, together with some of the *Cassandra's* cargo, should be given to Macrae. Before he could recover from his alcoholic stupor, Macrae had sailed off. As soon as the pirates had vanished in the *Victory* and *Cassandra*, Macrae began work to patch up the *Fancy*, and in a few days sailed for Bombay, with 41 of his ship's company, among whom were two passengers and 12 soldiers. After 48 days of terrible suffering, half-naked, starving, and reduced to a daily pint of water each, Macrae reached Bombay on 26 October 1720. He made Captain Kirby's shameful desertion known to the East India Company.

England and Taylor now thought they spotted the Angria pirate fleet, but it turned out to be an English naval squadron sent from Bombay to chase pirates. When the fleets became accidentally intermingled, England blasted a broadside and the English fled. England and Taylor took an English ship, the *Elizabeth*, and on 12 December, Governor Boone of Bombay again despatched Captain Brown to search for the pirates, needing protection for the vessels bringing valuable pepper from southern factories. Brown commanded a squadron including the 42-gun *Greenwich*, 40-gun *Chandos*, 26-gun *Victory*, 24-gun *Britannia*, 16-gun *Revenge* and a fireship, and took Captain Macrae with him. England and Taylor had sailed to the Laccadives, needing water and provisions, before heading northward again to Cochin.

There, the Dutch authorities entertained the wealthy pirates, and supplied them with all they required, including a present from the governor of a boat loaded with arrack (alcohol), and 60 bales of sugar. A superb clock and gold watch, found in the *Cassandra*, were sent as a present to the governor's daughter, and formal salutes were fired on both sides as they entered and left the harbour. On leaving Cochin, they took a small vessel sailing under a Bombay pass, and learned from its master that the Bombay squadron, 'with Macrae in command', was cruising in search of them. Before long they were sighted by Brown, but by superior sailing lost their pursuers. Taylor, incensed that Macrae had been freed, organised a vote to remove England from command of the fleet. England was marooned on Mauritius with three loyal followers, without adequate provisions. They took about four months to build a small boat of scrap wood, and sailed across the Indian Ocean to St Augustine's Bay, Madagascar. One of these men was the man whom Long John Silver seems to be based upon. In poor health after the voyage, England survived for a few months, living on the charity of other pirates, possibly some of Henry Every's former crew. Johnson (Defoe) wrote:

He had a great deal of good Nature, and did not want for Courage; he was not avaricious, and always averse to the ill Usage of Prisoners received: He would have been contented with moderate Plunder, and less mischievous Pranks, could his Companions have been brought to the same Temper, but he was generally over-ruled, and as he was engaged in that abominable Society, he was obliged to be a Partner in all their vile Actions.

John Taylor (*fl.*1721–1723) – Taker of 'the Richest Plunder ever Captured by any Pirate'

Taylor was a vicious pirate, fond of torture, who mutinied against and marooned Edward England, as outlined in the previous entry. Taylor next sailed to Cochin, a Dutch port, to reprovision his ships, and was forced to pay heavy bribes there. He next careened his ships at Mauritius and St Mary's Island. Now captain of the *Cassandra*, Taylor pirated the Indian Ocean, sailing in consort with Olivier Levasseur (*la Buze*). At St Mary's Island, command of the *Victory* was given to *la Buze*, and they were off Bourbon (Réunion) when they spied a great treasure ship. The Conde de Ericeira, former Viceroy of Goa, sailed for Lisbon in January 1721, in the 70-gun carrack *Nostra Senhora della Cabo* (Our Lady of the Cape). The 700-ton vessel was carrying a consignment of jewels to Lisbon for the Portuguese Government, and the viceroy's own wealth gained during three years in Goa. A heavy storm dismasted the ship, forcing many guns to be thrown overboard, and she returned to Réunion to refit. In April 1721 Taylor discovered her fate, and while she was being repaired, sailed into the anchorage under English colours, where the *Cassandra* received a welcome salute from the viceroy's ship. Taylor and the Buzzard in return fired real broadsides, and in the confusion, the Portuguese ship was easily boarded.

It was stripped of silver, gold, diamonds, gems, pearls, silks, spices, art and Church regalia, and the pirates sailed off with treasure valued at between £100,000 and £875,000, with some accounts of £1,000,000, wildly different figures but even the lowest is impressive. Jan Rogoziński called the *Nostra Senhora della Cabo* 'the richest plunder ever captured by any pirate', estimating its reported treasure of £875,000, the high end, to be worth more than $400 million today. The former viceroy was forced to raise another 2,000 crowns as his ransom, which would have been higher had he not convinced them that part of the jewels and money on board was his own property. Réunion's French governor had allowed pirates virtually free access over the years, needing income for the island, and *la Buze* was to later settle on the island. Taylor had only detained one of Macrae's crew from the *Cassandra* – the carpenter's mate, Richard Lazenby, whom he had forced unwillingly to go with him. Lazenby later wrote of

> ...the cruel tortures inflicted on all captured natives; how on the Malabar coast they had friends, especially among the Dutch at Cochin, who bought their plunder, supplied them with provisions, and gave them information of armed ships to be avoided, and rich prizes to be intercepted. Those who wished to retire from the trade were given passages to Europe with their ill-gotten gains, in French ships; and finally, after witnessing the capture of the Portuguese Viceroy, to be related presently, he was put ashore at Bourbon; whence, in time, he made his way to England.

Taylor sailed off in the *Cassandra*, capturing a great Ostend ship, and sailing her to St Mary's Island. However, the Dutch captives overpowered the small guard while the crew were ashore celebrating, and sailed off with their ship. The pirates divided their loot and the *Victory* was burned and replaced with the *Nostra Senhora de Cabo*, again named the *Victory*. In December 1722 Taylor and *la Buze* argued and Taylor sailed for the Caribbean. In May 1723 the *Cassandra* was next recorded off Portobello, Panama, as Taylor was negotiating for a pardon with the captain of an English man-of-war. A Jamaican letter records that Taylor's crew bragged that each man possessed £1,200 in gold and silver, plus diamonds and other rich goods. The negotiations fell through, and instead Taylor was given a pardon by the Spanish Governor of Portobello in exchange for the *Cassandra*. Taylor may have become a captain in the Panamanian *costa garda*.

Howell Davis (*c.*1690–19 June 1719) – 'The Cavalier Prince of Pirates'

The career of this pirate is one of the more interesting of Defoe's case studies – he met some of the pirates who served with Davis and Black Bart Roberts, and Davis is recorded in far more detail in this author's biography of Black Bart. Davis was born in Milford Haven, Pembrokeshire, Wales. He was first mate aboard Captain Skinner's Bristol slaver, the snow *Cadogan*, which was taken off Sierra Leone by Edward England on 11 July 1718. (As mentioned earlier, a snow, snaw or snauw is a square-rigged vessel with two masts.) Although the *Cadogan* surrendered, Skinner was pelted with broken bottles and shot dead by some of England's men. Skinner was a brutal man, who had previously dismissed them without pay from a voyage after a disagreement. The remaining men on the *Cadogan* were given the option to turn pirate and sign England's articles. Davis refused, saying he would rather be shot. England was impressed by his bravery and gave him back command of the *Cadogan*, allowing him to sail off on 18 July. England had instructed him to set sail for a certain latitude, and then open a sealed letter, which contained a deed of gift of the ship and its cargo to Davis and his crew. They were told to sail to Brazil, where the cargo could be sold and the profits shared equally. However, the crew mutinied and took the *Cadogan* to Barbados, and Davis was thrown into jail for piracy. After three months, Davis was released for lack of evidence, but ship owners now refused to employ him. Davis thus went to Nassau, where its new governor, Woodes Rogers, took pity on him, offering Davis a place on board the merchant sloop *Buck*. The *Buck* sailed for Martinique in consort with the *Mumvil Trader* and the *Samuel*, with many of the crews being pirates pardoned by Rogers. Anchored off Martinique, one night Davis and 35 men overpowered their crewmates and transferred anything of value from the *Mumvil Trader* to the better ship *Buck*, before sailing off.

Davis was elected captain of a crew including the former pirates Walter Kennedy, Dennis Topping, Christopher Moody and Thomas Anstis. Articles were written up for the pirates to sign, and Defoe wrote that: 'He made a short speech, the sum of which was a Declaration of War against the whole World.' They set up their base at Coxen (Coxon's) Hole, Roatán Island, Honduras.

Off Hispaniola, he took a large 10-gun French vessel, and almost immediately spied a 24-gun French sloop with 60 crew. Davis knew that it would make a terrific and powerful flagship, but did not have the men or firepower to take it. Instead, he ran a black flag up on the new 10-gun French prize, and sailed the *Buck* to hailing distance of the French sloop. She fired a broadside, but he shouted in response that if they continued to fight, his commander on the other approaching ship (his captured prize), would kill everyone aboard. The captured Frenchmen on the other ship had been placed upon its deck, to demonstrate Davis' 'superior' force. The subterfuge worked and the French captain surrendered. Davis favoured mercy to captured crews, but often forced men to join him. On one prize, the Welshman Richard Jones refused to sign articles, and was slashed across the leg with a sword. He was then lowered on a rope into the shark-infested waters of the Caribbean until he capitulated.

Being now hunted, Davis and his trusted lieutenants, senior pirates and former captains known as 'The House of Lords', sailed across the Atlantic to the Cape Verde Islands. Davis sailed into the port of Sao Nicolau pretending to be an English privateer fighting the Spanish and was welcomed by the Portuguese garrison. He stayed for five weeks, briefly meeting up with Edward England again, reprovisioning, and with the crew enjoying themselves so much that five remained on the island. The pirates were soon to sail down the African coast, looking for ships full of slaves, which they could trade for gold, or for ships carrying gold and goods to buy slaves, ivory and the like. He took seven prizes, among them a two-masted brigantine off Cape Verde, upon which Davis placed 26 cannon, and renamed it the *Royal James*. Failing in a raid on the Portuguese settlement of Santiago (St Jago) in the Cape Verde Islands, he targeted the recently rebuilt Fort James, now known as Gambia Castle, on the Gambia River. It was an English slave trade station of the Royal Africa Company, holding African slaves for transport to the New World.

Davis knew that he would lose men by attacking the fortifications, so posed as a Liverpool merchant, with a few companions all dressed in fine clothes. Davis told the governor that he had been attacked by pirates while making for Senegal to buy ivory. Barely escaping, he did not wish to return to Senegal, but wanted to purchase slaves instead. The governor showed Davis and his men around as honoured guests, with Davis making a mental note of the fort's defences, and invited the 'traders' for dinner that evening. Davis next sent some of his men to quietly take the only other vessel in the harbour, so it could not raise any alarm. Twenty pirates were heavily armed and waited aboard the *Royal James* for Davis' signal, as Davis and his 'companions' arrived for dinner. Davis drew a pistol at the startled governor and told him to surrender, and then fired his second pistol through a window, as the signal to attack. His companions had positioned themselves between the governor's guards and their weapons, and pulled out their own concealed weapons and captured the guards, locking them in a room. Having captured the entire garrison, Davis then took down the flag, which was the sign for his 20 pirates to come into the castle. The men spent a day carousing at the castle, drinking all the rum and shooting the castle's cannons. Davis even convinced some of its soldiers to join them. They looted gold, ivory and about £2,000's-worth of silver from the castle before setting it on fire.

The celebrating pirates spotted another ship, and battle was just avoided when they realised that it was another pirate, captained by

Olivier Levasseur, known as 'the Buzzard'. They agreed to sail in consort and headed for Sierra Leone, where they came across the pirate Thomas Cocklyn. The three pirate ships then attacked the Royal African Company's fort at Bence Island, later to be known as Freetown. After prolonged bombardment, it was taken and looted. Shortly after, William Snelgrave's *Bird* was captured. Snelgrave attempted to defend his ship and would have been killed by Cocklyn, had not the crew of the *Bird* pleaded for his life. Davis personally protected Snelgrave from being tortured by Cocklyn and his crew, and took him for safety to the *Royal James*.

The pirates soon discovered claret and brandy in the hold, and a massive party was held aboard the *Royal James*. In their drunken state, no one noticed that a lantern had been dropped near the rum store, and a fire was spreading, near a store of 18 tons of gunpowder. Snelgrave organised a chain gang with buckets of water to put out the fire, and as a reward, Davis gave him the Buzzard's old ship to sail home.

Soon, there was an alcohol-fuelled argument about the next destination amongst the three captains, and they parted. Davis next fought and took the Dutch *Marquis del Campo*, when a large number of his men were killed and injured. The *Marquis* was renamed *Royal Rover*, which Davis equipped with 32 cannon and 27 swivel guns. Davis then captured three slavers at the Bay of Annamaboe (Anomabu), Ghana.

One was called the *Princess of London*, or possibly the *Princess*, out of London, and its third mate was a Pembrokeshire man like Davis, a former pirate captain called John Robert. Robert was to transmogrify into the greatest pirate of all time, 'Black Bart' Roberts, subtly altering his surname to avoid recognition.

The pirates were forced to abandon the rotting *King James*, which needed a new hull, and Davis sailed his *Royal Rover* to the Portuguese island of Principe, off the west coast of Africa. En route, he captured a Dutch ship, with the Governor of Accra and more than £15,000 on board. At Principe, the island's governor gave Davis and his crew an official welcome, believing their claim that they were Royal Navy pirate-hunters, sent to clear the region of piracy. A small French ship entered the harbour, and Davis quickly took it, saying he had been chasing it for trading with pirates.

Davis had the trust of the governor, and made him a gift of 12 black slaves. He wished to lure the governor aboard *Royal Rover*, where he could be held for ransom for £40,000. Although Davis invited the governor of Principe to dine on board the *Royal Rover*, the governor was informed the night before that they were pirates by a Portuguese black who had escaped and swum from Davis' ship. The governor set up an ambush of his own. Davis was invited to call at the governor's fort for a glass of wine, prior to escorting the governor to his ship. On 19 June 1719 Davis arrived at Government House with nine of his men, leaving John Robert in charge of the *Royal Rover*. The building was empty, and the pirates set off back to the ship, but were ambushed by a platoon of musketeers. Seven of the pirates were killed, including Howell Davis. According to Defoe, he was hit by five bullets and was killed only when his throat was cut: '…just as he fell, he perceived he was follow'd, and drawing out his Pistols, fired them at his pursuers: Thus like a game Cock, giving a dying Blow, that he might not fall unavenged.' Snelgrave described Davis as someone who, 'allowing for the Course of Life he had been unhappily engaged in, was a most generous humane Person.' Davis took 15 ships with a value today of millions of pounds. The crew selected another captain, not from among the 'House of Lords' of senior pirates, but the new recruit, John Robert. On 20 June John Robert attacked the Portuguese fort, looted it and threw its cannons into the sea. The town was bombarded and destroyed, and two anchored Portuguese ships were looted and burned. 'Black' Bart's career had begun in earnest (*see* next entry).

John Robert (c.May 1682–10 February 1722) – Black Bart Roberts, 'The Black Pyrate', 'The Black Captain', 'The Great Pyrate', 'The Greatest Pirate of All Time', *Barti Ddu* (Welsh), 'The Last and Most Lethal Pirate', the original 'Jolly Roger'

'No, not I,' said Silver. 'Flint was cap'n; I was quarter-master, along of my timber leg. The same broadside I lost my leg, old Pew lost his daylights. It was a master surgeon, him that ampytated me – out of college and all – Latin by the bucket, and what not; but he was hanged like a dog, and sun-dried like the rest, at Corso Castle. That was Roberts' men, that was, and comed of changing names of their ships – Royal Fortune and so on. Now, what a ship is christened, let her stay, I says.'

Treasure Island, 1883

It is interesting that only five factual pirates are mentioned in *Treasure Island* – Captain Edward England; Israel Hands; the two Welsh captains, 'Black Bart' Roberts and Howell Davis; and Roberts'

Bartholomew Roberts' flags. 'ABH' is a Barbadian head, 'AMH' a Martinican.

surgeon. Israel Hands was hanged after serving with Roberts, and Roberts' Welsh surgeon, Peter Scudamore, was said by R.L. Stevenson to have amputated Long John Silver's leg. Scudamore amputated the leg of Black Bart's second-in-command, Captain James Skyrme, and if he is the model for Silver, it makes six real pirates in *Treasure Island*.

John Robert was born in the tiny hamlet of Little Newcastle (Casnewydd Bach) in Pembrokeshire. Roberts is the most important of all Caribbean pirates, and first comes to light in a book by a contemporary naval officer. In 1737 Clement Downing wrote the life of John Plantain, in his *A compendious history of the Indian wars*. Downing was serving in East Indian Company vessels from 1716 to 1722 including the *King George*, in conflict with Angria and Indian Ocean pirates, and knew of Roberts, Plantain (*q.v.*) and Edward England (*q.v.*) being pirates in the area. Downing also served on the East India Company sloop *Emilia* in 1717, and wrote:

He [John Plantain] followed this Course of Life till he was near 20 Years of Age, when he came to Rhode-Island; there he fell into company with several Men who belonged to a Pyrate Sloop. These try'd to persuade him, with several others, to go with them; shewing great Sums of Gold, and treating him and others in a profuse and expensive Manner. His own wicked Inclinations soon led him to accept the Offer, without much Hesitation. At the same time, he acknowledged that he had no Occasion to go with them, as he belonged to a very honest Commander, and one that used the Sailors very well on all Accounts.

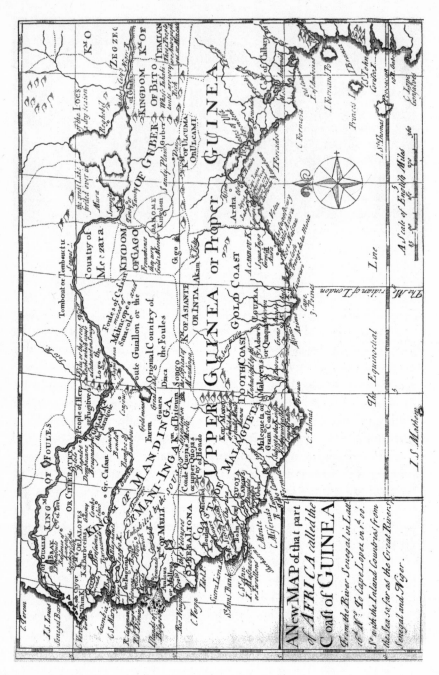

Map of the Slave Coast where Bart Roberts operated.

But being of a roving Disposition, he could not bear being under any Restraint. They soon went on board this Pyrate Sloop, and were entertained in a handsome manner, being presented to the Captain, who seem'd to like them very well, and told them if they would sail with him, they should have the same Encouragement as the other People had, and that they mould in a short time take a Voyage which would prove the making of them all; after this they design'd to accept the first Act of Grace, and leave off. They left Rhode-Island in this Sloop which they called the *Terrible*, commanded by John Williams; and one Roberts being a bold and resolute Man, was made Quarter-master. With John Plantain entered the following five, viz John James of Boston in New England and Henry Millis of Falmouth in the Weft of England; Richard Dean of Stepney in London; John Harvey of Shadwell; and Henry Jones of St Pauls London; all young Men, the oldest not being above 23 Years of Age.

Whenever any enter on board of these Ships voluntarily, they are obliged to sign all their Articles of Agreement; which is in effect, to renounce Honour, and all human Condition, for they seldom shew any Mercy to those who fall into their Hands. Frome Rhode-Island and they shaped their Course for the Coast of Guinea, and in their way took three Ships, amongst the Crews of which was Mr. Moore the Surgeon, spoken of in the *Account of Commodore Matthews's Transactions*. They pretended to give Liberty to those Ships Crews either to go or stay with them. The Boatswain of the Ship to which Mr. Moore belonged entered voluntarily, and would have used his Captain and several of the Men very barbarously, but [Bart] Roberts who was then Quarter-master, would not allow of it. They kept the Surgeon and Carpenter by Compulsion, when they found they chose to leave them; and took one of the Ships, which prov'd to be the best Sailor, and called her the Defiance. Now they had got a Ship of near 300 Tuns, which mounted 30 Guns, well mann'd and well stored with Provisions. They usually are at no certain Allowance amongst themselves, till they are in a Likelihood of being short of Provision, but every Man is allowed to eat what he pleases.

Then they put all under the care of their Quarter-master, who discharges all things with an Equality to them all, every Man and Boy faring alike; and even their Captain, or any other Officer, is allowed no more than another Man; nay, the Captain cannot keep his own Cabbin to himself, for their Bulk heads are all down, and every Man stands to his Quarters, where they lie and mess [eat], tho' they take the liberty of ranging all over the Ships. This large Ship they took was bound for Jamaica, called the *Prosperous* of London one Capt. James Commander; whom, and so many of his Crew as were not willing to go with them, they put on board those two other Vessels they let go. The *Prosperous* had on board a considerable number of East-India Bales, which they hoisted up on Deck, and slit open; the Quarter-master distributing the fame amongst the Pyrates. They arrived in a short time on the Coast of Guinea and kept all the trading Ships from carrying on any manner of Commerce at Gambo, and the other Ports on that Coast. Here they met with the Onslow whom they fought a considerable time; but the Pyrates being well mann'd, boarding her, made sad Havock of her Crew, and brought them to cry out for Quarter, which is but very indifferent at best; so when they had taken her, they made one of their number whose Name was [Edward] England a Man who had been Mate of several good Ships, Captain of her.

Plantain and his Companions were daily increasing their Store; for not long after they took the Onslow they mastered a Dutch Interloper, with whom they had a smart Battle, and had not the Sloop come to their Assistance, they would have been obliged to let her go. But the Sloop coming up, and pouring a great number of Men on board, they soon over-powered them. This Ship they liked exceeding well, and were resolved to keep her, calling her the Fancy and Capt. England having a mind to her, they allowed him to command her. They daily now increased their number, and were not for keeping so many Ships, imagining they should soon have a Squadron of Men of War after them, which they did not care to have any Correspondence with.

Now Capt. England proposed a new Voyage to them, which might be the making of them all very rich; and as they had got such good Ships under their Command, they were resolved to make the best of their present Situation. First they proposed to burn the Terrible Sloop, being old and leaky, and not fit to beat about the Cape, So having finished their Cruise on the Coast of Guinea they were resolved to steer another way. These Pyrates had now got the Fancy under the Command of Capt. England and a small Brigantine called the Unity which they named the Expedition and gave the Command to one Johnson that was with them, tho' one Quarter-matter serv'd for them all. And being in great Dispute how and which way they should dispose of each other, they went on shore on the Coast of Guinea and there held a fresh Consultation, when some were for going with Capt. England and some with Capt. Roberts.

These Disputes lasted for some time, but it was left to a committee to choose from among them, on whose Determination they resolved to rely. They had now six or seven Ships with them, on which account it was resolved, that England and Roberts should separate, for fear of a Civil War amongst themselves. England was to take the *Fancy*, the *Snow*, and the Ship they called the *Victory*, and go away for the East Indies; and Roberts and the rest were to continue and range about those Seas, as they thought fit. Roberts afterwards fell into the Hands of Sir Chaloner Ogle, and by him was brought to Justice, and he and his Crew were hung up in Chains along the Coast of Guinea, from Cape-Coast-Castle. Capt. England took to the Eastern Seas, and came away for St. Augustine's Bay, on the Island of Madagascar...

We shall see that Black Bart Roberts was not hanged, and that Edward England assisted Howell Davis into piracy. Somehow by spring 1719, Roberts was third mate on a slaver, having abandoned piracy for a few months. He may have been pardoned under an Act of Grace, when captured on the Slave Coast of Guinea by Howell Davis (*see* preceding entry). Davis was killed shortly after, and senior pirates, the infamous 'House of Lords', chose John Robert to succeed him as their captain. According to Defoe, the fearless Robert accepted the honour,

...saying, that since he had dipp'd his Hands in Muddy Water, and must be a Pyrate, it was better being a Commander than a common Man... In an honest service said he, there is thin commons [poor food and drink], low wages and hard labour; but in a pirate life there is plenty and satiety, pleasure and ease, liberty and power, and who would not balance creditor on this side when all the hazard that is run for it, at worst, is only a fore-look or two at choking [dying]. No, a merry life and a short one shall be my motto... Damnation to him who ever lived to wear a halter.

This seems to be the origin of the phrase 'a short life and a merry one'.

The senior 'Lords' who accepted Robert included the former pirate captain Christopher Moody, whose personal pirate flag was bright red, and featured an arm with a sword flanked by a winged hourglass and a skull and crossbones. Howell Davis knew Edward England, who had sailed with Roberts, and Valentine Ashplant strongly vouched for Robert as the new captain, probably knowing that he had been a former pirate.

The teetotal John Robert was soon to become known as Bartholomew Roberts, after avenging Davis's death by sacking Principe. He quickly took a Dutch Guineaman and the English *Experiment*, and he decided

The crimson flag of Christopher Moody.

to cross the Atlantic, cruising the coast of Brazil without success for nine weeks. The crew was becoming restless, and Roberts was close to becoming deposed when he decided to attack the Portuguese treasure fleet of 42 ships anchored in the Bay of All Saints off Salvador, Brazil. It was waiting for a few more ships to join and make the Atlantic crossing, and for the men-of-war to complete their preparations. The fleet was protected by two 70-gun men-of-war, and initially his men did not wish to make the attempt, but Roberts explained his plan to infiltrate the ships at night. His two ships joined the fleet at dusk, flying Portuguese flags, and were accepted as latecomers. Quietly approaching, a longboat then took over one of the ships anchored on the fringe of the fleet, and its captain was asked to take the pirates to the most valuable prize. Roberts then drew near the great 40-gun, 170-men flagship *Sagrada Familia,* but the captured captain shouted out a warning instead of the expected greeting.

However, the pirates quickly boarded the unsuspecting flagship, locking most of the crew below decks, and began towing both of their prizes out of the centre of the fleet. A Portuguese man-of-war began chasing Roberts' ships and two prizes, and Roberts fired at her. She fell off, and a sailor in the crow's nest shouted that she was waiting for the other man-of-war, stationed on the other side of the fleet, to join her. By dawn the pirates had escaped to the open seas. The *Sagrada Familia* held 40,000 gold *moidores* (*moeda d'ouro* means gold coin), pearls, silver and jewellery. For his personal use, Roberts took a thick gold chain holding a cross of diamonds set with a huge emerald, designed for King João V of Portugal. Now admired by the House of Lords, 'Black Bart' began dressing in crimson silk from head to toe, with a scarlet ostrich-plumed hat, and the royal emerald chain when going into battle. The tall captain was known as '*le joli rouge*' by his French victims, 'the pretty man in red', the origin of the 'Jolly Roger', and the sight of 'the great pirate Roberts' meant that most ships surrendered rather than fight. The tall Roberts seems to have been called 'black' because of his dark skin, probably weathered at sea for over 20 years.

Gosse, in his 1932 *The History of Piracy* notes that Black Bart Roberts

... seems to attain most nearly to the popular pirate of fiction... He was remarkable, even among his remarkable companions, for several things. First of all, he only drank tea, thus being the only recorded teetotaller known to the fraternity [of pirates]. Also he was a strict disciplinarian and on board his ships all lights had to be out by 8pm. Any of the crew who wished to continue drinking after that hour had to do so upon the open deck. But try as he would this ardent apostle of abstemiousness was unable to put down drinking entirely. If Roberts had lived today, he would probably have been the leading light on the council of a local vigilance society. He would allow no women aboard his ships; in fact he made a law by which any man who brought a woman on board disguised as a man was to suffer death. Nor did he permit games of cards or dice to be played for money, as he strongly disapproved of gambling. Being a strict Sabbatarian, he allowed the musicians to have a rest on the seventh day. This was as well, for the post of musician on a pirate ship was no sinecure, since every pirate had the right to demand a tune at any hour of the day or night. He used to place a guard to protect all his women prisoners and it is sadly suspicious that there was always the greatest competition amongst the worst characters in the ship to be appointed sentry over a good-looking woman prisoner. No fighting was permitted amongst his crew on board ship. All quarrels had to be settled on shore, the duellists standing back-to-back armed with pistol and cutlass, pirate fashion. Bartholomew dressed for action, surprisingly, was the very beau of pirates. A tall, dark man, he used to wear a rich damask waistcoat and breeches, a red feather in his cap, a gold chain round his neck with a large diamond cross dangling from it, a sword in his hand and two pairs of pistols hanging at the end of a silk sling flung over his shoulders.

Roberts took more than 400 recorded prizes in three years, across the Atlantic and Caribbean, and was famed as 'The Great Pyrate' – far better known at the time than Blackbeard, Captain Kidd, Edward Low and any other pirates. A teetotaller with many blacks in his crews, he did not fear attacking naval vessels belonging to Spain, France, Portugal, the Low Countries or England, whereas other pirates would flee from such powerful ships. Roberts sailed his *Royal Rover* to Devil's Island off Guiana to careen and celebrate, and soon after took a sloop on the estuary of the Surinam River. Sighting a brigantine, Roberts chased it in his sloop, with 40 men, and left Walter Kennedy in command of the treasure-laden *Royal Rover*. Roberts was becalmed at sea for eight days, and returning to the *Royal Rover*, discovered that Kennedy had sailed off with her treasure. Kennedy was a poor navigator, and tried to sail to Ireland but instead landed in Scotland, where 17 of his crew were arrested. In Dublin, Kennedy squandered his money, then becoming a brothel-keeper in London before being recognised, tried and finally executed on 21 July 1721. Swearing never again to take on any Irishman, Roberts renamed his sloop the *Fortune* and agreed a new pirate code, with his remaining crew signing articles.

In February 1720, Roberts took four ships off Barbados, and he was then joined by French pirate Montigny la Palisse in the sloop *Sea King*. The Governor of Barbados sent out two well-armed ships, the *Summerset* and the *Philipa*, to attack Roberts and on 26 February la Palisse and the *Sea King* quickly sailed off from the action, leaving Roberts to fight them alone. The *Fortune* sustained severe damage and only escaped by jettisoning guns to lighten the ship. Nearly all of Roberts' crew were wounded, and 20 died while sailing to Dominica to repair the *Fortune*. In March 1720, two armed sloops were sent by the Governor of Martinique to take Roberts, but he had just sailed north. Roberts thus swore vengeance against Barbados and Martinique, and had another personal black flag made of himself with his emerald chain standing upon two skulls, one labeled ABH (a Barbadian's Head) and the other AMH (a Martinican's Head). The heads represented the respective governors of the islands. One of his three other flags showed Roberts sharing an hourglass symbolising one's shortening time on Earth, with a skeleton representing Death.

Roberts began referring to himself as the 'Admiral of the Leeward Islands', and such was his fame that he was sought out on one occasion by two ships full of would-be pirates looking for advice. He gave them guidance, weapons and ammunition. Knowing that his *Fortune* was no longer powerful enough to cruise the West Indies seas, and being undermanned, Roberts sailed north to less dangerous waters, to recruit and take a better ship. The *Fortune* next raided Canso, in northern Nova Scotia, 'the oldest fishing port on mainland North America'. It was still being fought over by the Native Americans, French and English and was a centre for fur trading, where the English were building a fort. Roberts then took a few ships on the Newfoundland banks and off Cape Breton, before sailing into Ferryland, looting around a dozen ships. On 21 June 1720, the pirates flew Roberts' flags to enter Trepassey harbour, and 22 merchant ships and 150 fishing ships were immediately deserted by their panic-stricken crews. The pirates became masters of Trepassey without any resistance being offered. Roberts was angered by the cowardice of the 22 captains who had abandoned their ships, and each morning he fired a cannon to force the captains to attend him on board the *Fortune*. They had been informed that anyone who was absent would have his ship burnt.

A fine Bristol brig was fitted out with 16 guns to replace the small sloop *Fortune*, being given the same name. The pirates left in late June, setting fire to all vessels in the harbour. In July, a flotilla of six French ships was taken on the Newfoundland Banks. Roberts immediately made one, a square-rigged brig, yet another new flagship, replacing the Bristol brig. She was equipped with 26 cannons and renamed the *Good Fortune*. His French prisoners were placed on the old *Fortune* sloop and left behind. Roberts wished to punish Barbados and Martinique for their temerity in trying to capture him with armed ships disguised as simple merchant traders. There was also little left to take on the Northern American coastline and Atlantic shipping was scarce, partially because of his depredations. With his powerful new flagship, Roberts took four more ships and a few boats as he returned to the West Indies, there meeting up with Montigny la Palisse's *Sea King*, which Roberts allowed to rejoin his pirate flotilla. By this time Black Bart had taken more than 100 merchant ships – French, English, Dutch, Spanish, Danish and Portuguese – and 150 fishing vessels.

He careened his ships at Desirada (now Désirade), off Guadeloupe, and re-rigged his brig *Good Fortune* to make her faster and more manoeuvrable, renaming her *Royal Fortune*. On 26 September 1720 he hoisted his flags, and with his musicians playing, sailed into St Kitts harbour, where nearly all the moored ships struck their flags. He looted seven ships, burnt two for their minimal resistance and took two to join his fleet. The next day his sails were ripped by cannon from Basseterre Fort as he returned to put some prisoners ashore. He sailed to St Barts to repair his ship, sell cargo and for his men to get drunk and visit the local brothels.

Off Tortola in the Virgin Islands, the pirates took a 22-gun French brig from Martinique, which again Roberts chose as his new flagship *Royal Fortune*, adding 10 cannon. He left her French captain with an old sloop saying 'exchange is no robbery.' Between 23 and 26 October, 14 English and French ships were taken and their valuables placed in sloops acting as store ships.

The 32-gun *Royal Fortune* and 18-gun *Sea King*, firing their guns, with 350 pirates, black flags flying and musicians playing, next sailed into the harbour at St Lucia, having spotted a 42-gun Dutch 'interloper'. (An interloper was a ship, usually heavily armed, that trespassed on a trade monopoly, by conducting unauthorised trade in an area designated to a chartered company. Colonists of all nations could buy smuggled goods from them far more cheaply than from the national trade monopolies). However, its 90 men did not surrender, using booms to prevent the pirates from grappling their ship, and a four-hour fight ensued. Roberts could have blown the ship apart, but did not wish to sink her, as he desired yet another new flagship, and the smugglers were known to carry large amounts of gold. Eventually all the Dutch crew were killed, while la Palisse looted another 15 ships in the harbour. Roberts' men, thirsty for vengeance for their losses, went aboard all these boats, killing every Dutchman they could find. The Dutch ship became yet another new flagship, again the *Royal Fortune*, now with 44 guns and 124 hardened pirates. The fleet also included the French brig taken off Tortola, a St Lucia sloop and the *Good Fortune*.

Yet more ships were taken and with naval vessels of all nations after him, Roberts decided to head back to Africa. Off the Cape Verde Islands, he came across 2 fully laden merchant ships, escorted by 2 Portuguese men-of-war, one with 40 cannon and the other with 80 guns. He decided to attack, and as previously, the treacherous la Palisse sailed quickly away. However, Roberts failed to catch them, and prevailing winds meant that he was pushed away from reprovisioning at the Cape Verde islands. Roberts had no chance of a landfall and calculated that the nearest point would be at Surinam,

2,100 miles away, using the trade winds. He had just one barrel of 63 gallons of water, and men began drinking their own urine or seawater, as the water blackened and ran out. They were now provisioned to a swallow a day. After a terrible voyage, Roberts made Surinam, having lost some men, and reprovisioned at Tobago in December 1720.

More ships were taken, including the great Dutch brigantine *El Puerto del Principe* from Flushing. On 18 February 1721, there was a long battle with another Dutch interloper, and all her crew were killed. Roberts now hoisted their Dutch flags and sailed up and down the Martinique shoreline, enticing boats to come out and trade with his false 'interloper'; 14 boats, filled with gold and coin for barter, were tempted out from various ports. Each was taken and its crew whipped or killed, such was Roberts' hatred of the Martinicans who had wanted him dead.

After 13 of the ships were burnt and the survivors put on the remaining vessel, Roberts sent a message to the governor that he 'hoped we should always meet with such a Dutch trade as this was'. A Danish ship was then taken, its captain reporting that Roberts' ship had 180 white men and 48 French Creole blacks, with 42 cannon, from 4-pounders to 12-pounders, and another 7 guns. HMS *Rose* was ordered to take Roberts, but its captain, Witney, kept well away from the feared 'Great Pyrate'. Yet more ships were taken, and in April 1721 Roberts took a French naval 32-gun man-of-war with 9 swivel guns and 140 crew off the Windward Islands. Walter Kennedy said at his own trial that the Governor of Martinique was on the ship and Roberts swung him from the yardarm. Roberts was almost alone among pirates in attacking naval warships. On 18 April, Thomas Anstis secretly sailed off in the *Good Fortune*, which was storing most of the loot, with 100 white and 40 black crew.

Black Bart now sailed back across the Atlantic for the Cape Verde Islands, taking Dutch and English ships. The *Royal Fortune* was found to be unseaworthy and was abandoned on the islands. The pirates transferred to the *Sea King*, which was renamed as yet another *Royal Fortune*. Roberts made landfall off the Guinea coast in early June, near the mouth of the Senegal River. Two French warships, one of 10 guns and one of 16 guns, gave chase, thinking Black Bart was a Dutch interloper, but surrendered when his black flags were run out. One, the *Comte de Toulouse*, was renamed the *Ranger*, while the other was named the *Little Ranger* and used as a storeship. Thomas Sutton was made captain of the *Ranger*, and James Skyrme became captain of the *Little Ranger*.

HMS *Swallow* and HMS *Weymouth* had been expressly instructed to kill Roberts, and a deserter from the *Swallow*, Robert Armstrong, joined the pirates, informing Roberts of their mission. On 8 August, the pirates took two large ships off Liberia, including the frigate *Onslow* transporting soldiers, a number of them asking to join the pirates. The *Onslow* was converted to become the fifth *Royal Fortune*. In November and December, Roberts careened his ships and the crews caroused at Cape Lopez and Annobón Island in the Gulf of Guinea.

Black Bart took several ships in January 1722, then sailed into Whydah (Ouidah) harbour, where 10 of the 11 slavers at anchor immediately struck their colours. Each ship was ransomed, and eight pounds of gold dust per ship was paid. The remaining vessel was set on fire at night by some angry pirates, with approximately 80 enslaved Africans dying on board. On 5 February 1722, HMS *Swallow*, captained by Chaloner Ogle, sighted the *Royal Fortune*, *Ranger*, and *Little Ranger* careening at Cape Lopez. She veered away to avoid a shoal, and thinking she was a fleeing merchant ship, Roberts sent James Skyrme and the *Ranger* in pursuit. Over the horizon, the *Swallow* opened her gun ports and killed 10 pirates in a broadside. Skyrme had his leg smashed off by a cannonball, but refused to leave the deck. Many of the crew did not fight, being drunk, and believing the invincible Roberts would rescue them. On 9 February Roberts captured the *Neptune*, and his crew celebrated through the night. On 10 February, the drunken pirates thought they saw the *Ranger* returning, but it was the *Swallow*. Robert Armstrong, the deserter from the *Swallow*, recognised his old ship and ran to inform Roberts who was breakfasting in his great cabin, with Captain Hill of the captured *Neptune*. Defoe describes Bart dressing for action:

> Roberts himself made a gallant figure, at the time of the engagement, being dressed in a rich crimson damask waistcoat and breeches, a red feather in his hat, a gold chain round his neck, with a diamond cross hanging to it, a sword in his hand, and two pairs of pistols slung over his shoulders...

Roberts knew that if he sailed past the *Swallow*, he would be exposed to just one broadside from her, but once past, the wind would allow him a good chance of escaping, while the *Swallow* would have to turn about in shallow waters. However, his inebriated helmsman steered exactly the opposite course, becalming the *Royal Fortune* and allowing the *Swallow* to deliver a second broadside. Roberts had moved to sit astride a cannon, expecting death, and was killed instantly, struck by grapeshot in the throat. His crew wrapped his bejewelled body in sailcloth and weighted it with chains, throwing him overboard, as he had wished never to be taken. Only three pirates were killed and 272 men captured. There occurred the greatest pirate trial of all time at Cape Corso Castle, resulting in 52 pirates being sentenced to death by hanging, and 20 men to a fairly rapid death sentence in the Cape Coast mines. During the passage to London, 13 of 17 died; 72 black pirates were returned to slavery.

Of the 52 hanged men, the 18 greatest pirates, such as his 'Lords' Ashplant, Sutton, Simpson, Magness and Hardy, were executed first. These 18 most important pirates were all dipped in tar and hung in chains to rot, as an example to ships outside the port. Among them was 'Israel Hinde' who had only three months earlier joined Roberts. The manner of his treatment must mean that he was the 'Israel Hande/ Hands' who had been in Blackbeard's crew. He was thought to have died in poverty in London, after turning king's evidence against Blackbeard.

Governors of colonies from the North Americas and the Caribbean to Africa and India wrote letters giving thanks for the destruction of 'The Black Pyrate', who had almost brought transatlantic trade to a standstill. Daniel Defoe, under the nom-de-plume Charles Johnson, had the opportunity to talk to Woodes Rogers and some of Bart's crew, and wrote in his 1724 *A General History of Pyrates* that 'the account of Roberts runs to a greater length than that of any other pyrate ... because he ravaged the seas longer than the rest ... having made more Noise in the World than the others.' In the film *The Princess Bride*, the name 'Dread Pirate Roberts' is a reference to him.

Patrick Pringle, in *Jolly Roger*, puts the Welshman's career as a pirate into true perspective:

Most of the Guinea pirates were exceptionally daring, and one of them was possibly the most daring pirate who ever lived. His name was Bartholomew Roberts, and he bestraddles the Age of Piracy like a colossus. A Welsh poet has honoured 'Black Barty', but he has never become a household name like Kidd or Blackbeard. I cannot imagine why. Not only was he immeasurably bolder, braver, and more successful – not only is his story far more exciting and dramatic – but in his lifetime he achieved a far greater fame. For nearly three years he was feared more than any other man at sea. Moreover, Johnson, on whose history most popular pirate books are based, did Roberts full justice, giving him five times as much space as Blackbeard or any other pirate ... the story of Roberts (is) one of the best documented in pirate history. This is very fortunate, for Roberts was of considerable historical as well as personal importance. He was not only the greatest of the pirates, but he was virtually the last... Captain Ogle was knighted for destroying Roberts. I think this is the only case of such an honour being granted for taking pirates, and it is a measure of the importance that was attached to the event. Bartholomew Roberts was indeed the terror of the seas, and the news of his death was acclaimed by Governors in places as far apart as New York, Port Royal, and even Bombay... It was said that the end of 'the great pirate' would be the end of the great days of piracy. It was, too.

The Ballad of Barti Ddu (or 'Black Bart's Shanty')
A reworking by this author of the poem in Welsh about Black Bart (Barti Ddu) by I.D. Hooson.

Howel Davis in the *Royal Rover*
Was the Cavalier Prince of Pirates
With his House of Lords he roamed the seas
To the King's discomfit.
He took Bartholomew Roberts
In the *Princess* on the Gold Coast
And the mate from Casnewydd Bach
Soon led the Brethren's great host

Baa Baa Bartholomew
The great pyrate Roberts
Baa Baa Bartholomew
In his coat of scarlet

Cap'n Davis soon was killed
At the Isle of Princes
The House of Lords chose Bart as cap'n
To scour the sea's provinces.
Barti Ddu, he sailed the seas
The ship's band always playing
'A short life and a merry one'
Was his favourite saying.
Baa Baa Bartholomew etc.

Black Bart sailed the Seven Seas
In his silk scarlet costume
Crimson would not show the blood
As the Spanish met their doom
Baa Baa Bartholomew etc.

Black Bart took 400 ships
In his great *Royal Fortune*
The House of Lords sang and caroused
While the ship's band played the old tunes.
From Africa to the Caribbean
And up to Newfoundland
He stopped Atlantic shipping
His cutlass in his hand.
Baa Baa Bartholomew etc.

His ships were full of gems and gold
But Black Bart became tired
He was the lone teetotaller
He could see his funeral pyre
Baa Baa Bartholomew etc.

The House of Lords drank more and more
Black Bart was losing patience
He seemed to be seeking his death
He'd had enough of vengeance.
He sailed straight for the royal ship
With his drunken crew
The cannon blew him half apart
There was nothing left to do
Baa Baa Bartholomew etc.

His frightened crew wrapped Bart in chains
And threw him overboard
Still wearing his diamond cross
To go and meet his Lord.
Le Joli Rouge still sails the seas
Teacup in one hand
Looking for adventure
And for a freer land
Baa Baa Bartholomew etc.

Thomas Anstis (*fl.*1718–April 1723) – a Member of 'the House of Lords', Murdered in his Hammock

In 1718 Anstis, Howell Davis, Dennis Topping, Walter Kennedy and two other seamen shipped out of Providence in the sloop *Buck*, and began pirating. Upon the killing of Howell Davis, Anstis served as a member of 'The House of Lords' under Bart Roberts until 18 April 1721, when Anstis and John Fenn slipped away in the night and sailed to the West Indies in the brigantine *Good Fortune*, taking most of Roberts' loot. In 1721 he captured the larger *Morning Star* off Newfoundland, taking on her carpenter, John Phillips, and refitting her with 32 guns and 100 men. He then gave the *Good Fortune* to John Fenn.

In June 1721 Anstis and Fenn took several ships in the vicinity of Hispaniola, Jamaica and Martinique, from which they increased the size of their crews and reprovisioned. His pirates were suspected of 'abusing and wounding' one Colonel Doyle of Montserrat, for having attempted to prevent the pirates from brutalising a female passenger. The woman in question, probably taken off the *Irwin*, was gang-raped and flung overboard.

However, many of the crew wished to quit pirating, claiming they had been 'forced' by Roberts or Anstis. Fighting broke out, and a petition was drawn up to request a pardon, which they sent via a merchant ship. The pirates awaited an answer, living for some months on an uninhabited island off Cabo San Antonio, south-west Cuba. In August 1722 they found that their petition had drawn no interest, and that Admiral Flowers had been instructed to capture them. They thus sailed out in the *Morning Star*, but she was wrecked upon the Grand Cayman Islands, and it may have been at this time that Fenn lost his right hand.

While anchored to recover, Fenn and the crew of the badly damaged *Good Fortune* were set upon by the English men-of-war HMS *Hector* and HMS *Adventure*. Anstis cut his anchor cable ('cut and ran') and was chased for some time, escaping by rowing the ship during a calm in the wind. The *Good Fortune* was sailed to the Bay of Honduras to careen and refit, and Anstis took three more ships and burned them all to leave no trace. Some of his prisoners, including one Captain Durfey, attempted to take over the pirate ship, but luckily escaped with their lives. In early December 1722, the pirates took a large frigate and mounted her with 24 guns. The one-handed Fenn, although having wrecked the *Morning Star*, was given command of this larger ship.

After taking two more prizes, the pirates sailed to the Bahamas, taking more ships.

Anstis put into Tobago to clean and refit in April 1723, but was surprised by the arrival of the man-of-war HMS *Winchelsea*. Anstis and his men burned their prizes to destroy evidence, and set out to sea. Fenn and others on shore fled into the island's interior, but the *Winchelsea*'s marines captured them. Fenn and six pirates were hanged in May 1723 on Antigua. Anstis and several of his henchmen had escaped in the *Good Fortune,* but some members of his discouraged crew murdered him as he slept in his hammock, and took prisoner all those who remained loyal to Anstis.

The mutineers sailed for Curaçao, where they received amnesty, and their pirate prisoners were hanged. With the pirate carpenter John Phillips (*see* next entry), Brigstock Weaver escaped into the woods and hid from searching marines. The penniless Weaver now managed to return to England while Phillips found employment on a merchant ship. Gosse writes:

> This period of prosperity came to an end, for in May, 1723, Weaver, dressed in rags, was begging charity at the door of a Mr. Thomas Smith in Bristol, telling a plausible tale of how he had been taken and robbed by some wicked pirates, but had lately managed to escape from them. The kindly Mr. Smith, together with a Captain Edwards, gave Weaver £10 and provided him with a lodging at the Griffin Inn. Being now dressed in good clothes, Weaver enjoyed walking about the streets of Bristol, until one day he met with a sea-captain who claimed former acquaintance and invited him into a neighbouring tavern to share a bottle of wine with him. Over this the captain reminded the pirate that he had been one of his victims, and that Weaver had once stolen from him a considerable quantity of liquor; but at the same time he had not forgotten that the pirate had used him very civilly, and that therefore, if he would give him four hogsheads of cider, nothing further would be said about the matter. Weaver would not, or could not, produce these, and was apprehended, brought to London, and there tried and sentenced to death, and hanged at Execution Dock.

John Phillips (d.18 April 1724) – The 'Sea-Artist' turned Pirate

On 19 April 1721, Phillips was a ship's carpenter (a 'sea-artist', one of the skilled members of a crew) sailing to Newfoundland, when taken by the pirate Thomas Anstis in the brigantine *Good Fortune*.

Phillips was taken on by Anstis, staying with him until April, 1722, when Anstis sent Phillips and some others ashore on Tobago to careen a captured frigate. The English man-of-war HMS *Winchelsea* spotted the pirates, forcing Anstis to put to sea and abandon his men ashore. Most of the crew were captured, but Phillips hid in the forest from the searching marines, and later sailed to Bristol with a few other survivors. However, some of his former comrades were arrested in Bristol, and Phillips escaped by taking a ship bound for Newfoundland. On 29 August 1723 he seized a schooner named the *Revenge*, with a few other crewmates. The ship belonged to William Minott, sailing out of Petty Harbour. Phillips now had a crew of John Nutt (sailing master), James Spark (gunner), Thomas Fern (carpenter) and William White (tailor and sailmaker). They then agreed a pirate code of articles, only one of four which have survived (including Black Bart's).

Before leaving north-east America, Phillips took several fishing vessels and added to his crew, then took two prizes off Barbados, one by subterfuge. On one of the fishing boats was John Rose Archer, who had sailed with Blackbeard, and he became Phillips' quartermaster. On 5 September 1723, Phillips took the sloop *Dolphin*, with John Fillmore, great-grandfather of U.S. president Millard Fillmore, aboard, and forced him into piracy. When Phillips took a Martinique ship at the end of 1723, he was said to have flown a red flag, signifying no quarter if the ship defended herself, so her larger and more heavily armed crew surrendered without firing. His personal flag was later found on the *Revenge*, described at the time as: 'their own dark flag, in the middle of which an anatomy, and at one side of it a dart in the heart, with drops of blood proceeding from it; and on the other side an hour-glass.'

At Tobago, the pirates careened the *Revenge*, and searched for some of Phillips' abandoned pirates from Anstis's crew, finding a former black comrade named Pedro who joined them. They then captured a snow, and Fern and some other pirates tried to make off with her, but Phillips caught up with them. Sailing north from Tobago, Phillips took a Portuguese ship and a couple of sloops. Again, Fern tried to make off in one of the sloops, and in accordance with his pirate articles Phillips killed him and another mutineer. On 25 March 1724 another two ships were taken, followed by a sloop and schooner in early April. Phillips now sailed for Newfoundland, to take on more crew from the fishery vessels that abounded there. En route, he replaced the battered *Revenge* with a sloop out of Cape Ann. On 1 April 1724 he arrived at Nova Scotia, robbing 13 New England fishing vessels over the next few days.

Phillips then took a sloop captained by Andrew Harradine, who conspired with some forced men to kill Phillips. On 18 April they made a surprise attack, killing Phillips, his sailing master, boatswain, and gunner. Phillips had been a pirate captain for less than eight months but had captured 34 ships. John Rose Archer was taken and with three other pirates was hanged at Boston on 2 June 1724. All four pirates gave widely reprinted speeches. Archer blamed not only drinking but also brutal merchant captains, who drove oppressed sailors to seek piracy as their only escape. The account by John Fillmore of life aboard the *Revenge* is an important eye-witness document of piracy.

John Evans (d.1723) – From a Row-Boat to a Pirate Ship Captaincy to an Unfair Duel

Defoe gives us a cameo of the Welshman Evans, the master of a sloop operating from Nevis until losing the post. For some time, he then worked as a mate on ships sailing from Jamaica, but with the end of war there was a continuing surplus of seamen. Berths were now few and far between, and wages had been lowered. About the end of September 1722, with a few seamen in a similar situation, he stole a rowing boat at Port Royal, and went ashore on the north side of the island to raid some houses. After a few burglaries the pirates took a small Bermudan sloop lying at anchor in Dunns Hole. Evans next put in at a small village and sacked a local tavern of all the goods that they would need, and renamed their ship the *Scowerer*. Sailing to Hispaniola, they captured a Spanish ship, with each man receiving about £150, and then set course for the Windward Islands. Off Puerto Rico, they took Captain Diamond's *Dove*, bound from New England to Jamaica. Evans forced the *Dove's* experienced mate to join them, with three other crew.

A former merchant captain, Evans was sympathetic to captured crews. He allowed the *Dove* to leave after looting her. After taking on fresh water and supplies, off the island of Disseada on 11 January 1723 Evans captured the 200-ton *Lucretia and Catherine*. Then, near the island of Ruby, he came across a fine Dutch sloop and captured her. He released the *Lucretia and Catherine* and kept the Dutch sloop. The *Scowerer* and the sloop next set sail for the north coast of Jamaica and captured a sugar drover (or drogher – a small West Indies bark transporting sugar from plantation to port).

The crew elected to sail to the Cayman Islands to careen and reprovision. However, Evans had been in constant dispute with his boatswain, and en route the pirate challenged his captain to a duel, with pistols and swords, when they landed. When they did reach land, Captain Evans reminded the boatswain of this, but the latter now refused to fight. Evans reminded him of the 'pirate code', but the boatswain still refused to fight. Angered at his cowardice, Evans began beating him with his cane, but the boatswain produced a pistol and shot Evans through the head, killing him instantly. The boatswain then jumped overboard and tried to swim to shore, but he was soon picked up by the *Scowerer's* crew. The crew, so angered at the death of their successful captain, resolved to torture the man, but were unable to do so, as two of the crew shot him first. Lacking a suitable volunteer to take over as captain, the crew set ashore at the Cayman Islands with £9,000 to be divided among 30 pirates.

Christopher Winter (fl. 1717–1723) – the Renegade Costagarda and Nicholas Brown (d.1726) 'the Grand Pirate' with the Rum-Pickled Head

It seems that Winter was captured by pirates and became one, as his name was on the roster of pirates at New Providence when Woodes Rogers arrived there. In 1717 Winter took a sloop off the coast of Jamaica and convinced its mate, Jasper Seagar (Edward England, *q.v.*) to join him in pirating. England's agreeable manner and sailing skills were such that Winter granted him his own sloop, sailing out of New Providence.

In August 1718 Winter accepted the king's offer of pardon to all pirates who surrendered, but soon afterwards not only returned to piracy but now approached the Spanish Governor of Cuba. Winter converted to Catholicism, working as a Cuban *costagarda* until at least 1723. From the Spanish perspective he was defending their lands from the English, but to the other nationalities he was a pirate, chiefly preying on English vessels. He also made raids upon the coast of English-held Jamaica, stealing slaves to take back to Cuba, receiving a commission for each slave. In 1722 the Governor of Jamaica, Sir Nicholas Lawes, sent Lieutenant Joseph Lawes in the snow HMS *Happy* to demand the surrender of Winter and another renegade, Nicholas Brown. The Spanish refused, and nothing resulted except an exchange of angry letters between Lieutenant Lawes and the Governor of Cuba. Winter was active in Spanish service through

1723, known as one of 'the most notorious rogues and renegades of all', but disappears from history.

Nicholas Brown raided and operated off the Jamaican coast, and was offered a pardon by Woodes Rogers in Jamaica, which he accepted. However, Brown continued pirating, known as 'the Grand Pirate', and used caves on the cliffs of Negril to store his booty. A bounty was placed on his head. Brown probably worked for the Spanish in attacking English shipping, as he was mentioned alongside Winter when the English tried to extricate Winter from Cuba. His childhood friend Captain John Drudge had become a pirate hunter, and tried to ambush Brown, who was badly wounded in a gun battle. Brown surrendered but died of his wounds. Drudge then cut off Brown's head, pickled it in rum, and handed it over for the £500 reward offered by the Jamaican governor.

William Lewis (*fl.*1687–1726) – The Captain with one of the longest pirating careers, believed to have 'a Pact with the Devil'

Defoe tells us that a young man named Bannister had run away from Port Royal in June 1684, to take part in a privateering venture on a 30-gun ship. Bannister was caught and brought back on the frigate HMS *Ruby*, and put on trial by Lieutenant-Governor Molesworth, but was surprisingly released by the jury on a technical point. For the next 30 months, Bannister became active in piracy, eluding Molesworth's frigates. However, in January 1687 Captain Spragge's corvette sailed into Port Royal with Bannister and three other pirates hanging at the yardarm.

Defoe reckoned that from the age of 11, William Lewis had learned his trade from Bannister, who treated him as his 'nephew'. Lewis and another boy Darby McCaffrey had been 'triced up' (secured with small ropes) to Spragge's mizzen-peak (the top of the aft-mast), hanging 'like two living flags', when he sailed in with Bannister's body. Lewis was released as he said he had been forced into servitude by Bannister at Boston Harbor, and with his childhood friend McCaffrey he joined a merchantman. They were captured by the Spanish and enslaved. It was said that Lewis was an accomplished linguist in French, Spanish and the dialects of the Indians of the Mosquito Coast. Lewis and McCaffrey escaped from Havana with six other prisoners, taking a piragua (canoe) and with it capturing a sloop used for the turtling trade.

With McCaffrey as his quartermaster, Captain Lewis had become, three decades later in 1717, one of the 'leading lights' in the pirate community of Nassau. With 40 men on his sloop, he had taken a pink, bound from Jamaica to Campeche Bay, some Bermudan sloops, then another 90-ton sloop. He called her the *Morning Star,* now carrying 80 men, and mounting 12 cannon. Several ships were taken in the Leeward Passage. When Lewis careened in a South Carolina creek, some of his forced men ran away to Charleston.

In 1726 he operated off Virginia and South Carolina, taking ships and selling the goods he had taken out of Atlantic shipping. (Only New York and Boston were bigger towns than the port of Charleston, South Carolina, at this time in North America.) Defoe records that Lewis had many French pirates with him, and the English crew were conspiring to maroon him and the French, so Lewis put all the Englishmen in an open boat with only 10 pieces of beef for sustenance, and sailed off to Newfoundland with a crew of only French and black seamen.

There he took several fishing boats, then careened, before anchoring in Trinity Harbour in Conception Bay. Several merchant ships were in harbour, including Captain Beal's 24-gun *Herman* galley, which Lewis captured. Beal told Lewis that if he sent his quartermaster McCaffrey ashore he would be able to furnish him with provisions, but the quartermaster was instead imprisoned in chains by Woodes Rogers, and cannon was pointed at the harbour entrance to prevent Lewis or his prize *Herman* leaving port. At night, Lewis rowed from the *Herman* to his sloop *Morning Star* and managed to sail out, although damaged in the hull by cannon fire. Laying off the port, Lewis captured two fishing shallops, the captain of one being Captain Beal's brother. Lewis told him that if his quartermaster was not released, all his prisoners would be executed, so McCaffrey was given a boat to row out to the pirates. The merchantmen in the harbour had sent a fast rider to St John's to summon the Welsh Captain Tudor Trevor in the HMS *Sheerness* man-of-war to capture Lewis's *Morning Star,* but Lewis sailed off just four hours before Trevor's arrival.

Lewis took larger and larger French and English vessels, ending up with a French prize of 24 guns. Now in command of 50 men, he made her his flagship and again named her *Morning Star.* From Newfoundland, he sailed to the coast of Guinea, taking English, Dutch and Portuguese ships. Sailing off the African coast with 200 men, he was chasing Captain Smith's slaver from the Carolinas when his mainmast and foremasts were carried away; he clambered into the main top, tore out a handful of his hair and threw it into the gale, shouting 'Good Devil, take this till I come!' He eventually overhauled Smith's ship and took it, but his superstitious sailors were unhappy with his 'consorting with the Devil'. They noted that after his appeal to the Devil, with a damaged ship, Lewis had caught up with his previously escaping prize. There was now another argument between the more numerous French pirates and the English crew, and the French decided to leave under Captain Barre in a large sloop that had just been captured. They believed Lewis's *Morning Star* to be riddled with the teredos worm. They took ammunition and goods off Lewis's ship and moved away to anchor off the coast in a strong wind, beginning to store their goods.

While they were thus occupied, the angry Lewis told his men,

> They were a Parcel of Rogues, and he would make 'em refund; accordingly [Lewis] run along Side, his Guns being all loaded and new primed, and ordered him to cut away his [Barre's] Mast, or he would sink him. Le Barre was forced to obey. Then he ordered them all ashore; they begged to have Liberty of carrying their Arms, Goods & co. with 'em, but he allowed 'em only their small Arms, and cartridge Boxes. Then he brought the Sloop along Side, put every Thing on board the Ship, and sunk the Sloop. Le Barre and the rest begged to be taken on Board; however, tho' he denied 'em, he suffered le Barre and some few to come, with whom he and his Men drank plentifully. The Negroes on board [with] Lewis told him, that the French had a Plot against him. He answered, he could not withstand his Destiny; for the devil told him in the great Cabin, he should be murdered that Night. In the dead of Night came the rest of the French on board in Canoes, got into the Cabin and killed Lewis; they fell on the Crew, but, after an Hour and a Half's Dispute, the French were beat off, and the Quarter-master, John Cornelius, an Irish Man, succeeded Lewis.

The English crew had believed Lewis had a pact with the Devil, viewing it as a bad omen and thought their lives were in danger. They had elected to draw straws behind Lewis's back and plotted his assassination. One of the crew members drew the shortest straw and he went into the cabin of the sleeping captain and killed him with a single shot. Defoe goes on to describe Cornelius' exploits; he took Joseph Williams' slaver off the Guinea Coast before dying in Madagascar.

John Gow *(c.*1698–11 June 1725) – 'The Orkney Pirate' and 'Lieutenant' James Williams (d.11 June 1725) – 'a Merciless, Cruel and Inexorable Wretch'

Also known as Smith and Goffe, Gow was probably born in Wick, Scotland, and from 1699 grew up in the then-important port of

Stromness, Orkney; Defoe gives a full account. Some time before August 1724 Gow sailed from London to Lisbon, and on the return voyage attempted to recruit other crew members to mutiny and take the ship. Back in London, loyal sailors reported the event and Gow escaped to Amsterdam, where he found a berth as a seaman. Being a skilled sailor, Gow was promoted to second mate and gunner on the 200-ton *George*, bound for Santa Cruz on the Barbary Coast. Taking on a cargo of leather, woollen cloths and beeswax, the *George* left Santa Cruz for Genoa on 3 November 1724. However, the crew were starving and discontented, with poor food and a vindictive Guernsey captain, Olivier Ferneau. Some of the crew complained, interrupting a meeting of the captain with merchants, one threatening 'as we eat, so shall we work.' Many of the 23 crew began refusing to obey Ferneau's orders, and with his first mate Ferneau decided to stash the ship's small arms in his own cabin, for defence in case of mutiny. The conversation between Ferneau and the mate was overheard and reported to Gow, who was then told by the captain to clear the arms from their store, load them and bring them to the captain's cabin.

Gow secretly conscripted around half the crew to follow his orders, all fearing the captain's next actions. At night Gow's mutineers crept to the cabins of the first mate, the surgeon and the supernumerary, cutting their throats while they slept. (A Supernumerary is a person in addition to the regular complement of crew, but having no shipboard responsibilities.) However, the surgeon managed to stagger to the deck before dying, and his shouts alerted the captain. Ferneau left his cabin and was attacked by three mutineers and severely wounded. Gow arrived on the quarterdeck, shot the captain and threw his body overboard.

The next morning, the rest of the crew were given the option of joining the mutineers, and all agreed. Gow was elected captain and James Williams as first mate. They set about preparing the *George* for piracy, arming her with 18 guns and renaming her *Revenge*. Gow began attacking British ships in the area, beginning with the *Delight* on 12 November. She was an English sloop with a cargo of fish from Newfoundland, bound for Cadiz, commanded by Captain Thomas Wise of Poole. Gow then took the *Sarah*, a Glasgow ship loaded with herrings and salmon, on 21 November.

Defoe reports that Gow and Williams now sailed to Madeira, where Gow presented its governor with three barrels of salmon and six barrels of herrings. Pretending to be an English merchant, Gow asked the Portuguese governor permission to take on water and provisions, which was granted. Defoe writes:

> The Governour very courteously granted their Desire ... went off himself, with about Nine or ten of his principal People, to pay the English Captain a Visit... However, Gow, handsomely dress'd, receiv'd them with some Ceremony ... for a while ... and when the Governour and his Company rose up to take their leave, they were, to their great Surprize, suddenly surrounded with a gang of Fellows with Musquets and an Officer at the Head of them, who told them in so many Words, they were the Captains Prisoners, and must not think of going on Shore any more, till the Water and Provisions, which were promised, should come on Board... The poor Governour was so much more than half Dead with the Fright, that he really Befoul'd himself in a piteous Manner; and the rest were in no much better Condition; they trembled, cry'd, begg'd, cross'd themselves, and said their Prayers and Men going to Execution...They were however well enough Treated, except the Restraint of their Persons, and were often ask'd to Refresh themselves, but they would neither Eat or Drink any more all the while they stay'd on Board... Having no better Success in this out of the way run, to the Maderas, they resolved to make the best of their way back again to the Coast of Spain or Portugal...

Around this time HMS *Ludlow Castle* was sent out to search for the pirates but after 15 days gave up the search and returned to Lisbon. On 18 December Gow took the *Batchelor*, another ship bound from Newfoundland to Cadiz, and as with the other captures, the pirates plundered her of all of value, and sank her to prevent any news of their operations. Near Cape Finisterre they took a Scottish snow and a French ship bound from Cadiz to Brest. Their next capture was the sloop *Triumvirate* around thirty leagues from Vigo, after which they spied a large French ship, which fired upon the pirates rather than surrender. Gow gave orders to sail away from her, but his first mate Williams was, according to Defoe, 'a merciless, cruel and inexorable wretch', and accused Gow of cowardice. Williams snapped his pistol in Gow's face, after swearing at him for passing up this chance of plenty of plunder. The weapon failed to go off, and two nearby pirates shot Williams, wounding him in the arm and belly. The crew approved of Gow's actions and the next day Williams, heavily manacled, was thrown into the hold of the *Triumvirate* with all the prisoners of earlier raids.

The former captives were now set free on the *Triumvirate*, but given orders that Williams should be surrendered as a pirate to the first English man-of-war they should encounter. Williams was given up to HMS *Argyle* in Lisbon and carried in chains to London. Over the next few months, Gow's *Revenge* attacked several other ships in the seas surrounding Spain, France and Portugal, and their names and contents are recorded by Defoe. 'Sea artists' such as carpenters and surgeons, and also experienced seamen, were given the option of joining the pirates, which some did. Running low on provisions and now chased by various naval ships, Gow decided to leave the Iberian Peninsula and sailed home to Orkney, thinking it a secure place to traffic stolen goods. In January 1725, his *Revenge* sailed into Hamnavoe, opposite his home town of Stromnesss.

Gow and his pirates explained that their vessel had been blown off course, on a journey from Stockholm to Cadiz. As 'Mr Smith', Gow pretended to be a wealthy trader, courting a Miss Gordon. He intended to lie low and when he felt the pressure was off to raid mansions on the various islands. He renamed his vessel the *George*, but it was eventually recognised by a merchant captain in port. Members of the merchant crew also recognised some of Gow's men. Ten of the *Revenge's* crew now fled to the Scottish mainland in the ship's boat, while Robert Reid managed to flee to Kirkwall. There, Reid gave himself up to the law, claiming he had been forced to piracy, and warned the Justices of the Peace that Gow was at large and had planned to raid the gentry's isolated mansions.

On 10 February 1725, Gow and nine others raided Robert Honeyman's Hall of Clestrain, on the shore of Hamnavoe, directly opposite Stromness. *The Complete Newgate Calendar* gives a full account of the attack:

> Nine of the gang went into the house to search for treasure, while the tenth was left to guard the door. The sight of men thus armed occasioned much terror to Mrs Honeyman and her daughter, who shrieked with dreadful apprehensions for their personal safety; but the pirates, employed in the search for plunder, had no idea of molesting the ladies. They seized the linen, plate and other valuable articles, and then walked in triumph to their boat, compelling one of the servants to play before them on the bagpipes.

Gow's next target was Carrick House, the residence of his old school friend James Fea, on the island of Eday. However, strong currents carried the *Revenge* aground on 13 February, just opposite Carrick House. The boatswain and five men went ashore and met James Fea, who took them to the local inn where they were seized, presumably the worse for wear. Soon after this, Fea trapped Gow and all the rest of his crew of 28 men. Assistance was sent for, and the *Greyhound* frigate took Gow and his crew to London, arriving on 26 March 1725. The prisoners were taken to the Marshalsea Prison in Southwark, and there found their former comrade 'Lieutenant' Williams in prison awaiting trial.

Gow refused to plead at his trial, so his thumbs were 'bound together and squeezed with whipcord.' Still refusing to plead after torture, Gow was transferred to Newgate Prison. He again refused to plead, and was therefore 'sentenced to be pressed to death in the usual manner'. This was the legal punishment for those who refused to enter a plea, whereby the defendant would be

> ...put into a mean house stopped from any light and he be laid upon his back, with his body bare; that his arms be stretched forth with cord, the one to one side, the other to the other side of the prison, and in like manner his legs be used, and upon his body be laid as much iron and stone as he can bear and more. The first day he shall have three morsels of barley bread, and the next he shall drink thrice of the water in the next channel to the prison door but of no spring and fountain water; and this shall be his punishment till he die.

Gow now opted to plead not guilty, and was tried at the Old Bailey, and found guilty of murder and piracy. Gow and seven accomplices were executed together at Execution Dock, Wapping. Gow had asked for a speedy end, and some of his friends 'pulled him by the legs, but so hard that the rope broke'. Gow, 'still alive and sensible enough to climb the ladder a second time' returned to the gallows, to be hanged for a second time. The bodies of the ringleaders Gow and Williams were left in the Thames for 'three tides', after which the corpses of the two ringleaders were bound in chains and tarred. The pair were gibbeted on the Thames, Gow at Greenwich and Williams at Blackwall.

The Flying Gang

The 'Flying Gang' is a name given to a group of ex-privateers who turned pirate when there was peace and resultant unemployment. They congregated at Nassau on the formerly unpopulated island of New Providence in the Bahamas. Most of the pirates had previously served as privateers out of Port Royal, before the 1713 Treaty of Utrecht. It became a sort of 'pirate republic' after Henry Jennings (*q.v.*) brought in incredible wealth. Benjamin Hornigold and Jennings, although enemies, virtually governed the island. The English authorities feared that this breakaway island in the West Indies would threaten their colonial power structure, and the Nassau pirates were suppressed by Woodes Rogers from 1718.

Benjamin Hornigold *(c.*1680–1719) – Founder of 'the Pirate Republic of the Bahamas', turned Pirate Hunter

Possibly from Norfolk, England, Hornigold is thought to have been a Jamaican privateer during the War of the Spanish Succession, until peace in 1712–13. By the winter of 1713–1714, Hornigold was using large sailing canoes and a sloop to loot Spanish ships off the Bahamas, despite the peace. He also raided plantations in Cuba and the Florida Straits, making a fortune. He sailed his prizes and plunder back to Nassau, where he claimed to have established a 'Pirate Republic'. Nassau had been completely destroyed in the war, but with John Cockram, Hornigold built the first foundations of pirate society there. Cockram moved 50 miles north of Nassau, to Harbour Island, marrying the daughter of its leading merchant. From there he set up a supply and smuggling network for Hornigold's growing operations, and also money laundered for his friend. Hornigold in turn used this laundered money to buy more sloops and sailing canoes for his fleet, and Edward Thache (Blackbeard) was one of his early crew members. In 1715, Hornigold threatened English authorities who tried to arrest Nassau pirates, and his personal pirate crews numbered more than 200 by early 1716.

Henry Jennings sailed to the island in 1716, and Hornigold suddenly had a wealthier, influential rival in Nassau. Hornigold hated a more successful competitor entering his sphere of influence. In turn, Jennings disliked Hornigold, as in April 1716 Hornigold had sheltered Samuel Bellamy and Paulsgrave Williams, who had stolen treasure from Jennings. In summer 1716, Hornigold was sailing with Bellamy, Williams and Olivier *la Buze* (*q.v.* Olivier Levasseur), but the three left him as he would not attack English shipping. However, throughout 1716 and 1717, Blackbeard still sailed with Hornigold as Horngold's second-in-command. By 1717, Hornigold had captured the 30-gun sloop *Ranger,* and on taking the *Ranger* as his flagship, Hornigold gave the captaincy of his former sloop to the loyal Blackbeard. In spring 1717 they took a merchant ship carrying 120 barrels of flour bound for Havana, a Bermudan sloop with a cargo of spirits, and a Portuguese ship out of Madeira with a cargo of white wine. By March 1717 Hornigold had a fleet of five ships and 350 men, and attacked an armed merchant pirate hunter sent by the Governor of South Carolina to take Nassau pirates. The pirate hunter only escaped by running itself aground. Hornigold next seized a sloop off Honduras. One of the passengers stated: 'They did us no further injury than the taking most of our hats from us, having got drunk the night before, as they told us, and toss'd theirs overboard.'

By not attacking English-flagged ships, Hornigold was able to mount a semi-legal defence that he was a 'privateer' operating against England's enemies. However, in November 1717 a vote was taken to attack any vessel, and Hornigold was replaced as captain. The loyal Blackbeard with his sloop was absent at the time. Hornigold sailed back to Nassau with a small crew upon a small, damaged sloop, and kept pirating until December 1717, when news came of a general pardon for those who gave up piracy. Hornigold became the leader of those who wished for a pardon. He sailed to Jamaica in January 1718 to receive his pardon, and became a pirate hunter for Woodes Rogers, the new Governor of the Bahamas. He re-outfitted Henry Jennings' former ship *Bathsheba*, becoming Rogers' trusted lieutenant. Pardoned pirates were also offered large sums of money for capturing anyone who was guilty of piracy, murder, and treason against the Crown. For every captain who was captured, the person responsible for it would receive £100, and for every lieutenant and boatswain captured, there was a reward of £40, and so on for all crew members caught or killed. Rogers commissioned Hornigold to hunt Blackbeard, Charles Vane, Jack Rackham, Stede Bonnet and others in the Bahamas, and wrote to London praising his efforts and those of Hornigold's long-time partner John Cockram. In late 1719, Hornigold's ship was caught in a hurricane somewhere between New Providence and Mexico and was wrecked. He may have died then, or been captured by the Spanish near Havana and died in captivity.

Henry Jennings (*fl.*1704–1718) – The Captain who took $20,000,000 in Two Hits

It is thought that during Queen Anne's War (the War of the Spanish Succession), Jennings was operating from Jamaica, probably as a merchant and privateer captain. He had an estate on Jamaica but with the peace following the 1713 Treaty of Utrecht, turned to piracy, as did many other unemployed seamen. He is also said to have been involved in the conspiracy to overthrow the German George I and replace him with James Stuart on the throne of England. On 31 July 1715, the Spanish Plate Fleet from Havana, led by the flagship *El Capitana*, was hit by a hurricane off Florida. The entire fleet was lost, and only a few Spaniards survived in longboats. Philip V declared that all the sunken treasure belonged to Spain, and demanded that no other country tried to salvage the wrecks. Spain was able to get salvage crews into the area and was intent on forcing all treasure hunters away. The *Urca de Lima* was quickly located in shallow waters, and to support salvage operations and protect its recovered gold, Governor Martinez of St Augustine built a small fort on the Florida coast near the salvage site. Jennings' friend, the pro-Stuart Governor of Jamaica, encouraged him to salvage loot from the wrecks of the fleet. Jennings armed his 80-ton sloop *Bathsheba* and at the end of 1715 sailed with three ships and 150–300 men. He launched a savage assault on the Spanish salvage camp at Palma de Ayz in early 1716, to take the poorly defended camp and all the treasure it had recovered. The pirates forced about 60 Spanish soldiers to flee the fort. The raiders set sail for Nassau carrying an estimated 350,000 pesos (worth £87,000 then, perhaps £15 million today). At Nassau, Jennings incurred the enmity of Benjamin Hornigold, and returned to Jamaica on 26 January 1716.

Although his raid was illegal, Jennings was not troubled by Jamaican authorities and sailed away again in March. Off Cuba on 3 April, he illegally seized a French merchant ship worth around 60,000 pesos with the help of a ship captained by 'Black Sam' Bellamy. Bellamy later stole a large portion of the treasure and slipped away to join Jennings' enemy Hornigold, who happened to be operating in the area. When Bellamy double-crossed him, Jennings was so angered that he killed over 20 French and English prisoners and burnt an English merchant sloop. After French diplomatic action, Jennings was declared a pirate by George I and could not return to Jamaica, being warned that he would be hanged by the very governor that he had supplied with bribes in the past. The crew elected to sail instead to the port of Nassau, on New Providence Island in the Bahamas, a favoured pirate haven. With the incredible wealth in gold and silver brought in by Jennings, the port expanded, and Jennings became the unofficial mayor of the growing pirate colony, which became 'the new Port Royal'. Like his enemy Hornigold, he would not target English ships. In late 1717 Woodes Rogers was appointed Governor of the Bahamas, commissioned to end all piracy in its waters. Jennings accepted the King's pardon in 1718, assuming the life of wealthy plantation owner in Bermuda. He may have been captured by the Spanish in his later years, dying in prison.

Samuel Bellamy (1689–1717) – 'Black Sam', the 'Prince of Pirates', Captain of 'Robin Hood's Men'

He was probably born in the village of Hittisleigh, Devon, and by the end of the War of the Spanish Succession (1702–1712) he was reportedly in Massachusetts. There he was supposed to have fallen in love with Maria (Mary) Hallet, at Eastham on Cape Cod. Bellamy went into partnership with a Rhode Island silversmith, Paulsgrave Williams, to salvage treasure from the Spanish treasure fleet sunk off Florida. Finding that much of the loot had already been salvaged from shallow waters by the Spanish, and that it was far more heavily guarded after Henry Jennings' recent raid, they decided to attack Spanish shipping. Bellamy and Williams recruited a gang of about 50 pirates and from March 1716 were in the Bay of Honduras in two large sailing canoes (*piraguas*) looting boats around the Yucatán Peninsula. In April 1716 they surprised an English merchant ship, and forced it to tow their boats to eastern Cuba. There they met Benjamin Hornigold, stole a large amount of booty from Jennings, and were given protection by Hornigold's pirate fleet, which included Olivier

Levasseur (*la Buze*) and Blackbeard. Hornigold was deposed as leader, after sailing around Cuba and Hispaniola, for refusing to take English ships. Bellamy, Williams, and *la Buze* sailed off in two ships and successfully pirated around the Antilles chain, their crews growing in number. In early 1717, with a fast French sloop of war, the *Marianne*, they took a slaver, the well-armed 300-ton *Whydah*.

They sailed the *Whydah* to careen her and equip her with 28 cannon for piracy in the Bahamas. Then Bellamy and Williams sailed up the Eastern coast of America to raid shipping. They were separated in dense fog but had a contingency plan to meet at Damariscove Island in Maine. Bellamy in the *Whydah* sailed to Eastham, Cape Cod, to see Maria Hallett, and Williams sailed the *Marianne* to his home at Block Island, Rhode Island. Bellamy was caught in bad weather near Eastham on 26 April 1717, and his ship ran aground. Bellamy died but two survivors, plus seven survivors of another wrecked pirate ship, were arrested and sent to Boston, where eight men were hanged. In just over a year, Bellamy was said to have captured more than 50 ships. He was called 'Black Sam' because he never wore a fashionable powdered wig, instead tying his long black hair with a band of cloth. Bellamy was regarded as a gentlemanly pirate, earning him a second nickname as the 'Prince of Pirates', and his crew called themselves 'Robin Hood's Men'. In 1984, the wreckage of the *Whydah* was discovered under just 14 feet of water.

Paulsgrave Williams (*c.*1675–*c.*1720) – The Bewigged Silversmith

His was one of the strangest decisions to take up a career of piracy, as his father was both a wealthy merchant and Rhode Island's attorney general. However, his father died when Williams was 11 and his mother remarried, moving from Newport to Block Island, notorious for smuggling and fencing stolen goods. One of his sisters was said to have married a friend of Captain Kidd, but Williams learned silversmithing, possibly using black market or pirate silver, married and had two young children. In 1715 the middle-aged Williams went into partnership with Sam Bellamy (*see* above), sailing a small boat down to Florida to salvage Spanish treasure. Failing, turning to piracy, and stealing Jennings' plunder, they were so successful that by 1716 about 250 pirates, including at least 25 former slaves, were in their crews. While the former seaman Bellamy commanded the *Whydah*, Williams captained the sloop *Marianne*, her hull painted in the blue and yellow of her original French owners.

Pirating gave Williams, like all seamen, a deep tan, which contrasted with the white powdered gentleman's wig that he habitually wore. The *Marianne's* crew was reported as 30 Britons, 5 Africans, 5 Frenchman, and an 'Indian', all with equal shares of any prize. Sailing north in March 1716, he parted company with the *Whydah* in heavy fog. Williams was now said to have visited his mother and sisters on Block Island, staying ashore for a short time, and probably disposing of some loot. It is not known if he met his wife and children. He expected to rendezvous with Bellamy at Damariscove Island, Maine, around 20 May, and waited two weeks, not knowing his partner had perished, before returning to Nassau. In February 1718 Williams was noted there, when Captain Vincent Pearse of HMS *Phoenix* visited the island, but Williams left that year for Africa prior to the arrival of the Bahamas' new governor, Woodes Rogers. Williams was sighted in April 1720 off Sierra Leone in April 1720, serving as an officer under the pirate *La Buze*, then disappears from history.

Charles Vane (d. 29 March 1721) – Leader of the Nassau Pirate Opposition

Living in Port Royal, Jamaica, Vane joined Jennings' pirate crew to assault the Spanish salvage camp in Florida, and was known to be in Nassau in February 1718, when Captain Pearse sailed HMS *Phoenix* into port to threaten the 'republic'. Soon after, Vane was known to be leading pirates in open boats, at night, taking anchored merchant ships off the Bahamas, and sailing them back into Nassau.

In July 1718, Vane had become the leader of the pirates who did not want a royal pardon, and wished to oppose the incoming Governor of the Bahamas, Woodes Rogers. Vane argued strongly against the pirates wanting to accept pardons, who were led by Hornigold and Jennings. On the night of 26 July 1718, Vane's men almost destroyed two of the naval frigates that had escorted Rogers into Nassau, before escaping in a sloop. Vane attempted to make Rogers leave the island by raiding Bahamian shipping and gathering resources for a pirate invasion of Providence Island. On 30 August 1718, Vane blockaded Charleston, South Carolina, capturing several ships.

It appears from recent research that Vane went to find Blackbeard, living in retirement in North Carolina, and asked him to join an assault on Nassau. Their crews were said to have partied on Ocracoke Island, on the Outer Banks, in September or October 1718. However, his crew deposed Vane in November 1718, as he refused to attack a

Charles Vane.

far better-armed French man-of-war in the Windward Passage, and Jack Rackham was elected in his place to command Vane's brigantine. Fifteen crew joined Vane on a captured sloop, with which they attacked shipping off Jamaica. Unfortunately for Vane, the Royal Navy's West Indies squadron was based in Port Royal, so he met with little success. In February 1719, Vane was shipwrecked on an island off Belize (then part of the Spanish Honduras). He was recognised by a merchant captain and taken in chains to Jamaica. After more than a year in prison, on 29 March 1721 Vane was hanged at Gallows Point, Port Royal.

Edward Thache (*c*.1680–1718) – 'Blackbeard' the Showman

His surname is also given as Thatch or Teach. Blackbeard's reputation as a fearsome pirate is unjustified; although he cultivated a terrifying appearance, fighting with burning fuses tied into his long black beard, there is no evidence of Blackbeard deliberately killing anyone. His appearance was intended to force merchant crews to surrender immediately. Blackbeard is believed to have been born in or around the port of Bristol. In 2015 Baylus Brooks examined government records and discovered that he was once known as 'Edward Thache, a respected resident of Spanish Town, Jamaica'. Sailing out of Jamaica, Thache was probably a privateer in the War of the Spanish Succession and at its end had no employment. Between 1714 and 1716 he joined Hornigold's pirates, becoming his most loyal lieutenant. In early 1717, Hornigold and Blackbeard, each captaining a sloop, took a boat out of Havana carrying 120 barrels of flour and then took 100 barrels of wine from a Bermudan sloop. Shortly after they took a ship sailing from Madeira to Charleston, and on 29 September off Cape Charles, Virginia, they took a cargo of Madeira from the *Betty* of Virginia, before scuttling her.

Captain Mathew Munthe led an anti-piracy patrol from North Carolina. He described 'Thatch' as commanding 'a sloop 6 gunns and about 70 men'. In September 1717 Blackbeard and Hornigold came across Stede Bonnet, whose crew of about 70 pirates were dissatisfied with his command. With Bonnet's permission, Blackbeard took the captaincy of Bonnet's ship *Revenge*. Hornigold commanded

Blackbeard, Courtesy Library of Congress.

Blackbeard in bloody action.
Wikimedia Commons.

the *Ranger*, and with Blackbeard's former sloop, in October they added another ship to the flotilla. On 22 October, they took the cargo from the sloops *Robert* of Philadelphia and *Good Intent* of Dublin. Hornigold was separated from the fleet, and Blackbeard now attacked vessels off the Carolinas, Virginia, and Delaware, before returning to the Caribbean.

On 28 November 1717, after crossing the Atlantic and only 100 miles from its destination of Martinique, the 250-ton French slaver *Concorde* was attacked by Blackbeard and his company. According to one report, the pirates were aboard two sloops, one with 120 men and 12 guns, and the other with 30 men and 8 cannon. The French had already suffered 16 deaths at sea, and another 36 were suffering badly from scurvy and dysentery, so Captain Dosset surrendered after the pirates fired two warning volleys. Blackbeard sailed *Concorde* to the island of Bequia in the Grenadines, where the French crew and slaves were put ashore. Blackbeard's men then ransacked *Concorde*, after Louis Arot, a French cabin boy, told them that gold dust was aboard. The pirates seized the gold, and Arot and three French sailors voluntarily joined the pirates; ten of the most useful crew were also taken by force including the cook, three surgeons, two carpenters, two sailors and a pilot.

Blackbeard decided to keep the *Concorde* and gave the French volunteers the smaller of the two pirate sloops. Blackbeard renamed his new ship *Queen Anne's Revenge* and equipped her with 22 cannon. With Stede Bonnet (*see* next entry) captaining the *Revenge* and another brigantine in his pirate flotilla, Blackbeard left the Grenadines in late November 1717, cruising the Caribbean, taking prizes and adding

Sign on the Ocracoke, courtesy of Cathy Helms, from *Pirates, Truth and Tales*, by Helen Hollick.

to his fleet. Blackbeard first sailed north along the Lesser Antilles, plundering ships near St Vincent, St Lucia, Nevis, and Antigua, and by early December he had arrived off the eastern coast of Puerto Rico. In December 1717, he burnt most of the boats harboured at St Kitts. Blackbeard also sacked and burnt Guadeloupe town, and his presence forced the English Governor of the Leeward Islands, aboard the frigate HMS *Seaford*, to send messages asking for help. (At this time Blackbeard did not battle HMS *Scarborough*, although some historians record the fight.) A former captive reported to authorities that the pirates were headed to Samana Bay in Hispaniola.

By April 1718, the pirates were off Turneffe Islands in the Bay of Honduras and captured the sloop *Adventure*, forcing her captain, David Herriot, to sail with him. Sailing east once again, the pirates passed near the Cayman Islands and captured a Spanish sloop off Cuba that they also added to their flotilla. After spending some time in Nassau, Blackbeard was forced to leave for the Carolinas. In May 1718, the pirates arrived off Charleston, South Carolina, with *Queen Anne's Revenge* and three smaller sloops, where Blackbeard blockaded the port of Charleston for almost a week. He took several ships attempting to enter or leave the port, and detained the crew and passengers of the *Crowley* as prisoners. As their ransom, he demanded a chest of medicine in return for the hostages. Pirates always took medicine chests, one of the main reasons being to procure mercury as a 'cure' for syphilis.

Shortly after leaving Charleston, the fleet attempted to enter Old Topsail Inlet (now Beaufort Inlet) in North Carolina, where *Queen Anne's Revenge* and the *Adventure* grounded on an ocean bar and were abandoned. David Herriot, the former captain of the *Adventure*, wrote: 'the said Thatch's ship *Queen Anne's Revenge* run a-ground off of the Bar of Topsail-Inlet' and that *Adventure* 'run a-ground likewise about Gun-shot from the said Thatch'. Captain Ellis Brand of the MS *Lyme* wrote in a letter to the Lords of Admiralty on 12 July 1718: 'On the 10th of June or thereabouts a large pyrate Ship of forty Guns with three Sloops in her company came upon the coast of North Carolina ware they endeavour'd To goe in to a harbour, call'd Topsail Inlet, the Ship Stuck upon the barr att the entrance of the harbour and is lost; as is one of the sloops.' Herriot claimed in his deposition that Blackbeard intentionally grounded the two ships in order to break up the company, which had grown to more than 300 pirates. Blackbeard marooned most of his pirates, including Stede Bonnet, and sailed away with a few handpicked men in the sloop holding most of the treasure. Blackbeard sailed his favoured crew to Bath, then the capital of North Carolina, and accepted the king's pardon from Governor Charles Eden, who probably received some reward. Blackbeard also married a local woman and ran a virtual pirate mafia under Governor Eden's protection.

However, his continued piracy angered Alexander Spotswood, the Governor of Virginia, who organised an illegal military invasion of North Carolina. An armed contingent led by Royal Navy Lieutenant Robert Maynard engaged Blackbeard at Ocracoke Inlet on the North Carolina coast. Spotswood sent armed men overland, to attack in tandem with the two sloops commanded by Maynard. On 2 December

1718 Maynard arrived at Ocracoke with about 60 men. They attacked Blackbeard's force of about 20 pirates the following morning. Attempting to close up and board, one of Maynard's sloops went aground upon a sandbar. Blackbeard fired a broadside, disabling her and killing about 20 men. Maynard hid his men below deck as Blackbeard's men threw grenades, which were ineffective as only Maynard's pilot and helmsman were on deck. Maynard's men tried to board Blackbeard's ship as they had no cannon, and according to Defoe, Blackbeard raised a glass and toasted Maynard with the oath: 'Damnation seize my soul if I give you quarters, or take any from you.' Blackbeard now boarded Maynard's sloop with about a dozen pirates, but around 30 of Maynard's men swarmed up onto the deck, where Maynard and Blackbeard met and fought. Blackbeard was shot by Maynard but did not fall, and he broke Maynard's cutlass, then moved forward to kill him. However, Blackbeard was attacked from behind, being wounded in the throat and neck. With blood flowing, Blackbeard swung his cutlass, but was encircled by Maynard's men, being shot five times and receiving 20 sword wounds before collapsing. Maynard then decapitated him. Governor Spotswood thought he would become rich, but only about £2,238 of booty was collected at Ocracoke. Maynard returned to Virginia with the surviving pirates and the trophy of Blackbeard's severed head hanging from his sloop's bowsprit.

In 2014, archaeologists brought up an 8-foot-long, 2,000-pound cannon, the 13th so far salvaged from the 24 guns on the wreck of Blackbeard's flagship in North Carolina's Beaufort Inlet. After the ship's discovery in 1996, experts found more than 280,000 artefacts including the 13 cannon, an anchor, assorted weapons, shackles and gold dust. Of the cannon pulled from the site, four were found to be loaded, meaning that the pirates were primed for battle when the ship went down. One contained spikes designed to slash sails and maim crew.

Stede Bonnet (1688–18 December 1718) – The Gentleman Pirate

The son of an influential family of Barbados sugar planters, Bonnet had a wife, children, and a 400-acre estate on Barbados. He was orphaned as a child and his first son died in infancy, after which Bonnet was said to have developed 'a disorder of the mind', caused 'by some discomforts he found in a married state'. He had no knowledge of seamanship, but for some unknown reason, allegedly because he could not stand his wife, one night in April 1717 Bonnet left Barbados in secrecy. He sailed in the *Revenge*, an armed sloop he had ordered built at a local yard in 1716, having probably informed the authorities that it was to be used as a privateer. Sailing as 'Captain Edwards', Bonnet plundered vessels near the entrance to Charleston Harbour in August 1717. However, he lost the esteem of his crew by attacking a more powerful Spanish warship. Half his crew was killed or wounded, including Bonnet, who was now confined to his cabin. The remaining crew managed to out-sail the larger ship, and took the *Revenge* to safety at Nassau. Hornigold took on the crew, but gave the *Revenge* to Blackbeard, while Bonnet, with an extensive library, remained confined in his cabin. Bonnet, a former major in the local militia on Barbados, now and again strolled the decks in his night gown.

Two months later, Blackbeard captured a French slaver which became his new flagship, the *Queen Anne's Revenge*. He handed the *Revenge* back to Bonnet, but Bonnet remained under his close supervision, while Blackbeard's expanding fleet burnt towns and shipping across the Antilles, the Gulf of Mexico and the Central American coast. Not until late March 1718 did Blackbeard allow Bonnet to operate independently. Bonnet now attacked an armed Boston merchantman and was repulsed. His crew sailed and found Blackbeard at Turneffe Atoll. They voted to replace Bonnet with one of Blackbeard's officers. The shamed Bonnet was placed under 'house arrest' on the *Queen Anne's Revenge*. However, in June 1718 Blackbeard double-crossed many pirates, leaving them stranded on an island in North Carolina. Bonnet had been sent to Bath, North Carolina, to accept a pardon, but

The pirate flag flown by Stede Bonnet.

then came to rescue the marooned men, taking control of the *Revenge*, which Blackbeard had abandoned.

A pardoned man, Bonnet intended to sail to the Danish colony of St Thomas and obtain a privateering commission to attack Spanish shipping. However, he lacked the authority to control his men, who instead voted to secure vital supplies by returning to piracy. Bonnet was again a wanted man when in September pirate hunters from South Carolina surprised him anchored at Cape Fear, North Carolina. Bonnet was taken after fighting courageously. Awaiting trial in Charleston, Bonnet escaped with the assistance of the smuggler Richard Tookerman. A large mob soon attempted to free the rest of Bonnet's crew, but failed and the pirates were brought to trial and executed. Bonnet was later recaptured and found guilty, but received several stays of execution as the result of pleas from Charleston merchants. He was hanged at White Point in Charleston on 18 December 1718.

John Rackham (d.18 November 1720) – 'Calico Jack'

Rackham acquired his nickname from wearing an outfit of brightly coloured Indian Calico cloth, and was one of Vane's pirates who opposed the arrival of Woodes Rogers in Nassau. On 23 November 1718, Rackham was Vane's quartermaster when Vane refused to tackle a French warship. He was elected in his place as captain of Vane's brigantine, while Vane sailed off in a smaller sloop. Rackham was initially brave, trying to take prizes off Jamaica, but operated too near the Jamaica Station naval base to have any real success. In December 1718 Rackham took the *Kingston*, with a rich cargo, just off Port Royal, prompting the Royal Navy to search for him; Jamaican merchants also outfitted several privateer ships to take him. In March 1719, the privateers discovered Rackham south of Cuba at Isla de Los Pinos. The *Kingston* prize was anchored near his brigantine, and Rackham and most of the pirates were sleeping ashore in tents. Their ships were taken while the pirates quickly hid in the dense forest. Rackham and just six pirates took three months to sail back to Nassau in a small boat, and claimed they had been forced into piracy by Vane. Governor Rogers pardoned the pirates, and Vane was also pardoned.

In Nassau, Rackham began an affair with Anne Bonny (*see* below), whose ex-pirate husband John had become one of Woodes Rogers' most trusted informers. In summer 1720, Rackham and Anne planned to marry. They arranged with John Bonny that Rackham would give John

'Jack' Rackham.

Bonny cash for Ann and John's marriage to be annulled, but Rogers refused to allow this to happen. The lovers, unable to wed, recruited six ex-pirates and stole a swift ship. One of Anne's closest friends, the cross-dressing Mary Read, joined them as they stole the armed sloop and secretly sailed out of Nassau on the night of 22 August 1720. In October, Rackham, showing a remarkable lack of intelligence, headed once more for the most dangerous place in the Caribbean, Jamaica, and sacked vessels in various harbours. After a short engagement, privateers took Rackham and his crew into custody. On 18 November 1720 he was hanged at Gallows Point, Port Royal. His body was gibbeted on a small sandbar in the harbour, now known as Rackham's Cay.

Anne Bonny (born 1700) and Mary Read (d.1721) – the Female Pirates of the Caribbean

Johnson's account of Anne Bonny and Mary Read in his 1724 *The General History of the Pyrates* is incorrect: Johnson (Defoe) states that Bonny and Mary Read disguised themselves as men to become sailors, and then sailed with John Rackham, each woman believing the other was a man. However, they had known each other at Nassau before going to sea, and by the time they were noted as pirates, had been

Anne Bonny and Mary Read, convicted of piracy November 18th, 1720 at the court of St Iago de la Vega, in the Island of Jamaica, engraved by B. Cole.

named by Woodes Rogers as being in Rackham's crew. Rogers' notice was published in *The Boston Gazette*. Bonny was from Charleston, and had come to Nassau in 1716 as the 16-year-old wife of the pirate James Bonny. She may have been the daughter of the influential William Cormac, and seemingly gained a reputation in Nassau for extra-marital affairs. In 1718, James Bonny took advantage of a royal pardon and began working for Woodes Rogers, while his wife Anne began an affair with 'Calico Jack' Rackham. Woodes Rogers halted their negotiations with James Bonny for an annulment and they began pirating with Anne Bonney's friend Mary Read and a few others. On 22 August 1720, they stole a ship from Nassau harbour.

Some of Rackham's captives reported that the women dressed as men and swore like pirates. One former prisoner stated that 'they were both very profligate, cursing and swearing much, and very ready and willing to do anything on board.' Another stated that he only knew they were women 'by the largeness of their breasts'. A few months later, owing to Rackham's stupidity, they were captured and thrown into a Jamaican gaol. Anne Bonny was reported to have seen Rackham on his day of execution, and said 'I am sorry to see you here, but if you had fought like a man, you need not have hanged like a dog.' She and Mary Read were also sentenced to be hanged, but had a stay of execution by revealing they were pregnant. We have no idea if Anne Bonny was hanged – there is no record – but one writer believes her father managed to secure her release, and she returned to Charleston, giving birth to Rackham's son there.

Defoe tells us Mary Read had preferred to wear male clothing since childhood, and her mother had raised her as a boy to try and pass her off as another man's son. Read then served as a sailor and foot soldier, according to Defoe's account, before joining Calico Jack and her friend Anne Bonny. Spared execution because she was pregnant, she died from a fever, and the records of St Catherine's church in Jamaica recorded her burial on 28 April 1721.

The Corsairs of the Gulf
of Mexico

William C. Davis, in his extensively researched *The Pirates Laffite: The Treacherous World of the Corsairs of the Gulf*, demonstrates that the brothers Jean and Pierre were not exactly the pirate heroes depicted helping the Americans at the Battle of New Orleans. Instead, they were acting in their own interests, keeping the United States from interfering with their trade. Because of the revolutionary movements sweeping across South and Central America, hundreds of adventurers attempted to make their fortunes. Privateers were given 'commissions' from various governments to attack 'enemy' commercial shipping in the Gulf of Mexico and the Caribbean. The brothers sometimes attacked Spanish shipping, and when it was convenient, also French or English vessels. They also helped rebels launch revolutions against Spain's New World territories, especially Texas. At the same time, they were being paid by the Spanish government, reporting on rebel movements. Legitimate governments, such as the USA, constantly mounted campaigns to stamp out the privateers. In Davis's view, they were not the 'gentlemen pirates' of historical tradition, but certainly with other privateers helped shape the course of history in the region from Florida to Texas.

Jean Lafitte (*c.*1760–6 February 1823) – Leader of the Barataria Pirates, the Pirate who made New Orleans a Boom Town, Hero of the Battle of New Orleans

Jean Lafitte (Laffite is the USA spelling) was born either in France or in its colony, Saint-Domingue, now Haiti. From 1803–1806, the Lafitte brothers Jean and Pierre ran a successful smuggling operation, but after the 1807 Embargo Act moved their activities to the Grand Terre islands, in Louisiana's Barataria Bay, about 100 miles south of New Orleans. Jean quickly became a popular figure as his smuggling and sale of captured goods helped to turn New Orleans into a boom town. The brothers would not attack American ships, but took cargo from any ships they considered as enemies of the USA. They often returned captured ships to their owners after looting them, presumably so they could take them again. Many men joined the prosperous Lafitte crews, and Jean Lafitte became the indisputable leader of the Barataria pirates. Lafitte claimed to have been given a letter of marque to attack English and Spanish ships, but also on occasion plundered French vessels.

By 1810, the Lafitte Brothers were extremely wealthy from their illegal trading and piracy, and had begun to deal in the even more profitable slave trade. However, in 1813 the Governor of New Orleans, William Claiborne, issued a $750 reward for the Lafitte brothers' arrest, and they left New Orleans. Within a week, Jean Lafitte offered $1,500 for anyone who could capture the governor and bring him to Barataria. In 1814, the English Captain Lockyer negotiated with Lafitte, offering $30,000, captaincy of an English naval frigate and other privileges, to join him in an attack on New Orleans, needing his expertise of the local marshes and bayous. Jean refused to co-operate and instead revealed information about the impending raid to the Americans. The Americans did not believe him, however, and instead, Commodore Daniel Patterson of the US Navy invaded Barataria Bay in 1814 to put an end to piracy and smuggling. However, officials now realised that Lafitte had been correct, and that capturing the Lafittes would leave Louisiana undefended from an expected invasion. Jean Lafitte conferred with General Andrew Jackson, and they agreed to defend New Orleans together, in return for a complete pardon for the Lafittes and their men.

On 23 December 1814, the van of the English fleet reached the Mississippi River, and Lafitte realized that Jackson's defensive line was too short. It needed to be extended into a nearby swamp to prevent encirclement of the American troops. Therefore Jackson altered the line, and on 28 December, the English were repulsed by an artillery crew manned by Lafitte's former lieutenants, Dominique Youx and Renato Beluche. On land and sea, Lafitte's expert gunners earned praise as the battle continued. On 21 January 1815, Jackson praised his troops, especially the 'cannoneers' and 'Captains Dominique and

Beluche, lately commanding privateers of Barataria, with part of their former crews and many brave citizens of New Orleans ... stationed at Nos. 3 and 4.' Jackson also named Jean and Pierre Lafitte for having 'exhibited the same courage and fidelity'. At the Battle of New Orleans in 1815, victory secured pardons for the brothers and their crews, but any further pirate activity was strictly forbidden in Barataria Bay.

It appears that the Lafitte brothers, from at least 1815, were also acting as informers for the Spanish against Mexican revolutionaries, being code-named 'Number Thirteen'. Pierre was to inform them about New Orleans, and Jean was asked to take the small inland port of Galveston, Texas. Despite being paid by Spain, from 1816 Jean began supplying the French Corsair Luis-Michel Aury (*see* following entry) in Galveston, from Louisiana, aiding General Francisco Mina and the revolution against Spain. In March 1817 Jean Lafitte arrived in Galveston to take over Aury's 'Campeche operation'. Aury was absent, on Mina's expedition to take over Soto La Marina, Mexico, and Jean gained control of Galveston in less than two weeks, while Pierre stayed overseeing operations in New Orleans.

Jean had a large house built for himself in Galveston, painted red and named *Maison Rouge*, and erected another 200 or so buildings. All newcomers took loyalty oaths to Jean Lafitte, which he rewarded by issuing letters of marque, allowing ships leaving Galveston to 'legally' prey upon merchant ships. Like Barataria, Galveston was an island that protected a large inland bay, and also became a pirate haven. As part of Spanish-held Mexico it was largely uninhabited, except by the Karankawa tribe.

From 1817 to 1821 Lafitte was privateering from Galveston, including taking some Spanish ships, although also giving the Spanish intelligence which may have led to the capture and execution of General Mina. He also built up his slave trade business, copying his Barataria operation. In 1818 a September hurricane sank four of his ships, and wrecked all but six houses in Galveston. In the same year 300 local Karankawa attacked *Maison Rouge*, as the pirates had kidnapped a Karankawa woman and were holding her in its compound. Lafitte's men were outnumbered but killed most of the Karankawa men with artillery. The tribe is now extinct. In 1821, one of Lafitte's captains raided an American merchant ship, which was the final straw for the Americans. After the Adams-Onís treaty between the USA and Spain, both nations stepped up attempts to prevent piracy and privateering, and many of the new South American republics also stopped issuing letters of marque. Jean's sources of revenue began to dry up and he came to an agreement to leave Galveston. The USS *Enterprise* was sent to ensure his removal. Knowing that any defence was hopeless, Jean Lafitte sailed out of Galveston in 1821 on his sloop the *Pride*, first burning *Maison Rouge*, the fortress and all other buildings in his settlement to the ground. Galveston was initially abandoned, then became part of Mexico, and then independent Texas, and finally the United States.

Lafitte continued taking ships, but admitted to his crew that he did not have a legitimate letter of marque from any nation, making them pirates, not privateers. About half of his men left, and he gave them the large brig *General Victoria*. That night his remaining men boarded the brig, destroying its masts and spars, crippling the ship, but they left the crew unharmed. In 1822 an English naval brigantine destroyed his small fleet off Cuba. Jean swam ashore and was imprisoned in Puerto Principe, but became so sick that he was taken to hospital, from where he escaped on 13 February. On 19 March he was reported as captaining 30 men in a pirate *guairo*, a small two-masted vessel with 'leg-of-mutton' sails. In June 1822, Lafitte approached Colombian officials, who had begun commissioning former privateers as officers in their new navy. He was granted a commission and given a new ship, a 43-ton armed schooner, the *General Santander*.

In February 1823, Lafitte was cruising off Honduras near Omoa, a Spanish fort that had been built to guard the Spanish shipments from silver mines. He tried to take what appeared to be two Spanish merchant vessels. They fled in poor visibility. Lafitte chased them, but the Spanish ships were heavily armed privateers or warships, and turned and attacked him. Badly wounded, Lafitte is believed to have died just after dawn on 6 February 1823, being buried at sea. One extraordinary legend is that he did not die but sailed to St Helena, rescued Napoleon, and settled down with him in Louisiana. There was some discussion among Gulf pirates about rescuing the emperor in 1820, but he died in May 1821. There have been many searches for Lafitte's 'buried treasure' in Louisiana and Texas.

Pierre Lafitte (1770–1821) – the Smuggler, Merchant and Pirate who Sold Male Slaves to Jim Bowie for a Dollar a Pound

The elder brother of Jean Lafitte, he was also possibly born in the French colony of Saint-Domingue, now Haiti, but Davis believes that the Lafittes were born near Pauillac, France, before emigrating with their parents to Haiti. Because of ongoing revolution, many French settlers had moved to New Orleans, which, although in Spanish possession for 30 years, had formerly been part of French colonial Louisiana and was thus mainly French-speaking. In 1803, Louisiana became part of the United States under the Louisiana Purchase, and the following year Pierre Lafitte moved to Baton Rouge, Florida, still under Spanish control, then moved to Pensacola in Florida. From 1804, he began working in the slave trade, foreshadowing the Lafitte brothers' future enterprise. In 1805, he took a new mulatto mistress, Marie Louise Villard, with whom he had several children over the next 15 years.

In New Orleans, Pierre used his legitimate business running a blacksmith's shop, at the corner of St Philip and Bourbon Streets, as a cover for piracy, slave trading, smuggling, and selling goods captured by himself and his brother Jean. Alongside his brother, Pierre Lafitte worked as a smuggler under the banner of a privateer ship authorised by the new Republic of Cartagena to pillage Spanish ships. However, the Lafitte brothers did not limit their prey to Spanish vessels but were known to capture ships of all nations. Despite their reputation as pirates the brothers were popular and extremely influential in New Orleans, helping build its trade and prosperity. In January 1808 the US Government began actively enforcing the 1807 Embargo Act, preventing American ships from docking at foreign ports. This damaged the trade of New Orleans merchants, who had very much relied on illicit trade with Caribbean colonies for their prosperity. Pierre and Jean now needed another port from which they could smuggle goods to the merchants. They set up at Barataria Island, where ships could easily smuggle in goods without being noticed by customs officials. Goods were then reloaded into smaller vessels, to secretly sail through the bayous into New Orleans. Perhaps more than 1,000 men worked for the Lafitte brothers, with Jean specialising in pirating, capturing slaves and smuggling, and Pierre handling the slave trade and fencing stolen goods. The USA had banned the international slave trade in 1807, so it was now highly lucrative. With Jean, Pierre led hundreds of men, being mentioned several times for his prowess at the Battle of New Orleans in 1814–15.

Jean left New Orleans for Galveston around 1817 but Pierre remained in New Orleans, often commuting to Galveston to help keep the brothers' empire growing. At this time Jim Bowie sold timber to purchase slaves and built up an illegal slaving trade. Bowie and his brothers bought smuggled slaves from the Lafittes, declaring that they had 'found' them, so they could keep the money when they were sold. In fact, the Lafitte brothers sold male slaves for 'a dollar a pound' to Bowie, and Bowie would avoid American laws against slave trading by reporting his purchased slaves as having been 'found' in the possession of smugglers or hiding in the forests. The law allowed Bowie to collect a fee on these 'recovered' slaves, and he would then immediately re-buy the slaves from the authorities, selling them for a further profit.

Pierre Lafitte spied for Spain, through agents in Cuba and in Louisiana, but he and Jean only supplied information to the Americans or Spanish which suited their own interests. By May 1820, the United States had persuaded the Lafittes to stop all operations, or be forced to close down by the American navy. Jean therefore destroyed the Galveston settlement, and set off with three ships to become a privateer for a junta in Colombia. Pierre closed their dealings in New Orleans and travelled to Charleston, South Carolina, to buy a ship and enlist a crew for privateering. In March 1821, he established a base of operations at Isla de Mujeres off the Yucatán Peninsula and took a few prizes, but on 30 October the Spanish attacked and captured Pierre and a few others. He escaped, but Pierre may have been wounded or ill, as he almost immediately fell into a severe fever. Pierre died on 9 November 1821, and the following day was buried in the churchyard of the Santa Clara convent at Dzidzantún, Yucatán.

Dominique Frederic Youx (*fl.*1806–1830) – the 'Most Trusted Lieutenant' of the Lafitte Brothers

Youx may have served in the French artillery, putting down a slave revolt in Haiti, but we first hear of him as a French privateer sailing out of Guadeloupe in 1806. (The terrible war of Haitian independence from France lasted from 1791 to 1804, led by Toussaint L'Ouverture. The leading French general Donatien de Rochambeau drowned Haitians in bags and mass executed perhaps thousands by using the 'fumigational-sulphurous bath' in the holds of ships, burning sulphur to make sulphur dioxide to gas them). According to Davis, Youx took part in defending the port of Baracoa in eastern Cuba against the English. He took his prizes to the Lafitte brothers at Barataria, and developed the relationship to become their 'most trusted Lieutenant'. He was also the close friend of another of the Lafittes' associates, Renato Beluche. However, by 1810 Guadeloupe and Martinique had fallen to the English, and Youx and other French sailors made for

Cartagena, Venezuela, to request a letter of marque to allow them to sail as privateers in the Gulf of Mexico.

By 1813, Youx was prominent in all the Lafitte operations, and Vincent Nolte, a leading New Orleans merchant who had lost business to the Lafittes, complained about them and their friends strolling the streets arm-in-arm, with no fear of the law. He wrote of seeing Jean Lafitte with 'Beluche, Dominique [Youx] and Gambi ... walking about publicly. They had ... their depots of goods &c., in the city and sold, almost openly, the wares they had obtained by piracy.' On 16 December 1814 General Andrew Jackson, expecting an English attack, imposed martial law on the City of New Orleans. Warshauer writes:

All who entered or exited the city were to report to the Adjutant General's office. Failure to do so resulted in arrest and interrogation. All vessels, boats and other crafts desiring to leave the city required a passport, either from the General or Commodore Daniel T. Patterson. All street lamps were ordered extinguished at 9:00 p.m., and anyone found after that hour without a pass was arrested as a spy. New Orleans was officially an armed camp and General Jackson the only authority.

Commodore Daniel T. Patterson of the New Orleans Naval Station was given almost equal authority with Andrew Jackson but was an English sympathiser. Jean Lafitte told him that the English were anchored off Mobile Point and about to attack Fort Bowyer, offering to help him fight them. Jackson trusted Lafitte implicitly, but Patterson instead attacked the Baratarian privateers, destroying their base, and capturing their ships and sailors in September 1814. The Lafittes seem to have been tipped off and had sailed away, leaving Youx in charge, telling him not to fight the Americans. When Patterson approached, Youx set about burning stolen cargoes and warehouses and was placed in chains. In an agreement with the Lafitte brothers, General Andrew Jackson agreed to release Youx and his fellow pirates to assist at the Battle of New Orleans. Youx needed time to recover from the brutal treatment he had suffered because of his actions at Barataria. At New Orleans, the final battle of the War of 1812 with England, on 8 January 1815, Dominique Youx and Renato Beluche each commanded an expert Baratarian crew working two 24-pound cannon. They were in control of Battery Number 3, which decimated the English and was praised by General Jackson in a public address.

Youx is found next operating with Beluche around Jamaica in 1816, probably bringing prizes into Galveston, which was used by the Lafittes between 1816 and 1821. In 1823, he bought a small house in the Faubourg Marigny district of New Orleans, starting a coffee shop, but was still suffering from wounds. He died in pain in 1830, having spent all his wealth, and the city and local Freemasons paid for his funeral. His gravestone reads:

> This warrior bold on land and rolling sea, in hundred battles proved his bravery. Nor had this pure and fearless Bayard known one tremor, though the world were overthrown.

Renato Beluche (15 December 1780–4 October 1860) – 'A Patriot in the Eyes of Eight American Nations'

Renato's father was a French emigrant to New Orleans, who used a wig-making business as a front for smuggling. Beluche was born on his family's nearby Chalmette plantation. In 1787 his father died, leaving six children, the house and a heavily mortgaged plantation with several slaves. Around 1801–1802 Beluche sailed as a pilot's mate in the Spanish Navy on Governor Casa Calvo's flagship *Catalina*, and by 1805–1809 he was master of trading schooners for four New Orleans merchants. In 1809 he could afford to buy the pilot-boat schooner *Camillus*, but was in debt and was forced to sell her in Pensacola. Captaining the *Jenny* to Bordeaux, she was captured and he spent a month in prison at Plymouth, England, in 1812. Returning to New Orleans just before the War of 1812 broke out, he accepted command of the *Fly*, described as 'the only successful United States privateer of the six commissioned at New Orleans during the War of 1812'. In November 1812 he took the English *Jane*, carrying logwood and mahogany from Honduras. Like Youx (*see* above entry), Beluche next sailed to Cartagena on the coast of Venezuela, which had declared itself a republic in 1811, and offered his ship, crew and their services to join its new navy. Beluche could now sail under Cartagena's letters of marque, and he commanded a fleet of at least three privateers, the *La Popa*, *Las Piñeras* and the *General Bolivar*.

Flying the French flag, Beluche captured Spanish and English ships. The Lafitte brothers had a smuggling base at Grande Terre on the Louisiana coast, and Beluche sent his ships and booty to them, and also back to Cartagena. From 1812 to 1814 he also scuttled more than a million dollars' worth of Spanish shipping in the Gulf and

Caribbean. In 1813, Beluche became associated with the Venezuelan revolution against Spain, and with its leader, Simón Bolívar. He spent the next decade fighting for Venezuelan independence, except for a brief intermission when he gained fame for his role as a master gunner, alongside Dominique Youx, at the Battle of New Orleans (23 December 1814–8 January 1815). After that battle, he returned to Cartagena in *La Popa*, said to be the fastest ship in the Gulf and Caribbean, and managed to slip into the blockaded port before escaping back through the Spanish cordon to Jamaica.

On 19 December 1815 Beluche carried Simón Bolívar on *La Popa* from Kingston, Jamaica, to Aux Cayes, Haiti, to organise a fleet of seven privateers. This was a crucial step towards the freedom of half a continent from Spanish rule. Beluche defeated a Spanish fleet off Margarita Island, Venezuela, allowing Bolívar to land in Venezuela. In its eight-year battle for independence, Beluche's privateers were invaluable. His first wife, Marie Milleret, a native of Port-au-Prince, filed for divorce in 1822, but by the time it was finalised she had died aged 40. Beluche already had two children by a New Orleans woman, Maria Boudri. In 1823 Beluche took part in both the Battle of Lake Maracaibo (which virtually signalled Venezuelan independence), and in the successful siege of Puerto Cabello, the last Spanish Royalist stronghold.

In 1824, Beluche settled his family in Puerto Cabello and initially worked as a coastal shipping captain. He married Maria 'Mezelle' Boudri in 1824, legitimising their children, aged six and four; they had another child in 1828. He soon became active in the navy of Bolívar's Colombia (consisting of Ecuador, Colombia and Venezuela), being promoted to Brigadier-General in 1827, with headquarters at Puerto Cabello. With the Peruvian Navy threatening Ecuador, Bolívar sent letters to the Governor of Venezuela urging him to send 'General Beluche' to sea commanding the 'Pacific Squadron of Colombia' because of his 'ability and enthusiasm'. Beluche sailed the 60-gun frigate *Colombia* from Puerto Cabello on 25 August 1829, made one stop of 14 days in Rio de Janeiro and on 1 February 1830 anchored near Guayaquil. Ecuador was in the throes of its battle for independence against Colombia, Venezuela had seceded in 1829. In April 1830 Bolívar resigned. Beluche entered Panama and became involved in a losing revolution, being expelled. He and 'Mezelle' had another son in 1832.

In 1836 Beluche fought on the losing side of a rebellion against the Venezuelan government and was exiled for nine years. In 1840, his wife died, aged 49. He returned in 1845 and helped crush a revolt that lasted from 1848 until 1850. He died peacefully in Puerto Cabello in 1860, being buried alongside Mezelle. His burial stone reads simply: 'General Renato Beluche – Octobre 4, 1860 – 79 años'. Considered a pirate by the English and Spanish, he is regarded as 'a patriot in the eyes of eight American nations', and his remains were re-interred in the National Pantheon of Venezuela on 22 July 1963.

Louis Michel Aury (*c.*1788–1821) – Rival of the Lafittes and Freedom Fighter

Born in Montrouge, Paris, Aury served both in the French Navy and on French privateers from about 1802 until 1810. Aged 15, he left his French warship at Guadeloupe, joining privateers. Aged 22, his prize money enabled him to own and captain his own ships. In 1810, in New Orleans, American officials confiscated his vessel and in 1811, at Savannah, North Carolina, a mob torched his second ship. Both events may have been initiated by the Lafitte brothers resentment over his success. In 1812, the rebel government of Cartagena commissioned Aury as captain of a refitted privateer. He sailed from North Carolina in April 1813, reaching Cartagena in May, and with Cartagena as his headquarters he harassed Spanish shipping lanes with great success.

From August 1813 Aury commanded the Republic of Granada's privateer schooners, a service that ended in January 1816. In December 1815, as Commodore in the navy of New Granada (Colombia), he ran the Spanish blockade of Cartagena. The siege had left the inhabitants in desperate conditions, and Aury evacuated hundreds of people at great personal expense. After successfully passing through the Spanish blockade he reached Aux Cayes, Haiti, where Renato Beluche was assembling a fleet for Simón Bolívar. However, Aury quarrelled with Bolívar over payments for his services, supposedly about $25,000. Also, a rivalry had developed between Aury and Luis Brión, the commander of Bolívar's Venezuelan squadron. Aury thus refused to serve under Brión, and instead accepted a letter of marque from Mexican rebels, funded by a group of merchants in New Orleans. The merchants wished to gain access to the Mexican silver mines, as well as take control of Florida from Spain. They were initially planning to create a Mexican rebel port on the Texas coast, and attacked Mexican Royalist ports as part of the Mexican revolt against Spain. Leaving Haiti on 4 June 1816 Aury took several vessels en route to Belize, where he arrived on 17 July, before sailing to the island port of

Galveston. Unfortunately, most of his prize vessels and cargo were lost or damaged trying to make it into the narrow harbour in strong winds.

Dissatisfied sailors mutinied on the night of 7 September, wounding Aury, and sailed back to Haiti with considerable loot. However, assistance from New Orleans soon arrived, and José Manuel de Herrera, the Mexican rebel, proclaimed Galveston Island a port of the Mexican republic, making Aury its resident commissioner. The rebel flag was raised at Galveston on 13 September 1816 and Aury's fleet captured many prizes, including one with a cargo of indigo and goods worth about $778,000. Such cargoes were transferred from Galveston through New Orleans customs in unlabelled bales, or were smuggled direct into Louisiana. Aury backed General Xavier Mina, a young Spanish insurgent, and in late 1816, Mina arrived in Galveston to organise an overland invasion of Mexico. Aury disagreed, and instead in April 1817 they attacked the port of Tampico and took it easily.

Against Aury's advice, Mina then marched inland anyway, but was captured and executed by the Spanish in October 1817. When Aury returned to Galveston he discovered that Jean Lafitte and his Baratarians had moved in and taken control of 'his' island. Aury tried to re-establish himself, but failed, and resigned as commissioner of Galveston Island on 31 July 1817.

From Galveston, Aury sailed for Fernandina, Amelia Island, Florida, where the Scot Gregor McGregor had established the Republic of Florida, styling himself 'Brigadier-General of the United Provinces of the New Granada and Venezuela and General-in-Chief of the armies of the two Floridas'. The intention was to use the island as a springboard to attack Spanish Florida. McGregor had himself been trapped in the siege of Cartagena, and had helped organise the evacuation that Aury led on 5 December 1815.

However, McGregor, who called himself the authorised agent of the rebel colonies of Venezuela, New Grenada (Colombia), Mexico, and La Plata (Argentina), had left two weeks earlier, so two of his lieutenants turned over Amelia Island to Aury, as a representative of the Mexican insurgents. Aury used the island as a base for privateering, moving slaves into Georgia along with captured merchandise, so in December 1817 the Americans shut down his activities. With 400 men and 14 ships Aury now sailed for Providencia (Old Providence Island, of Nicaragua), capturing it on 4 July 1818. He set up his new base of operations and tried to reconcile with Simón Bolívar, but still refused to serve under Luis Brión, so accepted letters of marque from the governments of Buenos Aires and Chile. In May 1819 Aury made a successful raid on Izabal, Guatemala, and began plotting to free Central America from the control of Spain. In April 1820 he attacked the Spanish fortresses at Trujillo and Omoa, Honduras, but failed. In August 1821, Aury passed away at the young age of 33, supposedly after falling off a horse.

José Gaspar *(c.1756–1821)* – 'Gasparilla', the Invisible, 'Last of the Buccaneers'

Before the early 20th century, no mention of Gaspar appears in writing, and there is neither physical nor literary evidence of his existence. The Spaniard was said to have sailed the Caribbean and operated off Tampa Bay, Florida, being credited with taking more than 400 ships from 1789 to 1821, but none seem to have been actually recorded. The story is that he was planning on retiring from a life of piracy, dividing treasure among his crew, when they spotted an English merchant ship offshore. Seeing easy plunder they took to sea, but the merchant vessel was the disguised USS *Enterprise*, on a pirate-hunting mission. Too late, Gaspar realised that it was a trap. His ship caught fire and was about to be boarded, and rather than surrender and be hanged for piracy he wrapped a heavy chain around his waist and jumped off the bow of his ship. However, Gaspar had left his treasure on shore with some of his trusted crew, and they took the treasure inland and buried it in different places along the west coast of Florida. For more than a hundred years, Tampa Bay has celebrated José Gaspar with a great parade with more than 120 pirate crews in floats for a festival called the Gasparilla Pirate Fest or Gasparillafest. In excess of 500,000 people attend annually, and the world's 'only fully-rigged pirate ship', the *José Gasparilla*, sails into Tampa Bay accompanied by hundreds of small boats. The ship is crewed by 'pirates' firing cannons, intent on capturing the city.

Ángel García (b.1800) – *Cabeza de Perro* (Dog Head)

Ángel García was said to be born in Igueste de San Andrés, Tenerife, in 1800 (others believe he flourished in the late 19th century) and from his youth was possibly engaged in smuggling and piracy. He was nicknamed 'Dog Head' because he had a thick and stubby snub nose, small eyes, sunken mouth with long, wide-apart teeth, dark blond hair and a very bulky, misshapen head. He used a black hood to disguise his appearance. He pirated from the African Coast to the Caribbean, and with his wealth built a huge mansion, stacked with money and jewels, in the San Lázaro district of Havana. There, 'rooms communicated with secret doors leading to the basement of death, when his faithful servant, Placido the Mulato, waited for their victims.' Presumably captives were tortured to reveal where they had hidden valuables, or kept there for ransom. From the house, his son Luis García controlled the entrance and exit of wealthy clients of his father, come to fence and source goods and money. When sailing to the African coast for slaves, ships loaded with ivory and wood, they never attacked the boats that sailed Canary Island waters.

A Spanish website tells us that in his flagship *El Invencible*, García took the brig *Audacious*, which was sailing from Havana to New York, stabbing to death all the crew and passengers except for a woman and her son, who had hidden below decks. When discovered, they were thrown into the sea. Some sources state that they drowned, but it is also said that an Italian ship *Centauro* picked them up from the waters. According to some, García's attitude changed after seeing the crying infant being thrown overboard. Unable to sleep, he is said to have been wracked with guilt, asking his wealthy high-ranking partners in Havana if he could give up pirating and turn himself in. However, his son dissuaded him, as it would mean that he and all of the crew would also be imprisoned and executed. García began to attend church regularly and befriended a local cleric, also a native of Tenerife, who told him that he should leave Havana and return to his old home at Igueste de San Andrés in Tenerife and begin farming, forgetting his pirate days and giving thanks to God. García bought a suit, hat, a pair of glasses and shaved his beard, and as a 'respectable man' secretly boarded the *Triton* to sail home to become a farmer.

All the way from the Caribbean to the Canary Islands, he did not leave his cabin, not wishing to be seen by other passengers, until there was a cry that Mount Teide, Tenerife, was spotted. He soon could see his village from the deck, and before arrival at the port of Santa Cruz de Tenerife he had completely transformed his appearance. He now wore baggy pants above the ankles, a large shirt, a large straw hat with a wide brim to try to hide his misshapen head, and carried an umbrella and a cage with a parrot. However, Dog Head's appearance meant that he was mocked by a crowd of youths, who threw rocks at him, and wounded, he fell to the ground. When guards arrived to protect him, they found García trying to defend himself with a knife. Its handle was shaped like a dog's head, and he was arrested, and imprisoned at the

Castillo de Paso Alto de Santa Cruz de Tenerife. He spent a long time there before trial, distracting himself by smoking and building model ships, and never speaking to his warders. Upon learning of his death sentence, crowds gathered to see his walk from the fortress between bayonets. Before he faced the firing squad, he is said to have ordered a cigar, and to have given a model of a brig to the Church of the Virgin of Mount Carmel. Wrapping a red scarf around his head, he was smiling when shot.

As with another Tenerife pirate, Amaro Pargo, García is said to have hidden treasure in the 'Water Cave' on a black sand beach, just over a mile from Igueste. However, Manuel de Paz, Professor of American History at the University of La Laguna, in *Piracy in the Canary Islands*, writes that there is no record in the Canaries or America of the existence of such a pirate. However, it is a good story – and a great name for a pirate.

Hippolyte Bouchard (15 January 1780–4 January 1837) – The Argentinean Corsair, 'California's Only Pirate'

Born near St-Tropez, and also known as Hipólito de Bouchard, he served on French merchant ships and then joined the French Navy, fighting the English in the Battle of the Nile (1798) and taking part in Bonaparte's Saint-Domingue (Haiti) Expedition (1801–03) to retake the colony after Toussaint L'Ouverture's rebellion. Napoleon had instructed his brother-in-law Charles Leclerc to kill anyone older than 12 and to restore slavery in Saint-Domingue, Martinique and Guadeloupe; about sixty per cent of the black population was exterminated. Disenchanted with Napoleon, Bouchard arrived in Argentina in 1809 to join the May Revolution, where he joined Azopardo's naval squadron. In 1811, he was in the Argentine Republic's flotilla defeated by the Spanish, and was noted for his leadership defending Buenos Aires from a Spanish blockade. In March 1812 Bouchard joined San Martín's Regiment of Mounted Grenadiers, and in the 1813 Battle of San Lorenzo captured the Spanish flag and was granted citizenship of the United Provinces of the River Plate (now the Argentine Republic).

In 1815 he returned to the Navy under the command of Admiral Guillermo (William) Brown, being given a corsair licence to fight the Spanish aboard the corvette *Halcón*. Brown commanded the fleet of four ships. Heading to rendezvous, Bouchard suffered damage rounding Cape Horn and one ship was lost with all hands. In 1816, the three ships attacked villages in Chile, then Callao, Peru's main port, and then Guayaquil (now in Ecuador), seizing seven ships. In February, Guillermo Brown was captured near Guayaquil, and the corsairs traded him for four ships and five correspondence chests. Bouchard's ship, still in a bad state since rounding the Horn, was close to sinking, and his officers wanted to sail back to Buenos Aires. Abandoning the *Halcón*, he returned via the Horn in the *Consecuencia*.

In 1817 he circumnavigated the globe in *La Argentina*, harassing Spanish merchant ships wherever he found them. In July, a great fire aboard ship meant that he had to head for Madagascar under little sail. He spent two months repairing his ship. With many of the crew dying or suffering from scurvy, Bouchard sailed through Indonesia to the Philippines, being attacked by *Lanun*, Malayan pirates. He took their largest ship with a boarding party and the other three ships fled. The prisoners were all sentenced to death, save for the youngest. They were returned to their ship, locked below decks, and their damaged ship hit by cannon fire until she sank beneath the waves with her prisoners.

On 31 January 1818, Bouchard was off Manila, a heavily fortified city with excellent artillery. Staying clear of its cannon range, Bouchard blockaded it, plundering nearby vessels. Over the next two months *La Argentina* captured 16 ships, and in Manila the price of food tripled. Bouchard left just before Spanish ships arrived to relieve Manila.

On the return trip, at Hawaii, Bouchard recruited 80 more men to replace those lost to scurvy. There he recovered a Spanish frigate, the *Santa Rosa*, whose crew had mutinied and had tried to sell the vessel to King Kamehameha. Leaving Hawaii, he anchored at Kauai Island and he captured the *Santa Rosa* mutineers, executing the leaders and giving the rest 12 blows with a lash in the face. Bouchard next began raiding the coast of Spanish Alta, California. In October 1818 his fleet raided the Presidio of Monterey in California. Bouchard, commanding *La Argentina*, along with the rebuilt *Santa Rosa*, under the command of Englishman Peter Corney, entered Monterey Bay. The *Santa Rosa* suffered substantial damage from the shore batteries and was listing heavily, so Corney ordered a surrender and the firing stopped. His crew quickly moved all of the cannon to the undamaged side, raising the damaged side higher out of the water to save the ship. Manning the lifeboats, they did not head for surrender on the shore but instead rowed to join Bouchard, out of range of the Spanish guns.

Bouchard sailed a couple of miles away to land 400 men and two cannons to capture El Castillo, forcing the governor to abandon the

Presidio. Spanish troops fled with their families, while the pirates looted the Presidio, Castillo and town, before setting fire to the place. Bouchard destroyed the Spanish cannons by loading them, burying them barrel-down half-way into the ground, then firing them. The governor sent for reinforcements from the San Francisco and Santa Barbara Presidios, but after six days the pirates had repaired the *Santa Rosa* and sailed away.

Next Bouchard threatened to attack Santa Bárbara Mission, California, and the nearby town. The 50 Presidio troops were outnumbered by 285 pirates, but began marching along the beach, then changing their clothes behind scrub and marching back again, to make it appear there were more defenders. Fooled by the masquerade, the *La Argentina* and the *Santa Rosa* sailed farther down the coast, and on 14 December 1818 attacked and severely damaged the Mission of San Juan Capistrano. It had refused to supply the pirates with supplies, having heard of the raids farther up the coast, and Bouchard ordered an assault by 140 men with three cannon to take the needed provisions. The Mission guards were overwhelmed and the governor's house, the king's stores and barracks were damaged.

From 25 January 1719 Bouchard blockaded San Blas, on the west coast of Mexico, after taking the brig *Las Animas*. He also took the British *Good Hope*, confiscating her cargo of Spanish goods. On 18 March his fleet took a brig off El Salvador. On 2 April Bouchard led two boats with cannons and 60 men to attack El Realejo, which was protected by four ships. Bouchard managed to take the ships after an intense battle and burned the brig *San Antonio* and the schooner *Lauretana*, as their owners had not offered enough money for their return. He retained the lugger *Neptuno* and the second schooner *María Sofía*. Soon after, the *Santa Rosa* was attacked and about to be boarded by the schooner *Chileno* when she raised the Chilean flag. She was commanded by a corsair named Croll, who sailed off when Bouchard commanded that he gave him his surgeon to tend to his wounded. Bouchard's long privateering expedition around the world ended on 3 April 1819, at Valparaiso in Chile, when he joined San Martin's campaign to liberate Peru. According to Daniel E. Cichero's biography of Bouchard, he marked each door of any American's house with a red cross. These were to be left alone during any depredations, protecting the interests of the Americans. This corsair from the young free state of the 'United Provinces of Rio de la Plata River' is honoured as a patriot and hero in Argentina today.

Unclassifiable Pirates

Lope de Aguirre (8 November 1510–27 October 1561) – the Limping Conquistador, 'Keeper of the Dead', El Loco (The Madman), who styled himself 'Wrath of God, Prince of Freedom, Prince of Peru, and King of Tierra Firme'

Lope de Aguirre was the son of a Basque nobleman, born in the province of Gipuzkoa, in north-eastern Spain. Living in Seville in his twenties, he saw the conquistador Francisco Pizarro bring back incredible Inca treasures from Peru, and was inspired to seek his fortune in the Americas. He joined an expedition of 250 men, arriving in Peru in 1536/37. Aguirre was involved in the plotting and fighting between the Spanish factions, and in 1551 was arrested and flogged. After the trial judge left office, he frequently changed his home, as Aguirre, now with a small army of followers, was trying to kill him, in revenge for the dishonour of a noble being whipped. After three years, he found the judge sleeping in his library in Cuzco. The former judge, fearful for his life, always slept in armour, so Aguirre stabbed him in the temple and fled.

In 1555, Hernández Girón rose in rebellion and the Governor of Peru, Alonzo de Alvarado, needed men to fight. He thus pardoned Aguirre and all those who had followed him. Aguirre was wounded by two musket balls fighting Girón at the battle of Chuquinga, resulting in an incurable limp that made his peers ostracise him.

Aguirre next joined Pedro de Ursúa's expedition of September 1560. They weighed anchor with three brigantines, various barges, 300 soldiers and hundreds of Indians. The Spanish were enticed by the news that Brazilian Indians ruled over the riches of Omagua and

El Dorado, so went in search of great treasures such as those found at Cajamarca and Mexico City, also with good land to settle. Governor Ursúa appointed the Seville nobleman Fernando de Guzman as general, and Lope de Aguirre as 'the keeper of the dead', caring for the goods of those that died during the expedition. However, the whole mission was simply a plot by Governor Ursúa to rid himself of trouble-making veterans from the Peruvian civil wars. The force descended by the river Huallaga to the Amazon, but by December the soldiers, having not encountered a single trace of promised riches, became discontented.

The expedition was in Mocomoco and soldiers wanted to turn back. Aguirre, who enjoyed prestige among the troops, planned the death of Pedro de Ursúa, which occurred on 1 January, 1561. Lope de Aguirre then surrounded himself with a ferocious bodyguard, which would follow any order, and took command of the expedition. However, for a temporary figurehead he decided to appoint Fernando de Guzman 'General of the Marañones and King of Peru, and Chile Tierrafirme'. The document has been called the 'First Act of American Independence'. Through this, and by subsequent arrangements by Aguirre, his followers left the rule of Philip II of Spain. Guzman was barely 21 years old and was convinced of the madness of Aguirre, and wished to kill him, but did not dare to give the order. Lope de Aguirre knew his men desired to return to Peru. His small army destroyed native villages on their way to the Atlantic.

Aguirre now killed the young Guzman and other opponents and in March 1561 Aguirre made his remaining 186 soldiers sign a statement acknowledging him as 'Prince of Peru, Tierra Firme, and Chile'. Aguirre acquired a reputation for torture, treachery and brutality on his journey. At the beginning of July, the expedition reached the Atlantic. Imposing an iron rule, he constructed two brigantines. On 21 July Aguirre took Margarita Island, Venezuela, by surprise, exterminating all opposition and killing its governor. They left the island at the end of August, after Aguirre sent a letter which defied Philip II of Spain, declaring an independent state of Peru. He also took and plundered Nueva Valencia on the Venezuela coast. Venezuela had lived in terror before the impending arrival of '*el loco*' Aguirre, and even the governor, Pablo Collado, had fled. On 22 October, Aguirre's men entered Barquisimeto, Venezuela, where pardons for them were found in the deserted homes. Soldiers initially joked about them, but many secretly hid the pardons and later deserted. The defections came to a head when the mad Aguirre's trusted captain Tirado rode off overnight.

Only a few old conquistadors were left with the 'Wrath of God'. On 27 October, abandoned by most of his force, he killed his daughter Elvira, 'because someone that I loved so much should not come to be bedded by uncouth people'. He then killed several of his own troops who had intended to capture him. He was eventually taken and shot to death. Aguirre's body was beheaded and cut into quarters, with pieces being sent to nearby towns as a warning. Lope de Aguirre has been represented in film in 1972 (*Aguirre, the Wrath of God*) and 1988 (*El Dorado*), and the character of the renegade Colonel Kurtz in *Apocalypse Now* was in part inspired by his story.

Dixie Bull (*fl.*1630–1632) – New England's First Pirate, 'the Dread Pirate'

Dixie, or Dixey, Bull was born in London, apprenticed as a skinner and joined the Worshipful Company of Skinners (the Skinner's Guild), which controlled the English fur trade. Bull left for the Americas around 1630, intending to trade 'coats, rugs, blankets, biskettes, etc.' with the Native Americans, in exchange for highly valued beaver pelts. (Biskettes are twice-cooked bread.) In 1631 he was associated with Sir Ferdinando Gorges in the development of a large land grant, east of Agamonticus at York, Maine. In June 1632, Bull was known to be sailing a shallop along the coast of Maine and trading in furs but, at Penobscot Bay, he was attacked by French pirates in a pinnace, who robbed him of all his money and trade goods. Destitute, Bull wanted his wealth back, and travelled between the few settlements from Penobscot to Boston, recruiting 15 men for his shallop. (A shallop is a two-masted, gaff-rigged ship, ideal for shallow waters.) Not finding the French, and needing provisions, Bull instead plundered two or three small merchantmen. Having made his first step into piracy, with 20–25 men he next attacked an English trading post at the mouth of the Damariscotta River, Pemaquid, Maine. It was a centre for fish processing and the fur trade, and about 85 families lived there. Sailing into its harbour, now possibly with three ships, he opened fire on the stockade. Bull led his men ashore and there was little resistance. They sacked the trading station, taking about $2,500's-worth of goods, then burnt it. There is a legend that as the pirates were sailing away, the fisherman Daniel Curtis fired a musket shot that killed Bull's second-in-command. Few pirates had the courage to attack a defended town, and his fame as 'the dread pirate' stems from this 1632 raid.

Fear spread along the Maine coast. Bull did not seem to target French shipping, presumably because English merchantmen were more valuable. A Salem ship was later captured by Bull, and its captain reported that the pirates were 'afraid of the very Rattling of the Ropes', which seems to indicate hanging. From Boston, Governor Winthrop sent a flotilla of three shallops and two pinnaces, under Samuel Maverick, to hunt the English pirates, but Bull had vanished. Early in February 1633, three of Bull's crew secretly returned to their Maine homes, and said that Bull had sailed eastward and joined the French, his former enemies. Captain Roger Clap stated that Bull eventually returned to England. One report is that he was hanged at Tyburn, but there is no record and his fate (and real name) are as yet a mystery. The contemporary ballad, *The Slaying of Dixie Bull*, describes a duel with swords between Dixie Bull and Daniel Curtis, in which Curtis kills him. One of his treasure troves was reputed to be worth $400,000 at the time of its burial on Damariscove Island, and another of his hoards is supposed to have been buried on Cushing Island, also off the Maine coast.

Hiram Breakes (1745–*c*.1780) – 'Dead Men Tell No Tales'
Breakes was a son of a councillor on Saba, the smallest island in the Netherlands Antilles, south-east of Puerto Rico. In 1764, aged just 19, he was appointed to a Dutch merchant ship sailing between Saba, the Caribbean, and Amsterdam. He later commanded a trading ship that operated between Schiedam, Holland, and Lisbon. Breakes fell in love with a married woman named Mrs Snyde. Mr Snyde was poisoned and Breakes and the Mrs Snyde went on trial but were acquitted of the murder. Next, Breakes stole his employer's ship and renamed it the *Adventurer*. Having turned to piracy, he raided Vigo, the port in Galicia, northwest Spain. There he took the *Acapulco*, which had sailed from Valparaiso, Chile, with a load of 20,000 small gold bars. He murdered her crew and refitted the *Acapulco* for piracy to sail the Mediterranean. From there, Breakes used some of the booty to buy a letter of marque from the governor of English-held Gibraltar and turned to pillaging throughout the Mediterranean and the Atlantic Ocean.

According to Gosse, Breakes ordered a stop to piracy on Sundays, and would often preach a sermon 'after the Lutheran style'. Breakes plundered a nunnery on Minorca in the Balearic Islands and decided that it was inappropriate for his crew to be unmarried, so he had each of his men select a nun from the convent, who was then kidnapped and brought to the ship. Wealthy, he retired from piracy to return to Amsterdam to marry his mistress, Mrs Snyde. However, he discovered that she had been hanged for poisoning their young son. In a state of depression, according to Gosse, Breakes 'turned melancholy mad' and drowned himself in a dyke. There is little independent information upon Breakes apart from Gosse's account, but Breakes has been credited with coining the phrase 'dead men tell no tales.'

John Paul (6 July 1747–18 July 1792) – John Paul Jones, 'Father of the American Navy'

Later taking on the surname of Jones, John Paul is regarded as an American hero, but was thought a common pirate by the English. Born at Arbigland, Scotland, he was an estate gardener's son, who spent much of his childhood talking to sailors at the small harbour of Carsethorn on the Solway Firth. Aged 13, he took a ship for the larger port of Whitehaven in England to sign a seven-year seaman's apprenticeship. As a ship's boy he sailed to Barbados and Fredericksburg, Virginia, on the *Friendship*, but was released from his apprenticeship and, in 1764, the 17-year-old was third mate on the Whitehaven slaver *King George*. By 1766 Jones was first mate on the Kingston, Jamaica, brigantine *Two Friends*. Only 50 feet long, its crew of six took 77 blacks from Africa to the West Indies in terrible conditions, and he left what he called the 'abominable trade' in disgust. Jones was given free passage home on the *John* of Kirkcudbright, whose captain and mate died of fever en route. Jones took command and the owners were so pleased they appointed him captain, in charge of buying and selling the cargo for the *John* to sail back to America.

A short and 'dandy' man, Jones always displayed a vicious temper, once flogging excessively with a cat-o'-nine tails the ship's carpenter Mungo Maxwell, at Tobago. Maxwell died of the wounds across his back on the way back to Kirkcudbright.

Jones next commanded the *Betsy*, and accumulated considerable sums in the West Indies. However, in 1773 he had to leave the Caribbean after a dispute over wages. He had killed the ringleader of the complainants with his sword. He fled to Virginia, now changing

John Paul Jones, courtesy
of the Rijksmuseum.

his name to John Jones and later to John Paul Jones, probably to
escape retribution. In the War of Independence, Jones offered his
services to the new 'Continental Navy' formed by Congress, being
commissioned as first lieutenant on 7 December 1775, sailing on
the *Alfred*. In November 1777 he captained the *Ranger* to France
and met the American Commissioner, Benjamin Franklin. In April
1778, Jones left Brest for the Irish Sea, capturing and destroying
small shipping. After another near mutiny by his crew, he made a
night raid on Whitehaven, spiked the fort's guns and burnt some coal
ships. Jones then tried to capture the Earl of Selkirk, but the lord
was away from home. Off Carrickfergus, Ireland, Jones fought the
20-gun sloop HMS *Drake* for more than an hour, killing its captain
and second-in-command. The raid made Jones' name a household
word throughout Britain.

Back in Brest, Brittany, Jones was given command of a French
East Indiaman, the *Duc de Duras*, which he converted into a

John Paul Jones
sculpted from life
by Frenchman
Jean-Antoine
Houdon, courtesy
U.S. Naval Academy.

warship and renamed *Bonhomme Richard* (in honour of Benjamin
Franklin's translated book, *Les Maximes du Bonhomme Richard.*)
In August 1779 Jones led a squadron of seven ships with the
mission of destroying British commerce in the North Sea. Jones
sailed around Ireland and into Leith harbour, Scotland, on
16 September. Jones wanted to ransom Leith for £50,000, but a
storm forced his fleet out of the Firth of Forth. On the evening of
23 September 1779, Jones was off Yorkshire when his fleet fought
HMS *Serapis* and the *Countess of Scarborough* off Flamborough
Head. On a millpond sea, *Serapis* had better artillery, but Jones
managed to lash the *Bonhomme Richard* to her. More than half of
the crews of the ships were killed, wounded or horribly burned.
In the course of a three-and-a-half hour battle, the wounded Jones
was asked if he wished to surrender, and replied that he had 'not
yet begun to fight'. Jones then transferred his surviving crew to
the captured *Serapis*, and with the *Pallas*, which had captured the
Countess of Scarborough, Jones sailed to the Texel in Holland
with more than 500 prisoners.

He became the toast of Paris and later received a gold sword and the Order of Military Merit from Louis XVI. In 1781 he sailed back to America in the *Ariel* and Congress passed a vote of thanks and awarded him another gold medal. With peace, Jones returned to Paris to collect prize money for the officers and men of the *Bonhomme Richard*. Thomas Jefferson, the new American Ambassador, recommended him for service in Russia, and in 1788 the Empress Catherine II created Jones a Rear-Admiral in the Russian Navy. Thus 'Pavel Ivanovich' Jones served under Prince Potemkin against the Turks in the Black Sea campaign. At the Battle of Liman, he destroyed 15 Turkish ships, killing about 3,000 men, and took more than 1,600 prisoners, just losing one frigate and 18 dead. In 1789, after a brief audience with Catherine, Jones left Russia after a scandal. Returning to Paris in poor health, he died of pneumonia, his body being discovered by Gouverneur Morris. Jones's body lay in an alcohol-filled coffin in an unmarked grave, in a cemetery for foreign Protestants, for over a century. In 1905 it was rediscovered, and in 1913 his body was interred in a marble sarcophagus in the chapel crypt of Annapolis Naval Academy.

William Williams (*c.*1727–1791) – the Marooned Privateer, Artist, Polymath and 'Author of the First American Novel', the 'Forgotten Genius'

Around 1786, an elderly impoverished artist was befriended by the literary critic, the Reverend Thomas Eagles, who found him lodgings in the Merchant Venturers Almshouses in Bristol. The painter's bedroom can be visited today. The old man had been a successful painter in colonial America, and became known to Eagles as 'Llewellin Penrose'. Penrose became very friendly with Eagles' family, and in 1791 Eagles was surprised to be Penrose's sole beneficiary in his deathbed will. It was only then that the family discovered that 'Llewellin Penrose' was actually William Williams. Williams had been forced to leave New York because the War of Independence left him with no livelihood from teaching music and painting – many of his paintings are now in art galleries.

Williams left the Reverend Eagles a manuscript written in the Americas, detailing how he joined a Bristol privateer and was captured by the Spanish, imprisoned in Havana, and finally joined a privateer again before being marooned off the Miskito Coast of Nicaragua. Williams left all his possessions to Thomas Eagles, including this factional *The Journal of Penrose, Seaman*. In 1805, fourteen years after Williams' death, the great American artist Benjamin West RA was visiting Thomas Eagles' London townhouse. Luckily, as he waited for Eagles, West happened to notice William's manuscript lying upon a table. West then borrowed the manuscript, telling Thomas Eagles' son John that he had known Williams, aka 'Penrose', both in America and London. Williams had initially inspired and indeed then taught West to paint. West honestly believed the *Journal* to be a true account of Williams' life as a privateer, and that Williams had been marooned among the Caribbean Indians. The places mentioned in the text – the islands, reefs, caves and coastline – have all been identified in Nicaragua. John Eagles himself had heard 'Penrose' recounting his years on the Nicaraguan coastline.

Written perhaps around 1775 by the unknown privateer and polymath, William Williams, the book is an account of living among the Rama Indians of the Miskito Coast. It is a superb evocation of an almost idyllic existence and, in effect, an astonishing natural history of the area – its jungle, shoreline, sea and islands. At least 36 different species of birds are described, 48 different trees, shrubs, fruit and vegetables, 36 fish, 14 mammals, 24 reptiles, 20 insects, 7 turtles and tortoises, plus crustaceans and invertebrates totalling about 200 known animals and plants. All these fish, plants and animals mentioned by Penrose are native to the Atlantic seaboard and rainforest of Nicaragua. The indigenous Rama tribe that supported him is now facing extinction, and their customs are described in some detail.

Williams' *The Journal of Penrose, Seaman* contains entries covering 27 years spent on the rainforest shoreline, and reads almost as if it is written in the 21st century, with strong feelings against slavery and religious bigotry running as themes throughout the book. The author's attitudes towards racial and female equality, in a time of universal slavery, are simply astonishing, as is his positing of a 'savage' native civilization being far more humane and rational than many aspects of the Christian church. The Reverend Thomas Eagles and his son John altered the original manuscript to produce a book, not published until 1815, 24 years after Williams' death. It was the literary sensation of its day. Proofread by Sir Walter Scott, this was a heavily expurgated edition, but was still highly lauded by the Poet Laureate Robert Southey, who believed it to be true. The *Journal* was ecstatically reviewed by Lord George Byron. 'I have never read so much of a book in one sitting in my life. He [Penrose] kept me up half the night, and made me dream of him the other half ... it has all the air of truth, and is most interesting and entertaining in every point of view.' It is thought that Penrose's *Journal* influenced Lord Grey to later enact the first anti-slavery laws when he became Prime Minister. It is also the first novel written in America by around 15 years, and should be on all academic syllabi, and it would be suitable for a film script. It was widely praised as being vastly superior to *Robinson Crusoe* (published in 1719), as Daniel Defoe had never experienced the vicissitudes of William Williams.

The book is a plea for racial and religious tolerance, but much more than that, a marvellous adventure story based upon its author running away from Caerphilly, Wales, to sea in 1744, and being marooned in the coastal rainforests of Central America until his death in 1775. In 1946 the art critic James Thomas Flexner wrote of 'The amazing William Williams: Painter, Author, Teacher, Musician, Stage Designer, Castaway ... The activities of this forgotten genius spread across almost every branch of American culture ... he will stand out as a significant figure in the development of American culture.' This forgotten author was a polymath – a privateer, poet, music teacher, naturalist, writer and painter who inspired and taught Colonial America's greatest artist, Benjamin West, built America's first permanent theatre and wrote America's first novel.

Of special importance in the text is the discovery of mammoth bones in the rainforest by Penrose (aka Williams), along with basalt pillars with hieroglyphics. These have only been discovered in Nicaragua in the last 40 years. The book itself is superbly written faction, and contains the 'first story of buried treasure', which inspired Edgar Allan Poe to write *The Gold Bug* and saved him from bankruptcy. It is also the first known account of a message in a bottle. *The Journal of Penrose, Seaman* was strongly anti-slavery at a time when Presidents Washington, Jefferson and Adams had slaves. America's first novel, written by a privateer polymath, is an astounding piece of writing, an exciting adventure story worthy of international renown. Why it is still barely known is a mystery. The author has studied and rewritten in a modernised form the original manuscript (in the holdings of the Lilly Library, Indiana University, Bloomington), with notes and a biography of Williams, as *The First American Novel: The Journal of Penrose, Seaman by William Williams, & the Book, the Author and the Letters in the Lilly*

Library (2007), and a rewritten modernised version as *The Journal of Penrose, Seaman – the New Robinson Crusoe* (2014).

Edward 'Ned' Jordan (1771–1809) – The Pirate Jordan, the Black Irishman

From County Carlow, Ireland, Jordan had fought the English in the 1797–98 Irish Rebellion, but was captured and sentenced to death. He escaped but was again arrested, and turned informer to receive a royal pardon. Jordan married, but when his former allies discovered his betrayal he was forced to flee with his wife Margaret. They disembarked in New York in 1803, moving to Montréal, and then to Gaspé, Newfoundland. He borrowed money for a small schooner to set up as a fisherman, calling it the *Three Sisters* after his daughters. A run of bad luck meant that he could not repay his creditors, and he sought more financial assistance from Halifax merchants J. & J. Tremain. However, his debts mounted, and in 1809 the merchants sent Captain John Stairs to retrieve the 1,000 quintals of fish promised by Jordan to repay his debt (1 quintal being approximately a hundredweight, so Jordan owed 112,000 pounds weight of fish). Stairs found only 100 quintals, and took the *Three Sisters* in lieu of the debt. However, Stairs offered Jordan and his family passage on the schooner to Halifax, so he might find employment more easily than in Gaspé.

On 10 September 1809 the *Three Sisters* sailed under Captain John Stairs, with Edward Jordan, his wife Margaret, their three daughters and son, and three crew – John Kelly, Tom Heath and Ben Matthews. On 13 September, Jordan drew a pistol and shot at Stairs, but instead killed Tom Heath, standing next to him. Jordan and his wife then fought with Captain Stairs and Ben Matthews, while John Kelly remained at the wheel in heavy seas. Matthews was killed by Jordan, and the injured Stairs leapt into the sea, with a hatch cover as a float. Jordan shouted to Kelly to alter his course to make sure that John Stairs was 'finished.' However, Kelly refused to endanger the ship by tacking, shouting that the wounded Stairs could never make the swim back to the coast in the heavy seas, and it would be impossible to locate the captain in the swell. Jordan, his family and Kelly landed in Newfoundland to hire a crew and sail on to Ireland, but incredibly, a schooner sailing to Massachusetts had rescued Stairs after four hours in the sea.

At Halifax, Stairs reported events, and instructions were sent along the coast to 'arrest Jordan and Kelly, whenever found, on charges of piracy and murder'. A reward of £100 was offered and the *Three Sisters* was captured by the schooner HMS *Cuttle* in Bay of Bulls, Newfoundland. Jordan, reported as the 'Black Irishman', was convicted and sentenced to be hanged, but Kelly was acquitted. Margaret Jordan was discharged, as she had acted out of 'duress or fear of her husband'. Jordan was executed on 23 November 1809, and his body was tarred and gibbeted in Point Pleasant Park at Black Rock Beach, Halifax. Earlier that year, the Royal Navy had hanged in chains four men from the brig HMS *Columbine*, just across the harbour from Black Rock Beach. The tarred corpses served as a warning to wrongdoers at sea, and by 1844, only Jordan's skull remained and was given to the Nova Scotia Museum.

Benito Soto Aboal (22 April 1805–25 January 1830) – Benito de Soto, Captain of the *Black Joke*

Known as Benito de Soto, he was born in a small village near La Coruña, Spain, and took to piracy in 1827 in Buenos Aires. He was hired by the captain of the *Defensor de Pedro*, who was taking cheap rum to West Africa in exchange for slaves. A few months later, the captain was ashore in Angola, leaving his mate in charge. En route from South America, de Soto had planned with the mate to take over the *Defensor de Pedro* at the first opportunity. The pair told their shipmates that they had five minutes to decide whether to take to piracy or be set adrift in boats. One version is that 18 men decided against piracy and were given a longboat to sail away. Another is that those who disagreed were simply thrown overboard for the sharks. The alcoholic mate elected himself as captain, and after a heavy drinking session, de Soto entered the new captain's cabin and shot him through the head. The rest of the crew elected de Soto to take over as captain from the dead drunkard. De Soto renamed the *Defensor del Pedro* as *La Burla Negra* (Black Joke) and usually sailed under Colombian colours.

He seems to have criss-crossed the Atlantic, selling cargoes of stolen slaves across the Caribbean, and attacking English, American, Spanish and Portuguese ships along the coast of South America. From 1830 *La Burla Negra* also sailed eastwards into the Atlantic to take ships returning from India and the East Indies. It is said that de Soto sacked almost a dozen ships, among them the *Topaz*, *Cassnock*, *New Prospect*, *Melinda* and *Simbry*. De Soto also killed or injured about 100 prisoners. On 19 February 1828 *La Burla Negra* captured the British *Morning Star* just off the Ascension Islands, sailing from Ceylon to England. After killing some of the passengers and crew with cannon, they took the ship. Grappling hooks fastened the ships and de Soto politely asked the captain and his mate to come aboard, assuring them that they were safe. Once on board, they were hacked to death, and the pirates raped some women. De Soto now instructed one of his lieutenants, named Barbazan, to board the *Morning Star* with some other pirates and kill everybody. Barbazan realized that there were more females aboard the *Morning Star*. After slaughtering many of the crew, he imprisoned the rest in the main hold and took the finest women for de Soto's entertainment. Barbazan had fastened down the hatches of *Morning Star*, trapping the surviving men and women inside the hold, and bored a series of holes below the water line so that the ship would sink, leaving no evidence or survivors. *La Burla Negra* sailed off, but one of the women escaped and managed to free the rest of the crew. A passing vessel rescued the survivors of the slowly sinking *Morning Star.*

Sailing for La Coruña, Spain, the crew of *La Burla Negra* boarded a small brig and murdered the whole crew, except for one sailor who had told de Soto that he knew the fastest route to La Coruña. A few weeks later de Soto asked him: 'Amigo, is that really the harbour of La Coruña?' His pilot affirmed the fact, and de Soto smiled at him, saying 'In that case, you have done well and I thank you for your service.' He then shot the man in the head and threw him overboard. Soon after, de Soto was caught in a great storm and forced to abandon ship. The pirates came ashore near Cadiz, but the authorities were suspicious, and de Soto managed to escape to a tavern in Gibraltar. The pirate historian Charles Ellms met de Soto in Gibraltar, and says that he dressed expensively in silk stockings, white trousers, a blue frock coat and a clean white hat of the best English quality. However, de Soto was recognised by one of the survivors of the *Morning Star*. He was arrested, put on trial, found guilty of piracy, sentenced to hanging and his head placed on a pike.

'Don' Pedro Gibert (*c.*1800–11 June 1835) – The Last American Pirate, 'Dead Cats Don't Mew'

Gibert (also Gilbert) was possibly South American, but after he captured the brig *Mexican* in 1832, stated that he was born in Catalonia, Spain. He was a captain in the last recorded act of piracy in Atlantic waters off the USA coast. Gibert had been a privateer in

PEDRO GIBERT, *Captain.*

(CONVICTED.)

Born in Catalonia.—Married.—Age, 38.   Pedro Gibert.

the service of Colombia, then commanded the large schooner *Panda*, a former slaver, raiding American merchant ships off the coast of Florida. He sometimes operated out of Havana. His first mate, and the owner of the *Panda*, was Bernardo de Soto. Gibert and his crew of around 12 men would wait for passing ships, sometimes starting a fire on the shore to attract a ship's attention, pleading for help, and then attacking their rescuers. Soon he had about 40 crew, consisting of Spaniards, Portuguese, South Americans, mixed-race, and at least one West African. On 21 September 1832, off the coast of what is now Martin County, Florida, he boarded the American brig *Mexican*, sailing from Salem to Rio de Janeiro. Following her capture, and after locking the crew inside the fo'c'sle, Gibert's men ransacked the ship, finding $20,000 in silver. The pirates looted the stores and stripped the ship of anything valuable. His men then slashed the rigging and sails, and filled the ship's galley with combustibles. A pirate asked Gibert what to do with their prisoners, and he reportedly answered: 'Dead cats don't mew. You know what to do.' He set fire to the ship with the crew trapped inside, but they freed themselves and allowed smoke to billow until Gibert had vanished over the horizon. Six weeks later, the *Mexican* limped into Salem, where the incident was reported.

Two years later Gibert was off West Africa, loading slaves, when his ship was spotted by the British sloop HMS *Curlew,* captained by Henry Dundas Trotter. On 4 June 1833 Trotter seized the *Panda* in the Nazareth River, but its crew escaped to the shore. Trotter succeeded in capturing most of them, blew up the *Panda* and took possession of the Portuguese schooner *Esperanza,* which had been helping the fugitives. Gibert and 12 crew were extradited to Boston for trial, and in 1834 all were charged with piracy. The wife of Bernardo de Soto, the first mate and the owner of the *Panda,* crossed the Atlantic and prostrated herself before President Andrew Jackson, who gave the condemned de Soto a free pardon on 6 July 1835. A defence lawyer managed to procure not-guilty verdicts for five of the crew on grounds of following a superior's orders, including the cabin boy and the West African. Four were hanged together in June 1835: Pedro Gibert, Juan Montenegro, Manuel Castillo, and Angel Garcia. Manuel Boyga slashed open his carotid artery with a sharp piece of tin just before the hanging, and his unconscious (possibly dead) body was later taken in a chair to the scaffold to be hanged along with his four comrades. Two pirates received stays of execution. The ship's carpenter Francisco Ruiz pretended to be mad, but Spanish-speaking doctors said he was 'acting', and he was hanged on 12 September 1835. Gilbert's Bar, a sandbar off Stuart, Florida, near where the *Mexican* was taken, was named after Gibert.

George Fielding (1804–1844) – The Last Nova Scotia Pirate

George Fielding was baptised at St Mary's, Jersey (Channel Islands, UK) on 22 November 1804. Fielding supposedly started his working life fishing off the coast of France, possibly being involved in smuggling. In 1829 at St Helier, George married Sophie Le Sueuer, and on 18 February 1835, their son John was buried, aged just three years. His 32-year-old wife Sophie was buried five days later on 23 February 1835, probably dying in childbirth, as their daughter Anne Sophie had been buried just 11 days earlier, aged four days. Cholera was raging, and after these three tragedies in the space of 11 days, the widowed Fielding left St Helier for St Mary with his remaining child, another George Fielding. In August 1836 he was master of the 39-ton cutter *Samuel and Julia.* Fielding sailed for several years from Liverpool to Newfoundland and became well known. He sailed the 510-ton

Actaeon, but treated his crews badly, bullying, and providing poor food. 'It was a rare circumstance for him to bring back the same crew which sailed,' as they usually deserted on shore. Fielding was abusive, but spoke French, Spanish, Portuguese and Dutch, which helped him negotiate deals for his merchant employers. Fielding married at least twice, being known to be violent towards a wife at Liverpool.

Fielding next captained the *Vitula*, a recently built barque of 460 tons burden, sailing to Buenos Aires with his 12-year-old son George and a crew of 16. Finding no cargo to take on, he sailed around Cape Horn for Valparaiso, Chile, again finding nothing to purchase. He next landed at the Peruvian Island of Chincha, to buy and smuggle a cargo of guano. When the *Vitula* was fully laden, 50 Peruvian soldiers arrived and prevented Fielding from giving his crew guns. The crew had fled below decks, but the abrasive Fielding was badly injured by a gunshot wound in his shoulder. He was taken by a schooner to hospital in Pisco, and the *Vitula* was seized. With the schooner as escort and the crew under guard, the *Vitula* was sailed to Callao, Lima's harbour. The Peruvian authorities found out that Fielding was planning to take back the *Vitula*, and placed him in prison, but his son was left free.

Young George now smuggled a punch (a large cloak) into the gaol, and Fielding escaped wearing it. For two days he hid under debris at the dockyard of the South Pacific Steam Company, emerging only to seek a British vessel. The Fieldings secured a passage on the *Essex* for England, but after a row between the argumentative Fielding and Captain Oakley, the father and son were put ashore at Valparaiso. Knowing Fielding's quarrelsome reputation, two English captains refused to take them aboard, but Thomas Byerly, the mate of the Newcastle 550-ton barque *Saladin*, bound for London, took pity on them. Some of the *Saladin's* crew had deserted and young George and his injured father would have helped on the homeward voyage. The 1844 voyage was planned to be Captain Alexander ('Sandy') McKenzie's last. The *Saladin* carried a crew of 11 men plus the Fieldings, with 90 tons of copper, 13 silver bars, bags of gold, a chest holding between $7,000 and $20,000 in coins, and a hold full of valuable guano.

Its Scottish captain was a cruel alcoholic, and like Fielding lost crew wherever he docked. Setting sail on 8 February 1844, within a few days he and Fielding could not talk to each other, nor even share a table. Fielding began sounding out the crew to find out who hated their drunken captain, and once safely past the dangers of Cape Horn, he assembled his chosen mutineers to take over the *Saladin*. The firearms were locked away, so they took axes, an adze (large axe) and hammers from the carpenter's chest. Around midnight on 15 April, the mate Thomas Byerly was at the wheel, in charge of the night watch. He was feeling unwell and was resting on a hen coop, when crewmen Jones, Tregaskis, Hazelton and Anderson hit him in the head with axes and threw him overboard. They then went to kill the captain, but his dog Toby began barking, which woke the carpenter, Allen, who rose to investigate. He was attacked and mortally wounded, but cried out before he was thrown into the sea. The mutineers used his call as a pretext to shout 'man overboard!' and Captain McKenzie emerged from his cabin. Fielding and the others axed him to death. Samuel Collins and Thomas Moffat left their bunks and were also butchered and thrown overboard.

George Fielding asked the surviving six crew to swear an oath of loyalty on McKenzie's Bible, and he set a course for Newfoundland, to sell the cargo and scuttle the *Saladin*. Fielding then threw overboard axes, firearms and any harmful weapons, to assure the crew that all were now safe. However, they discovered that he had hidden a brace of pistols and some dangerous hand tools in his cabin. The crew immediately suspected that Fielding was going to kill them, so seized him and his son. They were tied hand and foot and locked in a cabin overnight, and tossed overboard next morning. The cabin boy John Galloway was 'the only man who could take the sun and work out the reckoning', so he navigated the *Saladin* towards the Gulf of St Lawrence, but she ran aground on 21 May at Country Harbour, Nova Scotia.

Captain William Cunningham on the schooner *Billow* boarded the ship to assist the stranded crew. The six remaining members of *Saladin*'s crew told Cunningham that their captain had died seven to eight weeks earlier, the first and second mates shortly after, and that the other crew members had drowned. It was obvious to those who boarded the barque, with her decks littered with empty bottles, papers destroyed, and no entry in the log since 15 April, that the survivors' claims were untrue. The large amount of money and silver aboard also made Captain Cunningham suspicious, and the six survivors were taken to Halifax to be tried for piracy and murder. The money, silver bars and some of the copper were recovered before the *Saladin* broke up and sank. At a Vice-Admiralty court trial on 22 July 1844, four of the crew – George Jones, William Tregaskis aka Johnson, John Hazelton and Charles Anderson – were found guilty of murder and piracy, and publicly executed on 30 July. William Carr (the cook) and John Galloway stated that they were forced to join the pirates and were released, probably for being co-operative. It was to be the last piracy trial in Nova Scotia and the bodies of the pirates were buried rather than being gibbeted for public display. News of the mutiny, wrecking and trial soon appeared across the world.

Modern Piracy

Mohamed Abdi Hassan (born about 1956) – *Afweyne* (Big Mouth), the First Pirate Leader to be Prosecuted by the International Community

Also known as Maxamed Cabdi Xasan, and commonly known as Afweyne, Somali for 'Big Mouth', Mohamed Abdi Hassan is said to be the pirate leader behind the greatest modern act of piracy, the hijacking of the *Sirius Star* in 2008. Afweyne is from the port of Harardhere, and his son Abdiqaadir worked closely with him in his 'entrepreneurial' operations. Afweyne began his piracy in 2005, making millions over the next eight years. The UN Monitoring Group on Somalia and Eritrea linked him to more than seven vessel hijackings in 2009 alone, and it is alleged that he was also involved in the capture of dozens of other ships, including in 2008 the Ukrainian MV *Faina* and the supertanker MV *Sirius Star*. On 25 September 2008 the *Faina* was captured by about 50 of Afweyne's Somali pirates, in the 26th such attack in the first nine months of 2008. The *Faina's* crew consisted of 17 Ukrainians, three Russians and a Latvian.

Three days after its capture, on 28 September, the ship's Russian captain died from a stroke. Leaving the Ukraine, the ship was ostensibly making for Mombasa, Kenya, with 33 Soviet tanks, plus anti-aircraft guns, ammunition and rocket-propelled grenades, but documents on board show that the arms were destined for the Sudan civil war. The Somalis demanded a ransom of $35 million and threatened to blow up the ship, but the demand diminished to $5 million over a few weeks. They anchored the *Faina* off Somalia, but the US destroyer *Howard*

Cargo ship the MV *Faina*, ransomed for $3,200,000. Did the pirates know she was carrying armaments, including RPGs, anti-aircraft guns and tanks?

ensured that no munitions were landed. On 5 February 2009 it was announced that a ransom of $3.2 million had been paid to the pirates and the *Faina* was released.

Naval vessels from Russia, India and NATO began patrolling the Horn of Africa region in response to the *Faina* hijacking, but seven weeks later there came Afweyne's greatest success. The VLCC (Very Large Crude Carrier) MV *Sirius Star*, with a length of 1,089 feet and a capacity of 2.2 million barrels of crude oil, was registered in Monrovia under a Liberian flag of convenience. Built in Korea, it was launched in March 2008 and was en route from Saudi Arabia to the United States with 25 crew, its tanks fully loaded with oil. About 450 nautical miles south-east of the coast of Kenya, it was taken on 15 November 2008, allegedly under the orders of Afweyne, being the largest ship ever captured by pirates. Because she was fully laden, the freeboard was only about 30 feet, which meant it was easier to climb aboard for the pirates. This was the farthest out to sea Somali pirates had ever targeted a vessel, having travelled for three to four days to intercept it. Its cargo was valued as $100 million, and the *Sirius Star* was estimated to be worth around $150 million. Owned by the Saudi Arabian state oil company, the ship was sailed to be anchored off Afweyne's home port of Harardhere.

On 19 November, the alleged pirate leader, Farah Abd Jameh, asked for a ransom by an audio tape broadcast on Al-Jazeera television. An unspecified cash ransom was to be delivered to the *Sirius Star*, to be counted using machines that were able to detect counterfeit bills. On 20 November, the cash demand was $25 million, with a 10-day deadline given to the Saudis. On 24 November, the pirates had reduced the demand to $15 million and the *Sirius Star* was released on 9 January 2009, after payment of a $3 million ransom by a parachute drop. Five of the pirates drowned after their boat capsized in a storm after leaving the *Sirius Star*, and the body of one was later washed ashore with $153,000 in cash in a plastic bag. Somali pirates, having captured better boats, were now operating in an area of more than 1.1 million square miles, beyond established international patrols, and the attack raised crude oil prices in global markets.

Afweyne became a cult figure to many, with Colonel Gaddafi hailing him as a national hero, and inviting the pirate to a 2009 four-day celebration in Libya. From 2010 Afweyne entered into a formal agreement with Al-Shabaab militants, agreeing to hand over a $100,000 tax per hijacking ransom, in return for no interference from the insurgents in his operations. In 2010 Afweyne received an official pardon from Mohamed Aden ('*Tiiceey*'), the governor of Somalia's south-central region. Afweyne now handed over his piracy operations to his son Abdiqaadir, to focus on his growing business empire, including smuggling operations. In 2012 a UN report stated that Afweyne was 'one of the most notorious and influential leaders of the Hobyo-Harardhere Piracy Network', being specifically 'responsible for the hijacking of dozens of commercial vessels from 2008 to 2013'.

In April 2012 Malaysian authorities captured Afweyne, but he was released, as a former Somali president had reportedly given Hassan a diplomatic passport as an incentive to quit the piracy business. Belgium and Seychelles now issued an INTERPOL notice for his arrest, and in January 2013 Afweyne announced that he had renounced all crime to retire. After months of talks, he and Tiiceey flew to Brussels to take part as consultants in a film documentary about Somali piracy exploits. Belgian prosecutors had determined that an international arrest warrant was insufficient for detaining them, and undercover agents were used in a sting operation to get the Somalis on Belgian soil and arrest them. They were said to be the masterminds behind the hijacking in 2009 of Belgian dredger *Pompei*. The pair were arrested in Belgium in 2013 for taking the ship, as well as abducting the ship's crew and belonging to a criminal organisation. Afweyne was sentenced in Bruges in March 2016 to 20 years' imprisonment for leading the hijacking. Tiiceey received only five years, and because of a legal technicality, no attempt was made to confiscate any of their gains from piracy.

Three other VLCCs have been ransomed by pirates. On 29 November 2009 the Greek-flagged VLCC, MV *Maran Centaurus* was boarded by Somali pirates 570 nautical miles north-east of the Seychelles. It had left Kuwait for the Louisiana Offshore Oil Port in the Gulf of Mexico with nearly two million barrels of crude oil, worth more than $150 million. The ransom of the ship and crew on 18 January 2010 was, according to Reuters, $5–7 million, parachuted to the pirates. Reuters reported that rival pirate gangs fired shots at each other on 17 January in a dispute over how to split the ransom. If the oil tanks of the ship had been breached, any oil spill would have been an environmental disaster, with no prospect of any help to clean up the Somali coast. *Samho Dream,* a South Korean supertanker, carrying crude from Iraq to the USA, was hijacked by Somalis on 4 April 2010. On 6 November 2010, the ship was released for a ransom of about $13.5 million. The Greek-owned supertanker *Irene SL* was taken by Somalis on 9 February 2011, 350 miles southeast of Muscat, Oman, en route to the USA, loaded with 2 million barrels of crude oil with an estimated value of $200 million. The *Irene SL* was captured one day after the pirates took control of another tanker, the bulk oil carrier Italian MV *Savina Caylyn.* After 11 months in captivity, the *Irene's* crew and the ship were released for $11.5 million. It had been attacked by Somalis in skiffs with rocket-propelled grenades, 500 miles west of India.